International Review of RESEARCH IN MENTAL RETARDATION

VOLUME 15

Consulting Editors

International Review of RESEARCH IN MENTAL RETARDATION

EDITED BY

NORMAN W. BRAY

UNIVERSITY OF ALABAMA AT BIRMINGHAM
BIRMINGHAM, ALABAMA

VOLUME 15

ACADEMIC PRESS, INC.
Harcourt Brace Jovanovich, Publishers
San Diego New York Berkeley Boston
London Sydney Tokyo Toronto

ACADEMIC PRESS, INC.
San Diego, California 92101

United Kingdom Edition published by
ACADEMIC PRESS, INC. (LONDON) LTD.
24-28 Oval Road, London NW1 7DX

LIBRARY OF CONGRESS CATALOG CARD NUMBER: 65-28627

ISBN 0-12-366215-X (alk. paper)

PRINTED IN THE UNITED STATES OF AMERICA
88 89 90 91 9 8 7 6 5 4 3 2 1

Contents

Mental Retardation, Analogical Reasoning, and the Componential Method

J. McConaghy

Application of Self-Control Strategies to Facilitate Independence in Vocational and Instructional Settings

James E. Martin, Donald L. Burger, Susan Elias-Burger, and Dennis E. Mithaug

Family Stress Associated with a Developmentally Handicapped Child

Patricia M. Minnes

Physical Fitness of Mentally Retarded Individuals

E. Kathryn McConaughy and Charles L. Salzberg

Contributors

Numbers in parentheses indicate the pages on which the authors' contributions begin.

Donald L. Burger (155), *School of Education, University of Colorado, Colorado Springs, Colorado 80933*

Susan Elias-Burger (155), *School of Education, University of Colorado, Colorado Springs, Colorado 80933*

Hans Kreitler (81), *Department of Psychology, Tel Aviv University, Ramat Aviv, Tel Aviv 69978, Israel*

Shulamith Kreitler (81), *Department of Psychology, Tel Aviv University, Ramat Aviv, Tel Aviv 69978, Israel*

James E. Martin (155), *School of Education, University of Colorado, Colorado Springs, Colorado 80933*

J. McConaghy (125), *C.S.I.R.O. Division of Human Nutrition, Adelaide, Australia*

E. Kathryn McConaughy (227), *Developmental Center for Handicapped Persons, Utah State University, Logan, Utah 84322*

Patricia M. Minnes (195), *Department of Psychology, Queen's University, Kingston, Ontario, Canada*

Dennis E. Mithaug (155), *School of Education, University of Colorado, Colorado Springs, Colorado 80933*

Ernesto Pollitt (33), *Department of Applied Behavioral Sciences, University of California, Davis, California 95616*

Charles L. Salzberg (227), *Developmental Center for Handicapped Persons, Utah State University, Logan, Utah 84322*

Herman H. Spitz (1), *Edward R. Johnstone Training and Research Center, Bordentown, New Jersey 08505*

Preface

This series was established under the editorship of Dr. Norman R. Ellis in 1966. As a result of his editorial efforts and the contributions of many authors, the series came to be recognized as the area's best source of reviews of behavioral research on mental retardation. From the beginning, active research scientists and graduate students in mental retardation have looked to this series as a major source of critical reviews of research and theory in the area.

I had the pleasure of serving as co-editor with Dr. Ellis beginning with Volume 12 in 1984. In 1986, Dr. Ellis retired from the series and I became editor. This volume reflects the editorial policies originally developed by Dr. Ellis and builds on this solid base.

The seven chapters in the present volume represent one sample of the current breadth of research and theory in mental retardation. The first four deal with diverse aspects of mental development and the last three with aspects of adaptation.

In the first, Herman Spitz develops a rationalist approach to the nature of mental retardation, reviewing research in support of a position that mental retardation is a disorder in thinking with biologically imposed limits. He reviews and rejects the empiricist appeal to aberrations in learning history as the mechanism underlying mental retardation, and outlines an approach to narrow the gap between laboratory studies and the special education classroom.

Next, Ernesto Pollitt reviews research on nutrition and behavioral development, focusing on forms of undernutrition and the effect of constituents of the daily diet of children in the United States. He examines the latest evidence indicating that even mild to moderate nutritional deficits during the prenatal and postnatal period may have adverse affects on mental development.

Also concerned with aspects of mental development, Shulamith Kreitler and Hans Kreitler review research on the influence of cognition on motivation. They review empirical research, much of it conducted in their own laboratories, showing that the cognitive intentions of mentally retarded individuals influence their pattern of motivation and actual behaviors. Such cognitive motivations can be used to predict behavior in mentally retarded individuals with a precision not obtained by competing theoretical approaches.

Julie McConaghy examines research, including her own, on analogical reasoning in mentally retarded individuals. This is a particularly important aspect of reasoning, one included on virtually every major intelligence test. She concludes that clearer patterns of quantitative and qualitative differences in analogical reasoning will depend on the use of research methodologies based on specific rather than general process analyses.

The last three chapters deal with several important areas of research related to personal and social adaptation of mentally retarded individuals. James Martin, Donald Burger, Susan Elias-Burger, and Dennis Mithaug review the growing literature on self-control strategies designed to facilitate independence in vocational and instructional settings. Their review indicates that there are a variety of self-control techniques that can be used successfully by mentally retarded individuals and that these procedures are more effective than traditional trainer-based approaches.

Patricia Minnes reviews the recent literature on family stress associated with a handicapped child, including families with a mentally retarded child. She emphasizes the importance of understanding the complex relationships between family resources, coping strategies, and stress in families with a handicapped child. She calls for further movement away from questionnaire-oriented methodologies to more focused observational studies and theoretical frameworks.

In the last chapter, E. Kathryn McConaughy and Charles Salzberg review the literature on physical fitness of mentally retarded individuals. Their review indicates that most mentally retarded individuals have serious deficits as compared to nonretarded individuals of the same age, and that the magnitude of these deficits is inversely related to level of retardation. They note that, although most current fitness research is plagued with many methodological limitations, physical fitness programs hold the promise of enhancing the integration of retarded persons into society and may result in increased adaptation and productivity.

As exemplified by these chapters, this series will continue to publish integrative reviews addressing theoretical and methodological issues in mental retardation research. Appropriate topics include the psychological and social nature of mental retardation, the biological and neurological bases of behavioral and psychological problems associated with mental retardation, and the nature of problems of adaptation encountered by mentally retarded individuals. Reviews of both basic and applied research will be included. The majority of chapters are written by invitation but unsolicited manuscripts will be considered.

NORMAN W. BRAY

Mental Retardation as a Thinking Disorder: The Rationalist Alternative to Empiricism

HERMAN H. SPITZ

EDWARD R. JOHNSTONE TRAINING AND RESEARCH CENTER
BORDENTOWN, NEW JERSEY 08505

I. INTRODUCTION

In the experimental psychology of mental retardation there are two distinct competing hypotheses around which researchers of different persuasions can rally. Similar dichotomies have been immensely productive in other areas of science: the big bang vs. the steady state theory of the origin of the universe and the wave vs. the particle explanation of the nature of light transmission are just two of the better known examples. Our duality has little of the earth-shaking features of these examples, but nevertheless can provide a framework for mental retardation researchers who, it seems, have not yet fully recognized its import or, in some cases, even its existence.

The opposing camps to which I refer represent two theoretical views of the nature of mental retardation: one that it is primarily a learning disorder, the other that it is primarily a thinking disorder. Note the use of the qualifier "primarily." No one can doubt that mental retardation is both a learning and a thinking disorder and that these two processes overlap, but we should not permit anyone to use these bromides to escape the responsibility of taking a position on the relative importance of deficiencies in learning vs. thinking as most descriptive of mental retardation. For this reason, and for the sake of brevity, "primarily" will not be used henceforth to qualify the two positions, but it should be regarded always as a silent presence.

INTERNATIONAL REVIEW OF RESEARCH IN
MENTAL RETARDATION, Vol. 15

Learning is conceived of here as the process that allows us to acquire and store new information and certain new skills. *Thinking* (defined in more detail later) is the process that allows us to judge and reason about our inner and outer environment, providing us with some understanding of ourselves and the world around us. The capacity to learn and to think evolved into highly skilled functions that provide humans with effective means of coping with a complex environment. They are inborn process that act upon the material provided by particular environments.

The term *general intelligence* will be used frequently in this article. Elsewhere, I considered that general intelligence is "reflected in the pervasive manner in which we respond to everyday challenges, the speed with which we learn and the complexity and scope of material we can understand, the curiosity and interest we show in a range of subjects or in one engrossing problem, the intricacy of the problems we can solve, and so on" (Spitz, 1986, p. 5). It is in this descriptive sense that the term is used here.

Those who view mental retardation as a learning disorder are generally empiricists who, although they might concede that the most basic mechanisms of learning and thinking are innate, nevertheless minimize the effect of inborn constraints on learning and thinking and believe that individual differences in the efficiency of learning and thinking are due primarily to differences in environmental history. Furthermore, they stress learning rather than thinking as the dominant source of intellectual achievement. Indeed, they believe that we can learn to think, or at least learn to think more efficiently.

Those who believe that mental retardation is a thinking disorder emphasize that these basic processes are innately constrained and predisposed to function in certain ways. In this view, children are no more taught to think than they are taught to walk, although of course thinking is shaped and modified by the environment, within certain limits. Humans (and many other animals) are innately endowed with the capacity to think, which under normal conditions emerges in its various manifestations according to a genetic timetable. Furthermore, excepting the effects of pathologies and catastrophic deprivations, differences in how efficiently people learn and think are largely genetically determined (and, indeed, these and other types of individual genetic variability are important as mechanisms of evolutionary development; see Plomin, DeFries, & McClearn, 1980). Although learning and thinking may be separate (though interacting) modules, thinking is preeminent. That is, the greater the complexity of the to-be-learned task, the more must thinking be brought to bear upon it.

In this article I defend the position that mental retardation is a thinking disorder. Evidence is marshaled in favor of this position and against the position that mental retardation is a learning disorder, a position that has long dominated theory, research, and practice.

A. From Locke to Skinner—the Empiricist Domination

Jean-Marc-Gaspard Itard's (1801, 1806/1962) attempt to civilize Victor, the mute "Wild Boy of Aveyron," is usually given as the birth of the experimental approach to the understanding and training of persons who are mentally retarded. What is not so often recognized, however, is the philosophical background that inspired Itard. A confirmed empiricist, he wrote of his debt to the philosophers John Locke and Étienne Bonnot de Condillac, who had emphasized the dominant role that our sense organs play in the development of ideas, and it was this principle that he followed in his attempt to educate Victor. Locke and Condillac were, in turn, following Francis Bacon, whose emphasis on the senses as the primary source of ideas and knowledge was the foundation of the inductive scientific method.

But it was not this aspect of empiricism that was to become the source of controversy, for scientists generally agree that theories have to be supported by data. The source of disagreement was Locke's and, to an even greater extent, Condillac's stress on our senses as the source of *individual* mental development. Methodological empiricism as a scientific approach to understanding the natural world was one thing, but developmental empiricism as the source of a person's ideas was another, and it was the latter that clashed with Cartesian rationalism's stress on innate ideas, producing the dichotomy that has survived to this day (Boring, 1950; Robinson, 1976). For Descartes, there is nothing in an object perceived by the senses that contains within it the *idea* of the object; in this sense, all ideas are innate. As Katz (1981) puts it, "The rationalists claimed that our concepts originate in principles that form the inborn consitution of the mind, and the empiricists claimed that all our ideas come originally from experience" (p. 282).

Consistent with his empiricist orientation, Itard believed that intellectual dullness is a result of poor or inadequate education and, consequently, that Victor—who obviously had no formal education—could be civilized and taught to speak by intensive sensory training. By educating Victor, Itard would prove the validity of empiricist philosophy.

> We are indebted to the works of Locke and Condillac for a just estimation of the powerful influence that the isolated and simultaneous action of our senses exerts upon the formation and development of our ideas.... These were the principles I followed, when, after completing the main projects which I had first proposed and which are made known in my first work, I devoted all my attention to the exercise and individual development of young Victor's sense organs. (Itard, 1801, 1806/1962, p. 55)

Itard believed that education had not taken into account children's individual differences, but that now, guided by medicine, education could be dramatically advantageous in training retarded individuals, "who for the most part are no different from other men save in their reduced sensory capacities, which can certainly be developed. . . . Up to a certain point [we] can blunt or sharpen nervous sensitivity and by this means influence man's intellect" (quoted in Lane, 1976, pp. 77–78).

Although Victor was transformed in many ways by Itard's extraordinary persistence and ingenuity, he never learned to speak nor could he be returned to society, and Itard harshly judged his experiment a failure. It is important to note that Itard was at that time resident physician at the National Institute for Deaf-Mutes in Paris, where the residents were taught to communicate by sign language. Sign language had been encouraged by the founder of the Institute, the Abbé de l'Epee, and by his successor, the Abbé Roche-Ambroise Sicard, who directed the Institute when Itard was given the task of educating Victor (Lane, 1976; Shattuck, 1980). It is curious, therefore, that Itard tried to teach Victor to speak rather than to use sign language, which might have proved more propitious. But Itard had been influenced by Condillac's assertion that ideas must be linked to signs (symbols), that ideas cannot be related to each other unless the signs are linked to each other, and that this linkage can occur more easily in speech than in sign language. Furthermore, Victor was not deaf and, in any event, Jacob Rodriguez Perèire had demonstrated 50 years earlier that it was possible to teach even deaf-mutes to speak.

Nevertheless, the training of deaf-mutes influenced the training of what was then termed *idiocy* in a manner that was to have profound and lasting effects. Until recently, the term for deaf-mutes was *deaf and dumb*, and it is no accident that the word dumb is synonymous with intellectual deficiency. If "dumbness" in deaf-mutes can be cured by using alternative senses, why not cure the dumbness of "idiocy" by the same means?

That this reasoning shaped the philosophy of Itard's famous pupil, Edouard Séguin, cannot be doubted. As support for his dictum that in training the senses the sense of touch is foremost, Séguin (1866/1907) cited Perèire's use of tactile sensations to teach deaf-mutes. Indeed, on the basis of evidence from the training of deaf-mutes, Séguin concluded that each of the senses can be given "physiological" training, one sense can be substituted for another, our most abstract ideas are generalizations of what is perceived through the senses, and "sensations are intellectual functions performed through external apparatus as much as reasoning, imagination, etc., through more internal organs" (p. 20). For Séguin, "*the physiological education of the senses is the royal road to the education of the intellect: experience, not memory, the mother of ideas*" (1870, p. 26, his italics).

Training the senses as a means of raising general intelligence took various forms in the following years. Maria Montessori translated into Italian and copied by hand the works of Itard and Séguin, "making for myself books as the old Benedictines used to do before the diffusion of printing. . . . I chose to do this by hand, in order that I might have time to weigh the sense of each word" (Montessori, 1912/1965, p. 41). She added many pedagogical innovations to their work, but evidence that her stated philosophy was guided by theirs can be found throughout her writings. As one example, she noted that "if one of the senses suffices to make of Hellen Keller a woman of exceptional culture and a writer, who better than she proves the potency of that method of education which builds on the senses?" (Montessori, 1914/1964, Preface).

In recent times the philosophical empiricism of Locke and Condillac, and the pedagogical empiricism of Itard and Séguin, are rarely given as the basis for particular training programs, but the doctrine that general intellectual development is dependent on sensory-motor development and that intelligence is, therefore, learned and can be trained through the senses flourishes. To mention just a few such programs (not all of equal merit or even of equal ethical standards), there is the patterning technique of Doman and Delacato and their colleagues (LeWinn, Doman, Doman, Delacato, E. B. Spitz, & Thomas, 1966), Kephart's (1971) perceptual-motor therapy, the visuomotor training advocated by Getman (1965), the sensory integrative training progam of Ayres (1978), Frostig's (1975) perceptual approach, and countless numbers of early intervention programs that have stressed not only sensory and motor training but also the behaviorist principles of B. F. Skinner, the ultimate empiricist (see Mann, 1979, for an extensive historical review of training the faculties of the mind).

I do not mean this list to be exhaustive, nor is it a criticism of the many dedicated workers who, it goes without saying, are bound by no single technique or philosophy. What I question only is the general notion that training the senses has any effect on intelligence in instances where all the senses are intact. When they are not all intact, as in the cases of deaf-mutes or blind deaf-mutes such as Helen Keller, reaching the brain by alternative senses is clearly the method of choice. But rather than proving that alternative (or combined) sense training can produce intelligent behavior, the intelligent performance of deaf-mutes actually provides evidence that intellectual potential is inherent in the brain, waiting to be tapped, not *given* by the environment. If it were produced by sensory training, 180 years of effort with retarded persons who have all their senses intact would have shown by now more favorable results.

The focus of this article, however, is empiricism's influence on mental retardation research, particularly in the United States. In experimental psychology, it descended, in broad outline, from Locke through Berkeley, Hume, Condillac, James Mill, J. S. Mill, Helmholtz, Wundt, Thorndike, Pavlov, British and American associationism, and the behaviorism of Watson and Skinner. Throughout, there have been opposing viewpoints, but only in the last 30 years has empiricism's influence diminished, due to a number of interesting developments.

B. The Erosion of Empiricist Principles

A mounting store of contrary evidence in various research domains placed the basic principles of empiricism in jeopardy. Findings in the fields of animal behavior, linguistics, and human perception were particularly significant.

1. ANIMAL STUDIES

In 1938, B. F. Skinner published a book, majestically titled *The Behavior of Organisms: An Experimental Analysis*, in which he examined a single organism, the white rat, producing a single kind of artificial behavior, pressing a lever for reinforcement. Skinner (1953) acknowledged diversity in animals, but only in the sense that different responses and different reinforcers are differentially effective for different species, not in the sense that the behavior of organisms is immensely rich and diverse and most productively studied by observing naturally occurring behaviors. For Skinner (1953), "Operant conditioning shapes behavior as a sculptor shapes a lump of clay" (p. 92).

For decades, proponents of this modern form of empiricism chose to ignore the ample evidence provided by ethologists that there are innate, species-specific behaviors fundamental to the organism, but finally they could not ignore the increasing instances of insubordination within their own ranks. In an article pointedly titled "The Misbehavior of Organisms," Breland and Breland (1961), who trained animals for commercial purposes, described the breakdown of conditioned operant behaviors when animals continually revert to innate behaviors. Raccoons being trained to put coins in a metal box held onto the coins for long periods of time, rubbing them together and dipping them into the box, thereby spoiling the display that was supposed to feature a raccoon putting money in a piggy bank. Similar breakdowns occurred with other animals. Pigs, for example, began to take a large wooden coin and instead of dropping it directly into a large piggy bank for for a food reward, would incessantly drop it and root it, toss it in the air and root it some more, and so on; this behavior increased to such a degree that the pig failed to get enough food in the course of the day.

The Brelands summarized their findings. "After 14 years of continuous conditioning and observation of thousands of animals, it is our reluctant conclusion that the behavior of any species cannot be adequately understood, predicted, or controlled without knowledge of its instinctive pattern, evolutionary history, and ecological niche" (p. 459).

By 1973, numerous constraints on learning had been documented (e.g., Hinde & Stevenson-Hinde, 1973; Seligman & Hager, 1972; Shettleworth, 1972). When another former disciple (Herrnstein, 1977a) reviewed the accumulating evidence that increasingly undermined many of the basic principles of Skinnerian behaviorism in 1977, Skinner (1977) replied that he had always occupied the middle ground between nativism and environmentalism. Subsequent rejoinders by Herrnstein (1977b) and by Robert Bailey and Marian Breland Bailey (1980) were cautiously hopeful—but with many reservations—about Skinner's acknowledgment of the role of nativism.

Unfortunately, the world of Skinnerian behaviorism changed very little (Garcia, 1981), and recent attempts to demonstrate that human cognitive behavior can be duplicated in pigeons illustrate, perhaps better than anything else, the absurdities to which radical empiricism ultimately leads (Gallup, 1984). Skinner and colleagues, using the usual fading, shaping, chaining, and discrimination techniques, produced an interacting chain of key-pecking responses in two pigeons, but WHAT COLOR? and THANK YOU were painted on two of the keys. On the basis of this, they concluded that "A similar account may be given of [the learning]. . .of comparable human language" (Epstein, Lanza, & Skinner, 1980, p. 545).

2. LINGUISTICS

Teaching pigeons "to engage in sustained and natural communication," as Epstein *et al.* (1980, p. 595) put it, was consistent with the logic of empiricism and with Skinner's long-held position that language is taught to children by the principles of operant conditioning (particularly response–reward contingencies) that had been delineated in laboratory studies with rats and pigeons. Indeed, all verbal behavior was said to be explained by those principles. When psychologist Charles Osgood (1958) reviewed Skinner's (1957) *Verbal Behavior,* he called it "one of the two or three most significant contributions to this field in our time" (p. 212). Linguist Noam Chomsky (1964), on the other hand, was simply mystified.

It is impossible to summarize briefly Skinner's book or Chomsky's review, but a sampling of a few quotations provides at least the flavor of the opposing viewpoints. For Skinner, the three important events to be taken into account are the stimulus, the response, and the reinforcement (p. 81). "Appropriate contingencies of reinforcement. . . bring verbal behavior under control of the nonverbal environment" (p. 204). Language cannot be learned or maintained without reinforcement not only for the speaker (learner, child), but also for the reinforcer (parent, listener). In the animal laboratory, the precise temporal relationship of stimulus, response, and reward determines the rate and persistence of the response. Reinforcement, and its temporal relationship to simulus and response, is a crucial variable. Yet Skinner wrote that "complex behavior is acquired at different speeds not because of great diffences in the effect of reinforcement, but because of interactions among responses and stimuli" (p. 204).

From this, we might assume that the laborious compilation of hundreds of schedules of reinforcement is irrelevant for complex behavior. But then, a few sentences later, we are told that "the availability of [verbal] behavior, its probability or strength, depends upon whether reinforcements *continue* in effect and according to what schedules" (p. 204). Further, "when reinforcements are abundant, the individual is likely to be called. . .voluble or talkative. When reinforcements are scarce. . .taciturn or silent" (p. 204). This places a heavy burden on the mechanism of reinforcement, a burden under which it collapses.

As Chomsky pointed out, the term *reinforcement* becomes a tautology, without explanatory power. For example, Skinner wrote, "A man talks to himself. . .because of the reinforcement he receives" (p. 163, see also p. 438). In this instance, the man is both speaker and listener, reinforcer and reinforced. Thinking is "behaving which automatically affects the behavior and is reinforcing because it does so" (p. 438). A person "engaged in verbal fantasy says [to himself] what he is reinforced by hearing or writes what he is reinforced by reading" (p. 439). "Verbal behavior receives intermittent reinforcement" (p. 205). For writers, verbal behavior may reach over centuries or to thousands of listeners or readers at the same time. "The writer may not be reinforced often or immediately, but his reinforcement may be great" (p. 206), even though, I might add, he is not alive to enjoy it.

As these quotes illustrate, Skinner did not, and could not, directly apply the findings of his laboratory to support his speculations concerning language. Precise control by reinforcement had disappeared.

Chomsky (1964) made this clear. "The notion of reinforcement has totally lost whatever objective meaning it may ever have had. . . . A person can be reinforced though he emits no response at all, [and] the reinforcing *stimulus* need not impinge on the *reinforced person* or need not even exist (it is sufficient that it be imagined or hoped for). . . . The phrase 'X is reinforced by Y'. . .is being used as a cover term for 'X wants Y,' 'X likes Y,' 'X wishes that Y were the case,' etc." (p. 558) "A term [*reinforcement*] borrowed from the laboratory, [which] is used with the full vagueness of the ordinary vocabulary, is of no conceivable interest" (p. 559).

Chomsky (1964) was also mystfied by the claim that children learn language by the same mechanisms that rats in a Skinner box learn to press a lever in response to a stimulus. "It is," he wrote, "simply not true that children can learn language only through 'meticulous care' on the part of adults who shape their verbal repertoire through careful differential reinforcement" (p. 562).

Whereas the work of Skinner and other learning theorists is in the Lockian empiricist traditon, Chomsky's approach descends (via Wilhelm von Humboldt) from Cartesian rationalism, although of course both Skinner and Chomsky depart appreciably from their intellectual predecessors. In his book *Cartesian Linguistics*, Chomsky (1966) noted approvingly Descarte's emphasis on the creative aspects of language, and his general view that, for humans, language "can serve as a general instrument of thought and self-expression rather than merely as a communicative device of report, request, or command" (pp. 11–12). Descartes, in fact, had raised a number of issues that continue to be debated. He pointed out that language is unrelated to the organic ability to form words, which parrots can do, and that what distinguishes humans is their ability to use "words or other signs made in regard to whatever subjects present themselves, without reference to any passion" (cited by Chomsky, 1966, p. 5). By passion, Descartes was referring to emotions and needs, and he went on to note that animals are trained by using their desire for food or by exploiting their fears, hopes, and joys. This contrasts with the fact that human language can be unrelated to external stimuli or physiological need and is free to serve as an instrument of thought and self-expression. Interestingly, Descartes remarked that even persons of low intelligence have language ability and that deaf-mutes will invent signs to make themselves understood.

Chomsky's own "generative grammar" has many aspects of von Humboldt's proposal, made some 200 years ago, that language must be generated or constructed from an underlying system of fixed elements according to certain intentions and rules, in this way accounting for the indefinite range that language displays (see Chomsky, 1966). That is, there are infinite possibilities of expression (the creative aspect of language) emerging from a finite and constrained set of rules and principles.

In terms of children's acquistion of language, the rationalist approach differs decisively from the empiricist approach. Although verbal behavior can be conditioned, just as the pecking behavior of pigeons can be conditioned, rationalists would argue that conditioning is not the source of language acquisition in humans, any more than it is of the disposition of pigeons to peck. There is, in fact, no learning theory of any kind that can adequately account for the acquisition of language. As Lenneberg (1964) noted: "We have neither a good theoretical model nor any practical insights into how we could teach an organism to respond to plurality, third-person-ness, past-ness, let alone how we could train him to use these responses in the correct order and verbal contexts within original sentence construction" (p. 599). Furthermore, Lenneberg (1966) rejected the idea that language develops in humans because of their general cognitive capabilities. He pointed out that the ability to acquire the basic syntax of a language is relatively independent of intelligence. Children learn language at 2 and 3 years of age, and retarded persons with IQs of 50 (and lower) have language competence despite limitations in their ability to reason logically.

It is a general proposition of Cartesian linguistics that the principles of language are inborn. When the brain matures to some predetermined state, language expression is triggered and molded by apropriate environmental stimuli. This accounts for the universality of all language, for the fact that in all cultures language begins to emerge at about 2 years of age (the "critical period") and that all children go through the same stages in the course of acquiring speech, for the fact that children quite rapidly produce a language that is much more complex than they could possibly have been taught (at the same time that it is constrained in very definite ways), and for the fact that children learn their first (natural) language, or even two languages, in a different way and apparently with greater ease than adults learn a new language.

Recently, Chomsky (1980) has referred to language metaphorically as a "mental organ" which can be studied in a manner analogous to the way one might study the eye or heart, seeking, among other things, its invariant properties, the course of its development in individuals, the genetic basis for its development, and its evolutionary origins. He proposed that there are a variety of initial states (S_0) that are fixed for all members of a species. Language is one such state. During development, individuals progress through a series of states until they reach a relatively stable steady state (S_S). Because experience is required to attain the steady state, the initial state is "in effect *a function that maps experience onto the steady state*" (Chomsky, 1980, p. 109, his italics).

For Chomsky, there are linguistic analogs for innate mechanisms already discovered or acknowledged in other domains. For example, individual nerve cells in the visual cortex of cats and monkeys respond maximally only to certain patterns, line orientations, and directions of movement; that is, some cells will respond selectively to vertical lines, others horizontal lines, and so on (Hubel & Wiesel, 1979). Presumably, the human visual cortex responds in a similar manner.

Consider another physical analogy. All normally developed human beings will, at about 12 or 13 years of age, develop secondary sexual characteristics which soon reach a final or steady state of development. These characteristics do not develop because of any specific experience during the preceding years, although they can be altered by malnutrition or other pathological conditions. They develop because the organism's initial state contains genes that trigger the development of these characteristics after a certain period of maturation. It is important to recognize that—had we not by now learned otherwise—an empiricist perspective would demand that we look for certain experiences or events during the first dozen years that would cause all humans to develop secondary sexual characteristics, just as empiricists search for the past experiences responsible for human language acquistion. But such a search will only find correlations that lead to incorrect attributions of causality, for it fails to consider innate mechanisms as causative agents.

From the viewpoint of Cartesian rationalism, environmental stimuli do not organize the nervous system; rather, organized, biological predispositions selectively act on environmental stimuli. Environment determines the specific manner in which the underlying language principles are expressed (such as the particular language spoken), but does not create or alter their basic structure. If this seems to be a radical approach, one might ponder why it is that most psychologists readily acknowlege genetic determination of physical development and physical capacities, but are unable to accept similar explanations for mental development and the acquisition of cognitive capacities.

It would be difficult at this time to find any serious student of linguistics who would consider that children are taught language as they are taught, for example, to write or to read (e.g., Wanner & Gleitman, 1982). Indeed, in the absence of pathological conditions or unnatural environments, it would be as difficult to *prevent* children from learning to speak as it would be to prevent them from learning to walk.

3. HUMAN PERCEPTION

Empiricists teach that the perception of objects is learned, a basic premise that, as we shall see, has been stretched to support the philosophy that the environment plays a dominant role in the creation of intelligence.

The mechanisms by which we learn to preceive have never been successfully determined by empiricists, but their explanations have never lacked ingenuity. Condillac, who influenced so greatly both Itard and Séguin, believed that we learn to see objects by generalizing from the sense of touch. Although this explanation is still considered plausible by some workers, it cannot be correct. For one thing, it merely transfers the problem from vision to touch, for we still must explain how the fingers construct shapes that are then recognized by the mind. For another thing, vision is prepotent, not touch. When Bower, Broughton, and Moore (1970) presented an object so that it appeared to be closer than it actually was, infants from as young as 7 days of age produced anticipatory hand shaping when reaching to grab it and became frustrated and tearful when they couldn't. When the object was actually placed in their hands (but out of sight) it produced a stereotyped hand closure rather than sensitive tactile exploration, and not until infants were 3 months old did they look at the object in their hand. When the experimenters presented a visual object that did not look hard or palpable (e.g., looked like a patch of film color in depth), 3.5-month-olds did not close their hands on it, but did produce exploratory hand behavior, something they had not done when the solid object was presented. None of these behaviors is consistent with tactile theories of the visual perception of objects. Furthermore, unfortunate infants born without limbs (e.g., some thalidomide babies) show no evidence that they cannot perceive objects (Decarie, 1969; Kopp & Shaperman, 1973).

Two books were particularly influential in disseminating the empirical viewpoint. One was Hebb's (1949) *The Organization of Behavior.* Hebb was not crystal clear about what features of a figure can be seen immediately (innately) and what features require a period of learning, but his theory emphasized that the organized structure of a perceived object was not automatic. It was built up (learned) by the organism's motor activity (eye movements). Although he conceded (p. 29) that the capacity to perceive figure from ground is innate, he argued that "identity" of the figure is not. For example, seeing a circle as a figural object may be innate (p. 28), but recognizing it as similar to other circles and associating it with other objects or with some action is a learned ability. Infants must *learn* to see figures as distinctive wholes (p. 35), which Hebb somehow distinguishes from seeing a figure as only a "single coherent object" (p. 28). This final percept of a figure or object, then, is learned very slowly and is dependent on multiple visual fixations.

According to Hebb, infants perceive lines and angles in a very primitive way. Only after repeated multiple fixations of the corners of a triangle, for example, can they finally come to perceive the triangle as other than an amorphous mass with several isolated foci (contours and angles). "Perception depends on learning first to see the parts of an object clearly, a process involving a series of visual fixations, and proceeds from seeing, at first, an amorphous mass containing several foci (the corners) to seeing a distinctive figure at a glance" (Hebb, 1949, p. 101).

Hebb's theory was very influential despite some strong criticisms, especially from Gestalt psychologists (e.g., Wertheimer, 1951; Zuckerman & Rock, 1957). His mistake was to base his theory almost entirely on Senden's review of reports, mostly from the eighteenth and nineteenth centuries, of congenitally blind patients whose vision had been restored by surgical intervention. Hebb wrongly assumed that perception in infants is acquired in the same manner that it is acquired in children and adults who are suddenly given sight.

As Wertheimer (1951) noted, when the bandages had been removed after the cataract operations, there were a number of physical effects that precluded immediate perception, effects such as painful "dazzle" from the novel brightness, narrowed visual field, and eye-muscle cramps. Uncontrolled nystagmus had to be overcome. Moreover, the inactivity of neurons selectively responsive to edges in particular orientations, as well as to other features of the visual world, will result in the degeneration of corresponding synapses, and this must have affected vision. In some of the cases reviewed, poor performance was apparently related to cognitive difficulties, such as remembering the names of objects. The patients' reports were anecdotal and, to add to the problem, Hebb's descriptions and interpretations of Senden's review were selective and often incorrect.

On logical grounds, too, it is entirely unlikely that infants learn to perceive objects by inspection of an amorphous mass containing isolated foci. Surely during evolution hominids would acquire or sustain the same foolproof visual mechanisms as exist in other, closely related members of the animal kingdom who show no evidence that they must gradually learn to see. Considering the vast number of extraordinary capacities that are genetically programmed, it must be obvious that nature would not be so remiss as to leave so basic a function as the perception of objects to the whims of learning. How could an organism survive in a world where every new or different shape was an amorphous mass until the required number of fixations was carried out?

Research with infants also raises serious problems for learning theory, for it appears that young infants can distinguish patterns and forms and do not successively fixate the corners of a triangle (Bower, 1971; Fantz, 1963; Fantz & Fagan, 1975; Salapatek & Kessen, 1966). In terms of Chomsky's proposals, then, there is an S_0 (initial state) that contains a genetic program for the perception of the visual world. For example, neural development during the first 3 months of life results in stereopsis by about 4 months of age in all normal human infants (e.g., Birch, Gwiazda, & Held, 1983). Pipp and Haith (1985) recorded the visual fixations of 48 infants from newborn to 8 weeks of age. Variations in the segmentation, thickness, and orientation of the lines presented to the infants produced different eye-fixation behavior depending on the particular stimulus configuration and the infant's age. Newborns scanned the stimuli with 22% larger eye movements than did the older infants. On the other hand, infants of all ages were apparently able to detect a small (1.3°) gap in segmented lines and made more fixations on segmented than on continuous lines. There were differences in the size and dispersion of eye movements to the horizontal compared to the vertical arrays; the authors related these to anatomical evidence that retinal cell concentrations, which are greatest in the central retina (fovea), fall off more rapidly in the vertical than in the horizontal direction. They suggested, in sum, that "young babies do not 'choose' stimuli to look at in any important sense of that term; rather, they engage in visual activity that partly reflects the ongoing sampling characteristics of the visual system and partly the constraints on that sampling that a visual stimulus invokes" (p. 393).

The evidence, then, is that a young infant's perceptual ability is quite good and improves with maturation untill it reaches S_S (the steady state). Maturation of the neural sytem includes increased myelination, foveal enhancement, and greater selectivity of feature-detecting, occipital-lobe neurons, refined by feedback from the visual world (Bronson, 1974). Of course, visual experiences are necessary if normal S_S is to be reached, but this experience can in no sense be equated with learning as it is conceived by empiricists.

Hebb did not confine his theories to perception alone. He suggested that the neural processes and systems ("cell assemblies" and "phase sequences" that developed in an organism's central nervous system as it learned to see objects) accompany all kinds of learnng and are ultimately responsible for the realization of an organism's innate intellectual potential. Learning in general was equated with perceptual learning, being slow at first as associations are built up and faster in mature individuals where it builds upon the earlier acquired connections and cell assemblies. In the final chapter of his book, he mentioned a pilot experiment comparing rats blinded during infancy with rats blinded during maturity. When both groups were compared at maturity on an "intelligence test" for rats, the group blinded later performed better, presumably because they had built up a fund of experiences (associations) before being blinded. This and other animal studies of early deprivation and early enrichment were cited by Hebb as evidence that early experience not only permanently affects visual perception, but also permanently affects intelligent behavior.

The other very influential book was J. McV. Hunt's (1961) *Intelligence and Experience.* Although by far the largest portion of this book described Piaget's work, it did include discussions of Hebb's theories and the work on early deprivation and enrichment. To a greater extent than done by Hebb, Hunt generalized from this work to the area of intelligence. "That the capacity and the readiness of stimulation to influence behavior depend upon appropriate past experience fits nicely the notion that such past experience is the *source* of the strategies for processing information which underlie intelligence" (p. 96, italics added).

Hunt's major targets were the concepts of predetermined development and fixed intelligence. Although he granted that heredity was important, the environment was said to have the major responsibility for individual differences in intelligence (pp. 264–265). In a later paper, cultural deprivation in humans was viewed as analogous to early deprivation in animals (Hunt, 1964, p. 242). In the course of two decades, then, there had been a progression from animal studies of perceptual (visual) deprivation, which were interpreted as showing that perception is a learned skill, to animal studies of general deprivation (e.g., cage-reared vs. pet-reared animals), to, finally, cultural deprivation in humans, as if all these domains were points along the same dimension. In fact, Hunt's work—the culmination of these events—provided a most important incentive and theoretical basis for early intervention programs, including Project Head Start (Cooke, 1979). Although the initial anchor (that perception is learned) for this chain of events had doubtful validity, the groundwork had been laid for the empiricistic idea that most mental retardation was due to cultural deprivation. The thinking was that if individual differences in intelligence are due to the environment, and if cultural deprivation is synonymous with early deprivation in animals, then most mentally retarded persons without central nervous system pathology must be retarded because they were culturally deprived. Mental retardation is, in this view, a result of faulty learning.

II. MENTAL RETARDATION AS A LEARNING DISORDER

Adherents of radical behaviorism are the most extreme group in claiming that mental retardation is best described as a disorder that results from inadequate or detrimental past experience. It is their contention that genetic processes cannot be directly responsible for retarded mental processes. In fact, mental processes are of little interest to behaviorists, and genetic processes contribute only to the extent that they produce pathological *physical* functions that impose restrictions on the senses and physical capacities of the individual or produce an abnormal physical appearance. These restrict a child's social interaction, which leads to behavioral retardation (Bijou, 1963, 1966). The primary reason a child is retarded, in this view, is related to the kinds and patterns of reinforcement given by the child's parents or parent surrogates.

Perhaps the strangest consequence of this philosophy is the attempt to raise intellectual performance by training retarded persons on the kinds of items used in intelligence tests using operant conditioning techniques (e.g., Farb, Cottrell, Montague, & Throne, 1977; Throne & Farb, 1978). Based on the dubious premise that intelligence-test behavior is identical with intelligence as an abstraction (there being no mental analog), raising intelligence-test performance in this way is said to be tantamount to reversing mental retardation, defined as a behavioral disorder.

Mainstream research in mental retardation has not been as extreme as this, but until recently it has been dominated by stimulus–response and association–learning theory, and it is still dominated by the point of view that mental retardation is, first and foremost, a learning disorder.

In their article "Mental Retardation as a Learning Disorder," Paris and Haywood (1973) defended this viewpoint. For them, the diagnosis of mildly retarded persons who have no demonstrable genetic, neurologic, or physiologic defect (that is to say, the majority of mildly retarded individuals) "must be based upon relative inefficiency in demonstrating the products of prior learning opportunities" (p. 643).

The difficulty with this approach, however, is that the inability to demonstrate a physical cause, especially if it is genetic, does not prove that it does not exist. For example, because of recent technological advances a number of new chromosomal abnormalities have been found, including the fragile X syndrome, rivaling Down's syndrome as a genetic cause of mental retardation (Hagerman & McBogg, 1983). The important point is that some afflicted individuals had previously been diagnosed as "cultural–familial" retarded because the syndrome usually does not produce any gross or obvious physical anomalies, particularly in prepubertal boys.

Paris and Haywood conceded that not all individual differences are environmentally caused, but objected to a purely congenital, pathologic model of retardation as being pessimistic and inappropriate for most retarded persons. They concluded, "Regarding mental retardation as a symptom of developmentally inappropriate learning strategies forces attention on environmental intervention and maximizing of learning opportunities for all children" (p. 650). In other words, they ask us to assume that mental retardation results from inadequate training (even though this cannot always, or even usually, be true) because such a stance will force us to maximize our training efforts. However, taking an opposing position is not incompatible with the need to maximize training.

In recent articles, Haywood and colleagues frankly attribute more of the variance in intelligence to genetic factors than they had in previous years. For example, "By far the largest part of one's basic ability that is measured on intelligence tests is the product of a polygenic system" (Haywood, 1985, p. 3). "Favorable environmental circumstances do not create intelligence. . .although it is possible that its growth can be stimulated or accelerated to some degree through such circumstances" (p. 11). Their approach is the reasonable and popular one that intelligence results from the interaction of genes and environment, with genes playing a prominent role, but in which strong environmental influences can deter development or possibly even stimulate or accelerate it to some degree.

But healthy differences still persist. Rationalists would take issue with the belief that "cognitive functions. . .are largely acquired" (Haywood, 1985, p. 11) by learning, and even with the assumption that motivational dispositions are primarily learned. According to Haywood and Burke (1977), who draw on Hebb's hypotheses of cell assemblies and phase sequences, individuals will learn efficiently if, during development, they had experienced high (but not too high) levels of stimulation and incongruity. Because of structural deficiencies, organically retarded children would be relatively limited in their ability to incorporate novel and complex information, whereas cultural–familial retarded children's low adaptation level for stimulation and incongruity would be limited because of the paucity of their opportunities to experience novel and complex events.

This appeal to learning as the source of motivational differences is central to their use of the concepts of intrinsic and extrinsic motivation to account for some of the performance variance that remains unaccounted for after intelligence (IQ) is partialed out (Haywood & Switzky, 1988). In general, retarded individuals are said to be more *extrinsically* motivated than nonretarded individuals; that is, they tend to avoid dissatisfaction by focusing on factors extrinsic to the task, such as money (rewards), comfort, safety, and so on. Individuals more *intrinsically* motivated, on the other hand, find their rewards within the task: in its challenge, in what they can learn from it, in the satisfaction it gives them, and in the sense of achievement they get from performing the task. Indeed, in one study a more intrinsically motivated retarded group (as measured by a picture-preference scale) scored higher on the Metropolitan Achievement Test than did a more extrinsically motivated retarded group. Since "intrinsic motivation is, to a large degree, a learned disposition" (Haywood, 1985, p. 12), it would follow that teaching retarded children to be more intrinsically motivated would eventually lead to better classroom performance.

Haywood and Switzky (1988) conjecture that all children, regardless of their native intelligence, "enter the world with a general motive to explore and gain some mastery over their world," and that children's motivational postures are conditioned by whether their exploration and attempts at mastery meet with relative success or failure. It is this conditioning, then, that is said to lead to the higher proportion of extrinsically motivated retarded than nonretarded individuals. Note that this work parallels in many ways much research on related concepts, such as learned helplessness, negative reaction tendencies, inner and outer directedness, reinforcer hierarchy, punishment avoidance, failure expectancy and failure avoidance, external locus of control, and effectance motivation, to name just a few (see Haywood & Switzky, 1986; Siegel, 1979), all of which are in the empiricist tradition.

To the extent that motivational differences can be shown to adversely affect retarded individuals—over and above differences accounted for by native ability—there would appear to be a path for rapproachment between the two camps. But even here, questions arise concerning the source of personality (motivational) dispositions. Although all children enter the world with a general motive to explore and gain mastery over it, there is evidence for individual differences in newborn infants' responses to stimulation (Birns, 1965), sucking responses (Kron, Ipsen, & Goddard, 1969), and general temperament and behavior (Freedman, 1974). Consequently, as infants mature these kinds of constitutional differences will influence their drive to explore and gain mastery over the world, bias the manner in which they react to failure, and affect their interactions with parents and strangers (Plomin & Rowe, 1979; Scarr, 1969). In this regard there is mounting evidence that the extent to which infants prefer visual novelty is directly related to their later intelligence (Fagan, 1984).

A recent popular expression of the empiricist philosophy is the work of Reuven Feuerstein and colleagues (Feuerstein, Rand, & Hoffman, 1979; Feuerstein, Rand, Hoffman, & Miller, 1980), which has been enthusiastically embraced by many workers in the United States. It is Feuerstein's contention that the crucial determinant of cognitive development is the "mediated learning experience"; that is to say, although children can develop intellectually from direct exposure to stimuli, only when a competent, caring person explains the experience (mediates between the experience and the child) will the child really benefit to the greatest extent possible. Feuerstein considers native intellectual endowment important only in the sense that more poorly endowed individuals require a larger investment of time and greater ingenuity on the part of the mediator than do less well endowed individuals (Feuerstein *et al.*, 1980, p. 8).

Lack of mediation during a child's early years is said to be the "proximal" cause of retarded performance. The "distal" causes, such as poor heredity, poverty, injury, and emotional disturbance, will result in retarded cognitive performance only when coupled with inadequate or absent mediation. Though Feuerstein disavows behaviorism, his theory has a similar empiricist bias; for example, in its contention that injury or poor genetic endowment is not totally responsible for producing retarded behavior, but rather that retarded behavior results because mediated learning is inadequate or nonexistent. Retarded behavior (a term Feuerstein uses as a general description for many kinds of exceptionality, eschewing the use of the term *mental retardation*) can be modified at any age, although the earlier an organism is given mediated learning experiences the greater the beneficial effects (Feuerstein *et al.*, 1980, p. 16).

Some of the enthusiasm for Feuerstein's methods stems from the reported success of his "instrumental enrichment" program, in which special training techniques are used with a series of paper-and-pencil exercises over a period of years, 3 to 5 hours a week, in order to supply poorly performing students with compensatory mediated learning (Feuerstein *et al.*, 1980). The population used by Feuerstein's group was quite special, consisting of young Israeli adolescents, 45% of whom were immigrants from Asia or Africa. In fact, more than 90% of the subject's parents were born in Asia or Africa. There is little doubt that these students' cultural and language differences deleteriously affected their performance on the intelligence tests given in the preexperimental evaluation; but even so, the mean preintervention IQ of all subjects was 80, which is above the retarded range. The further acculturation and schooling of these students very likely accounted for the finding that following the 2-year intervention the mean IQs of *both* the experimental group (intervention) and the control group (which received only regular schooling) had risen considerably, to about 103 and 97, respectively (Chance, 1981).

One series of studies in the United States is particularly interesting because one of the groups given the Feuerstein program consisted of the children of Mexican-American migrant workers in Phoenix, Arizona, who may well have had the same kind of cultural and language disadvantage as did Feuerstein's group (Arbitman-Smith, Haywood, & Bransford, 1984; Haywood and Arbitman-Smith, 1981). Following a pilot study, groups of students, including a group of mentally retarded children, were given the instrumental enrichment program during the school year. At year-end assessment, the mentally retarded group showed no change, whereas the Phoenix group improved by 6 IQ points relative to a control group, the same 6-point IQ gain shown by Feuerstein's Israeli immigrant group (see Spitz, 1986, p. 179). Consequently, these gains may as readily be ascribed to improved aculturation and language facility as to changes in intelligence. In sum, there is no good evidence that the Feuerstein program will satisfy the hope that intellect can be trained or that learning disabilities associated with mental retardation can be cured.

Feuerstein and colleagues consider that "the latitude of modifiability of intelligence, particularly in the culturally deprived, is so wide as to make for astounding growth of functioning, given proper training" (Feuerstein *et al.*,

1979, p. 76). And elsewhere, "Implicit in the conception of Instrumental Enrichment is the conviction that manifest low cognitive performance need not be regarded as a stable characteristic of an individual and that systematic intervention. . .will render the condition reversible by producing a change in the cognitive structure of the individual" (Feuerstein *et al.*, 1980, p. 1). The way to change cognitive structure is to train individuals on a series of exercises that presumably require the kinds of abilities associated with intelligent behavior. With the teacher as mediator, students are taught to focus on relevant attributes of a problem, to be active and selective, to plan, compare, evaluate, categorize, generalize, follow instructions, and so on, through just about every kind of intelligent behavior that has ever been listed. The supposition is that not only will success on the exercises make the students more motivated and confident, but that what they learn while doing the exercises will generalize to academic and other real-life challenges.

In the almost 200 years since Itard first worked with Victor, the most dedicated workers have been unable to show that this kind of generalization or transfer can be made by retarded persons, and we should not be beguiled by instances where initial evaluations are as apparently specious as Feuerstein's were. Indeed, many workers believe that difficulty in generalizing is one of the halllmarks of mental retardation (e.g., Campione & Brown, 1977). But here again, there are differences in approach and even in the definition of the term *generalization*. Moreover, generalization can be good in some instances (e.g., appropriately transferring to the solution of a novel problem a known solution from a related problem), but bad in others (e.g., treating a wild puma as if it were a house cat). What really matters in terms of intelligent adaptation is how well persons adapt to diverse circumstances and how appropiately they can apply a known skill or bit of knowledge to a new challenge. But the question is this: How do retarded individuals know when and how to apply what they know? They must recognize a new situation as amenable to a known solution.

Zeaman and House (1984), who see certain kinds of generalization as problems of attending to the identical relevant dimensions of the old and new situations (and ignoring the irrelevant dimensions) have mustered considerable evidence that this type of discriminative learning is related to intelligence. A multitude of related studies have assessed retarded persons' ability to transfer various learned strategies for improving the recall of words, pictures, numbers, or letters using techniques such as verbal elaboration, imagery, rehearsal, grouping according to category or redundancy, and so on (see Blackman & Lin, 1984; Borkowski & Cavanaugh, 1979; and Campione, Brown, & Ferrara, 1982, for reviews of this vast literature). Only rarely has there been interest in retarded persons' ability to generalize a strategy to solve problems (e.g., Minsky, Spitz, & Bessellieu, 1985), and only recently in their ability to apply a learned strategy to a broader range of skills (e.g., Campione & Brown, 1984).

Although there have been occasional successes, the bulk of the evidence from this ample literature is that retarded persons do not effectively and permanently transfer a learned strategy, certainly not to the extent that Feuerstein would lead us to believe is possible.

A currently popular approach to training assumes that the brain contains a separate faculty, usually referred to as the "executive function," that might be trainable even in retarded individuals. The notion of an executive function developed gradually in the field of general psychology and, in the 1970s, played an important role in theories of memory. Initially tied to computer programs, it soon became a homuncular mental process that guided the many subprocesses involved in intellectual functioning (e.g., Sternberg, 1984). In view of the fact that retarded individuals do not readily generalize what they learn and because there are limitless different strategies and adjustments required to meet successfully life's daily challenges, the hopelessness of training for every possible cognitive skill led to the proposal that it would be most efficient to train the executive function (Butterfield, 1983; Butterfield & Belmont, 1977; Butterfield, Wambold, & Belmont, 1973; Borkowski & Cavanaugh, 1979; Brown & Campione, 1979). Yet Brown and Campione (1982) warn that individual differences are not easily wiped out by training unless one is concerned only with specific cognitive skills, and to Blackman and Lin (1984) this approach is indistinguishable from attempting to raise general intelligence. Training a hypothetical executive function brings with it an aura of scientific respectability, but it will prove no easier than training the individual retarded person to be generally more intelligent, an endeavor that for two centuries has frustrated our greatest teachers (Spitz, 1986).

III. THE RATIONALIST ALTERNATIVE

There are many aspects of Descarte's philosophy with which I disagree, for example his sharp separation of humans from (lower) animals, whom he described as mindless mechanisms, or his dualism of mind (soul) and body. More agreeable is his view (which gives his philosophy its name) that for some problems the human mind, by rational and logical reasoning, can come to a correct conclusion without the necessity, and sometimes without the possibility (at least for the moment), of providing experimental (empirical) evidence. Indeed, the evidence of our senses, so dear to the empiricists, must always be considered suspect. Moreover, experiments that do not follow the rational creation of hypotheses are unlikely to advance our understanding. In modern times, Chomsky's (1965) conclusion that humans must be born with a "language acquisition device" is just such a logical conclusion, for which there is as yet no *direct* empirical evidence.

The other aspect of Cartesian rationalism that I believe has great merit is the concept of innate ideas or, more properly, the belief that infants are born with the disposition or propensity to develop certain ideas and certain ways of thinking that are triggered by experience. Since "nothing reaches our mind from external objects through the organs of sense beyond certain corporeal movements" (Descartes, as quoted by Kenny, 1967, p. 233), Descartes would like to be shown "what that corporeal movement is which can form any common notion in our mind; for example—*that the things which are the same with a third are the same with each other*, or the like. . . . These notions are *universal*, and possess no affinity with [corporeal] motions, nor any relation to them." Referring to "certain thoughts that did not proceed from external objects," Descartes "called them *innate* in the same sense in which we say that generosity is innate in certain families, in others certain diseases, as gout or gravel, not that, therefore, the infants of those families labour under those diseases in the womb of the mother, but because they are born with a certain disposition or faculty of contracting them" (these latter quotes are from the notes section of Veitch's translation of Descartes' *Discourse on Method*. See Descartes, 1637/1912, p. 251, original italics).

Continuing this tradition, the modern rationalist believes that human beings are born with a predilection to perform certain kinds of mentation. As noted, the development of language is a good example of an innate predisposition that is shaped and colored by experience. But even specific kinds of mental activity must also follow the same course. Consider the ability to group or categorize objects according to certain correlated physical features. There is ample evidence that infants at least as young as 7 to 10 months of age exhibit this capacity. Younger and Cohen (1985) reviewed a number of studies demonstrating that infants perceive stimuli as belonging to a variety of different perceptual categories. In these studies, resourceful investigators exploit the known fact that infants repeatedly exposed to the same picture or pattern will pay decreasing attention to it (habituate to it). When a novel stimulus is then introduced, visual attention is recovered, or when the habituated stimulus is paired with a new stimulus, infants look significantly longer at the new one.

In category studies infants are habituated to multiple stimuli belonging to the same category. Recovery from habituation by presentation of a stimulus from a different category is taken as evidence of categorization. Moreover, when a new stimulus from the old category is paired with a new stimulus from a new category, the latter captures the infant's attention. Variants of these procedures, using conditioning techniques, have also been used. Quinn and Eimas (1986), in their extensive review, reported that categories are formed by infants as young as 3 to 4 months of age and that infants form prototypical representations of categories, just as do adults. Based on these data, Quinn and Eimas (1986) are convinced of the innate nature "of the early development of categorization procedures and their underlying conceptual structures" (p. 356). Indeed, it is inconceivable that infants have been taught this ability, nor could it have been created by environmental contingencies. Usually, members of a category are seen together much less frequently than are members of different categories, so that frequency of pairings canot be invoked as a causal mechanism.

This ability to group material on the basis of some common features, or similarity to a prototype, reduces the chaos of an infinite variety of stimuli and permits the organism to deal more effectively with the environment. It is logical to conclude that this and many other such vital, adaptive skills had a high survival value and are genetically programmed into the structure and function of the central nervous system. In addition to the fact that these skills increase with the development and maturation of the brain, it is very likely that differences in aptitude for these skills are distributed in the population in a manner that approximates a Gaussian curve (as, for example, with physical height) and that they are adversely affected by neural damage. In this regard, Younger and Cohen (1985) cited unpublished studies by McDonough that developmentally disabled infants have more difficulty than age-matched peers in forming categories.

Another example is the propensity from early childhood to think metaphorically and analogically (Holyoak, 1984). Although not as proficient as older children, even 4 to 5 year olds can think analogically. In one study, many preschoolers successfully extracted and transferred a problem solution from a picture-book fairy tale to a similar (but disguised) manual problem (Holyoak, Junn, & Billman, 1984). We need no experiments to observe the daily use of analogies. People tell stories to illustrate a point, compare situations to win an argument or depict an event, use metaphors in poetry, apply the solutions of old problems to the solution of novel ones, and solve intelligence test items of the form: A is to B as C is to ______. Robert Oppenheimer (1965) has discussed the pervasiveness of analogies in human thought and in scientific discoveries, at the same time warning of the dangers of false analogies.

Many other illustrations of natural competencies can be found (recognition of and facility with numbers, for example, or the discovery of patterns in sequential events), and their universality, although hidden within cultural diversity, can usually be uncovered. Variations of strategic board games are played (and have been played for centuries) in almost every culture (Spitz, 1978). In Africa the game of mancala is very popular and easily set up by making shallow depressions in a board or in the ground and using objects such as pebbles or seeds as pieces. Mancala requires the same skills as are required by games such as chess or checkers: foresight, pattern analysis, position evaluation, general plans, memory, and persistence.

In the present view, the predilection to think in these and other ways is innate, although obviously certain thinking skills can be further developed by experience and training. The structure of the human central nervous system directs human thinking into certain channels, while within these constraints genetic diversity produces the individual differences (variety of genotypes) necessary to allow the species to adapt to a range of possible environments, enhancing the chances for species survival (Dobzhansky, 1972). For example, because retarded individuals generally make no automatic assumptions about the conservation of transformed material, their judgements of size and length following nonconservation can actually be more accurate than those of college graduates (Spitz, Borys, & Webster, 1982).

In experimental studies of developmental disabilities the use of prototypical problem-solving tasks that require analogical reasoning, logic, and foresight is relatively rare (Spitz, 1987), although quite a few studies of categorization ability can be found. Because the dominant empiricist concept is that we form ideas (and even learn to think) by the mechanism of association, far more mental retardation researchers have studied learning and memory than have studied problem solving. Even when experimenters claim to be interested in problem solving, learning has been the dominant procedure, the justification being that the ability to remember is related to the use of certain strategies. As Campione *et al.* (1982) put it , "The subject is presented with a problem—committing some material to memory—and must develop some method for solving that problem" (p. 432).

Rationalists put much less stress than do empiricists on the creative power of environment and experience, which are seen rather as indispensable grist for the intellectual mill. Much more interesting to neo-Cartesians are individual differences in how persons *act upon* the available information, how they organize it and relate it to past experience, how they solve problems (Goldman & Pellegrino, 1984), and so on.

If we approach the field of mental retardation research from the rationalist alternative, the way we define low intelligence and the kinds of research questions we ask are immediately altered. Mental retardation is considered a thinking disability, and the primary question becomes this: In what way are the thinking processes of retarded persons deficient? Research within this framework suggests that it is in the domain of problem solving that the processes associated with intellectual retardation are most explicitly revealed. In numerous experiments using problems whose solutions require logical reasoning, foresight, planning, mentally manipulating objects, and extracting sequential patterns, retarded groups generally perform at levels well below what we would expect based on their mental ages (Spitz, 1979, 1982, 1987; Spitz & Borys, 1984).

As a general term, *thinking* refers to an individual's consideration of any of an immeasurable variety of situations and subjects, not necessarily with any intention on the thinker's part other than as a silent soliloquy, an internal screening of events. But our interest here is thinking as it occurs in problem-solving situations (including the myriad problems that arise in daily life), where it is defined as the consideration, the weighing in one's mind, of the possible paths to solution or the kinds of rearrangements that will bring the problem from its present state to another, more desirable state. Although it is sometimes possible to follow one's thought processes, usually there is no way of knowing why or how these thoughts occur (cf., Meador & Ellis, 1987). That is, there is much that is automatic and spontaneous in this kind of thinking because (in this point of view) it springs from neural processes that are outside of awareness. Consequently, it is possible to teach people only certain of the conscious manifestations of these processes, which are peripheral expressions of an underlying capacity that remains untouched. For this reason, most retarded persons can be taught certain rather circumscribed mental skills without any change in their general level of intelligence (as defined on page 2). Whereas empiricists ignore the role of the central nervous system—believing that thinking is an entirely conscious process that can be imposed by a tutor—rationalists would counter that training does not affect the most important aspects of thinking; that is, that at the present time there is no way in which the efficiency of the central nervous system can be upgraded to any meaningful degree beyond the somewhat flexible but still limited restraints set by the individual's genotype. Of course in those instances where isolation, trauma, or metabolic disorders are the source of deficiencies, recovery can and does occur.

Thinking leads to *understanding*, which refers to the conscious grasping of relationships that makes things intelligible to the thinker (though the understanding may, in fact, be misunderstanding). In all but the simplest kinds of rote learning and memory, true understanding (and ultimately, therefore, thinking) is crucial to learning. Without it, learning and memory are meaningless. Indeed, laboratory experiments in which subjects must recall a list of words or pictures are often labeled learning experiments whereas in fact the subjects have already learned the words; that is, they can read the words or they know the names of the pictured objects presented in the list. Such experiments are more accurately described as episodic *memory* experiments in which subjects must remember, out of their total universe of words, the specific words presented by the experimenter (Tulving, 1972).

On this kind of rote memory task, mildly and moderately retarded groups do not show the kind of marked deficiency, relatative to matched mental age nonretarded groups, that they exhibit on problem-solving tasks, because rote-learning experiments are not fully tapping a crucial aspect of thought. When students of learning turn to the question of why they have such difficulty teaching mentally retarded individuals to read with comprehension at a sixth-grade level, to do arithmetic or algebra problems, or to do logic problems, then inevitably the problem of learning will become a problem of thinking and understanding.

Many present-day information-processing and cognitive theorists do not take the oversimplified view of the organism taken by behaviorists; they recognize and try to understand the complex thought processes behind behavior, an orientation that is vital for increasing our understanding of mental retardation (e.g., Campione *et al.*, 1982; Sternberg & Spear, 1985). On the other hand—perhaps because of the *zeitgeist*, as well as their intellectual kinship to the field of artificial intelligence—many of them tend to view mental processes as analogous to the functioning of a computer, with the result that their descriptions of mental processes mimic computer flow charts or contain specific interacting components. They show little interest in evolution's role in the structure and functioning of the brain or in genetic contributions to individual differences. According to Brooks and McCauley (1984), "most [cognitive] researchers seem to believe that the basic structure (hardware) of the system is the same for retarded and nonretarded individuals; it is the operation of the system that differs" (p. 480). In terms of the trainability of intelligence, then, most cognitive theorists would side with the empiricists. At the very least there are many workers who, though calling themselves cognitive psychologists, cannot entirely escape the strong pull of empiricism; the use of the oxymoron "cognitive-behavior modification" (Meichenbaum, 1977) is an illustration of this phenomenon.

As is evident, profound differences between empiricists and rationalists exist in their respective philosophies of the nature of mental retardation. From the rationalist perspective, if mental retardation is characterized as a thinking disorder, and if human thought processes develop naturally with the maturation of the brain and are triggered and shaped within a wide range of normal experiences (that is, excluding extreme environmental conditions such as infants and toddlers isolated in a single room or subjected to severe emotional and physical trauma), then manifest individual differences are perceived as the expression primarily of innate differences in competence rather than of different histories of environmental stimulation. Rationalists challenge the behaviorist contentions that thinking is a learned skill and that mental retardation is a learning disability that can be rectified by the judicious application of the principles of learning. They also would challenge the hope of information processing and cognitive theorists that, by training mental components, metacomponents, or executive functions, "it will be possible to train people in ways that will make them truly 'more intelligent' " (Sternberg, Ketron, & Powell, 1982, p. 170) or that "following thorough training, metacognitively and strategically deficient children (such as the. . . mentally retarded) should narrow the IQ gap, over time, when contrasted with uninstructed normal children" (Borkowski, Carr, & Pressley, 1987, p. 71). The modern rationalists that I have conjured up would not believe that mentally retarded persons can be made more intelligent by psychological or pedagogical techniques, although they would not deny that they can taught certain specific skills (e.g., Brown & Campione, 1982).

Even though rationalists do not believe it is possible to change the circuitry of the central nervous system, their approach is by no means a resigned or pessimistic one. In this regard, the best chance of rapproachment with empiricism is in the view that if we cannot train general intelligence (as defined on page 2), the alternative is to present material in such a way that persons of low intelligence can acquire some new material and specific skills. Such an approach requires extensive basic research into unearthing and, wherever possible, compensating for at least some of the thinking deficiencies that prevent retarded persons from the spontaneous acquisition of selected skills, an approach already taken by many cognitive and information-processing theorists. In a word, if we cannot change the central nervous system we at least can present material in such a way that retarded persons will learn to the limits of their potential, even though we deny that general intelligence is being changed.

There have been occasions when this approach has been used, and many other possible extensions have been suggested. In an attempt to close the gap between the research laboratory and the special education classroom, Mercer and Snell (1977) reviewed seven different laboratory-based theoretical approaches to the understanding of mental retardation and derived numerous possible teaching strategies from each of them. Gold (1972) developed techniques drawn from basic research on discrimination learning (Zeaman & House, 1963) to teach severely retarded individuals to assemble a 15-piece bicycle brake. In our own studies, we have stressed that mental retardation is, above all, a thinking disability and that one consequence of this fact is that retarded persons do not efficiently use organizational strategies to learn presented material (e.g., Spitz, 1979). For instance, no one can assume that retarded children will spontaneously recognize the redundancy in *cat*, *hat*, *mat*, *sat* when learning to spell these words. Wise teachers will isolate and emphasize this redundancy; they will, in other words, organize *for* their retarded students that which the students are unlikely to organize for themselves. As had been demonstrated two decades ago, organizing material for the mentally retarded student enhances episodic recall (Gerjuoy & Spitz, 1966). It will be no trivial achievement if we can develop a body of techniques to help retarded persons learn target material and specified skills at some increment above their present level of acquisition.

Although the goals set by rationalists may not excite the hopes that are kindled by the more ambitious assertions of many behaviorists and numerous other psychologists that intelligence levels can be appreciably raised, they are less likely to frustrate and disillusion the beleaguered parents and teachers who daily relate with retarded children and adults. And though the goals are relatively modest, they will nevertheless continue to require our most ingenious research efforts.

IV. SUMMARY

Research in mental retardation has been dominated by the philosophy of Lockian empiricism with its emphasis on associative learning and sensory experience as the source of cognition and intellect. The field continues to be dominated by this philosophy despite persuasive evidence that it does not accurately represent the origins of intelligence. The alternative philosophy of Cartesian rationalism argues for the innateness of the principles of mental operations and places the source of deficient knowledge acquisition on an individual's limited capacity for understanding, thereby directing our attention to thinking processes that unfold during maturation. Rationalism recognizes biological limits to raising general intelligence, but not to teaching specific, limited skills.

REFERENCES

Arbitman-Smith, R., Haywood, H. C., & Bransford, J. D. (1984). Assessing cognitive change. In P. H. Brooks, R. Sperber, & C. McCauley (Eds.), *Learning and cognition in the mentally retarded* (pp. 433–471). Hillsdale, New Jersey: Erlbaum.

Ayres, A. J. (1978). Learning disabilities and the vestibular system. *Journal of Learning Disabilities*, **11**, 30–41.

Bailey, R. E., & Bailey, M. B. (1980). A view from outside the Skinner box. *American Psychologist*, **35**, 942–946. (Comment)

Bijou, S. W. (1963). Theory and research in mental (developmental) retardation. *Psychological Record*, **13**, 95–110.

Bijou, S. W. (1966). A functional analysis of retarded development. In N. R. Ellis (Ed.), *International review of research in mental retardation* (Vol. 1, pp. 1–19). New York: Academic Press.

Birch, E. E., Gwiazda, J., & Held, R. (1983). The development of vergence does not account for the onset of stereopis. *Perception*, **12**, 331–336.

Birns, B. (1965). Individual differences in human neonates' responses to stimulation. *Child Development*, **36**, 249–256.

Blackman, L. S., & Lin, A. (1984). Generalization training in the educable mentally retarded: Intelligence and educability revisited. In P. H. Brooks, R. Sperber, & C. McCauley (Eds.), *Learning and cognition in the mentally retarded* (pp. 237–263). Hillsdale, New Jersey: Erlbaum.

Boring, E. G. (1950). *A history of experimental psychology* (2nd ed.). New York: Appleton-Century-Crofts.

Borkowski, J. G., Carr, M., & Pressley, M. (1987). "Spontaneous" strategy use: Perspectives on metacognitive theory. *Intelligence*, **11**, 61–75.

Borkowski, J. G., & Cavanaugh, J. C. (1979). Maintenance of generalization skills and strategies by the retarded. In N. R. Ellis (Ed.), *Handbook of mental deficiency* (2nd ed., pp. 569–617). Hillsdale, New Jersey: Erlbaum.

Bower, T. G. R. (1971). The object world of the infant. *Scientific American*, **224**, 30–38.

Bower, T. G. R., Broughton, J. M., & Moore, M. K. (1970). The coordination of visual and tactual input in infants. *Perception & Psychophysics*, **8**, 51–53.

Breland, K., & Breland, M. (1961). The misbehavior of organisms. *American Psychologist*, **16**, 681–684.

Bronson, G. (1974). The postnatal growth of visual capacity. *Child Development*, **45**, 873–890.

Brooks, P. H., & McCauley, C. (1984). Cognitive research in mental retardation. *American Journal of Mental Deficiency*, **88**, 479–486.

Brown, A. L., & Campione, J. C. (1979). Inducing flexible thinking: The problem of access. In M. P. Friedman, J. P. Das, & N. O'Connor (Eds.), *Intelligence and learning* (pp. 515–529). New York: Plenum.

Brown, A., & Campione, J. C. (1982). Modifying intelligence or modifying cognitive skills: More than a semantic quibble? In D. K. Detterman & R. J. Sternberg (Eds.), *How and how much can intelligence be increased* (pp. 215–230). Norwood, New Jersey: Ablex.

Butterfield, E. C. (1983). To cure cognitive deficits of mentally retarded persons. In F. J. Menolascino, R. Neman, & J. A. Stark (Eds.), *Curative aspects of mental retardation* (pp. 203–221). Baltimore: Brookes.

Butterfield, E. C., & Belmont, J. M. (1977). Assessing and improving the executive cognitive functions of mentally retarded people. In I. Bialer & M. Sternlicht (Eds.), *The psychology of mental retardation: Issues and approaches* (pp. 277–318). New York: Psychological Dimensions.

Butterfield, E. C., Wambold, C., & Belmont, J. M. (1973). On the theory and practice of improving short-term memory. *American Journal of Mental Deficiency*, **77**, 654–669.

Campione, J. C., & Brown, A. L. (1977). Memory and metamemory development in educable retarded children. In R. V. Kail, Jr. & J. W. Hagen (Eds.), *Perspectives on the development of memory and cognition* (pp. 367–406). Hillsdale, New Jersey: Erlbaum.

Campione, J. C., & Brown, A. L. (1984). Learning ability and transfer propensity as sources of individual differences in intelligence. In P. H. Broks, R. Sperber, & C. McCauley (Eds.), *Learning and cognition in the mentally retarded* (pp. 265–293). Hillsdale, New Jersey: Erlbaum.

Campione, J. C., Brown, A. L., & Ferrara, R. A. (1982). Mental retardation and intelligence. In R. J. Sternberg (Ed.), *Handbook of human intelligence* (pp. 392–490). New York: Cambridge University Press.

Chance, P. (1981). The remedial thinker. *Psychology Today*, **Oct.**, 62–73.

Chomsky, N. (1964). A review of B. F. Skinner's *Verbal Behavior*. In J. A. Fodor & J. J. Katz (Eds.), *The structure of language* (pp. 547–578). New York: Prentice-Hall. (Reprinted from *Language*, 1959, **35**, 26–58)

Chomsky, N. (1965). *Aspects of a theory of syntax*. Cambridge, Massachusetts: MIT Press.

Chomsky, N. (1966). *Cartesian linguistics*. New York: Harper & Row.

Chomsky, N. (1980). The linguistic approach. In M. Piatelli-Palmarini (Ed.), *Language and Learning* (pp. 109–130). Cambridge, Massachusetts: Harvard University Press.

Cooke, R. E. (1979). Introduction. In E. Zigler & J. Valentine (Eds.), *Project Head Start: A legacy of the war on poverty*. New York: Free Press.

Décarie, T. G. (1969). A study of the mental and emotional development of the thalidomide child. In B. M. Foss (Ed.), *Determinants of infant behavior* (Vol. 4, pp. 167–187). London: Methuen.

Descartes, R. (1912). *A discourse on method. Mediations and principles* (J. Veitch, Trans.). London: Dent (original work published 1637).

Dobzhansky, T. (1972). Genetics and the diversity of behavior. *American Psychologist*, **27**, 523–530.

Epstein, R., Lanza, R. P., & Skinner, B. F. (1980). Symbolic communication between two pigeons (*Columba livia domistica*). *Science*, **207**, 543–545.

Fagan, J. F. (1984). The intelligent infant: Theoretical implications. *Intelligence*, **8**, 1–9.

Fantz, R. L. (1963). Pattern vision in newborn infants. *Science*, **140**, 296–297.
Fantz, R. L., & Fagan, J. F., III. (1975). Visual attention to size and number of pattern details by term and preterm infants during the first six months. *Child Development*, **46**, 3–18.
Farb, J., Cottrell, A. W., Montague, J. C., & Throne, J. M. (1977). Update on research into increasing intelligence levels of mentally retarded children. In P. Mittler (Ed.), *Research to practice in mental retardation* (Vol. 2, pp. 129–136). Baltimore: University Park Press.
Feuerstein, R., Rand, Y., & Hoffman, M. B. (1979). *The dynamic assessment of retarded performers: The learning potential assessment device, theory, instruments, and techniques.* Baltimore: University Park Press.
Feuerstein, R., Rand, Y., Hoffman, M. B., & Miller, R. (1980). *Instrumental enrichment: An intervention program for cognitive modifiability.* Baltimore: University Park Press.
Freedman, D. G. (1974). *Human infancy: An evolutionary perspective.* Hillsdale, New Jersey: Erlbaum.
Frostig, M. (1975). The role of perception in the integration of psychological functions. In W. M. Cruickshank & D. P. Hallahan (Eds.), *Disabilities in children: Psychoeducational practices.* Syracuse, New York: Syracuse University Press.
Gallup, G. G., Jr. (1984). Will reinforcement subsume cognition? [Review of *Cognition, creativity, and behavior: The Columban simulations*]. *Contemporary Psychology*, **29**, 593–594.
Garcia, J. (1981). Tilting at the paper mills of academe. *American Psychologist*, **36**, 149–164.
Gerjuoy, I. R., & Spitz, H. H. (1966). Associative clustering in free recall: Intellectual and developmental variables. *American Journal of Mental Deficiency*, **70**, 918–927.
Getman, G. N. (1965). The visuomotor complex in the acquisition of learning skills. In J. Hellmuth (Ed.), *Learning disorders* (Vol. 1, pp. 49–76). Seattle: Special Child Publications.
Gold, M. W. (1972). Stimulus factors in skill training of retarded adolescents on a complex assembly task: Acquisition, transfer, and retention. *American Journal of Mental Deficiency*, **76**, 517–526.
Goldman, S. R., & Pellegrino, J. W. (1984). Deductions about induction: Analysis of developmental and individual differences. In R. J. Sternberg (Ed.), *Advances in the psychology of human intelligence* (Vol. 2, pp. 149–197). Hillsdale, New Jersey: Erlbaum.
Hagerman, R. J., & McBogg, P. M. (Eds.) (1983). *The fragile X syndrome: Diagnosis, biochemistry, and intervention.* Dillon, Colorado: Spectra.
Haywood, H. C. (1985). *The malleability of intelligence: Cognitive processes as a function of polygenic–experiential interaction.* Keynote address at the convention of the National Association of School Psychologists, Las Vegas, May.
Haywood, H. C., & Arbitman-Smith, R. (1981). Modification of cognitive functions in slow-learning adolescents. In P. Mittler (Ed.), *Frontiers of knowledge in mental retardation*: Vol. 1. *Social, educational, and behavioral aspects* (pp. 129–141). Baltimore: University Park Press.
Haywood, H. C., & Burke, W. P. (1977). Development of individual differences in intrinsic motivation. In I. C. Uzgiris & F. Weizmann (Eds.), *The structuring of experience* (pp. 235–263). New York: Plenum.
Haywood, H. C., & Switzky, H. N. (1986). Intrinsic motivation and behavior effectiveness in retarded persons. In N. R. Ellis & N. W. Bray, Jr. (Eds.), *International review of research in mental retardation* (Vol. 14, pp. 1–46). New York: Academic Press.
Hebb, D. O. (1949). *The organization of behavior.* New York: Wiley.
Herrnstein, R. J. (1977a). The evolution of behaviorism. *American Psychologist*, **32**, 593–603.
Herrnstein, R. J. (1977b). Doing what comes naturally: A reply to Professor Skinner. *American Psychologist*, **32**, 1013–1016.
Hinde, R. A., & Stevenson-Hinde, J. (Eds.) (1973). *Constraints on learning.* New York: Academic Press.
Holyoak, K. L. (1984). Analogical thinking and human intelligence. In R. J. Sternberg (Ed.), *Advances in the psychology of human intelligence* (Vol. 2, pp. 199–230). Hillsdale, New Jersey: Erlbaum.

Holyoak, K. J., Junn, E. N., & Billman, D. O. (1984). Development of analogical problem-solving skill. *Child Development*, **55**, 2042–2055.
Hubel, D. H., & Wiesel, T. N. (1979). Brain mechanisms of vision. *Scientific American*, **241**, 150–162.
Hunt, J. McV. (1961). *Intelligence and experience*. New York: Ronald Press.
Hunt, J. McV. (1964). The psychological basis for using pre-school enrichment as an antidote for cultural deprivation. *Merrill-Palmer Quarterly*, **10**, 209–248.
Itard, J.-M.-G. (1962). *The Wild Boy of Aveyron*. (G. & M. Humphrey, trans.). New York: Appleton-Century-Crofts (originally published in two parts, the first in 1801, the second in 1806).
Katz, J. J. (1981). Innate ideas. In N. Block (Ed.), *Readings in philosophy of psychology* (Vol. 2, pp. 282–291). Cambridge, Massachusetts: Harvard University Press.
Kenny, A. (1967). Descartes on ideas. In W. Doney (Ed.), *Descartes: A collection of critical essays* (pp. 227–249). Notre Dame, Indiana: University of Notre Dame Press.
Kephart, N. C. (1971). *The slow learner in the classroom* (2nd ed.) Columbus, Ohio: Merrill.
Kopp, C., & Shaperman, J. (1973). Cognitive development in the absence of object manipulation during infancy. *Developmental Psychology*, **9**, 430.
Kron, R. E., Ipsen, J., & Goddard, K. E. (1969). Consistent individual differences in the nutritive sucking behavior of the human newborn. In S. Chess & A. Thomas (Eds.), *Annual progress in child psychiatry and child development* (pp. 36–50). New York: Brunner/Mazel.
Lane, H. (1976). *The Wild Boy of Aveyron*. Cambridge, Massachusetts: Harvard University Press.
Lenneberg, E. H. (1964). The capacity for language acquisition. In J. A. Fodor & J. J. Katz (Eds.), *The structure of language: Readings in the philosophy of language* (pp. 579–603). New York: Prentice-Hall.
Lenneberg, E. H. (1966). A biological perspective of language. In E. H. Lenneberg (Ed.), *New directions in the study of language* (pp. 65–88). Cambridge, Massachusetts: MIT Press.
LeWinn, E. B., Doman, G., Doman, R. J., Delacato, C. H., Spitz, E. B., & Thomas, E. W. (1966). Neurological organization: The basis for learning. In J. Hellmuth (Ed.), *Learning disorders* (Vol. 2, pp. 51–93). Seattle: Special Child Publications.
Mann, L. (1979). *On the trail of process: A historical perspective on cognitive processes and their training*. New York: Grune & Stratton.
Meador, D. M., & Ellis, N. R. (1987). Automatic and effortful processing by mentally retarded and nonretarded persons. *American Journal of Mental Deficiency*, **91**, 613–619.
Mercer, C. D., & Snell, M. E. (1977). *Learning theory research in mental retardation: Implications for teaching*. Columbus, Ohio: Merrill.
Meichenbaum, D. (1977). *Cognitive-behavior modification: An integrative approach*. New York: Plenum.
Minsky, S. K., Spitz, H. H., & Bessellieu, C. L. (1985). Maintenance and transfer of training by mentally retarded young adults on the Tower of Hanoi problem. *American Journal of Mental Deficiency*, **90**, 190–197.
Montessori, M. (1964). *Dr. Montessori's own handbook*. Cambridge, Massachusetts: Robert Bentley (originally published 1914.)
Montessori, M. (1965). *The Montessori method*. (A. E. George, trans.). Cambridge, Massachusetts: Robert Bentley (originally published 1912.)
Oppenheimer, R. (1956). Analogy in science. *American Psychologist*, **11**, 127–135.
Osgood, C. E. (1958). A question of sufficiency. [Review of *Verbal Behavior*] *Contemporary Psychology*, **3**, 209–212.
Paris, S. G., & Haywood, H. C. (1973). Mental retardation as a learning disorder. *Pediatric Clinics of North America*, **20**, 641–651.
Pipp, S., & Haith, M. M. (1985). Infant visual responses to patterns: Which metric predicts best? *Journal of Experimental Child Psychology*, **38**, 373–399.

Plomin, R., DeFries, J. C., & McClearn, G. E. (1980). *Behavioral genetics: A primer.* San Francisco: Freeman.
Plomin, R., & Rowe, D. C. (1979). Genetic and environmental etiology of social behavior in infancy. *Developmental Psychology*, **15**, 62–72.
Quinn, P. C., & Eimas, P. D. (1986). On categorization in early infancy. *Merrill-Palmer Quarterly*, **32**, 331-363.
Robinson, D. N. (1976). *An intellectual history of psychology.* New York: Macmillan.
Salapatek, P., & Kessen, W. (1966). Visual scanning of triangles by the human newborn. *Journal of Experimental Child Psychology*, **3**, 155–167.
Scarr, S. (1969). Social introversion-extraversion as a heritable response. *Child Development*, **40**, 823–832.
Séguin, E. (1870). Idiocy, as the effects of social evils, and as the creative cause of physiological education. *Journal of Psychological Medicine and Diseasaes of the Nervous System*, **4**, 1–27.
Séguin, E. (1907). *Idiocy: And its treatment by the physiological method* (Rev. ed.). New York: Teachers College, Columbia University (originally published 1866.)
Seligman, M. E., & Hager, J. L. (Eds.) (1972). *Biological boundaries of learning.* New York: Appleton-Century-Crofts.
Shattuck, R. (1980). *The forbidden experiments: The story of the Wild Boy of Aveyron.* New York: Farrar Straus.
Shettleworth, S. J. (1972). Constraints on learning. In D. C. Lehrman, R. A. Hinde, & E. Shaw (Eds.), *Advances in the study of behavior* (Vol. 4, pp. 1–68). New York: Academic Press.
Siegel, P. S. (1979). Incentive motivation and the mentally retarded person. In N. R. Ellis (Ed.), *Handbook of mental deficiency: Psychological theory and research* (2nd ed., pp. 1–61). Hillsdale, New Jersey: Erlbaum.
Skinner, B. F. (1938). *The behavior of organisms.* New York: Appleton.
Skinner, B. F. (1953). *Science and human behavior.* New York: Macmillan.
Skinner, B. F. (1957). *Verbal behavior.* New York: Appleton-Century-Crofts.
Skinner, B. F. (1977). Herrnstein and the evolution of behaviorism. *American Psychologist*, **32**, 1006–1012.
Spitz, H. H. (1978). The universal nature of human intelligence: Evidence from games. *Intelligence*, **2**, 371–379.
Spitz, H. H. (1979). Beyond field theory in the study of mental deficiency. In N. R. Ellis (Ed.), *Handbook of mental deficiency, psychological theory and research* (2nd ed., pp. 121–141). Hillsdale, New Jersey: Erlbaum.
Spitz, H. H. (1982). Intellectual extremes, mental age, and the nature of human intelligence. *Merrill-Palmer Quarterly*, **28**, 167–192.
Spitz, H. H. (1986). *The raising of intelligence: A selected history of attempts to raise retarded intelligence.* Hillsdale, New Jersey: Erlbaum.
Spitz, H. H. (1987). Problem-solving in special populations. In J. Borkowski & J. D. Day (Eds.), *Memory and cognition in special children* (pp. 153–193). Norwood, New Jersey: Ablex.
Spitz, H. H., & Borys, S. V. (1984). Depth of search: How far can the retarded search through an internally represented problem space? In P. H. Brooks, R. Sperber, & C. McCauley (Eds.), *Learning and cognition in the mentally retarded* (pp. 333–358). Hillsdale, New Jersey: Erlbaum.
Spitz, H. H., Borys, S. V., & Webster, N. A. (1982). Mentally retarded individuals outperform college graduates in judging the nonconservation of space and perimeter. *Intelligence*, **6**, 417–426.
Sternberg, R. J. (1984). Macrocomponents and microcomponents of intelligence: Some proposed loci of mental retardation. In P. H. Brooks, R. Sperber, & C. McCauley (Eds.), *Learning and cognition in the mentally retarded* (pp. 89–114). Hillsdale, New Jersey: Erlbaum.
Sternberg, R. J., Ketron, J. L., & Powell, J. S. (1982). Componential approaches to the training

of intelligent performance. In D. K. Detterman & R. J. Sternberg (Eds.), *How and how much can intelligence be increased* (pp. 155–172). Norwood, New Jersey: Ablex.

Sternberg, R. J., & Spear, L. C. (1985). A triarchic theory of mental retardation. In N. R. Ellis & N. W. Bray (Eds.), *International review of research in mental retardation* (Vol. 13, pp. 301–326). New York: Academic Press.

Throne, J. M., & Farb, J. (1978). Can mental retardation be reversed? *British Journal of Mental Subnormality*, **24**, 63–73.

Tulving, E. (1972). Episodic and semantic memory. In E. Tulving & W. Donaldson (Eds.), *Organization of memory* (pp. 381–403). New York: Academic Press.

Wanner, E., & Gleitman, L. R. (1982). *Language acquisition: The state of the art*. London: Cambridge University Press.

Wertheimer, M. (1951). Hebb and Senden on the role of learning in perception. *American Journal of Psychology*, **64**, 133–137.

Younger, B. A., & Cohen, L. B. (1985). How infants form categories. In G. H. Bower (Ed.), *The psychology of learning and motivation: Advances in research and theory* (Vol. 19, pp. 211–247). New York: Academic Press.

Zeaman, D., & House, B. J. (1963). The role of attention in retardate discrimination learning. In N. R. Ellis (Ed.), *Handbook of mental deficiency: Psychological theory and research* (pp. 159–223). New York: McGraw-Hill.

Zeaman, D., & House, B. (1984). Intelligence and the process of generalization. In P. H. Brooks, R. Sperber, & C. McCauley (Eds.), *Learning and cognition in the mentally retarded* (pp. 295–309). Hillsdale, New Jersey: Erlbaum.

Zuckerman, C. B., & Rock, I. (1957). A reappraisal of the roles of past experience and innate organizing processes in visual perception. *Psychological Bulletin*, **54**, 269–296.

Developmental Impact of Nutrition on Pregnancy, Infancy, and Childhood: Public Health Issues in the United States

ERNESTO POLLITT

DEPARTMENT OF APPLIED BEHAVIORAL SCIENCES
UNIVERSITY OF CALIFORNIA
DAVIS, CALIFORNIA 95616

I. INTRODUCTION

This chapter reviews two major categories of research on nutrition and behavioral development. One relates to the effects of different forms of undernutrition prevalent in the United States while the other refers to the effects of a few selected constituents in the daily diet of American children. The first section also includes segments on the historical development of studies researching the effects of hunger and undernutrition on brain function and on conceptual and methodological changes that have taken place in the research approach in this area of work during the past several decades. This section covers the following major areas: low birth weight (LBW), growth retardation, food supplementation, and iron deficiency. The second section includes reviews on food additives (e.g., colorants and artificial flavors), sugar, and caffeine.

The literature reviewed in this chapter has been selected on the basis of (1) its concern with deficiencies of dietary origin or with potential adverse effects from ingredients in our daily diet, and (2) its relevance, in the author's opinion, to public health issues on mental development in the pediatric population of the United States.

INTERNATIONAL REVIEW OF RESEARCH IN
MENTAL RETARDATION, Vol. 15

II. UNDERNUTRITION

Different forms of malnutrition are well established causes of mental retardation. A dramatic example is iodine deficiency, which in some parts of the world (e.g., Ecuador, India, Peru) is the cause of endemic cretinism. This condition is characterized by severe impairment of the central nervous system and is often accompanied by deaf-mutism (Stanbury & Kroc, 1972). The prevalence of iodine deficiency and other nutritional deficiencies (e.g., niacin), which in their extreme form result in blatant mental deterioration (Carney, 1984), is negligible in the United States and other developed countries. Therefore, these forms of undernutrition are excluded from this chapter. Of greater relevance here are problems such as LBW, growth retardation, and iron deficiency, which occur relatively frequently in the United States.

Low birth weight, in conjunction with infant mortality, is generally considered in epidemiology as among the best indicators of the health and nutritional status of the pediatric population. LBW, particularly the form identified as intrauterine growth retardation (IUGR), generally results from a poor supply of nutrients from the mother to the fetus. The most recent statistical data on LBW for the United States are for 1984 (Hughes, Johnson, Rosenbaum, Simons, & Butler, 1987) and indicate that the prevalence for all races combined is 6.7%. There is, however, a broad range between states, the lowest being 4.8% for North Dakota and Alaska and the highest 12.5% for the District of Columbia. There are also dramatic differences between races; for whites the total prevalence is 5.6%, while for blacks it is more than double at 12.4%. Among blacks the lowest is 7.1% (Alaska) and the highest 14.2% (the District of Columbia and Michigan.)

Holding genetic background constant, growth retardation is generally determined by a dietary intake deficient in calories and protein; its prevalence is negatively correlated with socioeconomic status (Jones, Nesheim, & Habicht, 1985). In some states the prevalence can be as high as 18.1% (Brown, 1987). Among infants and children in the United States, the cause of iron deficiency anemia is generally a deficient intake of heme iron. In adolescent females causality is also attributed to monthly blood loss. The prevalence of iron deficiency anemia among infants was established at 9% by the last National Health and Nutrition Examination Survey (NHANES) of the United States (Pilch & Senti, 1984). In this as in the other nutritional deficiencies noted, however, prevalence varies inversely with the economic status of the subjects.

Thus, among low-income groups in this country, about 1 out of every 10 children are born with LBW, are growth retarded, or have iron deficiency anemia. The prevalence of these conditions is sufficiently high to be a major public health concern in a country that has enough resources to meet all the nutritional requirements of its population; the justification for action against these disorders will be even stronger if they are determined to be biological risk factors in the development of children.

A. Historical Background

Concern about the adverse effects of hunger and undernutrition on brain and behavioral development dates back to the early part of this century (Spargo, 1906; Laird, Levitan, & Wilson, 1931; Lininger, 1933). At that time wars and revolutions in Europe resulted in a painful scarcity of food, and as early as 1918 (Sorokin, 1975), dramatic descriptions of the effects of famine on social behavior and physical activity began to appear in the literature. After World War II, developed countries became concerned with nutrition in Third World populations, and clinical descriptions of the behavior of children with severe protein energy malnutrition (PEM) were published (Autret & Behar, 1954; Gerber & Dean, 1956). Apathy, irritability, anorexia, and withdrawal were commonly noted, while immobility was observed in the most severe cases. The prevailing view during the middle of this century was that the developing human fetus was relatively immune to the nutritional status of the mother. This view changed with the availability of data documenting the high prevalence of LBW (<2501 grams), prematurity, and mortality among infants born to mothers who had experienced famine conditions during World War II (Antonov, 1947; Smith, 1947). It was still unclear, however, whether less severe nutritional stress would result in similarly undesirable consequences. In the interest of ease of delivery, it was noted that intentional restriction of the size of the infant could be accomplished by controlling maternal dietary intake (Singer, Westphal, & Niswander, 1968). However, the risks to the infant involved in such a practice were not clearly identified. In the 1950s, prematurity and LBW were recognized as developmental risk factors in epidemiological studies and were associated with increased prenatal and infant mortality and early signs of neurological impairment (McKeown & Gibson, 1947; Corsa, Pugh, Ingalls, & Gordon, 1952; Knobloch, Rider, Harper, & Pasamanick, 1956). The data, however, did not differentiate between the relative risks of LBW in term infants versus pre-term infants, nor did it define the role played by maternal nutritional status.

In the 1960s a nutrition intervention study (see Section II,C,4) of pregnant, nutritionally at-risk women was launched in New York City to assess the impact of dietary supplementation during pregnancy on the growth and development of the offspring (Rush, Stein, & Susser, 1980). At about the same time, similar intervention studies were implemented in developing countries (Blackwell, Chow, Chinn, Blackwell, & Hsu, 1973; Klein, Arenales, Delgado, Engle, Guzman, Irwin, Lasky, Lechtig, Martorell, Pivaral, Russell, & Yarbrough, 1976; Waber, Vuori-Christiansen, Ortiz, Clement, Christiansen, Mora, Reed, & Herrera, 1981). A particular concern was whether maternal nutrition played a major role in the later development of metabolic inefficiency in the offspring (Chow & Lee, 1964). These field studies followed laboratory experiments involving female rodents subjected to a 50% dietary restriction during pregnancy and lactation. The results of such experiments showed that, as adults, the offspring were 20–30% smaller than the offspring of mothers fed ad libitum.

Systematic studies on the relationship between pre- and postnatal PEM and brain and behavioral development were initiated in the late 1950s and early 1960s. Data on laboratory rodents (Barnes, Cunnold, Zimmermann, Simmons, MacLeod, & Krook, 1966; Frankova & Barnes, 1968) and pigs (Barnes, Moore, & Pond, 1970) showed that experimentally induced undernutrition in early life adversely affected learning in later development. Experimentation with rats also demonstrated that early undernutrition retarded the division process of every type of proliferating brain cell and delayed migration of cells and myelination (Winick & Noble, 1966). Curtailment of brain-cell division was also documented in infants who died of severe undernutrition (Winick & Rosso, 1969).

These laboratory studies on the effects of undernutrition on behavior and brain morphology in animals were coupled with retrospective human studies. In developing countries children with histories of mild, moderate, or severe PEM in early life did not perform as well in tests of general intelligence, learning, and other cognitive tasks as did well-nourished children from the same communities (Brozek & Schurch, 1984; Galler, 1984b). In the United States a study reported results of developmental assessments among undernourished infants that concurred with those obtained in less developed countries (Chase & Martin, 1970). The possibility that such developmental differences could be causally related to social rather than nutritional factors was acknowledged. However, the statistical analyses required to rule out the possibility of confusion stemming from nonnutritional factors were not feasible.

One of the sociopolitical characteristics of the late 1960s was the concern shared by governmental agencies and the general public on the perceived high prevalence of undernutrition in the United States. The mental development of thousands of children was considered at risk because of undernutrition. Illustrative of such concerns were the report by the Citizen's Board of Inquiry into Hunger and Malnutrition in the United States (1969), the White House Conference on Nutrition and Health (1969), and the authorization by the U.S. Senate to conduct the Ten State Nutrition Survey (TSNS). The objectives of the TSNS was to determine the extent and severity of malnutrition in the respective states (1972). As such, sampling was intentionally targeted to at-risk groups.

Nutritional surveys with small samples targeted at low-income at-risk groups confirmed, in general, the perceived risk of malnutrition in the country. However, these observations did not concur with results from the TSNS or the Preschool Nutrition Survey (PSNS), which was based on a nationwide representative sample of 1 to 6 year olds (Owen, Kram, Garry, Lowe, & Lubin, 1974). These two large surveys did not present a picture of broad hunger and malnutrition in the country. The TSNS showed a high prevalence (30–50%)

of growth retardation among infants in the five low-income states included in the survey. However, growth retardation was generally not associated with clinical signs of malnutrition. The PSNS showed a low prevalence of stunting among infants. Still, both surveys documented that, although the perceived and assessed risks were not consistent with each other, the level of undernutrition in the country provided a strong reason for public concern.

The basic questions addressed by the initial research efforts on PEM and behavioral development have not yet been adequately answered; further research is needed to determine with a greater degree of precision the developmental risks of children with histories of protein–energy malnutrition. Fortunately, limitations in the availability of data have not precluded a significant heightening of interest in the relationship between nutrition and behavior. Questions are now being directed to the specific cognitive effects of selected micronutrients, such as iron (Lozoff & Brittenham, 1986; Pollitt, 1987), and to the effects that specific components of daily diet may have on levels of arousal and activity, mood and sleep cycles of well-nourished individuals (Wurtman & Wurtman, 1986).

B. Conceptual and Methodological Changes

Risk is defined as the probability of an individual's developing a given disease or experiencing a health status change over a specified period of time (Kleinbaum, Kupper, & Morgenstern, 1982). Biological risk factors are adverse environmental circumstances or events that occur during pregnancy, lactation, or the preschool period and increase the probability of diverting a child's growth and developmental trajectory from the course typically followed when physiological and emotional needs are adequately met.

Early studies on the relationship between prenatal and early postnatal nutritional deficits and subsequent brain function were guided by a main effect model that emerged from the biomedical sciences. This model, rooted in the early-trauma later-deficit hypothesis (Little, 1862), postulates that exposure to biological risk factors (e.g., anoxia, PEM) during critical periods of brain growth results in neurological trauma. This, in turn, leaves developmental sequelae such as mental retardation.

Estimation of a dose–response is also an objective derived from the main effect model. This is the quantification of varying degrees of change in a specific behavioral outcome after different degrees of exposure to a biological risk factor. An extreme example of this approach among studies on nutrition and development is the calculation of regression coefficients to determine the changes in protein intake required for a given change in an intelligence quotient (Taylor & Selowsky, 1973). This specific analysis may not be representative, but it conveys the flavor of the conceptual approach that dominated the field at the time.

In connection with the independent variable, it became apparent that the developmental deficits observed among undernourished children within populations where malnutrition was endemic resulted from a complex interaction between the nutritional insult and the socioeconomic surroundings in which the child was placed. Substantive differences were reported between studies in developing countries that focused on malnutrition resulting from dietary deficiencies and infection and those resulting from organic illness or famine. Most studies on children with organic illness showed that these forms of malnutrition did not leave sequelae in cognitive function (Beardslee, Wolff, Hurwitz, Parikh, & Shwachman, 1982; Berglund & Rabo, 1973; Klein, Forbes, & Nader, 1975). Likewise, a study in Holland on the effects of famine during World War II showed no effects of early undernutrition on subsequent IQ (Stein, Susser, Saenger, & Marolla, 1975). In contrast, results from retrospective studies in Third World countries consistently showed intellectual impairment among children with histories of moderate to severe undernutrition in early life (Galler, 1984b; Brozek & Schurch, 1984; Pollitt & Thomson, 1977). Recognition of the complex interactions between malnutrition, infection, and socioeconomic circumstances led many investigators to reject the main effect model and simple bivariate equations in studies on the effect of undernutrition on the development of economically impoverished children (Stein & Susser, 1985; Ricciuti, 1980; Pollitt & Ricciuti, 1969). A conceptual shift toward multivariate approaches has been made as the need to include social and environmental factors as key intervening variables became clear (Ricciuti, 1980; Balderston, Wilson, Freire, & Simonen, 1981).

The need for multivariate approaches has been further reinforced by studies on PEM and LBW infants, the results of which showed that the effects of early trauma are modified by socioenvironmental conditions. Children with similar types of early trauma differ in their developmental outcomes according to the nature of their social and familial environment (Richardson, 1980; Werner, Bierman, & French, 1971; Zeskind, Goff, & Huntington, 1984). Signs of intellectual impairment associated with early biological trauma, such as moderate or severe PEM, disappeared in some circumstances because of the favorable qualities of the child's environment (Winick, Meyer, & Harris, 1975; McKay, Sinisterra, McKay, Gomez, & Lloreda, 1978; Grantham-McGregor, Schofield, & Harris, 1983). An optimal environment might protect against, and in some instances rectify, the cognitive impairment that appears to accompany the insults of undernutrition on brain function (Winick *et al.*, 1975; Grantham-McGregor & Buchanan, 1982).

The second major conceptual change stemmed from the recognition of a selective and probably overemphasized focus on the measurement of behavioral outcomes, particularly on developmental and intelligence quotients. This had a limiting effect that prevented researchers from observing the interactions of undernutrition and behavioral development in their entirety. It is now becoming apparent that developmental risk factors do not need to have a *direct* influence on the central nervous system to affect behavioral development. There is likely to be a developmental cost in the behavioral adaptation reached by undernourished infants and children to maintain energy balance (Adair, 1984; Beaton, 1984; Prentice, 1984).

Continuous infection and low energy intake may have systemic effects affecting psychological domains such as motivation or emotionality. This, in turn, could shape critical developmental processes such as parent–infant interaction, attachment, or play behavior (Anderson & Mitchell, 1984; Chavez & Martinez, 1982; Kvalsvig, 1981; Lozoff, Klein, & Prabucki, 1986; Valenzuela & Araya, 1987). A series of investigations is now being conducted to examine these critical issues.

Recognizing the necessity for a change from bivariate to multivariate models and from outcome to process research does not guarantee that the main effect model and bivariate equations will not continue to be the prescriptions used in research on PEM and behavioral development. In fact, most of the research to be reviewed follows a main effect model. However, a multifactorial approach provides a conceptual umbrella to better understand the developmental meaning of the data that have been generated.

C. Selective Literature Review

1. INTRAUTERINE GROWTH RETARDATION

Intrauterine growth retardation is generally defined by a birth weight below the tenth percentile for a given gestational age (Lin & Evans, 1984). The pathogenesis of IUGR is generally associated with nutritional deficiencies, particularly in developing countries (Ounsted, Moar, & Scott, 1986; Villar, Khoury, Finucane, & Delgado, 1986). In 1980 the prevalence rate for IUGR in the United States was 2.76 per 100 live births. The rate for all low-birth-weight babies (IUGR plus preterm babies) was 6.31 [more recent data (Hughes *et al.*, 1987) yield a rate of 6.7], while that for preterms was 3.55 (Kessel, Villar, Berendes, & Nugent, 1984). Rates of LBW steadily declined from 1970 to 1980, particularly among IUGR cases (Kessel *et al.*, 1984). The pathophysiology of the preterm infants is generally not related to nutritional factors; therefore, this type of LBW is excluded from the present discussion. The issue of concern in this section is the case of retarded fetal growth secondary to a decreasing supply of nutrients from the mother to the fetus (Lin & Evans, 1984).

Two types of IUGR can be distinguished on the basis of the timing and extent of intrauterine retardation. Type I presents a fairly uniform retardation of body size in which no organ is spared. The infant is proportionally small in body size, body weight, and head size. When undernutrition is experimentally induced in laboratory animals throughout pregnancy, Type I IUGR results, with a 15–20% reduction in cell division in the placenta and all fetal organs. Congenital malformations are sometimes present, and microcephaly is generally part of the clinical picture, while placental size is often normal (Winick, Brasel, & Velasco, 1973). IUGR is particularly prevalent among undernourished women in developing countries and is the result of prolonged nutritional deficiencies throughout pregnancy (Lin *et al.*, 1984; Ounsted *et al.*, 1986; Villar & Belizan, 1982).

Type II growth retardation generally begins in the last trimester of pregnancy. Accordingly, the majority of the deficits are related to cell size rather than to cell division. In Type II, the head size is normal and the brain may be spared, but body weight is proportionately lower than body length (Rosso & Winick, 1974). Growth is, therefore, asymmetrical. In the United States the ratio of Type II to Type I IUGR infants is 4 to 1 (Lin & Evans, 1984).

Some studies have observed cognitive and developmental disabilities among term-LBW children during the preschool and school-age period (Fitzhardinge & Steven, 1972; Rubin, Rosenblatt, & Balow, 1973; Ounsted, Moar, & Scott, 1984). Other studies, however, failed to find differences in intelligence test scores between children born at term with LBW and those born at term without LBW (Babson & Kangas, 1969). In any case, most research on the developmental outcome of IUGR did not discriminate between infants with symmetrical (Type I) and asymmetrical (Type II) body proportions.

This difference in body proportions attests to different nutritional histories during fetal growth and is critical to an understanding of the developmental risk of IUGR infants. Symmetrical and asymmetrical body proportions at birth point to differences in the intrauterine histories of brain growth. In one recent study based on data from rural Guatemala (Villar, Smeriglio, Martorell, Brown, & Klein, 1984), IUGR infants were subdivided by ponderal index values (weight/length^3 $\times$ 100) into low ponderdal index [i.e., low weight for length (LPI)] and adequate ponderal index [i.e., adequate weight for length (API)]. The results indicated that head circumferences of the API (symmetrical-growth) infants were smaller and statistically different from those of the LPI (asymmetrical-growth) infants and control (birth weight $>$ 2500 grams) infants. In cognitive (e.g., discrimination-learning, memory, and vocabulary) tests infants with API scored significantly lower ($p < .05$) than the control group. The LPI infants, on the other hand, performed as well as the controls in all but one (digit span) of the cognitive tests.

To the author's knowledge there are no reported longitudinal data on LBW infants with symmetrical intrauterine growth. On the basis of related studies (Wilson, 1985; Eckerman, Sturm, & Gross, 1985), however, it would appear that the developmental risk associated with this type of early trauma decreases as a function of time. In one study (Wilson, 1985), for example, the difference between the mean IQ of a group of children with birth weights as low as $\leq$1750 grams and that of the reference standard was found to decrease significantly as a function of age. Likewise, on the basis of data already reviewed, the magnitude of the deficits can be expected to maintain an inverse relationship with the socioeconomic status of the family—i.e., the higher the socioeconomic level, the lower the magnitude of the deficit (Wilson, 1985; Hack & Breslau, 1986).

More studies on the developmental consequences of IUGR for infants born with symmetrical or asymmetrical anthropometric characteristics are needed. The developmental risks for infants who have experienced a nutritional insult during the first and second trimesters of pregnancy are different from those whose insult was restricted to the last two trimesters. In both cases the outcomes are probably different from what might have occurred had fetal undernutrition been present throughout the pregnancy. Moreover, it is important to establish the extent to which a supportive and stimulating postnatal environment might compensate for the developmental disabilities resulting from IUGR.

2. POSTNATAL GROWTH AND COGNITION

Growth retardation is one of the most commonly used indicators of nutritional history, and body length and weight are the most widely used measurements in nutritional surveys. Deficits in body length are an indication of deceleration or cessation of linear growth, while weight loss is an indication of depletion of adipose tissue and muscle (Martorell, 1984). One problem that arises in using a single anthropometric indicator is that it may provide a distorted picture of the child's current and past nutritional statuses. For example, low weight for a given age indicates a state of nutritional risk but fails to indicate the child's past nutritional history. Low weight for a given age can coexist with a normal or low height for the same age. The former suggests a current state of nutritional risk, while the latter points to a history of undernutrition.

On the basis of the World Health Organization reference standards, Waterlow (1978) has proposed a classification of undernutrition based on the cross-tabulation of deficits in linear growth ($\leq 90\%$ height for age) and weight for height ($\leq 80\%$). Deficits in height for age define stunting, while deficits in weight for height define wasting. The combination of wasting and stunting represents the most critical state of undernutrition.

The National Health and Nutrition Examination Surveys I (1971–1974) and II (1976–1980) have been used to monitor changes in nutritional status within the U.S. population. The two surveys included cross-sectional, representative samples of the population from 1 to 74 years of age and identified economically impoverished families on the basis of the Poverty Index Ratio (PIR). The PIR is used by U.S. government programs for various purposes and includes such parameters of social structure as total family income, family size and composition, sex of head of household, farm/nonfarm residence, and the current consumer price index. NHANES I and NHANES II showed consistent differences in height and weight between poor and nonpoor children (Jones *et al.*, 1985).

Growth data from NHANES I showed that, except for 12- to 17-year-old black females, the nonpoor children were taller than the poor children independent of race, sex, and age. NHANES II yielded similar findings, except that in this case only 8 of the 12 comparisons were statistically significant. However, the absolute differences between the poor and the nonpoor did not show a significant change from the 1971–1974 period to the 1976–1980 period. Moreover, the effects of poverty on height were the same for whites and blacks, males and females.

Two large-scale studies addressing the issues of nutrition, health, socioeconomic variables, and mental development in the United States found small but significant relationships between physical growth and cognitive test performance. One of the studies, the Collaborative Perinatal Project of the U.S. National Institutes of Neurological Diseases and Blindness (Broman, Nichols, & Kennedy, 1975), was a longitudinal investigation of 37,945 children from infancy to nearly 7 years of age. After controlling for the effects of various socioeconomic factors, anthropometric variables for black and white children of both sexes, measured at the time of testing and again at 1 year, explained a small (about 2%) but statistically significant portion of the variance in IQ at 4 years of age. For white children, the most significant anthropometric predictors were head circumference at 4 years and weight at 1 year. Among black children, the most important anthropometric variables were weight at 4 years and head circumference at 1 year.

A second large-scale study on the relationships between growth and intellectual development involved data from Cycles II (1963 to 1965) and III (1966 to 1970) of the National Health Examinations (NHE) Survey (Wilson, Hammer, Duncan, Dornbusch, Ritter, Hintz, Gross, & Rosenfeld, 1986). These two studies utilized national probability samples of noninstitutionalized youth. Cycle II included 7119 6- to 11-year-old children, while Cycle III was based on 6768 12- to 17-year-old adolescents; 2177 children were included in both surveys.

In addition to height the surveys also included bone age, which allowed investigators to calculate an index of relative physical maturity (bone age/chronological age). Intellectual functioning was measured using the Wechsler Intelligence Scale for Children (WISC) and the Wide Range Achievement Tests (WRAT). Family income data served to group the subjects into three income categories: <\$5,000.00; \$5,000–\$10,000; and >\$10,000.

A height Z score, which is a summary measure of nutritional status, was a statistically significant predictor of the two intelligence measures in both Cycles II and III (Cycle II, $r = .18$ with WISC, $r = .17$ with WRAT; Cycle III, $r = .20$ with WISC, $r = .19$ with WRAT; $p < .001$). Analyses within income groups showed that the correlations persisted; however, the lowest coefficients were found among the high-income groups (>\$10,000) (Cycle II, $r = .08$ with WISC, $r = .06$ with WRAT; Cycle III, $r = .12$ with WISC,

$r = .08$ with WRAT). Multiple linear regression models showed that height maintained its significant predictive value after controlling for income, race, and family size. However, the physical maturity index did not improve the predictive power of any of the regression models. Finally, there were no statistically significant associations between changes in height and changes in either the WISC or WRAT scores among the subjects included in the two NHE cycles.

These two large-scale studies in the United States concur with an array of other growth and cognition studies conducted among well-nourished populations (Tanner, 1969, 1970; Douglas, Ross, & Simpson, 1965; Humphreys, Davey, & Park, 1985; Pollitt, Mueller, & Leibel, 1982). In general the magnitude of these correlations tend to fall at about 10 years of age, but they generally remain statistically significant (Humphreys *et al.*, 1985).

The correlational nature of the studies on growth and cognition precludes conclusive inferences. One explanation is that intragroup differences in nutritional history mediate the correlations between anthropometry and intelligence test scores. Thus, slow growth and comparatively low intelligence among the subjects included in the Collaborative Perinatal Project and in the NHE surveys could be as much the result of a pre- or postnatal history of mild malnutrition as of concurrent malnutrition. Studies in populations where undernutrition is endemic yielded results similar to those reviewed above. Correlations between growth and cognition (Cravioto & DeLicardie, 1979; Klein, Freeman, Kagan, Yarbrough, & Habicht, 1972; Lasky, Klein, Yarbrough, Engle, & Martorell, 1981; Moock & Leslie, 1986) are similar to those reported for well-nourished populations, ranging from .15 to .30. Under endemic conditions of malnutrition, there is conclusive evidence that quantitative and qualitative deficiencies in dietary intake cause physical growth retardation (Martorell & Habicht, 1986).

Conceivably, the correlation between height and intelligence manifests only a common assortment of genetic factors. Accordingly, assortive mating would contribute to a between-family correlation of these traits (Jensen, 1980). Such an explanation would be appropriate for both undernourished and well-nourished populations. However, it is weakened by the fact that, in some clear cases, the magnitude of the correlations (Humphreys *et al.*, 1985) is significantly higher than what might be expected (i.e., .20) on the basis of strict assortive mating, indicating that something other than an assortment of genetic factors must come into play.

Tanner (1969, 1970) has reviewed part of the literature and suggests that among school-age children the mediating variable between growth and cognition is physiological maturity. This interpretation is not supported by the data from the NHE survey (Wilson *et al.*, 1986), which fail to show an association between an index of physiological maturation and intelligence test scores, but is supported by data from other sources. One recent study (Pollitt *et al.*, 1982) reported that measures of physiological maturation (e.g., weight for height) among well-nourished children in Cambridge, Massachusetts, were stronger predictors of mental development than measures of linear growth (i.e., height). Significant associations between bony chest diameter, a predictor of physiological maturation and IQ have also been reported (Kagan & Garn, 1963). Among 3 to 10 year olds, those with the largest chest diameters had the highest IQ. Similarly, among girls, the correlation between height at 8 or 9 years of age and intelligence test performance at age 11 or 12 is as high as .41 (Humphreys *et al.*, 1985). Since prepubertal height is a strong predictor of age at menarche, it would appear that children who are physiologically more advanced have an advantage in mental development.

Among nutritionally at-risk populations in developing countries or populations that fall below the poverty level in the United States, maturation is likely to be closely dependent on energy and protein intake as well as on some micronutrients, like zinc (Golub, Keen, Gershwin, & Vijayan, 1986). On the other hand, in populations where dietary intake meets all the nutritional requirements, such as in the middle- and upper-income segments in the United States, physiological maturation is likely to depend on genetics, among other factors (Mueller & Titcomb, 1977), but not on nutritional variation. Accordingly, although the magnitude of growth–intelligence correlations may be the same in undernourished and well-nourished populations, the reasons behind their apparent similarity differ. Nevertheless, it is currently impossible to reject the hypothesis that the association between growth and cognition among well-nourished populations is not mediated by minor variations in pre- and postnatal nutritional history.

In summary, the data pooled from developed and developing countries shows that a small but statistically significant association ($r \approx .20$) exists between physical growth measurements (height, weight) and performance in tests of mental development. This association tends to vary as a function of the social and familial environment of the children. Among well-nourished populations, this association may be mediated by physiological maturation, with a tendency for early maturers to have higher IQs. Among nutritionally at-risk populations, the correlations are likely to be mediated primarily by nutritional factors. Undernutrition in early life causes retarded physical growth and lower intellectual functioning. However, at present it is impossible to discard the possibility that the explanation for nutritionally at-risk populations may not also be applicable to well-nourished populations. Mild to moderate nutritional variations during the prenatal and early postnatal period could differentially effect mental development.

3. FAILURE TO THRIVE

Failure to thrive (FTT) is a general descriptive term for growth faltering originating from organic or nonorganic causes. Generally, however, this term is used to refer to infants or children whose growth retardation (i.e., weight and height less than the third or fifth percentile of the growth standards set by the National Center for Health Statistics) is associated with a nonorganic cause (NOFT) (Accardo, 1982; Drotar, 1985). For the purposes of this article, NOFT will also include cases of so-called psychosocial dwarfism, deprivation dwarfism, and faltering growth associated with child neglect.

To the author's knowledge there are no epidemiological data establishing the incidence and prevalence of NOFT in the United States, nor do national health and nutrition surveys such as NHANES I and II provide sufficient laboratory and clinical data to establish the prevalence of FTT. Nevertheless, NOFT is currently recognized as a common and frequently occurring pediatric problem in both rural and urban populations (Mitchell, Gorell, & Greenberg, 1980; Bithoney, 1985). In a comprehensive review of the literature, Drotar (1988) reports that NOFT accounts for 1 to 5% of pediatric hospital admissions of young children and for about 1% of all pediatric hospitalizations. The only prospective study for which there are currently published data found that 5.5% of a low-income sample of infants was diagnosed as having NOFT before 15 months of age (Altemeier, O'Connor, Sherrod, Yeager, & Vietze, 1985).

The term NOFT does not point to a specific causation. In most instances the causality chain is complex, involving causal factors at different levels of the ecological context of the child (Bronfenbrenner, 1979). Some cases are restricted to poverty and lack of food. Others involve socioenvironmental conditions (e.g., low family income), problems in mother–child interaction, and disturbances in feeding (Bithoney & Newberger, 1987; Kotelchuck, 1980; Kotelchuck & Newberger, 1983; Lieberman & Birch, 1985; Pollitt & Leibel, 1980). The problem of interaction often refers to a severe distortion of the physical and socioemotional relationship between mother and child (Powell, Brasel, & Blizzard, 1967; Pollitt, Eichler, & Chan, 1975; Bradley, Casey, & Wortham, 1984; Vietze, Falsey, O'Connor, Sandler, Sherrod, & Altemeier, 1980). The immediate causal antecedent is almost always a deficient energy intake, and the infant or child usually exhibits clinical signs and symptoms of moderate to severe undernutrition. Statistically significant correlations have been reported for weight gain and caloric intake during hospitalization among NOFT (Bell & Woolston, 1985).

Moderate (IQ $\simeq$ 80) to severe (IQ $<$ 70) developmental delays are generally a part of the NOFT syndrome. The sample of NOFT studied by Pollitt and Leibel (1980) included subjects from 13 to 60 months of age. The intelligence test data have not been previously reported; they included developmental and intelligence quotients ranging from 67 to 105, with a mean quotient of 85 (SD = 18). This quotient was significantly lower ($p < .01$) than that of their matched controls (IQ = 104). Other authors have reported similar findings (see Drotar, 1988). Follow-up studies of NOFT cases show that the developmental trajectories of these children vary depending on the availability of treatment after hospitalization as well as on whether the children are returned home after treatment or placed in foster care. In most cases, their level of intellectual functioning tends to fall below the reference standard (i.e., 100) months or even years after hospitalization (Field, 1984), but the magnitude of such deficits could either disappear—if exposed to appropriate therapeutic intervention (Drotar, 1988)—or become quite severe under some foster care conditions (Singer & Fagan, 1988).

The causes of cognitive deficits among NOFT children have not been defined, and this may prove to be an impossible task because the nutritional and socioenvironmental factors are hopelessly confounded. The very nature of the syndrome precludes the use of clinical trials, including randomization and double-blind procedures (Cook & Campbell, 1979). There are, however, data that strongly suggest that the nutritional factor plays a role in the observed developmental deficits. In his literature review, Drotar (1988) points out that differences in the degree of growth retardation at the time of diagnosis correlates positively with the degree of long-term developmental delay. In another study of NOFT, Drotar developed a predictive model incorporating physical growth (i.e., wasting and stunting) and family ecological variables (i.e., income, family size, and ratio of adults to children). Higher scores in the Bayley Scale were associated with a higher family income and lower wasting. These data go hand in hand with the results obtained from studies in developing countries on the mental development of children with histories of severe protein-energy malnutrition. Methodological problems notwithstanding, the studies consistently report that these children exhibit moderate degrees of intellectual deficits (Galler, 1984a; Pollitt & Thomson, 1977) in the absence of therapeutic interventions after hospitalization. The most detailed and comprehensive followup to date of children with severe PEM has documented that such deficits are still observed during the school years and in adolescence (Galler, 1984; Galler, Ramsey, & Forde, 1986).

As previously noted, there are no epidemiological data on the prevalence of FTT, and health and nutrition surveys pool FTT cases without distinguishing between organic and nonorganic causes. Furthermore, within the category of NOFT itself, it is impossible to distinguish between nutritional disorders that owe their existence to a pathological social environment and those that do not. These epidemiological data are needed before we can determine the nature and magnitude of severe undernutrition in the United States and predict the effectiveness and efficiency of food assistance programs such as the Special Supplemental Food Program for Women, Infants, and Children (WIC). [The WIC was authorized by a 1972 amendment (Public Law 92-433) to the Child Nutrition Act of 1966. This amendment mandates cash grants to state health departments and local health clinics for the provision of specified food supplements to pregnant and lactating women and to children through the age of 4 years.]

4. NUTRITIONAL SUPPLEMENTATION

The effects of fetal and postnatal malnutrition on the central nervous system and on behavioral development have been assessed through experimental manipulation of the dietary intake of pregnant women (Susser, 1981). Evaluations of food assistance programs (e.g., WIC) targeted to pregnant and lactating women and infants have also yielded information on the impact of early nutrition on behavioral development. In general, these attempts represent an extension of the early-trauma, later-deficit hypothesis (see Section II,B), which posits that early variations in nutritional status correlate with later variations in intellectual competence. The hypothesis proposes that such associations are mediated by changes in central mechanisms.

A well-controlled study on prenatal maternal supplementation and infant development in Harlem, New York (Rush *et al.*, 1980), involved placing women into one of three supplementation groups: high calorie–high protein (470 kcal, 4 g protein), high calorie–low protein (322 kcal, 6 g protein), or placebos. At conception all women enrolled in the study weighed under 140 lbs and met at least one of the following criteria: (1) prepregnant weight of less than 110 lbs, (2) previous delivery of an infant of low birth weight, (3) low initial weight gain at the first prenatal visit, and (4) low protein in the diet (<50 gm in the 24-hour period preceding the first interview). Supplementation began in the first trimester of pregnancy and ended at the delivery of the offspring. At 1 year of age there were no between-group differences in performance in any measure of behavioral development, such as the Bayley scales of mental and motor development. An exception was a visual habituation task, where the infants of the supplemented women habituated faster than those of women who were not supplemented.

A substantive problem with this study was that there was not strong evidence that the women enrolled in the trial were nutritionally at risk; in fact, critiques of the study have pointed out that the women were in good nutritional status (Haas, 1981). Therefore, the nutritional risk of their offspring was small. This may explain the lack of significant findings.

In Montreal, Canada, low-income women (N = 3,291) referred to a diet dispensary from a hospital prenatal clinic received free supplemental foods and nutritional advice during pregnancy (Susser, 1981). Women who were not referred to the dispensary were used as controls. In a followup at school age, there were no cognitive or educational differences between the children of women in the experimental group and those of the control group. This study, however, did not include randomization and the evaluations were not double blind; thus, critical flaws in design preclude conclusive inferences (Pencharz, Heller, Higgins, Strawbridge, Rush, & Pless, cited in Rush, 1983).

A retrospective study conducted in a parish in Louisiana reported dramatic differences in intelligence scores between siblings who participated for different lengths of time in the WIC program (Hicks, Langham, & Takenaka,

1982). The mean IQ of 21 children enrolled in WIC during the perinatal period was 13 points higher than the mean IQ of their older siblings who enrolled after 1 year of age. Mean ages at testing were 76 and 106 months, respectively. This IQ difference was attributed to the younger siblings' earlier enrollment and longer participation in WIC. However, the validity of this interpretation must be questioned because of problems in methodology and design. Adverse environmental factors may have cumulative effects on mental development (Jensen, 1974). In Louisiana, the older children may have had lower IQ scores because they were tested at a later age (106 vs. 76 months), after possibly having been exposed for a longer period of time to an environment deleterious to mental development than their younger siblings. In any event it must be recognized that the effects of supplementation and the potential influence of environmental conditions leading to the lower IQ of the older sibling are inextricably confounded in the sibling control design. Therefore, there is no way of testing the validity of any of the hypotheses underlying the study (Pollitt & Lorimor, 1983).

The Office of Analysis and Evaluation of the Department of Agriculture has recently made available the results from the National Evaluation of the WIC program (Rush & Seaver, 1986). This 5-year evaluation was conducted under the direction of D. Rush and included four major components: (1) a historical study of pregnancy outcome assessing the effects from 1972 through 1980 and including data from 19 states and the District of Columbia; (2) a longitudinal study of 3863 WIC pregnant women examining maternal dietary intake, weight gain, anthropometry, duration of gestation, birth weight, and infant length and head circumference; (3) a cross-sectional study of the effects of WIC on dietary intake and physical and psychological development, as well as the use of health services among a sample of 2619 preschool children (of whom one-third were enrolled in the WIC program, another third had been enrolled in the past, and the remaining third had never enrolled); and (4) a food expenditure study.

The WIC program was associated with improved intake of energy and protein as well as various micronutrients in women, infants, and children. The historical study showed that birth weight among WIC participants was increased by 15–60 g, reducing the rate of low birth weight by about 1–2%. On the other hand, the longitudinal study did not confirm these findings because it failed to demonstrate any effect of the program on either the rate of low birth weight or mean birth weight. However, the longitudinal study did show that the head circumferences of infants whose mothers enrolled in the WIC program were greater and significantly different from those of infants of women in the control group. The cross-sectional study also showed that the head circumferences of preschool children whose mothers enrolled in the program during pregnancy were similar to those of the controls. WIC participants were, in general, shorter than control children.

Children whose mothers enrolled in the program during pregnancy were found to have higher vocabulary scores and better performance in digit memory tests than the control children. However, the remaining WIC children did not show any evidence of a salutary effect from program enrollment in their cognitive test performance. Among all other children, cognitive test performance was not associated with WIC participation.

In general, nutrition intervention studies have not yielded the strong beneficial developmental results expected for the offspring. There are some studies that support the contention that prenatal nutrition supplementation of nutritionally at-risk women have beneficial effects on postnatal mental development (Rush *et al.*, 1980; Hicks *et al.*, 1982; Rush & Seaver, 1986). However, these data were generated from studies with serious methodological flaws, therefore they are far from conclusive. One case deserving particular attention is that of infants born to women who smoke. Two studies have shown that while supplementation during pregnancy had no significant effects on the mean birth weight of the offspring of all participating women, it did have a selective, statistically demonstrable effect on the offspring of smoking women (Rush *et al.*, 1980; Metcoff, Costiloe, Crosby, Dutta, Sandstead, Milne, Bodwell, & Majors, 1985). Infants born to smoking women who received supplementation had a higher and statistically different mean birth weight from that of children born to smoking women who received placebos. Among low-socioeconomic-class subjects, 8-month-old infants of mothers who smoked during pregnancy scored significantly lower on the Bayley Scale of Mental and Motor Development than did infants of nonsmoking mothers (Garn, Petzold, Ridella, & Johnston, 1980). It is possible that the developmental delay observed among low-socioeconomic-class infants of smoking mothers may disappear if the mothers were to receive nutritional supplementation (e.g., through WIC participation) during pregnancy. This possibility is strengthened by findings of a differential effect of nutritional supplementation during periods of nutritional stress among pregnant and lactating women (Prentice, Whitehead, Roberts, & Paul, 1981). A study in Gambia found that nutritional supplementation had statistical effects only during the hot, rainy months when energy intake decreased and expenditure increased. During these months, in the absence of supplementation, the mother's adipose tissue is depleted and the birth weight of the offspring is lower than in other seasons of the year.

Studies in Third World countries on the effects of nutritional supplementation of pregnant and lactating women, infants, and preschool children have shown statistically significant effects on mental development up to the first 36 to 48 months of life while the intervention was implemented. These effects subsequently "washed out" as the children grew older (Joos & Pollitt, 1984). However, as observed in early intervention studies among educationally disadvantaged children in the United States (The Consortium for Longitudinal Studies, 1983), the possibility of dormant effects still exists.

Social behavior may represent one exception to the effects of the supplementation restricted to the preschool period. Among children 8 to 10 years old (Barrett, Radke-Yarrow, & Klein, 1982) from three of four Guatemalan villages participating in a supplementation study, several aspects of social behavior (personal interactions with peers and adults, activity levels, response to the physical environment, and affect) appeared to be related to nutrition in early childhood. Controlling for socioeconomic status, high levels of supplementation between birth and 2 years of age were predictive of high levels of social involvement, happy and angry affect, and moderate levels of activity, while low supplementation was associated with passivity, dependency on adults, and anxious behavior.

A serious methodological problem in this Guatemalan study on socioemotional development is the self-selection in the frequency of participation in the supplementation program. Participation was likely to be influenced by the subjects' motivation to take advantage of the availability of the supplement. This sociobehavioral variable could have determined, at least in part, the variations observed in social development (Barrett, 1984).

The supplementation studies that focused on both the prenatal and postnatal periods are methodologically stronger than those that were primarily targeted to effects in utero. However, as already noted, the results have also been disappointing in terms of the magnitude of the developmental effects. Whenever the effects are present, they are not greater than 5% of the test score variance in question, and they are limited to the time when the intervention is implemented.

A critical issue in connection with food assistance programs in the United States and other developed and developing countries is whether school feeding (i.e., breakfast and lunch[1]) provides any educational benefits to the participants. In fact, Section 2 of the Child Nutrition Act—passed in 1966 to enable the Department of Agriculture to assume control over the breakfast, special milk, summer, childcare, maternal, and infant feeding programs—states that there is a "demonstrated relationship between food and good nutrition and the capacity of children to develop and learn, based on the years of cumulative experience under the national school lunch program with its significant contributions in the field of applied nutrition research. . ." (P.L. 80-642, 11 October 1966, 80 Stat. 885–890). Evaluations of school feeding programs in the United States (Pollitt, Gersovitz, & Gargiulo, 1978) and other countries (Levinger, 1983) have failed to reach definitive conclusions because of serious methodological shortcomings in the protocol. This is not surprising,

[1]The National School Lunch Program in the United States was authorized in 1946 by the National School Lunch Act. All public schools, private schools, and private nonprofit residential care institutions are qualified to receive benefits through this program. The School Breakfast Program was created in 1966 as part of the Child Nutrition Act and was authorized permanently in 1975.

since many confounding variables that cannot be adequately controlled come into play within classsroom settings. Moreover, the school feeding programs within the United States were implemented without consideration of the ways in which they could be evaluated. A recent evaluation of the national school feeding program conducted under the auspices of the Department of Agriculture estimated that 3 million children in the United States who now skip breakfast would not do so if the breakfast program were available to them (Radzikowski & Gale, 1984). Economically disadvantaged children who participated in the Head Start or free lunch programs did not show any comparative advantage in educational outcomes when compared to children from middle- and upper-income families (Gietzen & Vermeersch, 1980).

One way to bypass the problems of research design in the evaluation of school feeding has been to assess, under laboratory conditions, the cognitive function of school-age children following an experimentally induced period of short-term fasting. This experimental approach allows researchers to determine whether an 18- to 20-hour overnight fast is a risk factor for learning performance; its shortcoming, however, is its lack of ecological validity.

Two studies (Pollitt, Leibel, & Greenfield, 1981; Pollitt, Lewis, Garza, & Schulman, 1982–1983) using similar research designs indicate that an 18- to 20-hour overnight fast has an adverse influence on a child's performance in problem-solving situations. In each it was found that 9- to 11-year-old children made more errors at noontime in the Matching Familiar Figure Test (MFFT) on a day they did not eat breakfast than on a day they did. In one of these two studies (Pollitt *et al.*, 1982–1983), this decline in performance correlated with changes in glucose and insulin. Biochemical changes do not represent a deficit in brain fuel utilization, but indicate a physiological basis for the transient intellectual deficits observed. In keeping with this interpretation, the results from another study (Conners & Blouin, 1982–1983) showed that eliminating breakfast altered cardiac deceleration in a reaction-time task. Moreover, latencies and amplitudes of visually evoked responses were also affected during a no-breakfast condition. The types of cognitive effects observed among children who were experimentally placed on a no-breakfast condition are similar to those observed among subjects who have been exposed to such differing stressors as elevation of temperature or increased noise levels (Hamilton & Warburton, 1979). Changes in the arousal level of the organism may explain the observed cognitive effects.

In a study conducted in a boarding school, which also allowed for control over dietary intake during the morning, the elimination of breakfast appeared to have no effect on an array of cognitive measures (Dickie & Bender, 1982). In the first week, students were randomly assigned to two groups and tested after their normal breakfast routine for three consecutive days. The students were again tested on three consecutive mornings during the second week, but this time the experimental group omitted breakfast while the control group ate breakfast as usual. Cognitive performance was assessed by two short-term memory tests, a memory search test, a series of numerical additions, and an attention-demand test. There were no differences in performance between groups that could be attributed to the omission of breakfast.

In summary, there are no methodologically sound evaluations of the educational benefits of school feeding programs in the United States. Data obtained under laboratory conditions suggest that food assistance programs in schools are likely to prevent educational problems among children who would not otherwise have breakfast. Arousal changes resulting from a fasting state may interfere with attentional processes and problem-solving competence. However, the cognitive deficits observed under laboratory conditions might not be observed in the classroom setting.

5. IRON DEFICIENCY AND ANEMIA

Nutritional anemia is a hematological disorder defined by a depletion of hemoglobin concentration due to a deficit in the availability of nutrients essential for hematopoiesis. Depletion is generally defined by a hemoglobin (Hgb) value below the 95% reference range for age and sex. Iron deficiency anemia represents the end point in a continuum that may have taken place over a period of weeks or months. Depletion of iron stores and transport precede the hematological derangement (Bothwell, Charlton, Cook, & Finch, 1979).

Each stage in iron-deficiency can be measured by a different iron indicator. Ferritin in the serum is generally proportional to the abundance of storage iron. Thus, low serum ferritin (SF) or depletion of body iron stores defines a first stage. Serum iron is bound to transferrin, an iron-binding protein. Iron deficiency results in a decrease of serum iron and an increase of total iron-binding capacity. The ratio of these two values, defined as transferrin saturation (TS), is a sensitive measure of the second stage of iron deficiency. Iron is combined with protoporphyrin in red blood cells to form heme; when iron is deficient the accumulation of free erythrocyte protoporphyrin (FEP) increases. An increased value of FEP defines the last stage of iron depletion immediately before Hgb is affected (Bothwell *et al.*, 1979; Cook & Finch, 1979).

A critical issue related to the stages of iron deficiency is whether or not iron deficiency without anemia can interfere with cognitive function. If this were the case, it would be clear that the observed effects are not systemic or produced by a deficit in the oxygen-carrying capacity of the organism. The effects would have to be related to the role of iron in the brain.

Three major national surveys—the Preschool Nutrition Survey (PSNS), The Ten State Nutrition Survey (TSNS), and the first National Health and Nutrition Examination Survey (NHANES I)—conducted between 1968 and 1974 established iron-deficiency anemia as a serious public health concern among infants and young children (Owen, 1981). In both the PSNS and the NHANES I the prevalence of anemia (defined by low Hgb values) among

1 to 5 year olds was calculated to be 12% for blacks and 7% for whites. In the TSNS the prevalence for this same group was 25% for blacks and 14% for whites. The PSNS and the NHANES I included representative samples of the U.S. population. Conversely, the TSNS sample was biased toward low-income sectors of the population because its objective was to define the incidence and location of malnutrition in the United States. None of the three surveys, however, included comprehensive assessments of the iron status of the subjects examined.

The protocol of the second National Health and Nutrition Examination Survey (NHANES II), conducted from 1976 to 1980 on a sample representative of the U.S. population, included a fairly extensive assessment of the iron status of the subjects under study. Recently completed estimates of prevalence, using these data, have focused specifically on impaired iron status rather than on the more global hematological problem of anemia (Pilch & Senti, 1984). Of the three statistical approaches used to estimate prevalence rates, two included the use of different indicators of body iron, while the third was based on a measure of the deviations from the Gaussian distribution of Hgb values. The estimates based on these three approaches ranged from 9.2 to 9.4% for the 1 to 2 year olds, from 3.6 to 5.5% for the 3 to 4 year olds, and from 3.2 to 4.5% for the 5 to 10 year olds.

Comparisons between previous and more recent estimates based on NHANES II suggest that the prevalence of iron-deficiency anemia declined from the late 1960s and early 1970s to the late 1970s. More recent data (1982) from the Center for Disease Control's (CDC) Pediatric Nutrition Survey (Center for Disease Control Nutrition Surveillance, 1984) indicate that the prevalence of low Hgb (i.e., the percentage below the fifth percentile) among low-income children is higher than the estimates derived from NHANES II. Among the 2 to 5 year olds, the percentage of white and black children with low Hgb were 6.1 and 12.4%, respectively, while within the 6- to 9-year-old group those same estimates were 5.2 and 11%. The epidemiological information from the CDC pediatric nutrition survey, however, lacks the methodological rigor of the NHANES II data.

Even using the most auspicious epidemiological estimates, the conclusion to be drawn from this information must be that infants up to 2 years of age are particularly at risk of developing iron-deficiency anemia. It is during this age period that iron deficiency is generally related to a dietary intake inadequate to meet increased iron requirements.

Over the last decade the majority of experimental studies conducted with infants and children in Chile, Egypt, Guatemala, Indonesia, Israel, and the United States indicates that iron-deficiency anemia interferes with cognitive functioning. The following literature review is restricted to data from experimental studies conducted in the United States and other developed countries. Experimental study designs have allowed for cognitive evaluation before and after iron treatment and have controlled for related effects of other nutritional deficiencies, illness, and socioeconomic factors. Data from correlational studies or from studies in developing countries (e.g., Indonesia, Guatemala) with highly prevalent health and nutritional problems (e.g., diarrhea, protein-energy malnutrition) are excluded (for comprehensive reviews see Lozoff & Brittenham, 1986; Pollitt, 1987). In developing countries, the association of these conditions and iron deficiency creates an epidemiological condition that differs from that of the United States.

In one study (Oski & Honig, 1978) iron-deficient anemic infants (mean age of 14.3 months) received a dose of intramuscular iron while other infants (16.2 months) with the same micronutrient deficit received a placebo injection. The Bayley Scale of Mental and Motor Development (BSMMD) for infants and the Bayley Behavior Profile were administered before and after treatment. In the baseline evaluations, neither the mental nor the motor scales discriminated at a statistically significant level between groups. However, the delta (Δ) scores (13.1 points) in the mental scale between the pre- and post-treatment evaluation was statistically significant in the iron-treated group, while the upward change in the control groups (6.5 points) was not. There was a significant negative correlation between the magnitude of the increase in the mental development index and the baseline Hgb values in the iron-treated group.

The effects of intramuscular iron therapy on performance in the BSMMD of three groups of iron-deficient infants without anemia and their controls have also been assessed (Oski, Honig, Helu, & Howanitz, 1983). The mean values for Hgb, SF, FEP, and mean corpuscular volume for the controls were 11.9 gm/dl, 31.2 ng/ml, 20.4 μg/dl, and 77.3 fl, respectively. The mean Hgb value for the three other groups was ≥ 11 gm/dl; however, in contrast to the controls, their mean value for serum ferritin was <12 ng/ml. The mean FEP of Group 2 was <30 μg/dl, while that of Groups 3 and 4 was >30 μg/dl. Finally, the only group with a mean corpuscular volume <70 fl was Group 4.

The BSMMD mean values of the four groups before treatment were 90.8 (SD = 18.2), 94.6 (25.2), 83.9 (21.1), and 85.5 (17.3), respectively. The controls and Group 1 increased their developmental quotients (DQs) by 6.2 and 5.5 points from the pre- to the posttreatment evaluation. These changes were not statistically significant. On the other hand, the 20.1- and 23.6-DQ change in Groups 3 and 4, respectively, were statistically significant.

A recently reported study (Aukett, Parks, Scott, & Wharton, 1986) in Birmingham, England, was designed to determine the impact of oral iron on the psychomotor development of 17- to 19-month-old infants. Infants (97) diagnosed as iron-deficient anemic (Hgb = 8.0–11.0 gm/dl) were randomly assigned to either an iron treatment (24 mg ferrous sulfate) or a vitamin C treatment that lasted 2 months. The pretreatment Hgb and serum ferritin values were 9.9 gm/dl and 8.7 ng/ml for the iron-treated group, while those for the vitamin C group were 10.1 gm/dl and 7.7 ng/ml. The posttreatment values were 12.1 gm/dl and 12.9 ng/ml, and 10.4 gm/dl and 7.7 ng/ml, respectively. Psychomotor development was assessed via the Denver Developmental Screening Test (DDST).

The two groups did not differ in the mean increase of the DDST scores from the pre- to the posttreatment assessment. However, a more individualized analysis of the scores showed that, after treatment, "the average of the development was achieved by 15 of the treated children (31% but only 6 of the 49 (12%) in the placebo group ($p < .05$)" (Aukett *et al.*, 1986). Moreover, when the infants were classified by treatment and by change in Hgb (Δ Hgb >2 gm/dl and <2 gm/dl), the differences were more noticeable. The average rate of development was achieved by 42% of the children treated with iron, while only 13% of those treated with vitamin C achieved this level of success (50% of the test items for the respective chronological age are passed).

Results from a 6-month-long iron intervention (6 mg/kg/day elemental iron) on iron-deficient children with and without anemia and ranging in age from 18 to 60 months were recently reported in a study from Minnesota (Deinard, List, Lindgren, Hunt, & Chang, 1986). Selection criteria for this study included gestational age $\geq$ 38 weeks, birth weight $\geq$ 2500 g, anthropometry within ± 1 SD of mean values for age according to the U.S. standards from the National Center for Health Statistics, and no evidence of chronic conditions or central nervous system disorders.

Iron deficiency was defined by a free erythrocyte protoporphyrin $\geq$ 35 μg/dl and hematocrit (Hct) $\geq$ 34%. This group was matched with iron replete children (FEP $<$ 35 μg/dl and Hct $>$ 34%) serving as controls. Iron-deficiency anemia was defined by an FEP $\geq$ 35 μg/dl and Hct $<$ 33%; anemic children were also matched with a group of controls. The iron-deficient children and their controls were randomly assigned to either iron or placebo treatment, while all anemic children were treated with iron. The anemic and nonanemic iron-deficient children treated with iron were fully rehabilitated after the 6-month treatment. Surprisingly, the iron-deficient nonanemic children who received the placebo were also fully rehabilitated after 6 months of treatment.

The assessments of mental development included the administration of the BSMMD for children 19 to 24 months of age and the Stanford–Binet test for the older children. The iron-deficient children treated with iron had significantly higher baseline mental development scores than the controls. In contrast to their differing baseline scores, neither of these two groups experienced a significant change in their mental scores at 3 or 6 months. The baseline mental development scores of the iron-deficient children receiving placebos and the control group were not significantly different from each other. At 3 and 6 months the mean score of the control group was higher and significantly different from the baseline score, while in the placebo group a significant increase was noted only at 6 months. When the controls and the iron-deficient children treated with iron were matched for baseline mental development scores, there were no differences between these groups at 3 or 6 months. The iron-replete controls, however, had higher 3-month scores than the placebo children.

The authors claimed that the comparison between iron-deficient nonanemic children and iron-replete children showed an impaired ability of the former group to improve their mental development scores. However, it is important to note that the baseline scores of the iron-deficient children was higher and statistically different from that of the controls. Besides, these iron-deficient children had a mean development score approximately 10 points higher than that of the children with a similar iron status who received placebos. These placebo children did show an increase in the mental development score.

No intergroup differences in baseline scores were noted between the anemic children and their controls. The mean score of the control group was significantly higher than the mean score of the experimental group at 3 months and increased substantially over the baseline at 3 and 6 months. Group differences at 6 months were not significant. Iron-deficient anemic children, despite hematologic correction over 6 months, showed no significant improvement in their mean mental development score. When matching was done on the basis of baseline mental development scores, the control group showed a rise in mental development at 3 and 6 months compared to the baseline. These changes were not observed in the anemic children. Furthermore, the mean score of the control group was higher and significantly different from that of the anemic children at 3 and 6 months.

Although iron-deficient anemic children and their controls did not exhibit any significant differences in "responsiveness to examiner" at baseline, such differences became apparent by 3 and 6 months, with the control group rating as more responsive. Compared to the anemic children, the rating of "responsiveness to environment" was similarly higher among the controls in each of the three testing periods.

In a study of preschool children in Cambridge, Massachusetts (Pollitt, Leibel, & Greenfield, 1983), 3 to 6 year olds were given a battery of psychological tests, including the Stanford–Binet Intelligence Scale, discrimination-learning and oddity-learning tasks, and short-term recall; 15 children were defined (post hoc) as iron deficient. The criterion was a delta of transferrin saturation from 1 SD below the mean for the 100 subjects recruited for the study (T1) to 1.5 SD above the mean for only those subjects with a TS $\geq$ 20% after 3 months of oral iron therapy. The criteria for the selection of the control children included a TS $\geq$ 20% and Hgb $\geq$ 11 gm/dl. The mean Hgb and TS of the iron-deficient children were 11.2 gm/dl and 11.0%, respectively, while those of the control were 12.1 gm/dl and 26.1%.

Although no IQ differences were apparent between groups before or after iron treatment, there were statistically significant between-group differences in the number of trials required to reach a learning criterion in the three discrimination-learning tasks. The experimental children took more trials to reach the learning criterion than the controls. These differences suggest a deficit among the iron-deficient preschool children in the capacity to attend to relevant information in problem-solving situations. This deficit did not impair performance in the oddity-learning tasks, which tap conceptual learning and are considered to be more difficult than discrimination-learning tests. Thus, when the iron-deficient children were challenged by a complex problem-solving situation they responded as well as the controls. Moreover, the deficit in discrimination learning was reversed following iron therapy.

Although this review has excluded studies on school-age children conducted in developing countries, one such study is included because it is the only reported case based on a clinical trial research design (Soemantri, Pollitt, & Kim, 1985). In this study conducted in Semarang, Indonesia, iron-deficient 9- to 11-year-old schoolchildren obtained lower educational achievement test scores than iron-replete subjects. Following iron-repletion therapy for a 12-week period, the school achievement scores of the iron-deficient anemic children increased significantly above those of anemic children treated with placebo. The deficits in attention and concentration that were exhibited by the iron-deficient children disappeared following treatment. Nevertheless, the increase in achievement test performance among the iron-treated anemic children was not large enough to cancel the statistically significant differences with the iron-replete subjects, and the differences in test performance after treatment still remained quite substantial.

There is a striking consistency in the findings of the experimental studies comparing intellectual and educational test performance of iron-deficient anemic and iron-replete children. This is remarkable given the experimental nature of the research designs and the differences in the ages of the samples (i.e., infants, preschool, and school-age children). These findings concur with those of experimental studies of iron-deficient anemic children in developing countries to the extent that they show similar pretreatment differences between iron-deficient anemic and iron-replete subjects (see Lozoff & Brittenham, 1986; Pollitt, 1987). Compared to the results obtained by studies included in this review, some studies conducted in developing countries indicate that iron treatment is not accompanied by a significant improvement in test performance among the anemic subjects. Similarly, the differences observed between non-anemic iron-deficient children and iron-replete children in samples drawn from the United States have not been corroborated by studies in developing countries.

Existing differences in the general nutritional and health status of the children sampled may account for the discrepancies between studies in developed and developing countries. The differences between the iron-replete and iron-deficient subjects in the U.S. samples are likely to be restricted to one nutrient, while in developing countries these differences will probably include more than one nutrient. Therefore, in these latter conditions, the salutary effect of iron intervention is not likely to be observed in mental testing because of the limiting effect of other nutritional deficiencies. Similarly, milder and possibly more subtle effects of iron deficiency without anemia may not be captured under conditions where other forms of malnutrition and subclinical infection coexist.

Although biochemical and physiological mechanisms for the cognitive deficits resulting from iron deficiency with and without anemia remain unknown, the possible ways in which iron deficiency may affect the central nervous system are numerous (Leibel, Greenfield, & Pollitt, 1979). Iron is an important cofactor in various enzymatic activities in the brain, and depletion of iron results in alterations of brain neurochemistry (Sourkes, 1982; Mackler & Finch, 1982). Still, it is presently impossible to reject an alternative hypothesis that iron deficiency may have systemic effects that reduce the level of alertness of the organism, thus affecting attentional and learning processes.

III. DIETARY CONSTITUENTS

The effects of dietary quality (e.g., the amount of fat in daily intake) on the health and nutrition of children and adults has received considerable attention by the scientific community (Harper, 1978; Hegstead, 1978), policymakers (United States Department of Agriculture/Department of Health and Human Services, 1980), and the lay public in general. These concerns were well illustrated with the specific recommendations provided in the *Dietary Goals for the United States* (U.S. Senate Select Committee on Nutrition and Human Needs, 1977). These recommendations were quite specific regarding the amounts by which to decrease or increase specific elements (e.g., sodium, sugars) in the daily diet in order to prevent such conditions as hypertension, coronary artery diseases, or cancer. The validity of these recommendations have been challenged (Food and Nutrition Board, 1980) because of insufficient scientific data.

Concerns regarding the health value of the daily diet in the American family have broadened to include the potential adverse effects of such ingredients as food additives, sucrose, and caffeine on the central nervous system and on behavior. These three constituents are particularly noteworthy from a public health perspective because they are consumed daily by millions of children. Moreover, policies regarding any of these constituents would have to be based on solid scientific evidence, given the economic implications of regulatory control on the food industry.

The reviews that follow vary both in depth and in breadth. Substantive reviews on food additives are already in existence and the interested reader is referred to them: Lipton, Nemeroff, and Mailman (1979), Wender and Lipton (1980), Conners (1980), and Levitsky and Strupp (1985). The following presentation is limited to some of the main findings from this body of work. On the other hand, the literature on the effects of sugar and caffeine on children is relatively recent and reviews are scarce; this information is evaluated in more detail.

A. Food Additives

In a pioneering report to the American Medical Association (Feingold, German, Braham, & Simmers, 1973), Feingold and co-workers proposed that salicylates, artificial colors, and artificial flavors in foods were a cause of hyperkinesis in children. Feingold subsequently recommended a diet containing no artificial flavors and colors and the withdrawal of all natural foods high in salicylates (Feingold, 1975). In 1979, Feingold deemphasized the role of salicylates as a cause of hyperkinesis (Feingold & Feingold, 1979).

Subsequent studies aimed at testing the Feingold hypothesis have been classified into four major categories according to their research protocols: diet correlation studies, open trials, double-blind crossover studies, and challenge studies (Levitsky & Strupp, 1985; see also reviews by Lipton *et al.*, 1979; Wender & Lipton, 1980). These categories range from the weakest (correlational) to the most stringent (challenge) designs, and the frequency of positive findings among the studies varies accordingly. Two solid double-blind crossover studies showed that either parents or teachers, but not both, could discern the effects of an additive-free diet on hyperkinetic children (Conners, Goyette, Southwick, Lees, & Andrulonis, 1976; Harley, Ray, Tomasi, Eichman, Matthews, Chun, Cleeland, & Traisman, 1978). However, few of the experimental cases that responded to the Feingold diet also responded to the challenge of a food item, including additives (Goyette, Conners, Petti, & Curtis, 1978; Harley & Matthews, 1980).[2] Levitsky and Strupp estimate that only 1 out of approximately 25 children who respond to the Feingold diet show reliable behavioral responses to the challenge (Levitsky & Strupp, 1985, p. 364). Thus, the number of children who apparently increase their activity levels because of food additives is too low to constitute a major public health problem. The response of hyperactive children to the Feingold diet does not appear to be due to the elimination of additives. Here it is important to note

[2]In the challenge studies the subject is placed on the Feingold diet and, every so often, "challenged" with a food item containing the additive in question. Results from double-blind crossover and challenge studies show that among those children who respond to the Feingold diet, only exceptional cases respond consistently to the challenge of food additives.

that the Harley study did suggest that preschool children might be particularly sensitive to the effects of food additives.

B. Sugar (Sucrose)

To the author's knowledge, there are no double-blind crossover studies on the effects of sugar on children's behavior (see Milich, Wolraich, & Lindgren, 1986, for a recent comprehensive review of the literature), and the existing studies are restricted to correlational and challenge designs. Another problem is the obvious heterogeneity of the samples studied. For example, some investigators have focused on the effect of sugar on children diagnosed as having an attention-deficit disorder (i.e., hyperactive), while others have studied the same phenomenon on children free of developmental disorders.

In a correlational study of hyperkinetic children by Prinz, Roberts, and Hantzman (1980) a significant association was found between sugar intake and behavioral disturbances. This association was not observed among controls. In another correlational study (Lester, Thatcher, & Monroe-Lord, 1982), a negative association was also found between the consumption of refined carbohydrates and the intellectual functioning of 5- to 16-year-old children, after controlling for socioeconomic status variables. The results were interpreted as an indication that foods low in nutrient density and high in sucrose may contribute significantly to childhood learning disorders.

In an attempt to replicate the study by Prinz *et al.* (1980), 32 hyperactive boys were matched for age and sex with 26 controls (Wolraich, Milich, Stumbo, & Schultz, 1985). To improve accuracy in dietary methodology the investigators based their intake data on the weights of the nutrients. There were no between-group differences in the intake of any of the nutrient variables; a within-group analysis of the hyperactive children showed that only 4 of the 37 selected behavioral/cognitive variables correlated with sugar intake. The findings were interpreted as a failure to replicate the correlational evidence of a sugar effect on behavior.

Conners and Blouin (1982–1983) reported that a sucrose challenge increased "total movements" on actometer measures and decreased "appropriate behaviors" from direct observations among 13 children with varied behavioral diagnoses (e.g., attention-deficit disorders, conduct disorder, anxiety disorder). However, neither nurses nor teachers were able to detect any behavioral changes in the children during the challenge period. It is apparent that the heterogeneity in the sample precludes the drawing of any conclusive inferences from this study.

Two challenge studies on hyperactive children were recently reported by Wolraich *et al.* (1985). Similar research designs were used in which children were admitted to a clinical research center (CRC) for three successive days and placed on a sucrose-free diet. Baseline levels of the cognitive and behavioral tasks were established on the first day. Sucrose or placebo (aspartame) challenges were given in a flavored beverage on the second and third days. In the first study, the challenge drink was given 1 hour after lunch, with cognitive and behavioral performance measured 30 minutes after ingestion and continuing for 2.5 hours. The protocol for the second study included the same procedures beginning at 8:30 A.M. after an overnight fast. Selection criteria for the two studies included an IQ > 85, no neurologic or severe psychiatric disorders, a history of overactivity and attention problems as reported by parents and teachers, a diagnosis of hyperactivity by the local physician and corroborated by one of two developmental pediatricians in the study, and a teacher rating of ≥ 15 on the Conners Hyperkinesis Index. In the first study the children ranged from 7 to 12 years of age; in the second study the youngest children were 8 years old. Behavioral measures (37) were selected, including systematic playroom observations; laboratory measures of attention, learning, and impulsivity; and examiner ratings. Neither study yielded evidence to support the contention that variance in the behavioral and cognitive measures were explained by the variability in sugar intake.

Another sugar double-blind challenge study (Milich & Pelham, 1986) was conducted in a day treatment program for children with behavior and learning problems. It included 16 6- to 9-year-old boys diagnosed with an attention-deficit disorder, 9 of whom were also diagnosed as having conduct disorders. The children were randomly assigned to one of two treatment groups. During the study, which lasted for 4 days, parents were asked to withhold breakfast. At 8 A.M. each morning the children were given a challenge drink containing either 1.75 g/kg of sucrose (roughly the equivalent to the amount of sugar contained in a 16-oz sweetened beverage or a piece of cake) or aspartame of comparable sweetness. Each boy received 2 days of sugar beverage and 2 days of aspartame.

Cognitive/behavioral data were collected for the 3.5 hours following ingestion of the beverage. During this time, there were three 1-hour activities separated by two 15-minute rests. These activities consisted of two recreational periods and one classroom period. A highly structured token reinforcement program was used in which the children earned or lost points for appropriate or inappropriate behaviors. The dependent variables for this period included following rules, positive peer interaction, noncompliance, and negative verbalization. A classroom period included assignment of points for violation of class rules or being off task during periodic on-task checks. Results from math and reading tasks were also included in the assessment. None of the multivariate analyses performed detected differences in behavior between the sugar and aspartame challenges. Only 1 of the 16 children gave some evidence of sensitivity to the sugar intake; however, even in this case the evidence was restricted to 4 of the 25 measures collected.

The results of Wolraich *et al.* (1985) and of Milich and Pelham (1986) are consistent with each other. Neither study supports the hypothesis that sugar intake aggravates the behavioral symptoms or attentional disturbances of hyperactive school-age children.

Goldman, Lerman, Contois, and Udall (1986) recently reported a study on the behavioral effects of sucrose on four boys and four girls. All were healthy children ranging in age from 3 to 5 years. The study was conducted at a clinical research center at the Massachusetts Institute of Technology. Each child was seen three times, with a 1-week interim between visits. During the initial visit, a physical exam and dietary history were conducted, and the child was introduced to the playroom situation. Two subsequent visits were preceded by an overnight fast. At each visit the child received a 6-oz glass of sweetened orange juice containing a sucrose dosage of 2 gm/kg. The control condition included the same juice with an artificial sweetener, Equal (aspartame). Behavioral observations were conducted 15 and 90 minutes after the drink was ingested, and a battery of cognitive/behavioral tests were performed, including the continuous performance task (CPT), the walk-a-line task, draw-a-line task, and observations of "appropriate" and "inappropriate" behaviors during a free-play session.

A between-treatment condition analysis of the CPT yielded a statistically significant treatment by time interaction. In the sucrose condition, errors significantly increased as a function of time, while the opposite was true in the control condition. The differences between errors in the sucrose and control conditions were statistically significant 60 minutes after the ingestion of the juice. No statistically significant differences were found in the walk-a-line or draw-a-line tasks. In keeping with the results of the CPT, the children in the sucrose condition were more likely to exhibit "inappropriate" behaviors than in the control condition.

The results from the Goldman *et al.* (1986) study are in direct contradiction with those of the two other challenges (Wolraich *et al.*, 1985; Milich *et al.*, 1986) reviewed previously. It is important to note that while this study (Goldman *et al.*, 1986) was restricted to healthy preschool children, the other two studies included samples of hyperactive school-age children. A natural question that stems from these discrepancies is whether or not the age and the behavioral characteristics of the subjects determines, in part, the nature of the response to the sucrose ingestion.

In summary, there is no strong evidence of adverse behavioral or cognitive effects resulting from sucrose intake by normal school-age children or children with attentional deficit disorders. The supportive evidence is derived from studies with weak research designs (i.e., correlational) or striking sample heterogeneity. Well-controlled studies using "challenge" designs have yielded negative findings. One important exception is a study with preschool children (Goldman *et al.*, 1986) which did find an adverse effect of sucrose intake on performance in the CPT as well as on behavioral adjustment. This finding, in association with the findings from another study (Harley *et al.*, 1978) that showed an effect of the Feingold diet on preschoolers, suggests an inverse correlation between age and degree of risk for additives and sucrose intake.

C. Caffeine

Caffeine is recognized as a stimulant having side effects such as insomnia and restlessness (Institute of Food Technologists, 1987). It is also known to cross the placenta; pregnant women who consume large quantities of caffeine may also be risking exposure of their fetuses to the drug (Morris & Weinstein, 1981). Caffeine has been correlated with increased maternal serum epinephrine levels (Kirkinen, Jouppila, Koivula, Vuori, & Puukka, 1983). However, a detailed study of its potential effects on the behavior of neonates found little evidence of association between caffeine intake in the mothers and neurobehavioral measures of the offspring (Hronsky & Emory, 1987).

In the early 1970s, Schnackenberg (1973) proposed that caffeine be used, given its stimulant properties, as a substitute for methylphenidate hydrochloride and dextroamphetamine sulfate (*d*-amphetamine sulfate) in the treatment of hyperactive children. This was an attractive possibility because of the side effects (e.g., anorexia, weight loss, nervousness, abdominal pain) normally associated with those stimulants. He reported that in comparison to a baseline rating (i.e., without drugs) of hyperkinesis, 11 children with histories of hyperactivity had lower ratings when they were treated with either methylphenidate or caffeine (200 to 300 mg/day). Subsequently, Fras (1974, letter to editor) and Reichard and Elder (1977) reported findings that concurred with those of Schnackenberg (1973). On the other hand, Huestis, Arnold, and Smeltzer (1975), Arnold, Christopher, Huestis, and Smeltzer (1978), and Conners (1979) failed to find any evidence of a salutary effect of caffeine on hyperactive children. The study by Arnold *et al.* (1978) [the paper by Huestis *et al.* (1975) was a preliminary report based on a subsample of the cases used by Arnold *et al.* (1978)], which used a robust study design (i.e., Latin square), compared children exposed to placebo, methylphenidate, dextroamphetamine sulfate, and caffeine. A group of 29 children, ages 5 to 12 with high ratings on the David's Hyperkinetic Rating Scale and diagnosed as having minimal brain dysfunction, were exposed to each of the four treatment conditions. With the exception of the placebo condition, the children and testers were blind to the nature of the treatments. The duration of each treatment was 3 weeks, and each was closely monitored for compliance. The dosage of caffeine was about 240 mg/day. Following each treatment, ratings on schoolwork and behavior were obtained from teachers, parents, and psychiatrists. With the exception of the results from a "problem checklist" used by the parents, which found that the caffeine had a mild but significant effect on the children, the effects of the caffeine on the behavioral ratings were not different from those of the placebo. In this and in the five other statistical comparisons there were highly significant salutary effects of the two stimulant drugs. The authors were unable to explain the differences between their negative findings on the caffeine treatment and those reported by Schnackenberg (1973).

The controversy over the putative beneficial effects of caffeine on hyperactivity, which remained dormant during the first part of this decade, has been reawakened by a recently published study (Schechter & Timmons, 1985). In contrast to previous work that generally focused on behavioral rating, this report focuses on cognitive test performance. Children (15) between the ages of 6 and 10, some with histories of diagnosed hyperkinesis, were included. At the time of the study, 10 of the children scored at least 1 SD above published norms on the total scores of the Conners Abbreviated Parent Rating Scale for hyperactivity; the remaining 5 scored within the normal range. In addition to a predrug condition, the children were exposed to the following treatments in a Latin square design: caffeine (300 mg) twice daily, high *d*-amphetamine sulfate (5 mg) twice daily, low *d*-amphetamine sulfate (1.6 mg) twice daily, and low *d*-amphetamine sulfate and caffeine twice daily. Each of these treatments lasted for a 2-week period.

The results differed for the hyperactive and nonhyperactive children. Among the former, the four treatments resulted, compared to the predrug condition, in a significant increase in reaction time and a significant decrease in errors of commission in the CPT. All treatments resulted in a decrease in scores in the Conners questionnaire, placing the children within the normal range. However, there were no differences between treatments, and there was no evidence that the drugs had a significant beneficial effect upon the nonhyperactive children.

Two important differences in research design might explain the discrepancies between the results of Schechter and Timmons (1985) and those of others that have found no effect of caffeine. Most researchers followed Schnackenberg's (1973) suggestion of using 200–300 mg of caffeine daily and tended to focus on motor behavioral measures. Schecter and Timmons used 600 mg daily and looked at the effects on the continuous performance test (i.e., vigilance). Here, it should be noted that Conners (1979), using lower dosages of caffeine (a maximum of 180 mg), reported one significant effect of caffeine: a dose-related effect on the amplitude of the response in the occipital area on evoked potential. Moreover, he also observed a negative, nonsignificant association between the caffeine dosage and the errors of commission and omission in the CPT; dosages ranged from 75 to 180 mg daily.

In summary, the data are inconclusive and have failed to determine whether caffeine is beneficial for some and detrimental to others. A substantial number of studies on hyperactive children, using a daily dosage $\leq$ 300 mg of caffeine and focusing on motor behavior, have failed to find the expected helpful effects. Conversely, one recent well-controlled study found beneficial effects on vigilance. An explanation for this discrepancy is that the effects of caffeine are more likely to be observed in the cognitive rather than in the motor domain. This difference also indicates that caffeine does not have the spectrum of effects observed in the administration of *d*-amphetamine sulfate and methylphenidate.

Coverage of the effects of caffeine has not been as detailed for children free of developmental disorders as for hyperactive children. Moreover, a very well-controlled study has suggested that observed effects may depend on predisposition. Rapoport, Berg, Ismond, Zahn, and Neims (1984) conducted a challenge study on the behavioral effects of caffeine among normal children. The protocol included 10-year-old children classified as either "high consumers" (~500 mg/day) or "low consumers" of soft drinks. [The caffeine content (mg/12-oz serving) of soft drinks varies from 72.0 mg (Jolt) to 1.2 mg (i.e. Canada Dry Diet Cola) as reported by the Institute of Food Technologists' Expert Panel on Food Safety and Nutrition (1987)]. The data showed important psychological and behavioral differences between groups, even when they were not receiving caffeine. The high consumers tended to have lower levels of arousal and were more impulsive. Moreover, the challenge with a caffeine-free diet did not have any detectable effect in either group. As indicated by the authors these findings "are similar to findings from previous single-dose caffeine studies in college students in which adult male high consumers also had lower indexes of autonomic arousal" (p. 1078). Personality characteristics may predispose adults and children to the consumption of large quantities of caffeine.

IV. SUMMARY AND CONCLUSIONS

The introductory, historical section of this article noted that one of the sociopolitical features that characterized the late 1960s and early 1970s was the *perceived risk* of malnutrition in the United States. This perception led to the growth of already existing food assistance programs [e.g., Food Stamp Program (FSP)] and the creation of new ones (i.e., the Special Supplemental Food Programs for Women, Infants, and Children in 1979 and 1980). Evaluations of these and other food assistance programs have been criticized because of the lack of randomization and the inclusion of inappropriate controls. None of these programs wase implemented with consideration for the requirements of evaluations. However, the evaluations that do exist, particularly those of the WIC program, strongly suggest that these interventions are likely to have preventive effects and that the risk of malnutrition in this country decreased significantly in the 1970s and early 1980s because of these programs.

The pattern of improvement in the nutritional status of low-income groups in the United States, shaped in the last decade, has not been followed up in the 1980s. On the one hand, the growth of the food assistance programs has been arrested; on the other, the number of children below the poverty line has tended to increase (Children's Defense Fund, 1987). These changes in social policy and income distribution have exacted a toll on the health and nutritional status of the pediatric population, as indicated by the rates of infant mortality and low-birth-weight infants. Infant mortality rates in some segments of the population (such as among low-income black families in cities like Washington, D.C., or Detroit, Michigan, for example) are as high as rates in some developing countries (Hughes *et al.*, 1987). Thus, the concern for the developmental risk of nutritional deficiencies is again present.

A. Methodological Issues

The focus of this review has been on data from studies conducted either in the United States or in other developed countries. Our primary concern has been public health issues relevant to the pediatric population of this country, although inevitably some references had to be made to data from developing countries. This was the case when these data strengthened particular inferences.

As the review of studies on the effects of undernutrition progressed, it became apparent that a problem existed in the variability of the methodological rigor of the research. Research on LBW babies has been characterized by a lack of precision in the differential diagnosis among the various types of LBW babies and in the pathogenesis of the condition. Studies with well-defined cases of an inadequate supply of nutrients from the mother to the fetus are relatively new.

The studies on growth retardation and mental development are strictly correlational and, as such, provide weak basis upon which to establish lines of causality. A related problem is that the magnitude of the correlations between growth and cognition observed in populations where malnutrition is endemic are similar to those observed among well-nourished populations. It seems likely that the reasons for these correlations are not the same in the two types of populations.

Research on the effects of nutrition supplementation provide a stronger basis than the correlational studies as a source from which to draw inferential statements. However, most of the supplementation research has been done in developing countries. In these studies the general health and nutrition of the participant children differs substantively from that of the children in the United States. The external validity of such studies is, therefore, questionable. The most robust study designs on undernutrition and behavior are those on iron-deficiency anemia. This state of affairs is understandable because this nutritional disorder allows for the experimental manipulation of a single nutrient over short periods of time so that the requirements of a clinical trial can be met.

B. Substantive Issues: Undernutrition

With these caveats in mind we may proceed to draw some conclusions on the effects of undernutrition on behavioral development. First, however, the association between risk of undernutrition and socioeconomic status should be underscored. Although this association has not been discussed in detail, it has been pointed out that epidemiological data on LBW, growth retardation, and iron-deficiency anemia consistently show that the highest prevalence of these risk factors are found among the lowest income groups in this country. This is important because, as already noted, it is documented that the probabilities of deviation from a normal developmental course of children exposed to an early biological trauma varies as a function of socioeconomic status. The highest probability of finding a developmental sequela from early trauma is observed among the lowest income groups, where the chances for good health care and formal and informal educational opportunities are less available. Thus, the consequences of early trauma are not independent of the context in which the child lives. These conditions are interactive, and, as a result, what will be developmentally expressed depends upon the nature of the biological risk factor to which the child is exposed and the nature of the environment in which he or she grows.

1. IUGR

The information currently available on IUGR infants with symmetrical and asymmetrical body proportions is not sufficient to determine conclusively the probabilities of developmental risk from these conditions. However, on the basis of the data available and because of the nutritional implications of the proportional and the disproportional body measurements, it is justifiable to infer that the risk of both conditions are quite different. The highest risk is among the symmetrical infants, at least during the preschool years. A small infant with a small head circumference and low body weight is likely to have been undernourished throughout the period of gestation. Both cell multiplication and cell size were adversely affected. On the other hand, the probabilities of risk among cases with normal body size but low weight are likely to be low. In these cases cell multiplication is not likely to have been affected, while adipose tissue is lower than normal. Cases of small body size for a comparatively high body weight are rare; however, these cases are likely to be at high risk if the disproportionate body measurements are the result of a deficient supply of nutrients to the fetus during the first trimester of gestation.

2. GROWTH RETARDATION

Among infants and children in the low-income groups in the United States, growth faltering is generally associated with a qualitatively and quantitatively poor diet. Normal biological variability in physiological maturation does not explain why these children are consistently smaller than children of the same age but from higher income families. Although there is no epidemiological data on morbidity, it is reasonable to suspect that frequent diseases also play a part in the causality of small body size in these populations. Small bodies maintain a low but statistically significant correlation with both comparatively low intelligence test scores and low school achievement. These correlations are consistent across this type of population and are reasonably explained by the effects of nutritional history. However, these correlations *do not express the nature of the relationship between undernutrition and mental development*. Growth retardation is not a "proxy for nutrition"; it is only an index of nutritional status (Beaton, 1983). In other words it is not an intermediary between undernutrition and brain function; it is only *one* reflection of a nutritional deficiency. The correlation of growth and cognition among low-income groups only points toward the bidirectional effect of undernutrition: on physical growth and on mental development.

A dramatic example of growth retardation in the United States is the so-called failure-to-thrive syndrome, which generally implies growth faltering (i.e., weight and height below the third or fifth percentile of National Center for Health Statistics) without an organic illness (NOFT). There are no national statistics on this syndrome, but it is considered a routine pediatric problem. One characteristic of NOFT is slow psychomotor development in early life and low IQ in the school-age period. The magnitude of these developmental deficits is often similar to those observed among cases of severe protein-energy malnutrition in developing countries. The proximal and distal causal factors of NOFT are not constant across cases. In some instances the sole explanation might be insufficient food, whereas in other instances it entails a disturbed mother–infant interaction and/or other forms of a pathological social environment. However, in most if not all cases where the growth retardation is not constitutional, not associated with genetic factors, and not due to an organic illness, NOFT involves undernutrition. The specific role of a deficient intake or absorption of calories and micronutrients (e.g., iron) in the developmental delay observed among these cases is unknown. However, given the nature of the growth disorder, the involvement of nutritional factors, and the magnitude of the developmental deficit, it is reasonable to draw the general conclusion that the retardation of mental development is determined, in part, by undernutrition and social environmental circumstances. This is, unfortunately, a broad conclusion that is not helpful in terms of either prevention or solution. Much research is needed to establish the specific role of the different factors involved in the causation of this syndrome as well as in the developmental disorders observed. Likewise, a critical need exists for epidemiological studies to determine the prevalence and incidence of NOFT, and to measure the extent to which NOFT, together with a social pathological environment, form a part of the total undernourished population in the United States.

3. NUTRITIONAL SUPPLEMENTATION

Many cases of failure to thrive (particularly those associated with child neglect) and other nutritional deficiencies in this country will not be fully prevented through food assistance programs. Problems of coverage and implementation, and the less-than-optimal response of the potential beneficiaries, will surely interfere with the effectiveness and efficiency of these programs. However, even though these problems do exist, the fact is that, as previously noted, these programs have been partly successful in preventing malnutrition. To some extent we may also infer that they have made a small but important contribution to foster mental development among low-income, nutritionally at-risk children. In the United States there is not a single definitive work that has adequately tested the developmental impact of supplementation in early life. However, the results that do exist (given the methodological caveats noted) from this country and from developing countries suggest that, among nutritionally at-risk populations, supplementation will have a mild but important beneficial effect on mental development during infancy and the preschool years. In my opinion these data *alone* are not sufficiently strong to serve as the core or basis for an argument on behalf of the maintenance or increment of these programs. However, they should play a part in any argument in that direction.

4. IRON DEFICIENCY

On each of the topics covered in this review, data on both sides of a particular argument were presented whenever it existed—that is, most of the time. Indeed, it is generally difficult to find a question or issue in nutrition that does *not* present contradictory findings; this is generally the case in connection with the effect of a particular nutrient or food constituent on behavioral development. An important exception is iron-deficiency anemia. The experimental data in the United States and in other countries consistently show that iron-deficient anemic infants and children perform worse in developmental (e.g., Bayley) or other cognitive tests (e.g., attention) than their iron-replete peers. The data in this country also consistently show that iron-repletion therapy fully corrects the developmental delay. However, the specific neurophysiological and neurochemical mechanisms that mediate the cognitive effects observed remain unknown. Basic research on the effects of iron on the brain is urgently needed. This area of scientific inquiry offers unique possibilities for understanding the mechanisms whereby nutrients can affect the brain. From a public health standpoint it also offers a clear illustration in the ways in which undernutrition can affect the development of children.

C. Substantive Issues: Dietary Constituents

We turn now from the effects of undernutrition to the effects of food additives (e.g., the Feingold diet), sugar (i.e., sucrose), and caffeine on behavioral development. One important methodological distinction between this area of research and that devoted to undernutrition and behavior is that studies on dietary constituents may be fitted into the framework of a clinical trial, whereas most studies on undernutrition are correlational. (One exception, as previously noted, is the nutritional trials that test the effect of body iron on cognitive function.) Moreover, as indicated, studies of food constituents may also include the so-called challenge designs.

1. FOOD ADDITIVES

Research on additives seems to have peaked in the early part of this decade, and the issue appears to have been pretty well resolved. The data currently available strongly support the contention that food additives *do not* represent a public health risk for the pediatric population of the United States. This does not deny, however, the possibility that there may be individuals who are particularly sensitive (allergic) to selected food additives (i.e., artificial colors and flavors). Similarly, the available data does not support the contention that additive-free diets will reduce hyperkinesis or have a beneficial effect on cognition among children with a diagnosis of attention-deficit disorder.

2. SUGAR

Research on the effects of sugar on behavior is relatively new; it is expected that more data need to be generated before conclusive inferences, such as the ones for food additives, may be drawn. Nonetheless, the experimental data clearly point in the direction of no effects on both normal children and children with attention-deficit disorders. One important exception might be preschool children; a well-grounded study suggests that there may be some adverse effects on attention (i.e., vigilance) and social behavior.

3. CAFFEINE

The hypothesis that caffeine may replace *d*-amphetamine sulfate and methylphenidate in the treatment of hyperkinesis (i.e., attention-deficit disorders) is not supported by most of the available data—at least at a dosage of ≤ 300 mg daily. The final word is not yet in, however, given some promising findings at a higher dosage of caffeine (~ 600 mg) and focusing on specific cognitive functions (e.g., vigilance). The possibility that caffeine could explain the active (or disruptive) behavior observed among some "high" consumers is not supported by available data. Personality characteristics may lead to both the observed behavior and the "high" caffeine consumption.

In conclusion, there is at present no scientific reason to believe, using behavior and cognitive function as referent criteria, that additives, sugar, and caffeine represent public health problems for the pediatric population in the United States. The data, however, are definitive only for additives; further research is necessary on sugar and caffeine. However, let us bear in mind an important principle under which we live: substances, like persons, must be regarded as innocent unless proven otherwise.

REFERENCES

Accardo, P. J. (Ed.) (1982). *Failure to thrive in infancy and early childhood: A multidisciplinary team approach*. Baltimore: University Park Press.

Adair, L. S. (1984). Marginal intake and maternal adaptation: The case of rural Taiwan. In E. Pollitt & P. Amante (Eds.), *Energy intake and activity* (pp. 33–55) New York: Liss.

Altemeier, W. A., III, O'Connor, S., Sherrod, K. B., Yeager, T. D., & Vietze, P. M. (1985). A strategy for managing nonorganic failure to thrive based on a prospective study of antecedents. In D. Drotar (Ed.), *New directions in failure to thrive. Implications for research and practice* (pp. 211–222). New York: Plenum.

Anderson, R., & Mitchell, E. M. (1984). Children's health and play in rural Nepal. *Social Science and Medicine*, **19**, 735–740.

Antonov, A. N. (1947) Children born during the seige of Leningrad in 1942. *The Journal of Pediatrics*, **30**, 250–259.

Arnold, L. E., Christopher, J., Huestis, R., & Smeltzer, D. J. (1978). Methylphenidate vs dextroamphetamine vs caffeine in minimal brain dysfunction. *Archives of General Psychiatry*, **35**, 463–473.

Aukett, M. A., Parks, Y. A., Scott, P. H., & Wharton, B. A. (1986). Treatment with iron increases weight gain and psychomotor development. *Archives of Disease in Childhood*, **61**, 849–857.

Autret, M., & Behar, M. (1954) Sindrome policarencial infantil (Kwashiorkor) and its prevention in Central America. *FAO Nutritional Studies No. 13*. Rome: Food and Agricultural Organization of the United Nations.

Babson, S. G., & Kangas, J. (1969). Preschool intelligence of undersized term infants. *American Journal of Diseases of Children*, **117**, 553–557.

Balderston, J. B., Wilson, A. B., Freire, M. E., & Simonen, M. S. (Eds.) (1981). *Malnourished children of the rural poor*. Boston: Auburn House.

Barnes, R. H., Cunnold, S. R., Zimmermann, R. R., Simmons, H., MacLeod, R. B., & Krook, L. (1966). Influence of nutritional deprivations in early life on learning behavior of rats as measured by performance in a water maze. *Journal of Nutrition*, **89**, 399–410.

Barnes, R. H., Moore, A. U., & Pond, W. G. (1970). Behavioral abnormalities in young adult pigs caused by malnutrition in early life. *Journal of Nutrition*, **100**, 149–155.

Barrett, D. E. (1984). Methodological requirements for conceptually valid research studies on the behavioral effects of malnutrition. In J. Galler (Ed.), *Human nutrition: A comprehensive treatise:* Vol. 5, *Nutrition and behavior* (pp. 9–36). New York: Plenum.

Barrett, D. E., Radke-Yarrow, M., & Klein, R. E. (1982). Chronic malnutrition and child behavior: Effects of early caloric supplementation on social and emotional functioning at school age. *Developmental Psychology*, **18**, 541–556.

Beardslee, W. R., Wolff, P. H., Hurwitz, I., Parikh, B., & Shwachman, H. (1982). The effects of infantile malnutrition on behavioral development: A follow-up study. *American Journal of Clinical Nutrition*, **35**, 1437–1441.

Beaton, G. H. (1983). Energy in human nutrition: Perspectives and problems. *Nutrition Reviews*, **41**, 325–340.

Beaton, G. H. (1984). Adaptation to and accommodation of long-term low energy intake: A commentary on the conference on energy intake and activity. In E. Pollitt & P. Amante (Eds.), *Energy intake and activity* (pp. 395–403). New York: Liss.

Bell, L. S., & Woolston, J. L. (1985). The relationship of weight gain and caloric intake in infants with organic and nonorganic failure to thrive syndrome. *Journal of the American Academy of Child Psychiatry,* **24**, 447–452.
Berglund, G., & Rabo, E. (1973). A long-term follow-up investigation of patients with hypertrophic pyloric stenosis—with special reference to the physical and mental development. *Acta Paediatrica Scandinavica,* **62**, 125–129.
Bithoney, W. G. (1985). Prepared statements to the joint hearing before the Select Committee on Hunger and the Subcommittee on Health and the Environment. In U.S. House Committee on Energy and Commerce. *Health consequences of hunger on U.S. infants and children* Hearing, 23 May 1985 (Serial No. 99-3 and 99-10, pp. 25–32 and 65–67). Washington, D.C.: U.S. Government Printing Office.
Bithoney, W. G., & Newberger, E. H. (1987). Child and family attributes of failure-to-thrive. *Journal of Developmental and Behavioral Pediatrics,* **8**, 32–36.
Blackwell, R. Q., Chow, B. F., Chinn, K. S. K., Blackwell B.-N., & Hsu, S. C. (1973). Prospective maternal nutrition study in Taiwan: Rationale, study design, feasibility, and preliminary findings. *Nutrition Reports International,* **7**, 517–532.
Bothwell, T. H., Charlton, R. W., Cook, J. D., & Finch, C. A. (1979). *Iron metabolism in man.* Oxford: Blackwell.
Bradley, R. H., Casey, P. M., & Wortham, B. (1984). Home environments of low SES non-organic failure-to-thrive infants. *Merrill-Palmer Ouarterly,* **30**, 393–402.
Broman, S. H., Nichols, P. L., & Kennedy, W. A. (1975). *Preschool IQ: Prenatal and early developmental correlates.* Hillsdale, New Jersey: Erlbaum.
Bronfenbrenner, U. (1979). *The ecology of human development.* Cambridge, Massachusetts: Harvard University Press.
Brown, J. L. (1987). Hunger in the U.S. *Scientific American,* **256**, 37–41.
Brozek, J., & Schurch, B. (Eds.) (1984). *Malnutrition and behavior: Critical assessment of key issues.* Lausanne: Nestle Foundation.
Carney, M. W. P. (1984). Vitamin deficiencies and excesses: behavioral consequences in adults. In J. R. Galler (Ed.), *Human nutrition: A comprehensive treatise:* Vol. 5, *Nutrition and behavior* (pp. 193–222). New York: Plenum.
Center for Disease Control (1984). *Nutrition surveillance. Annual summary.* Atlanta: U.S. Department of Health, Education, and Welfare, Public Health Service.
Chase, H. P., & Martin, H. P. (1970). Undernutrition and child development. *New England Journal of Medicine,* **282**, 933–939.
Chavez, A., & Martinez, C. (1982). *Growing up in a developing community* (pp. 5-11). Guatemala City: INCAP-UNU.
Children's Defense Fund (1987). *A children's defense budget FY 1988.* Washington, D.C.: Author.
Chow, B. F., & Lee, C.-J. (1964). Effect of dietary restriction of pregnant rats on body weight gain of the offspring. *Journal of Nutrition,* **82**, 10–18.
Citizen's Board of Inquiry into Hunger and Malnutrition in the United States (1969). *Hunger USA: a report.* Boston: Beacon.
Conners, C. K. (1979). The acute effects of caffeine on evoked response, vigilance, and activity level in hyperkinetic children. *Journal of Abnormal Child Psychology,* **7**, 145–151.
Conners, C. K. (1980). *Food additives and hyperactive children.* New York: Plenum.
Conners, K. C., & Blouin, A. G. (1982–1983). Nutritional effects on behavior of children. *Journal of Psychiatric Research,* **17**, 193–201.
Conners, K. C., Goyette, C. H., Southwick, D. A., Lees, J. M., & Andrulonis, P. A. (1976). Food additives and hyperkinesis: A controlled double-blind experiment. *Pediatrics,* **58**, 154–166.
Cook, T. D., & Campbell, D. T. (1979). *Quasi-experimentation: Design and analysis issues for field settings.* Boston: Houghton.

Cook, J. D., & Finch, C. A. (1979). Assessing iron status of a population. *The American Journal of Clinical Nutrition,* **32**, 2115–2119.

Corsa, L., Pugh, T. F., Ingalls, T. H., & Gordon, J. E. (1952). Premature birth as a problem of human populations. *American Journal of the Medical Sciences,* **224**, 343–360.

Cravioto, J., & DeLicardie, E. R. (1979). Nutrition, mental development, and learning. In F. Falkner & J. M. Tanner (Eds.), *Human growth:* Vol. 3, *Neurobiology and nutrition* (pp. 481–511). New York: Plenum.

Deinard, A. S., List, A., Lindgren, B., Hunt, J. V., & Chang, P.-N. (1986). Cognitive deficits in iron-deficient and iron-deficient anemic children. *The Journal of Pediatrics,* **108**, 681–689.

Dickie, N. H., & Bender, A. E. (1982). Breakfast and performance in school children. *British Journal of Nutrition,* **48**, 483–496.

Douglas, J. W. B., Ross, J. M., & Simpson, H. R. (1965). The relation between height and measured educational ability in school children of the same social class, family size and stage of sexual development. *Human Biology,* **37**, 178–186.

Drotar, D. (Ed.) (1988). *New directions in failure to thrive. Implications for research and practice.* New York: Plenum.

Drotar, D. (1988). Failure to thrive. In D. K. Routh (Ed.), *Handbook of pediatric psychology.* New York: Guilford.

Eckerman, C. O., Sturm, L. A., & Gross, S. J. (1985). Different developmental courses for very-low-birth-weight infants differing in early head growth. *Developmental Psychology,* **21**, 813–827.

Falkner, F., & Tanner, J. M. (Eds.) (1979). *Human growth:* Vol. 3, *Neurobiology and nutrition.* New York: Plenum.

Falkner, F., & Tanner, J. M. (Eds.) (1986). *Human growth: A comprehensive treatise:* Vol. 3, *Methodology. Ecological, genetic and nutritional effects on growth* (2nd ed.) New York: Plenum.

Feingold, B. F. (1975). *Why your child is hyperactive.* New York: Random House.

Feingold, B. F., & Feingold, H. S. (1979). *The Feingold cookbook for hyperactive children.* New York: Random House.

Feingold, B. F., German, D. F., Braham, R. M., & Simmers, E. (1973). *Adverse reaction to food additives.* Paper presented at annual convention of the American Medical Association, New York.

Field, M. (1984). Follow-up developmental status of infants hospitalized for nonorganic failure to thrive. *Journal of Pediatric Psychology,* **9**, 241–256.

Fitzhardinge, P. M., & Steven, E. M. (1972). The small-for-date infant. II. Neurological and intellectual sequelae. *Pediatrics,* **50**, 50–56.

Food and Nutrition Board, Division of Biological Sciences, Assembly of Life Sciences, National Research Council (NAC/NRC) (1980). *Toward healthful diets.* Washington, D.C.: National Academy of Sciences.

Frankova, S., & Barnes, R. H. (1968). Effect of malnutrition in early life on avoidance condition and behavior of adult rats. *Journal of Nutrition,* **96**, 485–493.

Fras, I. (1974). Alternating caffeine and stimulants (Letter to the Editor). *American Journal of Psychiatry,* **131**, 228–229.

Galler, J. R. (1984a). The behavioral consequences of malnutrition in early life. In J. R. Galler (Ed.), *Human nutrition: A comprehensive treatise:* Vol. 5, *Nutrition and behavior* (pp. 63–117). New York: Plenum.

Galler, J. R. (Ed.) (1984b). *Human nutrition: A comprehensive treatise:* Vol. 5, *Nutrition and behavior.* New York: Plenum.

Galler, J. R., Ramsey, F., & Forde, V. (1986). A follow-up study of the influence of early malnutrition on subsequent development: 4. Intellectual performance during adolescence. *Nutrition and Behavior,* **3**, 211–222.

Garn, S. M., Petzold, A. S., Ridella, S. A., & Johnston, M. (1980). Effect of smoking during pregnancy on Apgar and Bayley scores. *The Lancet,* **Oct.,** 912–913.

Gerber, M., & Dean, R. F. A. (1956). The psychological changes accompanying kwashiorkor. *Courrier,* **6**, 3–14.

Gietzen, D., & Vermeersch, J. A. (1980). Health status and school achievement of children from Head Start and Free School Lunch Programs. *Public Health Reports,* **95**, 362–368.

Goldman, J. A., Lerman, R. H., Contois, J. H., & Udall, J. N. (1986). Behavioral effects of sucrose on preschool children. *Journal of Abnormal Child Psychology,* **14**, 565–577.

Golub, M. S., Keen, C. L., Gershwin, M. E., & Vijayan, V. K. (1986). Growth, development and brain zinc levels in mice marginally or severely deprived of zinc during postembryonic brain development. *Nutrition and Behavior,* **3**, 169–180.

Goyette, C. H., Conners, C. K., Petti, T. A., & Curtis, L. E. (1978). Effects of artificial colors on hyperkinetic children: A double-blind challenge study. *Psychopharmacology Bulletin,* **14**, 39–40.

Grantham-McGregor, S., & Buchanan, E. (1982). The development of an adopted child recovering from severe malnutrition. Case report. *Human Nutrition: Clinical Nutrition,* **36**, 251–256.

Grantham-McGregor, S., Schofield, W., & Harris, L. (1983). Effect of psychosocial stimulation on mental development of severely malnourished children: An interim report. *Pediatrics,* **72**, 239–243.

Haas, J. D. (1981). Nutrition during pregnancy. *Science,* **212**, 804–805.

Hack, M., & Breslau, N. (1986). Very low birth weight infants: Effects of brain growth during infancy on intelligence quotient at 3 years of age. *Pediatrics,* **77**, 196–202.

Hamilton, V., & Warburton, D. M. (Eds.) (1979). *Human stress and cognition: An information processing approach*. New York: Wiley.

Harley, J. P., & Matthews, C. G. (1980). Food additives and hyperactivity in children: Experimental investigations. In R. M. Knights & D. J. Bakker (Eds.), *Treatment of hyperactive and learning disordered children: Current research* (pp. 121–130). Baltimore: University Park Press.

Harley, J. P., Ray, R. S., Tomasi, L., Eichman, P. L., Matthews, C. G., Chun, R., Cleeland, C. S., & Traisman, E. (1978). Hyperkinesis and food additives: Testing the Feingold hypothesis. *Pediatrics,* **61**, 818–828.

Harper, A. E. (1978). Dietary goals—a skeptical view. *American Journal of Clinical Nutrition,* **31**, 310–321.

Hegstead, D. M. (1978). Dietary goals—a progressive view. *American Journal of Clinical Nutrition,* **31**, 1504–1509.

Hicks, L. E., Langham, R. A., & Takenaka, J. (1982). Cognitive and health measures following early nutritional supplementation: A sibling study. *American Journal of Public Health,* **72**, 1110–1118.

Hronsky, S. L., & Emory, E. K. (1987). Neurobehavioral effects of caffeine on the neonate. *Infant Behavior and Development,* **10**, 61–80.

Huestis, R. D., Arnold, L. E., & Smeltzer, D. J. (1975). Caffeine versus methylphenidate and *d*-amphetamine in minimal brain dysfunction: A double-blind comparison. *American Journal of Psychiatry,* **132**, 868–870.

Hughes, D., Johnson, K., Rosenbaum, S., Simons, J., & Butler, E. (1987), *The health of America's children: Maternal and child health data book*. Washington, DC: Children's Defense Fund.

Humphreys, L. G., Davey, T. C., & Park, R. K. (1985). Longitudinal correlation analysis of standing height and intelligence. *Child Development*, **56**, 1465–1478.

Institute of Food Technologists (1987). Evaluation of caffeine safety: A scientific status summary by the Institute of Food Technologists' Expert Panel on Food Safety & Nutrition. *Food Technology,* **41**, 105–113.

Jensen, A. R. (1974). Cumulative deficit: A testable hypothesis? *Developmental Psychology,* **10**, 996–1019.

Jensen, A. R. (1980). *Bias in mental testing.* New York: Free Press.

Jones, D. Y., Nesheim, M. C., & Habicht, J. P. (1985). Influences in child growth associated with poverty in the 1970's: An examination of HANESI and HANESII, cross-sectional US national surveys. *The American Journal of Clinical Nutrition,* **42**, 714–724.

Joos, S. K., & Pollitt, E. (1984). Effects of supplementation on behavioral development in children up to the age of two years: A comparison of four studies. In J. Brozek & B. Schurch (Eds.), *Malnutrition and behavior: Critical assessment of key issues* (pp. 507–519). Lausanne: Nestle Foundation.

Kagan, J., & Garn, S. M. (1963). A constitutional correlate of early intellective functioning. *The Journal of Genetic Psychology,* **102**, 83–89.

Kessel, S. S., Villar, J., Berendes, H. W., & Nugent, R. P. (1984). The changing pattern of low birth weight in the United States—1970 to 1980. *Journal of the American Medical Association,* **251**, 1978–1982.

Kirkinen, P., Jouppila, P., Koivula, A., Vuori J., & Puukka, M. (1983). The effect of caffeine on placental and fetal blood flow in human pregnancy. *American Journal of Obstetrics and Gynecology,* **147**, 939–942.

Klein, P. S., Forbes, G. B., & Nader, P. R. (1975). Effects of starvation in infancy (pyloric stenosis) on subsequent learning abilities. *The Journal of Pediatrics,* **87**, 8–15.

Klein, R. E., Arenales, P., Delgado, H., Engle, P., Guzman, G., Irwin, M., Lasky, R., Lechtig, R., Martorell, R., Pivaral, V., Russell, P., & Yarbrough, C. (1976). Effects of maternal nutrition on fetal growth and infant development. *Bulletin of the Pan American Health Organization,* **10**, 301–316.

Klein, R. E., Freeman, H. E., Kagan, J., Yarbrough, C., & Habicht, J.-P. (1972). Is big smart? The relation of growth to cognition. *The Journal of Health and Social Behavior,* **13**, 219–225.

Kleinbaum, D. G., Kupper, L. L., & Morgenstern, H. (1982). *Epidemiologic research: Principles and quantitative methods.* Belmont, California: Lifetime Learning Publications.

Knobloch, H., Rider, R., Harper, P., & Pasamanick, B. (1956). Neuropsychiatric sequelae of prematurity: A longitudinal study. *The Journal of the American Medical Association,* **161**, 581–585.

Kotelchuck, M. (1980) Nonorganic failure to thrive. The status of interactional and environmental etiologic theories. In B. W. Camp (Ed.), *Advances in behavioral pediatrics* (Vol. 1, pp. 29–51). Greenwich, Connecticut: JAI Press.

Kotelchuck, M., & Newberger, E. H. (1983). Failure to thrive: A controlled study of familial characteristics. *Journal of the American Academy of Child Psychiatry,* **22**, 322–328.

Kvalsvig, J. D. (1981). The effects of schistosomiasis on spontaneous play activity in Black school children in endemic areas. *South African Medical Journal,* **60**, 61–64.

Laird, D. A., Levitan, M., & Wilson, V. A. (1931). Nervousness in school children as related to hunger and diet. *Medical Journal Record,* **134**, 494–499.

Lasky, R. E., Klein, R. E., Yarbrough, C., Engle, P. L., & Martorell, R. (1981). The relationship between physical growth and infant behavioral development in rural Guatemala. *Child Development,* **52**, 219–226.

Leibel, R. L., Greenfield, D. B., & Pollitt, E. (1979). Iron deficiency: Behavior and brain biochemistry. In M. Winick (Ed.), *Nutrition, pre- and postnatal development* (pp. 383–439). New York: Plenum.

Lester, M. L., Thatcher, R. W., & Monroe-Lord, L. (1982). Refined carbohydrate intake, hair cadmium levels, and cognitive functioning in children. *Nutrition and Behavior,* **1**, 3–13.

Levinger, B. (1983). *School feeding programs in less developed countries: An analysis of actual and potential impact.* Washington, DC: Agency for International Development, Bureau for Food and Voluntary Aid, Office of Evaluation.

Levitsky, D. A., & Strupp, B. A. (1985). Nutrition and the behavior of children. In W. A. Walker & J. B. Watkins (Eds.), *Nutrition in pediatrics: Basic science and clinical application* (pp. 357–392). Boston: Little, Brown.

Lieberman, A. F., & Birch, M. (1985). The etiology of failure to thrive: An interactional developmental approach. In D. Drotar (Ed.), *New directions in failure to thrive: Implications for research and practice* (pp. 259–277). New York: Plenum.

Lin, C. C., & Evans, M. I. (Eds.) (1984). *Intrauterine growth retardation: Pathophysiology and clinical management*. New York: McGraw-Hill.

Lininger, F. F. (1933). Relation of the use of milk to the physical and scholastic progress of undernourished school children. *American Journal of Public Health,* **23**, 555–560.

Lipton, M. A., Nemeroff, C. B., & Mailman, R. B. (1979). Hyperkinesis and food additives. In R. J. Wurtman & J. J. Wurtman (Eds.), *Nutrition and the brain* (Vol. 4, pp. 1–27). New York: Raven.

Little, W. J. (1862). On the influence of abnormal parturition, difficult labours, premature birth, and asphyxia neonatorum on the mental and physical condition of the child, especially in relation to deformities. *Transactions of the Obstetrical Society of London,* **3**, 293–344.

Lozoff, B., & Brittenham, G. M. (1986). Behavioral aspects of iron deficiency. *Progress in Hematology,* **14**, 23–53.

Lozoff, B., Klein, N. K., & Prabucki, K. M. (1986). Iron-deficient anemic infants at play. *Journal of Developmental and Behavioral Pediatrics,* **7**, 152–158.

Mackler, B., & Finch, C. (1982). Iron in central nervous system oxidative metabolism. In E. Pollitt & R. L. Leibel (Eds.), *Iron deficiency: Brain biochemistry and behavior* (pp. 31–38). New York: Raven.

Martorell, R. (1984). Measuring the impact of nutrition interventions on physical growth. In D. E. Sahn, R. Lockwood, & N. S. Scrimshaw (Eds.), *Methods for the evaluation of the impact of food and nutrition programmes* (pp. 46–64). Tokyo: United Nations University.

Martorell, R., & Habicht, J. P. (1986). Growth in early childhood in developing countries. In F. Falkner & J. M. Tanner (Eds.), *Human growth: A comprehensive treatise* Vol. 3, *Methodology. Ecological, genetic, and nutritional effects on growth* (2nd ed., pp. 241–262). New York: Plenum.

McKay, H., Sinisterra, L., McKay, A., Gomez, H., & Lloreda, P. (1978). Improving cognitive ability in chronically deprived children. *Science,* **200**, 270–278.

McKeown, T., & Gibson, J. R. (1951). Observations on all births (23,970) in Birmingham, 1947. *British Medical Journal,* **2**, 513–517.

Metcoff, J., Costiloe, P., Crosby, W. M., Dutta, S., Sandstead, H. H., Milne, D., Bodwell, C. E., & Majors, S. H. (1985). Effect of food supplementation (WIC) during pregnancy on birth weight. *American Journal of Clinical Nutrition,* **41**, 933–947.

Milich, R., & Pelham, W. E. (1986). Effects of sugar ingestion on the classroom and playgroup behavior of attention deficit disordered boys. *Journal of Consulting and Clinical Psychology,* **54**, 714–718.

Milich, R., Wolraich, M., & Lindgren, S. (1986). Sugar and hyperactivity: A critical review of empirical findings. *Clinical Psychology Review,* **6**, 493–513.

Mitchell, W. G., Gorell, R. W., & Greenberg, R. A. (1980). Failure to thrive: A study in a primary care setting. Epidemiology and follow-up. *Pediatrics,* **65**, 971–977.

Moock, P. R., & Leslie, J. (1986). Childhood malnutrition and schooling in the Terai region of Nepal. *Journal of Development Economics,* **20**, 33–52.

Morris, M. B. & Weinstein, L. (1981). Caffeine and the fetus: Is trouble brewing? *American Journal of Obstetrics and Gynecology,* **140**, 607–610.

Mueller, W. H., & Titcomb, M. (1977). Genetic environmental determinants of growth of school-aged children in a rural Colombian population. *Annals of Human Biology,* **4**, 1–15.

Oski, F. A., & Honig, A. S. (1978). The effects of therapy on the developmental scores of iron-deficient infants. *The Journal of Pediatrics,* **92**, 21–25.

Oski, F. A., Honig, A. S., Helu, B., & Howanitz, P. (1983). Effect of iron therapy on behavior performance in nonanemic, iron-deficient infants. *Pediatrics,* **71**, 877–880.

Ounsted, M., Moar, V. A., & Scott, A. (1984). Associations between size and development at four years among children who were small-for-dates and large-for-dates at birth. *Early Human Development,* **9**, 259–268.

Ounsted, M., Moar, V. A., & Scott, A. (1986). Growth and proportionality in early childhood. III. Differences between babies of low birthweight in well-nourished and malnourished populations. *Early Human Development,* **14**, 167–178.

Owen, G. M. (1981). The nutritional status of the U.S. population. In P. J. Garry (Ed.), *Human nutrition: Clinical and biochemical aspects* (pp. 27–43). Proceedings of the Fourth Arnold O. Beckman Conference in Clinical Chemistry. Washington, D.C.: The American Association for Clinical Chemistry.

Owen, G. M., Kram, K. M., Garry, P. J., Lowe, J. E., & Lubin, A. H. (1974). A study of nutritional status of preschool children in the United States, 1968–1970. *Pediatrics,* **53** (Suppl.), 597–646.

Pencharz, P., Heller, A., Higgins, A., Strawbridge, J., Rush, D., & Pless, I. B. Effects of nutritional services to pregnant mothers on the school performance of treated and untreated children. Personal communication cited in Rush, D. (1983). In reponse to Hicks *et al.* *American Journal of Public Health,* **73**, 700–701.

Pilch, S. M., & Senti, F. R. (Eds.) (1984) *Assessment of the iron nutritional status of the U.S. population based on data collected in the second national health and nutrition examination survey, 1976–1980* (Contract Number FDA 223-83-2384). Prepared for Center for Food Safety and Applied Nutrition, Food and Drug Administration, Department of Health and Human Services, Washington, D.C. Bethesda, Maryland: Life Sciences Research Office, Federation of American Societies for Experimental Biology.

Pollitt, E. (1987). Effects of iron deficiency on mental development: Methodological considerations and substantive findings. In F. E. Johnston (Ed.), *Nutritional anthropology* (pp. 225–254). New York: Liss.

Pollitt, E., & Amante, P. (Eds.) (1984). *Energy intake and activity:* Vol. 11, *Current topics in nutrition and disease*. New York: Liss.

Pollitt, E., Eichler, A. W., & Chan, C. K. (1975). Psychosocial development and behavior of mothers of failure-to-thrive children. *American Journal of Orthopsychiatry,* **45**, 525–537.

Pollitt, E., Gersovitz, M., & Gargiulo, M. (1978). Educational benefits of the United States school feeding program: A critical review of the literature. *American Journal of Public Health,* **68**, 477–481.

Pollitt, E., & Leibel, R. (1980). Biological and social correlates of failure to thrive. In L. S. Greene & F. E. Johnston (Eds.), *Social and biological predictors of nutritional status, physical growth, and neurological development* (pp. 173–200). New York: Academic Press.

Pollitt, E., Leibel, R. L., & Greenfield, D. (1981). Brief fasting, stress and cognition in children. *American Journal of Clinical Nutrition,* **34**, 1526–1533.

Pollitt, E., Leibel, R. L., & Greenfield, D. B. (1983). Iron deficiency and cognitive test performance in preschool children. *Nutrition and Behavior,* **1**, 137–146.

Pollitt, E., Lewis, N. L., Garza, C., & Shulman, R. J. (1982–1983). Fasting and cognitive function. *Journal of Psychiatric Research,* **17**, 169–174.

Pollitt, E., & Lorimor, R. (1983). Effects of WIC on cognitive development. *American Journal of Public Health,* **73**, 698–700.

Pollitt, E., Mueller, W., & Leibel, R. L. (1982). The relation of growth to cognition in a well-nourished preschool population. *Child Development,* **53**, 1157–1163.

Pollitt, E., & Ricciuti, H. (1969). Biological and social correlates of stature among children in the slums of Lima, Peru. *American Journal of Orthopsychiatry,* **39**, 735–747.

Pollitt, E., & Thomson, C. (1977). Protein-calorie malnutrition and behavior: A view from psychology. In R. J. Wurtman & J. J. Wurtman (Eds.), *Nutrition and the brain:* Vol. 2,

Control of feeding behavior and biology of the brain in protein-calorie malnutrition. New York: Raven.

Powell, G. F., Brasel, J. A., & Blizzard, R. M. (1967). Emotional deprivation and growth retardation simulating idiopathic hypopituitarism: I. Clinical evaluation of the syndrome. *The New England Journal of Medicine,* **276**, 1271–1278.

Prentice, A. M. (1984). Adaptations to long-term low energy intake. In E. Pollitt & P. Amante (Eds.), *Energy intake and activity* (pp. 3–31). New York: Liss.

Prentice, A. M., Whitehead, R. G., Roberts, S. B., & Paul, A. A. (1981). Long-term energy balance in child-bearing Gambian women. *American Journal of Clinical Nutrition,* **34**, 2790–2799.

Prinz, R. J., Roberts, W. A., & Hantman, E. (1980). Dietary correlates of hyperactive behavior in children. *Journal of Consulting and Clinical Psychology,* **48**, 760–769.

Radzikowski, J., & Gale, S. K. (Eds.) (1984). Symposium on national evaluation of the school nutrition programs. *The American Journal of Clinical Nutrition,* **40** (Suppl.), 363–464.

Rapoport, J. L., Berg, C. J., Ismond, D. R., Zahn, T. P., & Neims, A. (1984). Behavioral effects of caffeine in children: Relationship between dietary choice and effects of caffeine challenge. *Archives of General Psychiatry,* **41**, 1073–1079.

Reichard, C. C., & Elder, S. T. (1977). The effects of caffeine on reaction time in hyperkinetic and normal children. *American Journal of Psychiatry,* **134**, 144–148.

Ricciuti, H., (1980). Developmental consequences of malnutrition in early childhood. In M. Lewis & L. A. Rosenblum (Eds.), *The uncommon child: Genesis of behavior* (Vol. 3, pp. 151–172). New York: Plenum.

Richardson, S. A. (1980). The long range consequences of malnutrition in infancy: A study of children in Jamaica, West Indies. In B. A. Wharton (Ed.), *Topics in Paediatrics:* Vol. 2, *Nutrition in childhood* (pp. 163–178). Tunbridge Wells: Pitman Medical.

Rosso, P., & Winick, M. (1974). Intrauterine growth retardation. A new systematic approach based on the clinical and biochemical characteristics of this condition. *Journal of Perinatal Medicine,* **2**, 147–160.

Rubin, R. A., Rosenblatt, C., & Balow, B. (1973). Psychological and educational sequelae of prematurity. *Pediatrics,* **52**, 352–363.

Rush, D. (1983). In response to Hicks *et al. American Journal of Public Health,* **73**, 700–701.

Rush, D., & Seaver, W. B. (1986). *National evaluation of the Special Supplemental Food Program for Women, Infants and Children (WIC), 1982–1985* Vol. 1–5, *Documentation*. Final report 1980–1985 (Contract USDA/FNS-53-3198-9-97). North Carolina: Research Triangle Institute, Research Triangle Park.

Rush, D., Stein, Z., & Susser, M. (1980). *Diet in pregnancy: A randomized controlled trial of nutritional supplements*. New York: Liss.

Schechter, M. D., & Timmons, G. D. (1985). Objectively measured hyperactivity. II. Caffeine and amphetamine effects. *Journal of Clinical Pharmacology,* **25**, 276–280.

Schnackenberg, R. C. (1973). Caffeine as a substitute for Schedule II stimulants in hyperkinetic children. *American Journal of Psychiatry,* **130**, 796–798.

Singer, J. E., Westphal, M., & Niswander, K. (1968). Relationship of weight gain during pregnancy to birth weight and infant growth and development in the first year of life. *Obstetrics and Gynecology,* **31**, 417–423.

Singer, L. T., & Fagan, J. F. (1988). The cognitive development of the failure to thrive infant: A three-year longitudinal study. *Journal of Pediatric Psychology*, in press.

Smith, C. A. (1947). Effects of maternal undernutrition upon the newborn infant in Holland (1944–1945). *The Journal of Pediatrics*, **30**, 229–243.

Soemantri, A. G., Pollitt, E., & Kim, I. (1985). Iron deficiency anemia and educational achievement. *American Journal of Clinical Nutrition,* **42**, 1221–1228.

Sorokin, P. A. (1975). *Hunger as a factor in human affairs*. Gainesville: The University Presses of Florida.

Sourkes, T. L. (1982). Transition elements and the nervous system. In E. Pollitt & R. L. Leibel (Eds.), *Iron deficiency: Brain biochemistry and behavior* (pp. 1–29). New York: Raven.

Spargo, J. (1906). *The bitter cry of the children*. New York: Macmillan.

Stanbury, J. B., & Kroc, R. L. (Eds.) (1972). *Human development and the thyroid gland relation to endemic cretinism:* Vol. 30, *Advances in experimental medicine and biology*. New York: Plenum.

Stein, Z., & Susser, M. (1985). Effects of early nutrition on neurological and mental competence in human beings. *Psychological Medicine,* **15**, 717–726.

Stein, Z., Susser, M., Saenger, G., & Marolla, F. (1975). *Famine and human development: The Dutch Hunger Winter of 1944–1945*. New York: Oxford University Press.

Susser, M. (1981). Prenatal nutrition, birthweight, and psychological development: An overview of experiments, quasi-experiments, and natural experiments in the past decade. *The American Journal of Clinical Nutrition,* **34**, 784–803.

Tanner, J. M. (1969). Relation of body size, intelligence test scores, and social circumstances. In P. Mussen, J. Langer, & M. Covington (Eds.), *Trends and issues in developmental psychology* (pp. 182–201). New York: Holt.

Tanner, J. M. (1970). *Education and physical growth*. New York: International Universities Press.

Taylor, L., & Selowsky, M. (1973). The economics of malnourished children: An example of disinvestment in human capital. *Economic Development and Cultural Change,* **22**, 17–30.

Ten State Nutrition Survey in the United States, 1968–1970 (1972). (U.S. Department of Health, Education and Welfare Publication No. (HSM) 72-8130-72-8134). Washington, DC: DHEW.

The Consortium for Longitudinal Studies (1983). *As the twig is bent... Lasting effects of preschool programs*. Hillsdale, New Jersey: Erlbaum.

U.S. Department of Agriculture/U.S. Department of Health and Human Services (USDA/USDHHS) (1980). *Nutrition and your health: Dietary outlines for Americans*. Washington, D.C.: U.S. Government Printing Office.

U.S. Senate, Select Committee on Nutrition and Human Needs (1977). *Dietary goals for the United States* (2nd ed.). Washington, D.C.: U.S. Government Printing Office.

Valenzuela, M., & Araya, M. (1987). *Attachment and developmental status of chronically undernourished infants*. Paper presented at the biennial meeting of the Society for Research in Child Development, April, Baltimore.

Vietze, P. M., Falsey, S., O'Connor, S., Sandler, H., Sherrod, K., & Altemeier, W. A. (1980). Newborn behavioral and interactional characteristics of nonorganic failure-to-thrive infants. In T. M. Field, S. Goldberg, D. Stern, & A. M. Sostek (Eds.), *High-risk infants and children: Adult and peer interactions* (pp. 5–23). New York: Academic Press.

Villar, J., & Belizan, J. M. (1982). The relative contribution of prematurity and fetal growth retardation to low birth weight in developing and developed societies. *American Journal of Obstetrics and Gynecology,* **143**, 793–798.

Villar, J., Khoury, M. J., Finucane, F. F., & Delgado, H. L. (1986). Differences in the epidemiology of prematurity and intrauterine growth retardation. *Early Human Development,* **14**, 307–320.

Villar, J., Smeriglio, V., Martorell, R., Brown, C. H., & Klein, R. E. (1984). Heterogeneous growth and mental development of intrauterine growth-retarded infants during the first 3 years of life. *Pediatrics,* **74**, 783–791.

Waber, D. P., Vuori-Christiansen, L., Ortiz, N., Clement, J. R., Christiansen, N. E., Mora, J. O., Reed, R. B., & Herrera, M. G. (1981). Nutritional supplementation, maternal education, and cognitive development of infants at risk of malnutrition. *American Journal of Clinical Nutrition,* **34** (suppl.), 807–813.

Waterlow, J. C. (1978). Anthropometric and biochemical findings in marginal malnutrition. In P. L. White & N. Selvey (Eds.), *Nutrition in transition: Proceedings, Western Hemisphere Nutrition Congress V* (pp. 273–280). Chicago: American Medical Association.

Wender, E. M., & Lipton, M. (Co-chairs) (1980). *National Advisory Committee on Hyperkinesis and Food Additives: Final report to the Nutrition Foundation*. Washington, D.C.: The Nutrition Foundation.

Werner, E. E., Bierman, J. M., & French, F. E. (1971). *The children of Kauai: A longitudinal study from the prenatal period to age ten*. Honolulu: The University of Hawaii Press.

White House Conference on Food, Nutrition and Health (1969). *Final report*. Washington, D.C.: U.S. Government Printing Office.

Wilson, D. M., Hammer, L. D., Duncan, P. M., Dornbusch, S. M., Ritter, P. L., Hintz, R. L., Gross, R. T., & Rosenfeld, R. G. (1986). Growth and intellectual development. *Pediatrics,* **78**, 646–650.

Wilson, R. S. (1985). Risk and resilience in early mental development. *Developmental Psychology,* **21**, 795–805.

Winick, M., Brasel, J. A., & Velasco, E. G. (1973). Effects of prenatal nutrition upon pregnancy risk. *Clinical Obstetrics & Gynecology,* **16**, 184–198.

Winick, M., Meyer, K. K., & Harris, R. C. (1975). Malnutrition and environmental enrichment by early adoption. *Science,* **190**, 1173–1175.

Winick, M., & Noble, A. (1966). Cellular response in rats during malnutrition at various ages. *Journal of Nutrition,* **89**, 300–306.

Winick, M., & Rosso, P. (1969). Head circumference and cellular growth of the brain in normal and marasmic children. *Journal of Pediatrics,* **74**, 774–778.

Wolraich, M., Milich, R., Stumbo, P., & Schultz, F. (1985). Effects of sucrose ingestion on the behavior of hyperactive boys. *The Journal of Pediatrics,* **106**, 675–682.

Wurtman, R. J., & Wurtman, J. J. (Eds.) (1986). *Nutrition and the brain:* Vol. 7, *Food constituents affecting normal and abnormal behaviors*. New York: Raven.

Zeskind, P. S., Goff, D. M., & Huntington, L. (1984). A developmental approach to the study of the behavioral effects of early malnutrition. In J. Brozek & B. Schurch (Eds.), *Malnutrition and behavior: Critical assessment of key issues* (pp. 428–440). Lausanne: Nestle Foundation.

The Cognitive Approach to Motivation in Retarded Individuals

SHULAMITH KREITLER AND HANS KREITLER

DEPARTMENT OF PSYCHOLOGY
TEL AVIV UNIVERSITY
RAMAT AVIV, TEL AVIV 69978, ISRAEL

I. INTRODUCTION

Motivation is still one of the domains about which we know the least in the sphere of mental retardation. This is astounding in view of the repeated reminders on the part of staunch supporters of the motivational view, such as Zigler and associates, that "besides having a head, children have a heart, a spirit, a personality" (Zigler & Cascione, 1980, p. 8) and "like nonretarded persons, the behavior of retarded individuals is affected by their emotions, motives, attitudes, and experiential backgrounds, as well as by intelligence" (Zigler & Cascione, 1984, p. 80). The far-reaching neglect of motivational factors in attempts to predict and understand the behavior in cognitive fields (Spitz, 1986) and other domains is due primarily to the overwhelming predominance of cognitive deficiencies in the daily performance of mentally retarded individuals. Cognitive defects are such a salient feature of mental retardation that other issues and aspects may seem negligible by comparison. Consequently, there is a tendency to consider cognitive subnormality as the major or sole cause of all phenomena in the realm of mental retardation (e.g., Stark, Menolascino, Albarelli, & Gray, 1987). The neglect of motivational factors may have been further reinforced by the glaring absence of motivational considerations in the two major frameworks that have affected cognitive studies in mental retardation, i.e., Piaget's epistemological theory and the information processing approach of most cognitive psychologists.

INTERNATIONAL REVIEW OF RESEARCH IN
MENTAL RETARDATION, Vol. 15

Notwithstanding our own attempts at devising and testing a purely cognitive method that led to appreciable improvement in the cognitive performance of retarded children (Kreitler & Kreitler, 1988), we found it promising to study the motivational variables as well. Different sets of findings indicate the important potential contribution of motivational factors to understanding and shaping the behavior of mentally retarded individuals. For example, most studies of social adjustment of retarded individuals following deinstitutionalization show that adjustment does not depend on intellectual level but is affected adversely by motivational factors, such as overdependency, jealousy, hostility, low self-esteem, and failure to comply with requests which were within one's intellectual competence (McCarver & Craig, 1974; Windle, 1962). Similar factors seem to determine the adjustment of intellectually subnormal individuals who have not been previously institutionalized (Granat & Granat, 1978; Saenger, 1960). Likewise, failure in vocational endeavors does not seem to depend as much on intelligence as on motivational factors, such as rebelliousness or critical disregard for others (Stephen, Peck, & Veldman, 1968). In general, motivation contributes most to the employment success of a retarded individual (Cohen & Close, 1975; Gifford, Rusch, Martin, & White, 1984; Gold, 1973). Further, in the domain of delinquency, the role of motivational factors overrides that of cognitive abilities (MacEachron, 1979; Menolascino, 1974). Motivation also plays a role in regard to academic achievements (Snyder, Jefferson, & Strauss, 1965). Finally, even the determination of the IQ is not free from the effects of motivational factors (Johnson, Bradley-Johnson, McCarthy, & Jamie, 1984; Zigler, Abelson, & Seitz 1973). Thus, regardless of whether motivation is considered as attenuating the achievements of retarded individuals (Zigler, 1973) or actually shaping them, it is important to study the impact of motivation, both in its own right and as a determinant of the performance deficit.

In order to study the impact of motivation on the behavior of retarded individuals, it would be necessary first to specify the motivational factors in question, then to examine whether their presence or absence influences behavior, and, eventually, to manipulate them in order to determine if they are causally related to behavior. Most research on motivational factors has not met these requirements, although it has yielded encouraging indications. In this article a conceptual framework for bridging the traditional gap between motivation and cognition will be presented. This framework may contribute to research on the role of motivational factors in the functioning of mentally retarded individuals.

II. MAJOR MOTIVATIONAL APPROACHES IN MENTAL RETARDATION

The goal of this section is to present briefly the major motivational approaches that have evolved in mental retardation research, focusing on their underlying assumptions, major findings, and implications for intervention and behavior change. The presentation will be selective, providing an overall orientation rather than an exhaustive review of findings.

A. The Behavioral Approach

From the viewpoint of a behaviorist, external events called reinforcers constitute the major motivational impact on behavior, increasing or decreasing its frequency. Hence, the focal issues for the study of motivation are (1) identification of reinforcers and (2) definition of behavioral units. Researchers in this tradition have demonstrated in many studies that mentally retarded individuals of all levels and ages are responsive to reinforcers of many kinds (Siegel, 1968, 1969). The behavioral approach has given rise to a set of practices which constitute the behavioral treatment of retarded persons (Yando, 1982). Common to these practices is the manipulation of reinforcers, their kind and the schedule of their presentation, so as to decrease the frequency of a specified behavior.

B. The Personality-Based Approach

Personality researchers have traditionally focused on personality traits of retarded individuals that are presumably a product of their subnormal cognitive functioning. One such trait is anxiety which, some time ago, was found to be higher in retarded subjects than in nonretarded ones (Cochran & Cleland, 1963; Feldhusen & Klausmeier, 1962). Another trait was elevated frustration, which could result in increased aggression (Gothberg, 1947; Rudolph, 1958) or enhanced resistance to extinction (e.g., Ryan & Watson, 1968; Viney, Clarke, & Lord, 1973).

In recent years the major motivational concepts of the personality-based approach have become personality traits or tendencies, such as rigidity, high needs for social reinforcement, strong social approach and avoidance tendencies, or high expectancy of failure. It is assumed that such traits are characteristic of mentally retarded individuals and have been acquired or strengthened through "severe social deprivation, institutionalization, and a lifetime of failure and ridicule" (Zigler, 1984). The major proponents of this approach are Zigler and associates. One focus of their work has been rigidity, reflected, for example, in the persistence, low satiation, and low rate of switching often found in retarded individuals. Originally, Lewin's (1936) thesis, tested by Kounin (1941a,b), was that the rigidity of retarded persons was due to structural features of their character (i.e., fewer regions and less permeable regional boundaries in their "life space"), which was reinforced through a history of failures. In contrast, Zigler *et al.* showed that rigid behavior observed in retarded children is a product of their motivation to maintain social interaction with adults and to obtain approval through compliant and persistent behavior. This conclusion was based, for instance, on studies showing that institutionalized retarded subjects evidenced more rigidity than noninstitutionalized subjects (Green & Zigler, 1962) or that retarded subjects spent more time playing simple games when social support was available than when it was not available (Zigler, Hodgen, & Stevenson, 1958; see a review in Zigler & Balla, 1982).

Thus, increased motivation to interact with supportive adults and to seek their attention is one personality trait of retarded persons that was thought to derive from their background of social deprivation. The Zigler group studied other personality traits of retarded persons which they also attributed to social deprivation. These include overdependency (Zigler & Balla, 1972), excessive wariness of adults (Shallenberger & Zigler, 1961) or peers (Harter & Zigler, 1968), an enhanced expectancy of failure or a lower expectancy of success (Ollendick, Balla, & Zigler, 1971), imitativeness (Yando & Zigler, 1971), and outerdirectedness, i.e., reliance on external cues to guide one's behavior (Achenbach & Zigler, 1968; Green & Zigler, 1962; see review by Balla & Zigler, 1979). Some of the findings were based on comparing retarded individuals in and outside of institutions and assumed that institutionalized subjects are deprived socially to a greater extent than noninstitutionalized ones (Balla & Zigler, 1982). Studies of this type led to the conclusion that "many of the reported differences between retarded and nonretarded persons of the same MA (mental age) are a result of motivational and emotional differences that reflect variations in experiential histories" (Zigler, 1984, p. 189).

A direct implication of this approach is that in order to change the motivation of retarded children, their environment must be improved. This involves providing favorable environments characterized by acceptance, affection, interaction, and adequate cognitive stimulation in infancy and early childhood when character is presumably shaped. In addition, it entails providing adequate institutions or other living accommodations for retarded individuals of all ages. Thus, social policy is one major means for preventing social deprivation and its ill effects on motivation.

C. The Psychodynamic Approach

The starting point for many of the different psychodynamic approaches to retardation is the high frequency of personality disorders and emotional maladjustment found among retarded persons (Jakab, 1982; Parton, Webb, & Clarke, 1974; Rutter, 1971; Stark *et al.*, 1987). Freudian investigators developed the conception that the basic defect in individuals of subnormal intelligence is poor ego functioning, which also results in a deficient superego (Hirsch, 1959; Pearson, 1942; Sternlicht, 1964; Webster, 1963). The defect in the organization of the ego is manifested in a relative failure of the defense mechanisms of repression and inhibition. It is also responsible for low control over aggression, delinquency, inability to delay gratification, deficient communication with others, and deficient attempts to attain one's goals. This state of affairs, often coupled with a history of rejection by parents and the environment at large, produces a low self-esteem and an increased sense of frustration which may, in turn, enhance hostility and rebelliousness as well as other pathological behaviors including self-injurious acts, suicide attempts, withdrawal, and apathy (Hutt & Gibby, 1976; Sternlicht & Deutsch, 1972). Whereas this line of thinking considers the personality disorder as an outgrowth of the mental retardation, or at least as its correlate, a different line of thinking considers mental retardation as the product of a basic personality disorder (Beier, 1964; Honig, 1966; Kanner, 1949; Rutter, 1971). In either case the resulting image is essentially clinical with mental retardation as one of the constituents of a complex personality–cognitive pathology.

So far, little research has supported these various assumptions. Studies showed, for example, that retarded individuals tend to have an unrealistic evaluation of their attainments (Ringness, 1961), a general expectaton of failure (Gardner, 1958), increased anxiety (Hutt & Gibby, 1976), and deviant emotional development (Vietze, 1985).

The major implication for change resulting from these approaches is psychotherapy. This treatment is used to counteract the deviant personality development and to strengthen the ego (Beier, 1964; Jakab, 1982; Sarason, 1959).

D. The Cognitive Approach

The approaches to motivation we call cognitive are based on the assumption that cognitive contents, namely, attitudes or beliefs, guide behavior. Most are focused on one or more constructs that are defined in terms of specific beliefs and the behaviors to which the beliefs presumably give rise.

Some of the early cognitive-motivated constructs were derived from Rotter's (1954) social learning theory. These included (1) "locus of control," the degree to which persons believe that their own behavior (vs. external forces and conditions) determines what happens to them (Bialer, 1961; Miller, 1961), and (2) "success-striving vs. failure-avoiding" modes of reaction to failure (Bialer & Cromwell, 1958; Moss, 1958).

As compared to the nonretarded, retarded individuals usually score higher on measures of external locus of control; and strive more for failure avoidance than for attainment of success (Cromwell, 1963). But the obtained relations were modest and sometimes inconsistent. The same was true for studies of the effects of failures and successes on the expectancies and performance of retarded persons. Though the effects were often different for retarded and normal individuals, they were not consistently favorable or unfavorable (Heber, 1957; Gardner, 1958; Ringelheim, 1958; Simpson, 1962).

Similar issues were examined more recently within the framework of attribution theory (Weiner, Frieze, Kukla, Reed, Rest, & Rosenbaum, 1972). Horai and Guarnaccia (1975) found that educable mentally retarded adults attributed their success more to their own ability than efforts but failure more to their insufficient efforts or bad luck than inadequate ability. In any case, they overlooked the role of task difficulty. Hoffman and Weiner (1978) also found that the effect of success on further performance in retarded persons depends on their previous causal attributions.

Learned helplessness is another construct that may be related to causal attribution. It is based either on the belief that actions cannot affect what happens (Seligman, 1975) or on the related belief that the required actions cannot be produced (Abramson, Seligman, & Teasdale, 1978). Learned helplessness was found to be more characteristic of retarded than nonretarded children when it was assessed through measures of beliefs (such as the Passive-Dependency Scale, Coping Behavior Questionnaire, and causal attributions for favorable and unfavorable outcomes) or through behavioral measures (such as low perseverance after failure) (Floor & Rosen, 1975; Gibson, 1980; Reynolds & Miller, 1985; Weisz, 1979, 1982). As expected, the retarded children tended to ascribe success more often to luck than to ability, but failure more often to low ability than to bad luck. Weisz (1982) presented evidence in favor of the thesis that it is the illogical attributions of adults concerning retarded children which promote helplessness in these children. In other words, the beliefs of adults breed corresponding beliefs in the children.

"Effectance motivation" is a cognitive–motivational construct similar to locus of control. It focuses on concern for maximal use of one's cognitive resources and for attaining mastery in the absence of reinforcement from an external agent (Harter, 1983; White, 1959). Retarded children scored lower than the nonretarded on different measures of effectance motivation including curiosity, variation seeking, mastery for the sake of competence, and preference for challenging tasks (Harter & Zigler, 1974). They also scored lower on intrinsic motivation on the Scale of Intrinsic versus Extrinsic Orientation in the Classroom developed by Harter for assessing this particular component of effectance motivation (Silon & Harter, 1985).

Low effectance motivation may be considered as one constituent of low intrinsic motivation. Haywood and associates have conducted the most extensive program of research on task-intrinsic and task-extrinsic motivation. Their dual motivational orientation refers to the extent to which individuals either seek their principal satisfactions through task-intrinsic factors (such as creativity, responsibility, learning, and aesthetic considerations) or seek merely to avoid dissatisfaction by focusing on task-extrinsic factors (such as ease, comfort, safety, and material gain). This motivational orientation can be assessed through observation of behavior (Herzberg, Mausner, & Snyderman, 1959), by means of scales that are usually based on vocational choices and the reasons for them (e.g., Haywood, 1968; Kahoe, 1966) or with the Picture Motivation Scale, which was developed for children and retarded individuals (Kunca & Haywood, 1969). In normal populations intrinsic motivation was found to be related to older age, lower task persistence, more exploration, greater responsiveness to task incentives, lower responsiveness to nontask incentives, higher school achievement, more effective and enduring learning of laboratory tasks, higher preference for self-monitored control of one's behavior, greater self-reliance, and lower need for externally provided reinforcement and feedback (Haywood, 1971; Haywood & Burke, 1977; Haywood & Switzky, 1986). The effects on learning, harder work, and persistence were also shown in samples of retarded persons (Haywood & Wachs, 1966; Haywood & Weaver, 1967; Switzky & Haywood, 1985). As expected, mentally retarded children and adults scored higher on task-extrinsic than on task-intrinsic motivation and were more task extrinsic than MA-matched nonretarded children (Haywood, 1971; Haywood & Weaver, 1967). The reason is assumed to be feedback from one's environment from early childhood onward, indicating incompetence and, thus, bringing about an increased withdrawal from novel stimuli and a resultant lower store of information (Haywood & Burke, 1977). There is suggestive though minimal evidence that the motivational orientation of children can be changed from extrinsic to intrinsic through verbal conditioning or cognitive enrichment (Haywood, Arbitman-Smith, Bransford, Delclos, Towery, Hannel, & Hannel, 1982; Haywood & Switzky, 1985).

Self-concept is another construct that could be considered as cognitive–motivational because it is usually assessed through cognitive contents (namely, evaluations of oneself) and probably affects the efficiency of learning and performance (Hardy, 1967; Wink, 1963). Findings, however, have been inconsistent. Some studies have found that, as compared with the nonretarded, retarded individuals have more negative or lower self-images (Pier & Harris, 1964; Zigler, Balla, & Watson, 1972), whereas others have found no differences (Collins, Burger, & Doherty, 1970). Again, an often quoted study found retarded persons to have an unrealistic evaluation of themselves (Ringness, 1961), but another found thay they have a realistic perception of themselves (Carr & McLaughlin, 1973). There is also evidence that retarded subjects have a lower ideal self and a smaller disparity between the actual and ideal selves than nonretarded ones (Zigler *et al.*, 1972). Such findings are usually interpreted as reflecting the adverse experiences of retarded individuals and their developmental defects.

E. Some Conclusions

This brief survey of motivational approaches in the domain of mental retardation shows that none is sufficiently elaborate to qualify as a major motivational theory. Some of the shortcomings are specific to the different approaches, others are shared by all of them. Elucidating the major shortcomings of these approaches may contribute to clarifying some of the objectives and elements of a new theory of motivation.

Let us indicate first some of the shortcomings characterizing each of the approaches separately. A major problem of the behavioral approach is that it defines reinforcement and its effects in purely external, "objective" terms without considering the subjects, their preferences, and the way they see the situation. Numerous studies have shown that the effectiveness of a so-called reinforcer cannot be accounted for in terms of its physical attributes or even drive-satisfying properties, but reflects its value for a particular individual (Siegel, 1979, pp. 1–5). For example, candy and verbal rewards are equally effective reinforcers for children, although only the first is presumably related to drive reduction (Tramontana, 1972). As it became evident that "a high proportion of the variability seen in dependent measures can be laid at the door of individual differences in the 'true' preference value of the incentive employed" (Siegel, 1979, p. 4), an increasing number of investigators backed away from the concept of reinforcement. Instead, they turned to incentive motivation, which relies on the individual's expectations and considers the effect of cognitive factors, such as beliefs and attitudes on the intensity, favorability, and impact of motivators (Bandura, 1986, Chap. 6). Yet even when reinforcement is replaced by incentive motivation, the conceptual analysis of motivation presented by the behavioral approach seems to be simplistic. It attempts to account for behavior in terms of only two factors—innate and mainly learned reinforcers or incentives and acquired habits. The resultant conception is that human beings acquire the available reinforcement if they have adequate habits. An account of this kind leaves out the possibilities of internal control, selection of incentives, selection of behaviors, and the planned construction of behavior modes for the attainment of envisaged outcomes. All of these possibilities have been amply documented in research (e.g., reviews in Bandura, 1986, Chaps. 8–10; Weiner, 1980).

A major limitation of the personality-based approach is that it infers motivation largely from the individual's social background. Such inferences are based on the unwarranted assumption that individuals experience the pressures of their environment the way an external observer (viz., the investigator) does. There is some evidence indicating that this is not necessarily so. For example, adults, who as children had been diagnosed as educable mentally retarded, were interviewed about the effect that learning in ungraded classes had on their careers (Ross, Begab, Dondis, Giampiccolo, & Meyers, 1985). The answers were contrary to the expectations of both the proponents and the opponents of special education; only about 19% reported that they had been made to feel stupid or inferior, and 44% reported it had no effect on them at all. These results, although not conclusive because of the retrospective design, suggest that the assumption of negative effects due to social background needs to be examined in detail.

The personality-based approach also claims that social deprivation leads both to wariness and to seeking social support without specifying the degree or duration of social deprivation necessary for the development of these personality characteristics. It is possible that other factors are involved in eliciting each of these tendencies as well as in determining the specific behavioral form these negative and positive tendencies will assume. Thus, wariness may become manifest in rigidity, withdrawal, aggression, or even concealing information about oneself (Edgerton & Bercovici, 1976), whereas support seeking may become manifest in dependence, conformity, helpfulness, learning, frequent smiling, etc. Ideally, a theory of motivation should predict which of these behaviors will actually occur. This is particularly important since behavior, like concealing information, may seem to reflect wariness but may actually be due to social support seeking if it concerns hiding some act the individual considers to be shameful (Edgerton, 1984). This example also highlights the difficulties introduced by deducing motivation from behavior itself, as is often done in this framework. It seems to us that behavior does not provide unequivocal information about the individual's motives, even if the behavior is simple and the individual is of subnormal intelligence. Thus, a subject may perform a task because he or she expects social approval or is afraid to stop or does not want to get another task. The subject's behavior as such would not disclose the underlying motives.

To us, the major limitation of the psychodynamic approach seems to be that it assumes too much and has so far proved too little concerning motivation. It also leads to nonspecific predictions about behavior without stating under which conditions early emotional or social deprivation would lead to particular responses, such as rebelliousness, apathy, or delinquency.

Finally, concerning the cognitive approaches it seems to us that, so far, they have dealt only with a highly circumscribed domain of behavior, focusing on helplessness, extrinsic control, and extrinsic motivation. The generalization of these cognitive approaches to other behaviors may seem doubtful because their proponents seem to assume that a few specific beliefs, such as those that concern causal attribution and intrinsic incentives, suffice for determining all or most behaviors. It is difficult, however, to evaluate this issue because the cognitive approaches have not provided an explanation of how beliefs exert their impact on behavior.

Beyond the limitations that characterize the specific motivational approaches, there are two shortcomings that seem to apply to all of them. One is the neglect of individual differences. With very few exceptions (e.g., Zigler, Balla, & Butterfield, 1968), the motivational approaches hardly deal with individual differences. The reason may be partly methodological. The common two-group research design that focuses on comparing mentally retarded subjects with MA- or CA(chronological age)-matched normals yields findings that apply to mentally retarded subjects as a group and support the misleading illusion of no individual differences in behavior within the groups. Another reason may be the paucity of constructs that may predict individual differences.

It is possible that overlooking individual differences may be one cause of inconsistent findings. For instance, studies of self-evaluation in retarded subjects have found them to be both unrealistic (Ringness, 1961) and realistic (Carr & McLaughlin, 1973); some studies have found them to have higher expectancy of failure than normals (Macmillan & Koegh, 1971) and others have not (Gardner, 1958; Heber, 1957; Ringelheim, 1958).

Another shortcoming shared by the different motivational approaches is their application to changing behavior. The behavioral approach has been applied to changing behavior more than the others, but an increasing number of studies have shown that the obtained behavioral effects are limited in their generalization (Schroeder, Mulick, & Schroeder, 1979; Whitman & Schibak, 1979). Successful attempts to increase generalization, for example, in the domain of training the use of memory strategies, have shown that generalization depends on factors such as awareness of the strategy's procedure and purpose, and beliefs about the requirements of the task (Belmont & Butterfield, 1977; Borkowski & Cavanaugh, 1979; Ross & Ross, 1978). These are essentially cognitive factors that are not incorporated in the behavioral approach. The personality-based approach has not dealt specifically with changing behavior. The attempts of the psychodynamic approaches have been limited to psychotherapy. Finally, the cognitive approach, though theoretically concerned with change, has neither devised a particular technique for attaining behavior change nor provided evidence for change which was beyond the "minimal" or "faint," to use Haywood's descriptions (Haywood, 1986, p. 12; Haywood & Switzky, 1986, p. 38).

These motivational approaches illustrate theoretical and methodological differences in the study of motivation in mentally retarded subjects as well as some of the limitations and unresolved issues. It is noteworthy, however, that all of the motivational approaches have assumed that motivation in mentally retarded individuals is subject to the same laws and processes as in nonretarded subjects. None of the motivational approaches includes any motivational constructs designed to cope with phenomena that occurred exclusively in retarded individuals. Moreover, at least three of the approaches (the only exception is, perhaps, the work of the Zigler group) were devised initially for dealing with motivation in nonretarded persons and were then applied to studying behavior in retarded individuals. This provides a precedent for the application of general motivational theories to mental retardation and promises the possibility of increased understanding of motivational processes in both retarded and nonretarded individuals resulting from such an application.

III. A COGNITIVE THEORY OF MOTIVATION

A. Reasons for Applying a Cognitive Theory of Motivation

One reason for using a cognitive theory of motivation was the encouraging evidence provided by studies performed within the framework of the four motivational approaches (see Sections II,A–II,D). Some of these studies directly or indirectly showed the potential motivational role of cognitive contents and processes, such as the impact of the expectation of failure.

Another reason was the existence of a pretested theory of cognitive motivation that has proven capable of predicting specific behaviors and enabled experimental change. The theory of cognitive orientation has been applied only to nonretarded populations (Kreitler & Kreitler, 1976, 1982). It enabled the prediction of behaviors such as arriving on time for appointments, pain tolerance, achievement, increasing or decreasing performance after success or after failure (Kreitler & Kreitler, 1976, Chap. 7, Studies IV, V, I, III; 1982), curiosity (Kreitler, Kreitler, & Zigler, 1974), quitting smoking after behavior therapy (Kreitler, Shahar, & Kreitler, 1976), recovering from pain following pain-relief therapy (Kreitler, Kreitler, & Carasso, 1987), applying different defense mechanisms (Kreitler & Kreitler, 1972; Zemet, 1976), overeating (Kreitler & Chemerinski, in press), assertiveness and orderliness (Lobel, 1982), decision making (Zakay, 1976), keeping commitments (Shmotkin, 1983), communicating with others about oneself (Kreitler, Schwartz, & Kreitler, 1987), slowness (Ziv Av, 1978), and planning (Kreitler & Kreitler, 1987a,b). The subjects in these studies were normal adults, adolescents, children, and adult schizophrenics. The theory also enabled modifying behaviors, such as curiosity, pain tolerance (Kreitler & Kreitler, 1976), and impulsivity (Zakay, Bar-El, & Kreitler, 1984).

Because of its success with the diverse behaviors and populations, the theory seemed promising for dealing with the problems of predicting and changing specific behaviors in the retarded. We expected that applying cognitive orientation theory to retarded individuals would serve three goals: (1) it would deepen our understanding of motivation in retarded individuals in general and of cognitive motivation in particular; (2) it would promote the study of individual differences in mental retardation; and (3) it would enable attaining changes in the behavior of retarded individuals by applying purely cognitive means.

B. The Cognitive Orientation Theory

The theory was developed as a conceptual framework for studying the chain of cognitive–motivational events and processes between initial input identification and output of human overt behavior. Our initial assumption, slightly modified during almost 20 years of experimentation, is that cognitive contents guide behavior by orienting the person toward some behaviors and away from others. The orientative impact is due to the representations of motivation-laden states (e.g., "I am hungry") and to the meanings assigned to these representations. The two do not necessarily orient the individual in the same direction. For instance, the motivational aspects of the cognitive contents "I am hungry" may orient the individual toward eating, but the meanings of "hunger" may include associations to obesity, high cholesterol levels, and heart arrest, all of which orient the person away from eating. This example is, in many respects, oversimplified. A more adequate understanding of the orienting properties of cognition requires tracing the chain of contents, processes, and interactions between initial input identification and behavioral output. In the present context, only a brief summary of the theory will be provided as an introductory background for the experiments to be presented in Section IV.

The theory describes the processes intervening between the occurrence of some external or internal input and the enactment of behavior. The first stage consists of initial input identification. Identification is carried out by retrieving and then assigning meaning to the input. Some of our previous studies have shown that normal adults use common shared meaning for input identification, but schizophrenic subjects use idiosyncratic meanings (Kreitler & Kreitler, 1984, 1986). In both cases, however, the identification process is the same.

The representation of every externally or internally elicited input is first checked against the representation of the immediately preceding stimulation (as in Sokolov's "neuronal model"). If no change is found, the ongoing processing continues. If a mismatch is registered, initial meaning assignment to this input sets in, leading to one of four possible outcomes:

1. The input is recognized as a signal for a defensive, adaptive, or conditioned reflex.
2. The input is recognized as a familiar signal for more complex action and, hence, stands in need of a more elaborate clarification of its meaning.
3. The input is known to be irrelevant to the present situation.
4. The input is new or has particular significance for the present situation and, thus, elicits an orienting response, which may provide sufficient information for identifying the input in line with alternatives 1, 2, or 3.

The transition from the level of initial input identification and reflex execution to a higher level of input elaboration takes place if one of three conditions is met: (1) the input was identified as a signal for an adaptive, defensive, or conditioned response, but feedback information indicates that the response was inadequate for coping with the situation; (2) the input was identified as a familiar signal for a more complex sequence of behavior; and (3) despite the orienting response, the input was not identified sufficiently for habituating the orienting response so that higher level exploration is required.

Using Pavlov's (1927) famous metaphor, the level of initial input identification may be characterized as an attempt to answer the question "What is it?" Correspondingly, the second stage of processing involves more extensive retrieval and elaboration of meanings and could be considered as attempts to answer the metaphoric questions "What does it mean?" and "What does it mean to me and for me?" (which are designed to clarify the input's behavioral relevance).

The second stage of cognitive orientation involves an extension of input identification called "meaning generation." It differs from its initial input identification both in its evoked meanings and in its function. More complex meaning combinations are processed, some of them indicating situational features and implications, others representing motivational factors. For instance, if the input was identified as the 12 strokes of a church bell, the situational implication could be "it is lunchtime," whereas the motivational representation might be "hunger." The meanings evoked at this stage are more highly individualized and reflect, in form and content, both interpersonally shared constituents as well as personal ones. The combinations of meanings, if verbalized, are equivalent to what are called "beliefs." All of the evoked beliefs concern the input directly or indirectly and are designed to clarify whether action is required or not. If the beliefs indicate that the input does require action or further consideration, the input is ignored with or without intentional storage in long-term memory, depending on the foreseen importance of that input. However, if at least one of the evoked beliefs indicates a goal, input elaboration continues. In case such an explicit goal belief comes to the fore, the cognitive processing becomes focused, as it were, on the question "What will I do?"

This third stage in the cognitive orientation model is characterized by a complex, mostly subconscious process of belief activation. Empirical studies and analyses (Kreitler & Kreitler, 1976) have shown that four types of beliefs are crucial for the guidance of molar behavior:

1. *Beliefs about goals of the subject.* If expressed in words, each goal belief would consist of the meaning "I," representing the subject, and other meanings that express a desired or disliked relation, e.g., "I want to be slim," "I hate dieting," "I want to go out," "I don't want to answer questions," etc.

2. *Beliefs about self.* These beliefs contain the meaning "I" and express information about the self, such as one's habits, traits, habitual actions, feelings, sensations, and abilities in the present, past, or future, e.g., "I am lazy," "I once fell and it hurt," "I did this task before," "In the evening I will go home," "I don't take moral rules seriously," etc.

3. Beliefs about norms and rules. Beliefs of this type are not explicitly self related. They express ethical, esthetic, social, and other norms and rules in regard to acts, events, etc. They concern the things a person considers as permitted, forbidden, or necessary. They reflect "the ought and should" relations that can be expressed in different forms, e.g., "one should not be lazy," "you must not put your hand in the fire," "it is detestable to dress sloppily," "a good boy never spills the milk," etc.

4. General Beliefs. Beliefs of this type express (in a nonpersonal form), usually by the use of an "is" or "is not" relation, information about people, events, objects, and situations that is assumed to be general knowledge, e.g., "tomorrow it is Sunday," "eating two eggs in the morning is not harmful," "if you fail once, you fail always," and "trying hard can sometimes help."

The four types of beliefs were selected from a larger number of belief types. These four were found to make significant contributions to the prediction of overt behaviors, such as achievement, arriving on time, and planning (Kreitler & Kreitler, 1976, 1987a,b). Control analyses showed that when all four belief types were pooled to form one score, the prediction of behaviors was poorer than when the four belief types were included as separate variables (Kreitler & Kreitler, 1982). Further, several studies indicate that each of the four belief types can be expected to make the largest contribution to prediction of behavior, depending on the type of situation (Kreitler & Kreitler, 1976, Chap. 13). An analysis of 117 published studies dealing with relations between attitude measures and overt behaviors indicated that studies in which a positive relation was found used attitude scales with at least three of these four belief types. Studies finding no relation between attitudes and behavior used attitude scales with only one or two of these belief types (Kreitler & Kreitler, 1976, Chap. 12). Findings of this nature provide support for the importance of the four belief types.

Beliefs of the four types are assumed to be activated mostly by a goal belief. Although beliefs of other types also may sometimes serve as focal beliefs, if no goal belief is activated, no overt behavior ensues. The activated beliefs undergo a process of clustering, in the course of which they interact with each other by mutually strengthening or weakening their support for some course of behavior. According to our findings, the beliefs of each belief type (that is, goal beliefs, beliefs about self, beliefs about norms, and general beliefs) function as a single vectorial component (Kreitler & Kreitler, 1976). Together, the four belief types form a belief cluster which orients action toward or away from the direction represented by the focal goal belief. This is the *cognitive orientation cluster,* probably the most important element of the cognitive orientation theory. It provides the basis for behavior prediction and constitutes the major locus of modification of behavior.

Some cognitive orientation clusters are stored for later retrieval, thus allowing a quick behavioral decision whenever they are activated. Regardless of whether they had been previously stored or not, they can be reconstructed by checking the beliefs of the subject or group of subjects that are likely to be pertinent to the theme of the situation in question (for more details, see Section IV,B).

If all four cognitive orientation components support the focal belief, or three support it and the fourth is neutral, a Behavioral Intent emerges. If the focal goal belief is supported by only one or two of the belief types whereas the others orient away from it, the behavior indicated by the goal belief is unlikely to occur. More complex situations occur when, for example, two cognitive orientation clusters are formed around two focal goal beliefs (viz., a conflict) or when no cognitive orientation cluster can be formed, for example, because not enough beliefs have been activated in any one cognitive orientation component. However, situations of this kind will not concern us in this chapter.

The behavioral intent represents the directionality of the total cognitive orientation cluster. It thus constitutes the answer to the metaphoric question "What will I do?" Whereas the process of clustering is not conscious, the behavioral intent may become so. If it is explicitly stated, it often assumes the external form of a belief about self (e.g., "I will read the report tomorrow") or a goal belief (e.g., "I want to read the report tomorrow"), but differs from both of them (Kreitler & Kreitler, 1976, Chap. 11).

Even if a behavioral intent is supported by all four congitive orientation components, overt behavior cannot occur if the person does not know how to do what he or she wants to do. Thus, the fourth stage of the model focuses, as it were, on the question "How will I do it?" The execution of overt behavior depends on the availability of a behavioral program or the ability to form it. A program is a hierarchical system of instructions, often sequential, which regulate action. Some programs are innate (e.g., reflexes), some are partly innate and partly learned (e.g., instincts, walking, defense mechanisms), some are learned (e.g., reading, going to a restaurant), and some are products of ad hoc planning. Planning is a complex cognitive activity, itself dependent on a cognitive orientation cluster, which takes place when no adequate program for implementing the behavioral intent is available (Kreitler & Kreitler, 1987a,b). When one or more programs are available, they are retrieved and the most adequate is selected. The program then undergoes adjustment to the current situation, which often involves resolving conflicts between programs in suspension and those in execution. Due to the importance of the program for executing actions, when predicting or changing behavior it is necessary to make sure that the subject can perform the behavior in question.

The final stage of the cognitive orientation model consists of enacting the behavior itself.

C. Availability of the Four Belief Types in Mentally Retarded Individuals

Our main methodological concern in the application of the cognitive orientation theory to predicting and changing the behavior of mentally retarded individuals was with their ability to express different belief types and to distinguish between them. Therefore, we will now review briefly studies suggesting to us that retarded subjects would be able to comprehend and express the beliefs that are necessary for successful predictions of behavior.

Studies of self-concept (see Section II,D) as well as studies about learned helplessness (e.g., Reynolds & Miller, 1985), anxiety (e.g., Levine, 1985) or causal attributions (e.g., Horei & Guarnaccia, 1975) indicate that retarded individuals have beliefs about self and can communicate them (see also Silon & Harter, 1985). Retarded individuals also have general beliefs as shown by evidence that they are aware of others and social problems (Blacher, 1982), consider food properties such as freshness, quality, or brand names while making purchasing decisions in the supermarket (Levine & Langness, 1985), have acceptable levels of knowledge about sexual issues (Edmondson, McCombs, & Wish, 1979) or political themes (Klein & Green, 1979), and can respond reliably to surveys (Sigelman, Schoenrock, Spanhel, Hromas, Winer, Budd, & Martin, 1980). Studies about the ideal self (Kniss, Butler, Gorlow, & Guthrie, 1962) and wishes (Sternlicht, 1967) indicate that retarded individuals have beliefs about goals. It is also clear that retarded individuals have beliefs about rules and norms. This is illustrated by studies on values in retarded adolescents (Sternlicht, 1967), acquisition of standards for performance by TMR (trainable mentally retarded) children (Litrownik, Cleary, Lecklitner, & Franzini, 1978), and observations of the reaction of retarded adolescents to various social climates of classrooms (Harris, 1953; Harris & Sievers, 1959).

There is also evidence about the ability of retarded individuals to distinguish between different types of beliefs. Studies of the real self, ideal self, and self-image disparity (e.g., Zigler *et al.*, 1972) show that retarded individuals are able to distinguish between beliefs about the self and beliefs about goals. Further, in studies by Miller and Gottlieb (1972) and by Hayes and Prinz (1976), retarded children were asked to select photos showing how they felt, how they wish they felt, and how the child in the picture or their teachers would feel about a certain task. The findings show that retarded children distinguished between questions about the self, about goals, and about others. Finally, studies of attribution (Horai & Guarnaccia, 1975) show that retarded persons can distinguish between beliefs about self (e.g., "you were not smart enough") and general beliefs (e.g., "the test was too hard").

The studies mentioned in this section show that retarded individuals, at least those who are moderately retarded, may provide the information required by the cognitive orientation theory for predicting behavior.

IV. PREDICTING BEHAVIOR IN THE RETARDED BY MEANS OF COGNITIVE ORIENTATION

A. Purpose and General Hypothesis

Previous findings (especially in Section II,D) and evidence about the availability of beliefs of the four types in retarded individuals (see Section III,C) were sufficiently encouraging to attempt an application of the cognitive orientation theory in predicting the behavior of retarded persons. Three previously unpublished studies dealing with four behaviors (the study in Section IV,F deals with two) will be described in this section. Their purpose was to predict behavior in retarded individuals on the basis of variables defined by the cognitive orientation theory.

All the behaviors selected for these experiments were overt. Further, they were behaviors commonly considered as characteristic of the retarded, e.g., rigidity, reactions to failure (see Sections II,B–II,D). By selecting these behaviors we hoped to show the extent of individual differences within the sample of retarded persons and to highlight the role of cognitive motivation in behavioral features considered as characteristic of the population as a whole.

Our general hypothesis was that beliefs of four types—about goals, the self, rules and norms, and general beliefs—would allow the prediction of behaviors in retarded individuals. We expected that the behavior in question would occur with greater intensity or strength in subjects in whom at least three belief types were oriented toward that behavior. The criterion, intensity or strength, was chosen because the studied behaviors were assessed by continuous variables.

B. The Cognitive Orientation Questionnaires

The major tool of prediction in all six studies was the cognitive orientation questionnaire. This questionnaire provides, for each subject, four scores: one on beliefs about goals, one on beliefs about self, one on beliefs about rules and norms, and one on general beliefs about others and the environment. The scores reflect the subject's answers to questions concerning the four types of beliefs. The questions do not refer directly to the behavior to be predicted, but only to themes which represent the meanings of that behavior. The meanings of the studied behavior for the particular population of subjects have to be established through pretests. The meaning probes are done by means of standard questions which refer directly to the studied issue or behavior. The first few questions are general (e.g., "What does it mean when the teacher gives you a candy?" and "What does it mean to go on doing something to the very end?"), whereas the later ones are more specific (e.g., "What happens when you stop doing something before the end?" and "Why do you stop?"). The answers of the children to both kinds of probe questions establish the meanings of the particular issue or behavior. Meanings that recur in at least 50% of the pretest sample were selected as themes for the particular cognitive orientation questionnaire.

In the pretests conducted with retarded individuals, the subjects were asked questions such as the following with regard to rigidity: "Mark (or Mary) likes to build with blocks. He always builds in the same way. Sometimes he wants to build in another way, but he doesn't. Why?" The children's answers pointed to three recurrent themes: (1) Mark is afraid of punishment by the teacher if he does not build the same way he was taught to build; (2) there is only one way to build with blocks; (3) in order to build differently, Mark would have to make an effort and try harder. Because answers of these types recurred in 70% of the pretest sample, the following themes, among others, were selected as themes for the Cognitive Orientation Questionnaire of Rigidity: (1) fear of punishment, (2) limited possibilities for doing things, and (3) trying harder.

For each behavior, separate themes were established. The number of themes for each behavior ranged from five to eight. In constructing the questionnaires, we used a simple version of the "focal situations" as is often done in cognitive questionnaires for children (e.g., see the questionnaire in Kreitler *et al.*, 1974). A focal situation is some concrete situation in which one or two children exemplifying a certain behavior are involved. The focal situation is presented verbally and, sometimes, also by means of a simple line drawing that is placed in front of the child. Beliefs of the four types are assessed by means of questions that refer to the focal situation. For example, the Cognitive Orientation Questionnaire of Intangible Rewards included getting attention as one of its themes. The focal situation for this theme was this: "Dan (or Mary) plays at school. He sees the teacher. She is busy. He screams so that she will come to him and see what he does." After the situation was presented, the child was asked the following questions: (1) "Should Dan make the teacher come to him or not?" (a question referring to beliefs about rules and norms); (2) "Do you want to make the teacher come to you and see what you do?" (a question referring to beliefs about goals); (3) "When you see the teacher, do you always make her come to you, like Dan or not?" (a question referring to beliefs about self); and (4) "When children play at school, do they make the teacher come and see what they do, like Dan, or not?" (a question referring to general beliefs).

After the questionnaire was constructed, it was administered to 20–35 subjects of the same population as the subjects of the study proper. The responses of the subjects were used for deleting or changing questions that were unclear or too difficult or did not allow for enough variability in responding. Item analyses performed with each belief type separately led to the deletion of items that reduced reliability (for more details concerning the standard procedure of constructing cognitive orientation questionnaires, see Kreitler & Kreitler, 1982).

Since the set of themes relevant for each behavior is unique to the behavior, four separate cognitive orientation questionnaires were constructed, one for each behavior. Each questionnaire included 15–42 questions, 4–11 for each belief type, grouped around 3 to 6 focal situations. The reliabilities of each questionnaire varied from $r = .80$ to $r = .91$ for the four belief types. The intercorrelations between the four belief types in each questionaire ranged from $r = .23$ (nonsignificant) to $r = .65$ ($p < .05$) (the mean of intercorrelations of the four belief types in the six questionnaires was $r = .39$, $p < .05$).

Each subject received four scores, one for each belief type. The four scores were used as predictors in regression analyses or were combined into one index score called a cognitive orientation score. The cognitive orientation score is the sum of the four binary scores (1 or 0) assigned to each belief type depending on whether the score was above (coded as 1) or below (coded as 0) the mean of the group. The cognitive orientation score ranges from 0 (when none of the four types of belief support the specific behavior) to 4 (when they all support the behavior).

C. General Information about the Studies

Several points concerning methods and procedures common to the three studies will be presented here and will not be repeated for each unless there are deviations (as in Studies 2 and 3).

A different group of subjects participated in each study. The subjects were of both genders. They were all of the familial type, i.e., there was no evidence of organic brain pathology for the subject and there was evidence that at least one other close member of his or her family was also retarded. The IQ was measured by the Stanford–Binet. The subjects were selected randomly from special education schools in Israel over a period of several years.

The experimenters were psychology students of both genders who did not know the hypotheses of the studies. Each subject was seen by an experimenter in two individual sessions 4 to 9 days apart. In one session the appropriate cognitive orientation questionnaire (constructed as described in Section IV,B) was administered, in the other the tasks designed to provide the behavioral measures. If there were two or more tasks for one session, they were administered in random order. In each sample, half of the children was given the questionnaire first, whereas the other half was tested with the behavioral measures first. No significant order effects were found in any of the studies, nor were there any significant differences between boys and girls. If more than one behavioral task was used, the findings of those who first received one of the tasks were compared to those who received the other first. But in no case were there any significant order effects. Therefore, in each study, all the data were analyzed without including order and gender variables.

D. Study 1: Predicting Rigidity

Retarded individuals have often been characterized as more rigid than nonretarded individuals, mostly because of structural characteristics or failure experiences (Zigler & Balla, 1982). In view of the cognitive orientation theory, the hypothesis was that the scores of retarded subjects on the four belief types of the Cognitive Orientation Questionnaire of Rigidity would predict the degree of rigidity manifested by the subjects in two tests of rigidity.

The subjects were 52 mentally retarded children (28 girls and 24 boys). Their mean age was 10.2 years, their mean IQ was 52.3, and their mean MA was 5.4. They were administered the Cognitive Orientation Questionnaire of Rigidity and behavioral measures of rigidity. The questionnaire focused on themes, such as "fear of punishment," "limited possibilities for doing things," "trying harder," and "change as the cause of forgetting." It included 29 questions and provided 4 scores, one for each belief type. The scoring was oriented toward nonrigidity so that the higher the cognitive orientation score, the lower the expected rigidity.

Rigidity was assessed by means of two behavioral tasks. One was a card-sorting task modeled closely after Kounin's (1941a) original test. The materials included 3 sets of cards: (1) 25 white cards of five different shapes, (2) 25 square cards in five different colors, and (3) 25 cards, 5 in each of the shapes, each in one of the five colors. The subject was first asked to sort the cards of the first 2 sets, presented in random order, into 5 groups in order to determine his or her ability to sort on the basis of color or form separately. Then the subject was asked to sort the cards of the third set into 5 groups. When the sorting was completed, the subject was asked to perform another sorting "different from the last one." The latter instruction was repeated 5 times at 5-minute intervals. The sortings were scored for completeness of change (ranging from 0 to 3; intercoder reliability 98%). The scores were multiplied by the number of trials on which the changes occurred, in descending order from 5 to 1, respectively. The weighted scores were summed across trials. On the card-sorting task all of the subjects showed they were able to sort on the basis of color or form alone. Therefore, their performance in the third and crucial part of the task could not be attributed to low discrimination between color and form.

The second rigidity task was route drawing. The subject was presented with a page on which there were crossed lines, and was asked to draw a route from a "start" point to a "house" point, using only segments of drawn lines. The task was repeated 5 times, at 5-minute intervals, each time on a new page. In each repetition the subject was requested to draw a new route "different from the former routes." The scores were based on evaluating the amount of change in the route drawn (ranging from 0 to 4; intercoder reliability was 99%). These scores were multiplied by the number of trials on which the changes occurred, decreasing from 5 to 1, respectively. The weighted scores were summed across trials.

In both rigidity tasks the lower the score, the higher the assessed rigidity. The scores of the two rigidity tests were correlated positively ($r = .41, p < .01$). They were also correlated ($r = .65, p < .01$) in a comparable group of subjects (age about 10 years, MA about 6.3) (Kreitler, Zigler, & Kreitler, 1988).

As expected, the results show that the higher the subjects' cognitive orientation scores, the lower the level of rigidity manifested in card sorting and route drawing (as reflected in the higher scores of subjects oriented toward nonrigidity). Table 1 shows that the children who had higher cognitive orientation scores, orienting toward nonrigidity, performed more changes and did so on earlier trials in both card sorting and route drawing. The differences between the five subgroups of cognitive orientation scores were significant in the case of both tasks. Notably, the means are ordered linearly, and the deviations from linearity are not significant in the two tasks. It is of interest to mention that the number of subjects with cognitive orientation scores orienting toward nonrigidity (scores 4 and 3, $n = 18$) was not significantly lower than the number of those with scores orienting toward rigidity (scores 0 and 1, $n = 28$).

Stepwise multiple regression showed that for prediction of rigidity on card sorting, all four belief types made significant contributions, whereas for prediction of rigidity on route drawing only three belief types made significant

TABLE I

MEANS, STANDARD DEVIATIONS, AND RESULTS OF ANALYSES OF VARIANCE ON THE RIGIDITY MEASURES OF CARD SORTING AND ROUTE DRAWING BY SUBJECTS WITH DIFFERENT COGNITIVE ORIENTATION SCORES[a]

CO scores[b]	N	Card sorting[c] M	Card sorting[c] SD	Route drawing[d] M	Route drawing[d] SD
4	7	30.05	6.03	54.21	6.10
3	11	30.00	5.89	50.86	6.04
2	8	18.72	5.07	42.21	5.12
1	12	12.33	4.78	24.66	3.25
0	14	10.00	1.06	22.73	3.12

[a]The lower the score the higher the rigidity.
[b]CO, Cognitive orientation.
[c]$F = 18.961, p < .001$, df = 4/47.
[d]$F = 16.382, p < .001$, df = 4/47.

contributions, i.e., beliefs about goals, self and norms (see, in Table II, the F values of each predictor separately). In both cases, beliefs about goals entered the prediction equation first. This reflects the fact that the relative contribution of this predictor to the explained variance was largest. The predictor with the least relative contribution was general beliefs. The multiple correlation coefficients of all significant predictors were $r = .70$ in card sorting and $r = .68$ in route drawing (see Table II, column 3). Accordingly, the variance accounted for by all of the significant predictors was 49% in card sorting and 47% in route drawing (see Table II, column 4).

The findings support the hypothesis. They show that beliefs of four or three types relevant for rigidity enable predicting manifestations of rigidity in retarded children.

E. Study 2: Predicting Responsiveness to Tangible and Intangible Rewards

It has been claimed that retarded individuals are more responsive to tangible than intangible rewards and that the reasons for this are their background of social deprivation (Byck, 1968; Clinton & Boyce, 1975; Zigler & deLabry, 1962; Zigler & Unell, 1962), their low IQ and ability level (McManis, 1967; Tramontana, 1972), or extrinsic motivation orientation (Haywood & Switzky, 1986). On the basis of the cognitive orientation theory, the hypothesis was that responsiveness to tangible and intangible rewards depends on cognitive orientation, so that children would respond best to the reward that corresponds to the one for which they have a higher cognitive orientation score.

The subjects were 44 retarded individuals (24 girls and 20 boys), ranging in age from 11.8–14.10 years ($M = 13.6$) with a mean IQ of 66.1 and a mean MA of 10.3. Two cognitive orientation questionnaires were administered: the Cognitive Orientation Questionnaire of Tangible Rewards (e.g., toys, food), which included 31 questions, and the Cognitive Orientation Questionnaire of Intangible Rewards (i.e., affective and informative feedback), which included 40 questions. The questionnaires were centered around themes, such as "getting attention," "relations between student and teacher," and "doing the right thing."

Responsiveness to rewards was assessed by performance on two tasks. One was the marble-in-the-hole game, which tested the effect of reward on performance of a familiar task. The subject was requested to put one kind of marble into one hole and another kind into another hole (the materials are described in Shallenberger & Zigler, 1961). The score, duration of performance in seconds, was transformed logarithmically for computations. The second task, cipher substitution, tested the effect of reward on learning. The subject was shown a series of forms printed on pages and was asked to write under each square the cipher 3. There were three rounds of "learning," each 15

TABLE II

MULTIPLE STEPWISE REGRESSION ANALYSES WITH BELIEF TYPES AS PREDICTORS AND THE BEHAVIORAL MEASURES OF RIGIDITY, POSTSUCCESS PERFORMANCE AND POSTFAILURE PERFORMANCE AS DEPENDENT VARIABLES[a]

Variables	Predictors	F	Multiple R	R^2	Beta
Study 1,	Goal	20.97***	.46	.21	.838
Rigidity:	Self	28.70***	.65	.43	.489
card	Norms	12.58***	.68	.47	.281
sorting	General	10.13***	.70	.49	.245
Study 1,	Goal	24.99***	.49	.24	.555
Rigidity:	Norms	22.65***	.64	.41	.336
route	Self	7.75**	.68	.47	.259
drawing	General	0.08	.68	.47	−.027
Study 3,	Goal	46.68***	.61	.37	.609
Postsuccess:	Norms	11.94***	.62	.39	.244
recall	Self	4.23*	.67	.46	.125
	General	0.02	.68	.46	.048
Study 3,	Goal	33.01***	.54	.30	.683
Postsuccess:	Self	11.24***	.62	.39	.330
copying	Norms	8.46**	.74	.55	.275
	General	4.15*	.82	.68	.021
Study 3,	Norms	42.27***	.37	.61	.579
Postfailure:	General	14.11***	.63	.40	.236
recall	Goal	4.10*	.65	.42	.136
	Self	1.01	.65	.43	.098
Study 3,	Norms	28.96***	.52	.27	.614
Postfailure:	Goal	27.29***	.74	.55	.432
copying	General	16.08***	.79	.63	.283
	Self	0.25	.79	.63	.039

[a]The predictors are presented in the order of their inclusion in the prediction equation. The F values refer to each predictor separately. The multiple R and R^2 are cumulative. The Beta values represent the standardized regression coefficients. Goal, Goal beliefs; Self, beliefs about self; Norms, beliefs about norms; General, general beliefs.

*$p < .05$.

**$p < .01$.

***$p < .001$.

minutes long with a 3-minute interval between each phase. The results of the first phase were used for evaluating the baseline performance. The crucial phase was the fourth, which also lasted 15 minutes. Each correct placement of the cipher was scored as 2 points, incorrect placements were 1 point.

The design was a 2 × 2 factorial. One factor was cognitive orientation scores (high cognitive orientation scores for intangible rewards *and* low scores for tangible vs. high cognitive orientation scores for tangible rewards *and* low scores for intangible). The second factor was the kind of reward (tangible vs. intangible).

About a month prior to the experimental sessions, the Cognitive Orientation Questionnaire of Intangible Rewards and the Cognitive Orientation Questionnaire of Tangible Rewards were administered to children of the same population as the study's sample, in random order, in two separate individual sessions, about a week apart. The subjects of the study selected from this group were those who had either a high cognitive orientation score (scores 4 or 3) toward intangible rewards *and* a low cognitive orientation score (scores 1 or 0) toward tangible rewards ($n = 22$) or a high cognitive orientation score (scores 4 or 3) toward tangible rewards *and* a low cognitive orientation score (scores 1 or 0) toward intangible rewards ($n = 22$). Each group was divided randomly into two equal subgroups ($n = 11$) (with an equal number of boys and girls); one subgroup received a tangible reward (i.e., a small toy and a candy) and the other received an intangible reward (i.e., "good, fine" and "right, correct"). The subjects of each subgroup were administered both tasks, in random order, in individual sessions 1 to 2 days apart. In the case of marble-in-the-hole, the reward was promised at the start ("I'll give you a toy and a candy" or "I'll tell you if you did right and good"); the cipher substitution task was administered at the end of each phase.

Comparing the means of the four subgroups in the first phase of cipher substitution showed that the differences were not significant. Hence, baseline performance could not explain the results in this task.

Two-factor analyses of variance with cognitive orientation scores and the kind of reward as independent variables and performance on the two tasks as the dependent variables showed that there was no significant main effect but, as expected, in both tasks the interaction between cognitive orientation scores and the kind of reward provided was significant (for marble-in-the-hole, $F = 35.80$, df $= 1/36$, $p < .001$, and for cipher substitution, $F = 14.57$, df $= 1/36$, $p < .001$). The means presented in Table III indicate that the subjects' responsiveness was highest when they got the reward that matched their cognitive orientation, and it was lowest when they got the reward that did not match it. Thus, the findings support the hypothesis. They show that responsiveness to tangible or intangible rewards is a function of the correspondence between the child's cognitive orientation and the provided reward.

TABLE III
MEANS AND STANDARD DEVIATIONS ON THE TASKS OF MARBLE-IN-THE-HOLE AND CIPHER SUBSTITUTION BY SUBJECTS HIGH AND LOW IN COGNITIVE ORIENTATION FOR INTANGIBLE AND TANGIBLE REWARDS WHO GOT INTANGIBLE AND TANGIBLE REWARDS[a]

	CO Scores (High for intangible rewards and low for tangible rewards)		CO Scores (High for tangible rewards and low for intangible rewards)	
Task	Intangible reward (n = 11)	Tangible reward (n = 11)	Intangible reward (n = 11)	Tangible reward (n = 11)
Marbles				
Mean	652.3	210.5	182.7	775.2
SD	150.9	74.3	60.2	240.5
Ciphers				
Mean	25.32	13.71	9.83	23.45
SD	3.81	2.94	2.01	3.16

[a]The means and standard deviations for marbles-in-the-hole represent seconds and for ciphers the index score reflects the number and correctness of cipher placement.

F. Study 3: Predicting Changes in Performance following Success and following Failure

It is usually assumed that success functions as a positive reward and, hence, improves the level of performance. In view of the evidence that, in normals, reactions to success vary with the subjects' cognitive orientation (Kreitler & Kreitler, 1976, Chap. 7), the first hypothesis of this study was that the scores of retarded children on the Cognitive Orientation Questionnaire of Postsuccess Performance would predict the degree to which their performance would rise or fall or remain unchanged following exposure to success.

Similarly, it is often claimed that failure exerts a negative impact on the level of performance. Since many retarded children probably have a long history of failures, it is assumed that repeated failures are one cause for their depressed level of performance (Balla & Zigler, 1979, pp. 148–149; Siegel, 1979, pp. 31–40). We found before that, in normals, reactions to failure vary with the subject's cognitive orientation (Kreitler & Kreitler, 1976, Chap. 7). Thus, the second hypothesis of this study was that the scores of retarded subjects on the Cognitive Orientation Questionnaire of Postfailure Performance would predict the degree to which their performance would rise or fall or remain unchanged following failure.

Because the manipulations of success and failure might interact, we used different groups of subjects for testing the two hypotheses. For predicting postsuccess performance we used 53 mentally retarded children (25 boys and 28 girls) with a mean age of 14.4, a mean IQ of 62.4, and a mean MA of 7.5. They were administered the Cognitive Orientation Questionnaire of Postsuccess Performance, and performance tasks. The questionnaire was focused around themes, such as "luck and chance," "the value of effort," and "durability of an achievement." It included 34 questions and provided 4 scores, one for each belief type. When the cognitive orientation score was high (Scores 3 or 4), performance postsuccess was expected to improve. When it was medium (Score 2), it was expected not to change; when it was low (Scores 1 or 0), it was expected to decrease.

There were two kinds of performance tasks. One, a free-recall task, had two parallel forms, each including 16 verbal items with 4 items in each of 4 categories (materials, furniture, geometric forms, and clothing). A fully correct recall was scored as 2 points, and a partially correct recall was scored as 1 point. The other task was a letter-copying task with two parallel forms. The score was the number of correctly copied letters in 10 minutes; fully correct copying received 2 points, and partially correct copying received 1 point.

Each subject was administered the Cognitive Orientation Questionnaire of Postsuccess Performance in one session, the recall tasks in another, and the copying tasks in a third, each 7 to 12 days apart. The order of the recall and copying tasks was random. One of the recall tasks was administered and the free-recall test was given immediately. After presumably checking the subject's responses, the experimenter provided both tangible and intangible rewards ("This is fine, you did very well" and a candy). After a pause of 5 minutes the procedure was repeated with the parallel recall task. The order of the two parallel tasks was randomized. The same procedure was followed for the tasks of copying letters, each of which lasted 10 minutes.

For predicting postfailure performance we used 58 mentally retarded children (28 boys and 30 girls) with a mean age of 13.9 years, a mean IQ of 68.2, and a mean MA of 8.1. They were administered the Cognitive Orientation Questionnaire of Postfailure Performance and two performance tasks. The questionnaire was focused around themes, such as "rejection by others," "luck and effort," and "changing one's image." It included 37 questions and provided 4 scores, one for each belief type. When the cognitive orientation score was high (Scores 3 or 4), performance after failure was expected to improve. When it was medium (Score 2), it was expected to remain unchanged; when it was low (Scores 0 or 1), it was expected to decrease. The same kinds of performance tasks were used as in testing the first hypothesis. Also, the procedure was the same except for one change: the success manipulation was replaced by a failure manipulation, which consisted of the experimenter saying to the subject, "This is not good, you did not do well." (At the end of the experiment all subjects were told they had done very well so as to give them a success experience.)

Concerning the first hypothesis, the findings show that before success there were no significant differences in the performance of the subgroups, but after success the differences were significant for both tasks (the covariance analysis showed no significant effect for the baseline, but a significant main effect for the cognitive orientation scores in Recall ($F = 7.269$, df = 1/48, $p < .001$) and Copying ($F = 12.267$, df = 1/48, $p < .001$). As expected, there was improvement after success in the performance of subjects with high cognitive orientation scores (Scores 3 and 4) in Recall (a rise of 52.17%) and Copying (a rise of 21.87%), and there was a decrease in the performance of subjects with low cognitive orientation scores (Scores 0 or 1) in Recall (a decrease of 44.84%) and in Copying (a decrease of 15.4%) (see Table IV). There were too few subjects to check stability of performance in the case of cognitive orientation Score 2 ($n = 2$).

As can be seen in Table II, the stepwise multiple regression analyses show that (1) for predicting recall postsuccess, all four belief types had a significant contribution (goal beliefs, norm beliefs, beliefs about self, and general beliefs, in that order), and (2) for predicting copying postsuccess, three belief types had significant contributions (goal beliefs, beliefs about self, and norm beliefs, in that order). All the predictors accounted for 46% of the variance in the recall task and for 68% of the variance in the copying task. The difference is probably due to the fact that purely cognitive factors play a larger role in recall than in copying. The findings support the first hypothesis. They show that beliefs of four or three types relevant for postsuccess performance enable predicting the increases and decreases of performance after success in retarded children.

Concerning the second hypothesis, the findings show that before failure there were no significant differences in the performance of the subgroups, but after failure the differences were significant for both tasks (the covariance analysis showed no significant effect for the baseline but a significant main effect for the cognitive orientation scores in Recall [$F = 9.420$, df = 1/51, $p < .001$] and Copying [$F = 11.473$, df = 1/51, $p < .001$]). As expected, there was improvement after failure in the performance of subjects with high cognitive orientation scores (Scores 4 or 3) in Recall (a rise of 18.27%) and in Copying (a rise of 12.39%), and there was a lowering in the performance of subjects with low cognitive orientation scores (Scores 0 or 1) in Recall (a decrease of 76.03%) and in Copying (a decrease of 52.58%) (see Table IV). The decreases after failure in subjects with low cognitive orientation scores were larger than the decreases after success in subjects with low cognitive orientation scores. In the group of Score 2 there were, as expected, only slight differences in performance, but the number of subjects was too small ($n = 4$) to permit analysis. The stepwise multiple regression analysis shown in Table II indicates that for predicting performance after failure in both tasks, three belief types made a significant contribution (i.e., norm beliefs, goal beliefs, and general beliefs). All of the predictors accounted for 42% of the variance

TABLE IV

MEANS AND STANDARD DEVIATIONS ON RECALL AND COPYING TASKS PRE- AND POSTSUCCESS OR -FAILURE BY SUBJECTS WITH DIFFERENT COGNITIVE ORIENTATION SCORES

Condition and CO scores	*N*	Recall task				Copying task			
		Pre		Post		Pre		Post	
		Mean	SD	Mean	SD	Mean	SD	Mean	SD
Success									
CO 4	13	3.7	1.12	5.9	1.54	36.45	3.72	48.17	4.15
CO 3	15	4.1	.89	6.0	2.13	33.12	4.12	37.12	5.09
CO 2	2	4.0	1.25	4.2	1.70	28.17	4.05	30.15	5.12
CO 1	14	4.3	1.50	2.0	.85	30.64	3.99	26.47	4.87
CO 0	9	4.2	1.07	2.9	1.01	28.44	4.10	23.14	4.90
Failure									
CO 4	6	3.6	.95	4.1	1.14	35.89	4.15	40.17	4.23
CO 3	9	3.8	1.17	4.6	1.15	32.35	3.96	36.46	4.21
CO 2	4	4.5	.85	3.4	1.34	27.79	4.51	30.50	3.87
CO 1	21	3.9	1.21	.8	1.01	28.16	4.10	12.41	4.02
CO 0	18	4.4	1.25	1.2	1.10	30.06	3.85	15.36	4.00

in the recall task and for 63% of the variance in the copying task. As in regard to postsuccess, the percentage is lower in the more cognitive task of recall than in copying. The findings support the second hypotheses. They show that beliefs of three types relevant for postfailure performance enable predicting the increases and decreases of performance after failure in retarded children.

V. CHANGING BEHAVIOR IN RETARDED INDIVIDUALS THROUGH COGNITIVE ORIENTATION

The purpose of this section is to describe briefly an exploratory study designed to examine the possibility of changing cognitive orientation clusters in retarded individuals in order to change the corresponding behaviors. Demonstrating that an experimentally induced change in beliefs leads to the expected change in behavior confirms the theoretical claim of the cognitive orientation theory that the direction of the causal impact is from cognitive contents to behavior. The major purpose of this study was not to provide evidence for this claim. As noted before (Section III,A), the cognitive orientation theory has already been applied successfully in normal individuals for changing different behaviors in the desired directions. This has been attained by systematically changing beliefs of the four belief types relating to the themes relevant for the target behavior. Rather, the study was performed mainly in order to investigate whether or not it would be possible to change beliefs of retarded individuals. The previous studies already showed that they had measurable beliefs and that these beliefs guide their behaviors. The problem, then, was whether or not they are also capable of changing these beliefs under the guidance of experimenters. Admittedly, we had some doubts. First, because at least some retarded individuals tend to be rigid and perseverant and may, therefore, find it difficult to give up familiar beliefs. Second, we thought that changing beliefs may perhaps require greater awareness of cognitive contents than many of the retarded individuals have.

Our hypothesis was that changing the beliefs of the four types that relate to rigidity would bring about a decrease in rigidity behaviors. For obvious reasons the study was designed only to decrease rigidity and not to increase it.

The subjects were 39 familial retarded individuals (19 boys and 20 girls) with a mean age of 11.9 and a mean IQ of 65.4. They were recruited randomly from different special education schools in Israel. The same Cognitive Orientation Questionnaire of Rigidity and the two performance tasks described in the previous study of rigidity (Section IV,D) were used. Rigidity was assessed by the same measures as in that study.

The subjects were divided into 2 groups and administered the Cognitive Orientation Questionnaire of Rigidity in one individual session and the two performance tasks in random order in another session, with 3 to 4 days between the sessions. Subjects (3) who received a cognitive orientation score of 4 were excluded from the sample because they already had the highest cognitive orientation score orienting toward nonrigidity. After the testing the subjects were divided randomly into two groups, one with 19 subjects (9 boys and 10 girls) and one with 20 subjects (10 girls and 10 boys). The subjects in one group served as experimental subjects, those of the other group as controls. The experimenter met with the experimental subjects in groups of 2 or 3 for 6 sessions twice a week (each session lasted 35 to 45 minutes). Each session was devoted to discussing one of the themes included in the Cognitive Orientation Questionnaire of Rigidity, i.e., change as the cause of forgetting, the existence of limited possibilities, difficulties involved in trying harder in order to change, etc. Concerning each theme, all four belief types were discussed. No reference was made to the performance tasks.

The cognitive orientation treatment sessions were conducted in accordance with carefully specified instructions. Some of the major techniques applied for attaining the change in beliefs were as follows.

1. The discussion was focused on the concrete figure of a child (a paper doll) who was described as nonrigid, and the children were requested to imagine his or her opinions concerning specific issues, e.g., "the existence of limited possibilities."
2. The desired target beliefs were introduced as the beliefs of the imaginary child, and the children were asked to supply arguments in favor of these beliefs. When they found it difficult, different arguments were presented and the children were asked to evaluate them and to adopt the best one.
3. Each session ended with some kind of decision in suppot of beliefs orienting toward nonrigidity.
4. The experimenter did not try to persuade the children to give up their beliefs but only to retrieve further beliefs from their own memories or learn new beliefs of nonrigidity.

The control group had the same number of sessions as the experimental group, but they were devoted to playing games.

The sessions lasted for three weeks. After an interval of one week, all children were retested individually on the Cognitive Orientation Questionnaire of Rigidity and the two performance tasks, following the same procedure as in the first stage of the experiment.

The findings show that the experimental and control groups did not differ significantly prior to the cognitive orientation treatment in cognitive orientation scores or rigidity as assessed by card sorting and route drawing (Table V). Covariance analyses showed no significant effect for the baseline performance, but significant main effects for the cognitive orientation scores prior to the treatment (for Sorting, $F = 4.72$, df $= 1/34$, $p < .05$, for Drawing, $F = 8.70$, df $= 1/34$, $p < .01$) and for the treatment itself (for Sorting, $F = 7.43$, df $= 1/34$, $p < .05$, for Drawing, $F = 11.51$, df $= 1/34$, $p < .01$).

TABLE V
MEANS AND STANDARD DEVIATIONS OF COGNITIVE ORIENTATION SCORES AND THE RIGIDITY MEASURES OF CARD SORTING AND ROUTE DRAWING IN THE EXPERIMENTAL GROUP AND IN THE CONTROL GROUP[a,b]

	Experimental group		Control group		*t* Test	*t* Test
Measures[c]	Pre	Post	Pre	Post	Pre/pre	Post/post
CO scores						
Mean	1.25	2.20	1.16	1.00	0.29	3.76***
Standard deviation	0.99	1.12	0.98	0.86		
Card sorting						
Mean	16.82	20.96	16.59	16.48	0.14	2.73*
Standard deviation	4.90	5.10	5.03	5.12		
Route drawing						
Mean	26.41	37.05	27.03	26.74	0.43	6.57***
Standard deviation	4.15	5.10	4.81	4.73		

[a]The experimental group received cognitive orientation treatment, the control group did not.
[b]For the experimental group, $N = 20$; for the control group, $N = 19$.
[c]For measures of card sorting and route drawing, the higher the score, the lower the rigidity.
*$p < .05$
***$p < .001$

Table V shows that the mean cognitive orientation scores of the subjects in the experimental group changed significantly from pre- to posttreatment sessions and became oriented more toward nonrigidity. No such changes occurred in the control group. More specifically, in 13 of the experimental subjects there was an increase in the cognitive orientation scores following the sessions, whereas in 7 subjects there was no change. In the control group, no subjects had increased their cognitive orientation scores, 2 had decreased, and 17 did not change ($\chi^2 = 12.216$, $p < .001$).

In view of these changes in cognitive orientation scores, the changes in the behavior of the experimental subjects should not be surprising. The means presented in Table V show that after the cognitive orientation treatment sessions the experimental subjects behaved less rigidly than before in both performance tasks. No comparable changes occurred in the control group. The findings support the hypothesis. They show that retarded individuals may change their beliefs orienting toward rigidity following cognitive orientation treatment sessions and that their rigidity behavior changes accordingly.

VI. CONCLUDING COMMENTS

A. Predicting Behavior in Retarded Individuals: Discussion of the Findings

The results of the three studies reported in Sections IV,D–IV,F show that, in every case, scores reflecting relevant beliefs of at least three of the four types of beliefs defined by the cognitive orientation theory enabled successful predictions of the assessed behaviors. These included rigidity (Section IV,D), responsiveness to tangible and intangible rewards (Section IV,E), and increase or decrease of performance after success and after failure (Section IV,F). Each of the behaviors was assessed in terms of two different measures. Thus, the results cannot be accounted for in terms of the characteristics of a specific measure. The broad range of findings, which refer to eight measures assessing four behaviors, supports the conclusion that cognitive orientation plays no less a major role in the motivation of retarded persons than it does in that of the nonretarded.

Notably, in all cases of prediction, three or four of the belief types had significant contributions. This is consistent with cognitive orientation theory and corresponds to the findings in nonretarded individuals. However, a closer examination of the regression analyses presented in Table II show that in four of the six cases (Study 2, Section IV,E, is not represented) only three belief types had significant contributions. The two exceptions were the card-sorting measure of rigidity and the recall measure of postsuccess performance. The involvement of only three belief types in the prediction of behavior has been observed in samples of nonretarded individuals under two conditions: (1) in adults when the fourth belief type does not orient in a direction opposite to that shared by the other three and (2) in children up to 8–9 years of age. It is tempting to conclude that our findings with retarded individuals are similar to those obtained with nonretarded younger children. Yet this conclusion should not be drawn before the first explanatory alternative has been thoroughly investigated.

The regression analyses (Table II) also show that each of the four belief types has a significant contribution to the prediction of the different behaviors. Further, the relative magnitude of the contributions differs across the six behavioral measures. These findings also correspond to those in nonretarded individuals (Kreitler & Kreitler, 1976, Chap. 13). Still, it seems that in the samples of retarded persons some belief types appear consistently earlier in the prediction equation than others. If we multiply each belief type by 4 if it occurs in the first place, by 3 if it occurs in the second place, by 2 if it occurs in the third place, and by 1 if it occurs in the fourth place, the sum of the products would yield an index of prominence in the regression equations. This index is 21 for goal beliefs and 18 for norm beliefs, but only 12 for beliefs about self and 9 for general beliefs. Thus, goal and norm beliefs play a more prominent role in the prediction equations than do beliefs about self and general beliefs.

According to the information we have at present about cognitive orientation, the consistent salience of some predictors could, in principle, occur in adults if the behaviors in question are highly similar. But even then it is rare and unlikely. Moreover, the studied behaviors do not seem to be so similar in the present case. On the other hand, it has been observed that the two belief types salient in the retarded individuals' data fulfil an important role in the development of the cognitive orientation cluster. Marom (1978) found that children 4 to 5 years old act in accordance with the orientation common to goals and norm beliefs and overlook beliefs about self and general beliefs unless there is a conflict between goal and norm beliefs. Hence, the salience of goal and norm beliefs in the prediction equations of the retarded individuals could indicate that their cognitive orientation clusters still have an affinity to an early developmental stage in the cognitive guidance of behavior.

There is still a third possible explanation. Goal and norm beliefs may be so salient in retarded subjects because they have the clearest orientational character of all four belief types. They point directly toward or away from a given course of behavior, mostly without the need to rely on inferences and combinations of beliefs, as is often the case with beliefs about self and general beliefs.

Finally, it is of interest to note that the range of variance accounted for by three or four belief types is from 43 to 68% with a mean of 52.7%. The percentage seems lower (M = 46%) for more purely cognitive behaviors (i.e., card sorting as a measure of rigidity, recall postsuccess and recall postfailure) than for the other behaviors (M = 59.3%). Yet, the number of involved behaviors is too small to allow for more than a suggestive hypothesis for future research.

B. Implications and Conclusions

The findings about predicting (Section IV) and changing (Section V) behavior in retarded individuals by means of cognitive orientation give rise to a number of implications and conclusions that may be organized into three groups.

1. IMPLICATIONS AND CONCLUSIONS CONCERNING MENTAL RETARDATION

The findings of the prediction studies (Section IV) demonstrate that there are sizable individual differences in mentally retarded persons in regard to behaviors often considered as main characteristics differentiating between mentally retarded and nonretarded groups. This implies that despite the temptation to compare mentally retarded with nonretarded groups, it is misleading to refer to mentally retarded individuals in global terms as if their motivation was cut along homogeneous lines. Though mental retardation may affect motivation, it does not eliminate motivation and perhaps does not even limit it.

Further, the findings show that the individual differences can be predicted on the basis of specific cognitive contents defined and combined in line with the cognitive orientation theory. In addition, the study of change (see Section V) showed that modifying the cognitive contents brings about the expected change in behavior, i.e., in that case a decrease in rigidity. Together, this set of findings indicates that cognitive contents and processes guide the behavior of mentally retarded persons. This conclusion is important theoretically. First, it implies that there is similarity in the motivational dynamics underlying behavior in both mentally retarded and nonretarded individuals. The particular beliefs constituting the cognitive orientation clusters may differ in retarded and nonretarded groups, as they also differ across individuals within the groups. Also, probably the meanings of the beliefs—their contents and range—differ in retarded and nonretarded individuals. But the major point of importance is that in both retarded and nonretarded persons, beliefs have an orientative function for behavior, and when combined they determine the course of behavior. Yet, emphasizing the guidance of behavior by belief clusters implies neither that behavior is controlled or voluntary nor that motivation is conscious or requires awareness on the part of the individual. It merely implies that the direction of behavior depends on the combined orientational directionalities of a great number of beliefs relevant for that behavior.

Second, the conclusion about cognitive motivation in retarded persons suggests that it is the cognitive processing of inputs that determines the impact that any external and internal force or condition will have on behavior. The cognitive processing includes meaning assignment in ever broadening circles, starting with input identification and proceeding toward elaboration of interpersonally shared and more personal meanings anchored on the emergence and specification of some course of action. Hence, no conclusions about motivation in the retarded can be drawn from their actual or presumed experiential history or environmental conditions without considering their meanings and orientational implications within the cognitive system of the retarded person himself or herself. Further, neither does behavior per se provide insight into the motivational dynamics of the retarded person. Behavior is the product of motivational forces like the cognitive orientation cluster and its product, the behavioral intent, but it is also shaped by behavioral programs. Since similar behavioral programs may implement different behavioral intents, inferring motives from behaviors is theoretically hazardous. But no less hazardous is inferring motives from single beliefs. As emphasized by the cognitive orientation theory, behavior neither derives from nor corresponds to one or two beliefs, but is elicited by a specific combination of beliefs that represents four different types of beliefs referring to different aspects of the behavior in question. It is important to recall that three to four belief types were shown to shape behavior in retarded individuals, just as they did in nonretarded individuals.

Finally, the evidence in favor of cognitive motivation in retarded persons implies that cognitive behavior is guided also by belief combinations, i.e., cognitive orientation clusters. In view of what is known about motivation of cognitive behaviors in nonretarded individuals (Kreitler, Maguen, & Kreitler, 1975; Kreitler & Kreitler, 1987a,b), it is likely that, also for retarded individuals, specific cognitive orientation clusters may determine cognitive behavior. More specifically, they may determine the extent to which a retarded person may utilize his or her cognitive potential. This includes applying one's potential as required by the various environmental and internal conditions. But it also includes the readiness to learn and, thus, expand and increase one's cognitive potential. Hence, by modifying relevant aspects of motivation it may be possible to increase, to some extent, the level of cognitive behavior of retarded individuals. But since their cognitive potential is so limited, their ability to apply it and, especially, to use it for learning is greatly restricted. Therefore it is unlikely that intervention focused on modifying motivation alone would dramatically raise the cognitive level of retarded individuals.

2. IMPLICATIONS AND CONCLUSIONS CONCERNING ASSESSMENT AND INTERVENTION IN MENTAL RETARDATION

Our research on predicting and changing behavior in retarded individuals by means of cognitive orientation leads to several conclusions of a more applied nature. We showed that beliefs relevant to a behavior predict that behavior. The beliefs were assessed by means of cognitive orientation questionnaires. Cognitive orientation questionnaires can be constructed for any behavior of interest for theoretical or practical reasons. The range of prediction of any cognitive orientation questionnaire within its domain is very broad. For example, the Cognitive Orientation Questionnaire of Curiosity was applied successfully for predicting 16 different curiosity behaviors and proved useful even for diagnosing whether or not a certain behavior was motivated by curiosity (Kreitler, 1976, Chap. 8; Kreitler *et al.*, 1974). Hence, it may be of importance to consider including cognitive orientation measures concerning basic behaviors in standard assessment programs of retarded persons as well as in any selection process involving retarded individuals (e.g., for the purpose of a special project or training). Cognitive orientation measures may be expected to help identify those individuals who, for motivational reasons, may benefit most or least from the available programs, services, or training.

Of even greater importance are the intervention possibilities suggested by our exploratory study (see Section V). This study showed that it is possible to change the behavior of retarded persons in a desired direction by modifying their cognitive orientation. The outlined method of cognitive orientation treatment has great potential for behavior modification in retarded individuals because of its broad range of generalization. Further research is needed to clarify techniques, processes, and outcomes of this new approach to changing behavior in retarded persons.

3. IMPLICATIONS AND CONCLUSIONS CONCERNING THE COGNITIVE ORIENTATION THEORY

The cognitive orientation theory has been applied successfully previously to predicting and changing behavior in normal (children, adolescents, and adults) and abnormal subjects (i.e., schizophrenics). Yet the successful application of the theory to mentally retarded subjects not only broadens the range of populations for which it was shown to be adequate. The evidence that the theory applies to mentally retarded individuals is a fact of major importance for the theory. As a theory of cognitive motivation it tends to be grasped as depending on the cognitive potential of the individual and, hence, as limited by this potential. The demonstration that even in retarded individuals with a low MA (e.g., 5, see Section IV,D) cognitive orientation processes guide behavior contributes to strengthening the conception of the cognitive basis of all motivation.

REFERENCES

Abramson, N. L., Seligman. M. E. P., & Teasdale, J. P. (1978). Learned helplessness in humans: Critique and reformulation. *Journal of Abnormal Psychology*, **87**, 49–74.

Achenbach, T., & Zigler, E. (1968). Cue-learning and problem-learning strategies in normal and retarded children. *Child Development*, **39**, 827–848.

Balla, D., & Zigler, E. (1979). Personality development in retarded persons. In N. R. Ellis (Ed.), *Handbook of mental deficiency, psychological theory and research* (2nd ed., pp. 143–168). Hillsdale, New Jersey: Erlbaum.

Balla, D., & Zigler, E. (1982). Impact of institutional experience on the behavior and development of retarded persons. In E. Zigler & D. Balla (Eds.), *Mental retardation: The developmental difference controversy* (pp. 41–58). Hillsdale, New Jersey: Erlbaum.

Bandura, A. (1986). *Social foundations of thought and action: A social cognitive theory.* New York: Prentice-Hall.

Becker, R. L., Schull, C., & Campbell, K. (1981). Vocational interest evaluation of TMR adults. *American Journal of Mental Deficiency*, **85**, 350–356.

Beier, D. C. (1964). Behavioral disturbances in the mentally retarded. In H. A. Stevens & R. Heber (Eds.), *Mental retardation* (pp. 453–487). Chicago: University of Chicago Press.

Belmont, J. M., & Butterfield, E. C. (1977). The instructional approach to developmental cognitive research. In R. V. Kail, Jr. & J. W. Hagen (Eds.), *Perspectives on the development of memory and cognition.* Hillsdale, New Jersey: Erlbaum.

Bialer, I. (1961). Conceptualization of success and failure in mentally retarded and normal children. *Journal of Personality*, **29**, 303–320.

Bialer, I., & Cromwell, R. (1959). Failure as motivation with mentally retarded children. *Abstracts of Peabody Studies in Mental Retardation, 1955–1960*, 1. Division of Human Development, George Peabody College for Teachers.

Blacher, J. (1982). Assessing social cognition in young mentally retarded and nonretarded children. *American Journal of Mental Deficiency*, **86**, 473–484.

Borkowski, J. G., & Cavanaugh, J. C. (1979). Maintenance and generalization of skills and strategies by the retarded. In N. R. Ellis (Ed.), *Handbook of mental deficiency, psychological theory and research* (2nd ed., pp. 569–617). Hillsdale, New Jersey: Erlbaum.

Borkowski, J. G., Reid, M. K., & Kurtz, B. E. (1984). Metacognition and retardation: Paradigmatic, theoretical, and applied perspectives. In P. H. Brooks, R. Sperber & C. McCauley (Eds.), *Learning and cognition in the mentally retarded* (pp. 55–75). Hillsdale, New Jersey: Erlbaum.

Byck, M. H. (1968). Cognitive differences among diagnostic groups of retardates. *American Journal of Mental Deficiency*, **73**, 97–101.

Carr, C. C., & McLaughlin, J. A. (1973). Self-concepts of mentally retarded adults. *Mental Retardation*, **11**, 57–59.

Clinton, L., & Boyce, K. (1975). Acquisition of simple motor imitative behavior in mentally retarded and nonretarded children. *American Journal of Mental Deficiency*, **79**, 695–700.

Cochran, J. L., & Cleland, C. C. (1963). Manifest anxiety of retardates and normals matched as to academic achievement. *American Journal of Mental Deficienty*, **67**, 539–542.

Cohen, M. E., & Close, D. W. (1975). Retarded adults' discrete work performance in a sheltered workshop as a function of overall productivity and motivation. *American Journal of Mental Deficiency*, **79**, 536–529.

Collins, H. A., Burger, G. K., & Doherty, D. (1970). Self-concept of EMR and nonretarded adolescents. *American Journal of Mental Deficiency*, **75**, 285–287.

Cromwell, R. L. (1963). A social learning approach to mental retardation. In N. R. Ellis (Ed.), *Handbook of mental deficiency* (pp. 41–91). New York: McGraw-Hill.

Edgerton, R. B. (1967). *The cloak of competence: Stigma in the lives of the mentally retarded.* Berkeley and Los Angeles: University of California Press.

Edgerton, R. B. (1984). Mental retardation: An anthropologist's changing view. In B. Blatt & R. J. Morris (Eds.), *Perspectives in special education: Personal orientations.* Glenview, Illinois: Scott, Foresman.

Edgerton, R. B., & Bercovici, S. (1976). The cloak of competence—years later. *American Journal of Mental Deficiency*, **80**, 485–497.

Edmondson, B., McCombs, K., & Wish, J. (1979). What retarded adults believe about sex? *American Journal of Mental Deficiency*, **84**, 11–18.

Feldhusen, J. F., & Klausmeier, H. J. (1962). Anxiety, intelligence, and achievement in children of low, average, and high intelligence. *Child Development*, **33**, 403–409.

Floor, L., & Rosen, M. (1975). Investigating the phenomenon of helplessness in mentally retarded adults. *American Journal of Mental Deficiency*, **79**, 565–572.

Gardner, W. (1958). *Reactions of intellectually normal and retarded bovs after experimentally induced failure.* Unpublished doctoral dissertation, George Peabody College for Teachers.

Gibson, B. J. (1980). *An attributional analysis of performance outcomes and the alleviation of learned helplessness on motor performance tasks: A comparative study of educable mentally retarded and nonretarded boys.* Unpublished doctoral dissertation, University of Alberta.

Gifford, J. L., Rusch, R. F., Martin, J. E., & White, D. M. (1984). Autonomy and adaptability in work behavior of retarded clients. In N. R. Ellis & N. W. Bray (Eds.), *International review of research in mental retardation* (Vol. 12, pp. 285–318) New York: Academic Press.

Gold, M. W. (1973). Factors affecting production by the retarded: Base rate. *Mental Retardation*, **11**, 41–45.

Gothberg, L. C. (1947). A comparison of the personality of runaway girls with a control group as expressed in the themas of Murray's thematic apperception test. *American Journal of Mental Deficiency*, **51**, 627–631.

Granat, K., & Granat, S. (1978). Adjustment of intellectually below-average men not identified as mentally retarded. *Scandinavian Journal of Psychology*, **19**, 41–51.

Green, C., & Zigler, E. (1962). Social deprivation and the performance of retarded and normal children on a satiation type task. *Child Development*, **33**, 499–508.

Hardy, H. A. (1967). The relationship between self-attitudes and performance on a paired-associates learning task in educable retardates. *Dissertation Abstracts*, **27**, 1657.

Harris, L. M. (1953). Reactions of adolescent, mentally deficient girls to a permissive atmosphere in an academic schoolroom. *American Journal of Mental Deficiency*, **57**, 434–446.

Harris, L. M. (1955). A method for studying and treating behavior problems in the schoolroom. *American Journal of Mental Deficiency*, **59**, 595–600.

Harris, L. M., & Sievers, D. J. (1959). A study to measure changes in behavior of aggressive mentally retarded adolescent girls in a permissive classroom. *American Journal of Mental Deficiency*, **63**, 975–980.

Harrison, R. H., & Budoff, M. (1972). Demographic, historical, and ability correlates of the Laureton Self-Concept Scale in the EMR Sample. *American Journal of Mental Deficiency*, **76**, 460–480.

Harter, S. (1983). Developmental perspectives on the self-system. In E.M. Hetherington (Ed.), *Handbook of Child Psychology: Socialization, personality and social development* (Vol. 4, pp. 278–386). New York: Wiley.

Harter, S., & Zigler, E. (1968). Effectiveness of adult and peer reinforcement on the performance of institutionalized retardates. *Journal of Abnormal Psychology*, **73**, 144–149.

Harter, S., & Zigler, E. (1974). The assessment of effectance motivation in normal and retarded children. *Developmental Psychology*, **10**, 169–180.

Hayes, C. S., & Prinz, R. J. (1976). Affective reactions of retarded and nonretarded children to success and failure. *American Journal of Mental Deficiency*, **81**, 100–102.

Haywood, H. C. (1968). Psychometric motivation and the efficiency of learning and performance in the mentally retarded. In B. W. Richards (Ed.), *Proceedings of the First Congress of the International Association for the Scientific Study of Mental Deficiency* (pp. 276–283). Reigate, Surrey: Michael Jackson.

Haywood, H. C. (1971). Individual differences in motivational orientation: A trait approach. In H. I. Day, D. E. Berlyne, & D. E. Hunt (Eds.), *Intrinsic motivation: A new direction in education.* Toronto: Holt.

Haywood, H. C. (1986). *The mental age deficit: Explanation and treatment.* Lecture at Conference of AAMD, Sweden, July.

Haywood, H. C., Arbitman-Smith, R., Bransford, J. D., Delclos, V. R., Towery, J., Hannel, M. V., & Hannel, L. (1982). Cognitive education with adolescents: Evaluation of instrumental enrichment. In A. M. Clarke & A. D. B. Clarke (Chairmen), *Psychosocial interventions: Possibilities and constraints.* Symposium, Sixth International Congress of the International Association for the Scientific Study of Mental Deficiency, Toronto, August.

Haywood, H. C., & Burke, W. P. (1977). Development of individual differences in intrinsic motivation. In I. C. Uzgiris & F. Weizman (Eds.), *The structuring of experience.* New York: Plenum.

Haywood, H. C., & Switzky, H. N. (1985). Work response of mildly mentally retarded adults to self versus external regulation as a function of motivational orientation. *American Journal of Mental Deficiency*, **90**, 151–159.

Haywood, H. C., & Switzky, H. N. (1986). Intrinsic motivation and behavior effectiveness in retarded persons. In N. R. Ellis & N. W. Bray (Eds.), *International review of research in mental retardation* (Vol. 14, pp. 1–46). Orlando, Florida: Academic Press.

Haywood, H. C., & Wachs, T. D. (1966). Size discrimination learning as a function of motivation-hygiene orientation in adolescents. *Journal of Educational Psychology*, **57**, 279–286.

Haywood, H. C., & Weaver, S. J. (1967). Differential effects of motivational orientation and incentive conditions on motor performance in institutionalized retardates. *American Journal of Mental Deficiency*, **72**, 459–467.

Heber, R. (1957). *Expectancy and expectancy changes in normal and mentally retarded boys.* Unpublished doctoral dissertation, George Peabody College for Teachers.

Herzberg, F., Mausner, B., & Snyderman, B. B. (1959). *The motivation to work.* New York: Wiley.

Hirsch, E. (1959). The adaptive significance of commonly described behavior of the mentally retarded. *American Journal of Mental Deficiency*, **63**, 639–646.

Hoffman, J., & Weiner, B. (1978). Effects of attributions for success and failure on the performance of retarded adults. *American Journal of Mental Deficiency*, **82**, 449–452.

Honig, A. (1966). Subnormal functioning in mental illness. *Psychoanalytic Review,* **53**, 112-133.
Horai, J., & Guarnaccia, V. J. (1975). Performance and attributions to ability, effort, task, and luck of retarded adults after success or failure feedback. *American Journal of Mental Deficiency,* **79**, 690–694.
Hutt, M. L., & Gibby, R. G. (1976). *The mentally retarded child: Development, education, and treatment* (3rd ed.). Boston: Allyn & Bacon.
Jakab, I. (1982). Psychiatric disorders in mental retardation, recognition, diagnosis and treatment. In I. Jakab (Ed.), *Mental retardation* (pp. 270–326). Basel: Karger.
Johnson, C. M., Bradley-Johnson, S., McCarthy, R., & Jamie, M. (1984). Token reinforcement during WISC-R administration. II. Effects on mildly retarded, black students. *Applied Research in Mental Retardation,* **5**, 43–52.
Kahoe, R. D. (1966). Motivation–hygiene aspects of vocational indecision and college achievement. *Personnel Guidance Journal,* **44**, 1030–1036.
Kanner, L. (1949). Child psychiatry; mental deficiency. *American Journal of Psychiatry,* **105**, 526–528.
Klein, N. K., & Green, B. B. (1979). Levels of political knowledge of mildly mentally retarded adults. *American Journal of Mental Deficiency,* **84**, 159-164.
Kniss, J. T., Butler, A., Gorlow, L., & Guthrie, G. M. (1962). Ideal self patterns of female retardates. *American Journal of Mental Deficiency,* **67**, 245–249.
Kounin, J. (1941a). Experimental studies of rigidity: I. The measurement of rigidity in normal and feebleminded persons. *Character and Personality,* **9**, 251–272.
Kounin, J. (1941b). Experimental studies of rigidity. II. The explanatory power of the concept of rigidity as applied to feeblemindedness. *Character and Personality,* **9**, 273–282.
Kreitler, H., & Kreitler, S. (1972). The cognitive determinants of defensive behavior. *British Journal of Social and Clinical Psychology,* **11**, 359–372.
Kreitler, H., & Kreitler, S. (1976). *Cognitive orientation and behavior.* New York: Springer.
Kreitler, H., & Kreitler, S. (1982). The theory of cognitive orientation: Widening the scope of behavior prediction. In B. Maher & W.B. Maher (Eds.), *Progress in experimental personality research* (Vol. 11, pp. 101–169). New York: Academic Press.
Kreitler, H., & Kreitler, S. (1986). Schizophrenic perception and its psychopathological implications: A microgenetic study. In V. Hentschel, G. Smith, & J. G. Draguns (Eds.), *The roots of perception* (pp. 301–330). New York: Elsevier.
Kreitler, S., & Chemerinski, A. (in press). The cognitive orientation of obesity. *International Journal of Obesity.*
Kreitler, S., & Kreitler, H. (1984). Meaning assignment in perception. In W. D. Froehlich, G. J. W. Smith, G. J. Draguns, & V. Hentschel (Eds.), *Psychological processes in cognition and personality* (pp. 173–191). Washington, D.C.: Hemisphere.
Kreitler, S., & Kreitler, H. (1987a). Plans and planning: Their motivational and cognitive antecedents. In S. L. Friedman, E. K. Scholnick, & R. R. Cocking (Eds.), *Blueprints for thinking: The role of planning in cognitive development* (pp. 110–178). New York: Cambridge University Press.
Kreitler, S., & Kreitler, H. (1987b). The motivational and cognitive determinants of individual planning. *Genetic, Social and General Psychology Monographs,* **113**, 81–107.
Kreitler, S., & Kreitler, H. (1988). *The cognitive rehabilitation of the retarded.* Unpublished manuscript.
Kreitler, S., Kreitler, H., & Carasso, R. (1987). Cognitive orientation as predictor of pain relief following acupuncture. *Pain,* **28**, 323–341.
Kreitler, S., Kreitler, H., & Zigler, E. (1974). Cognitive orientation and curiosity. *British Journal of Psychology,* **65**, 43–52.
Kreitler, S., Maguen, T., & Kreitler, H. (1975). The three faces of intolerance of ambiguity. *Archives of Psychology,* **127**, 238–250.
Kreitler, S., Schwartz, R., & Kreitler, H. (1987). The cognitive orientation of expressive

communicability in schizophrenics and normals. *Journal of Communication Disorders*, **20**, 73-91.

Kreitler, S., Shahar, A., & Kreitler, H. (1976). Cognitive orientation, type of smoker, and behavior therapy of smoking. *British Journal of Medical Psychology*, **49**, 167-175.

Kreitler, S., Zigler, E., & Kreitler, H. (1988). *Rigidity in the retarded and in normals.* Submitted manuscript.

Kunca, D. F., & Haywood, N. P. (1969). The measurement of motivational orientation in low mental age subjects. *Peabody Papers in Human Development*, **7**, Whole No. 2.

Levine, H. G. (1985). Situational anxiety and everyday life experiences of mildly mentally retarded adults. *American Journal of Mental Deficiency*, **90**, 27-33.

Levine, H. G., & Langness. (1985). Everyday cognition among mildly mentally retarded adults: An ethnographic approach. *American Journal of Mental Deficiency*, **90**, 18-26.

Lewin, K. (1936). *A dynamic theory of personality.* New York: McGraw-Hill.

Litrownik, A. J., Cleary, C. P., Lecklitner, G. L., & Franzini, L. R. (1978). Self-regulation in retarded persons: Acquisition of standards for performance. *American Journal of Mental Deficiency*, **83**, 86-89.

Lobel, T. E. (1982). The prediction of behavior from different types of beliefs. *Journal of Social Psychology*, **118**, 213-223.

Marom, S. (1978). *Examination of CO clusters in children based on the theory of cognitive orientation.* Master's thesis, Department of Psychology, Tel Aviv University (summarized in Kreitler & Kreitler, 1982).

MacEachron, A. E. (1979). Mentally retarded offenders: Prevalence and characteristics. *American Journal of Mental Deficiency*, **84**, 165-176.

Macmillan, D. L., & Koegh, B. K. (1971). Normal and retarded children's expectancy for failure. *Developmental Psychology*, **4**, 343-348.

McCarver, R. B., & Craig, E. M. (1974). Placement of the retarded in the community: Prognosis and outcome. In N. R. Ellis (Ed.), *International review of research in mental retardation* (Vol. 7, pp. 145-207). New York: Academic Press.

McManis, D. L. (1967). Marble-sorting persistence in mixed verbal-incentive and performance-level pairings. *American Journal of Mental Deficiency*, **71**, 811-817.

Menolascino, F. J. (1974). The mentally retarded offender. *Mental Retardation*, **12**, 7-11.

Miller, M. B. (1961). *Locus of control, learning climate, and climate shift in serial learning with mental retardates.* Unpublished doctoral dissertation, George Peabody College for Teachers.

Miller, M. B., & Gottlieb, L. H. (1972). Projection of affect after task performance by retarded and nonretarded children. *American Journal of Mental Deficiency*, **77**, 149-156.

Moss, J. (1958). *Failure-avoiding and success-striving behavior in mentally retarded and normal children.* Unpublished doctoral dissertation, George Peabody College for Teachers.

Nisbett, R. E. (1968). Taste, deprivation, and weight determinants of eating behavior. *Journal of Personality and Social Psychology*, **10**, 107-116.

Ollendick, T., Balla, D., & Zigler, E. (1971). Expectancy of success and the probability learning of retarded children. *Journal of Abnormal Psychology*, **77**, 275-281.

Parton, R. V., Webb, M. G. T., & Clarke, J. G. (1974). The psychiatric presentation and identification of mentally handicapped patients. *Irish Medical Journal*, **67**, 611-615.

Pavlov, I. (1927). *Conditioned reflexes.* Oxford: Clarendon.

Pearson, G. H. J. (1942). The psychopathology of mental defect. *Nervous Child*, **2**, 9-20.

Pier, E., & Harris, D. (1964). Age and other correlates of self-concept. *Journal of Educational Psychology*, **55**, 91-95.

Reynolds, W. M., & Miller, K. L. (1985). Depression and learned helplessness in mentally retarded and nonmentally retarded adolescents: An initial investigation. *Applied Research in Mental Retardation*, **6**, 295-306.

Ringelheim, D. (1958). *Effects of internal and external reinforcements on expectancies of mentally retarded and normal boys.* Unpublished doctoral disertation, George Peabody College for

Teachers.
Ringness, T. A. (1961). Self concept of children of low, average, and high intelligence. *American Journal of Mental Deficiency*, **65**, 453-461.
Ross, D. M., & Ross, S. A. (1978). Facilitative effect of mnemonic strategies on multiple associate learning in EMR children. *American Journal of Mental Deficiency*, **82**, 460-466.
Ross, R. T., Begab, M. J., Dondis, E. H., Giampiccolo, J. S., Jr., & Meyers, C. E. (1985). *Lives of the mentally retarded.* Stanford, California: Stanford University Press.
Rotter, J. (1954). *Social learning and clinical psychology.* New York: Prentice-Hall.
Rudolph, G., de M. (1958). The effects of children's television on behavior. *Mental Health*, **17**, 55-60.
Rutter, M. L. (1971). Psychiatry. In J. Wortis (Ed.), *Mental Retardation: An annual review* (Vol. 3, pp. 186-221). New York: Grune & Stratton.
Ryan, T. J., & Watson, P. (1968). Frustrative nonreward theory applied to children's behavior. *Psychological Bulletin*, **69**, 111-125.
Saenger, G. (1960). *Factors influencing the utilization of mentally retarded individuals in New York City.* Albany: New York State Interdepartmental Health Resources Board.
Sarason, S. B. (1959). *Psychological problems in mental deficiency* (3rd ed.). New York: Harper & Brothers.
Schachter, S. (1971). Some extraordinary facts about obese humans and rats. *American Psychologist*, **26**, 129-144.
Schroeder, S. R., Mulick, J. A., & Schroeder, C. S. (1979). Management of severe behavior problems of the retarded. In N. R. Ellis (Ed.), *Handbook of mental deficiency, psychological theory and research* (2nd ed., pp. 341-366). Hillsdale, New Jersey: Erlbaum.
Seligman, M. E. P. (1975). *Helplessness.* San Francisco: Freeman.
Shallenberger, P., & Zigler, E. (1961). Rigidity, negative reaction tendencies, and cosatiation effects in normal and feebleminded children. *Journal of Abnormal and Social Psychology*, **63**, 20-26.
Shmotkin, D. (1983). *Prediction of behavior following declaration concerning future behavior.* Unpublished doctoral dissertation, Tel Aviv University (in English).
Siegel, P. S. (1968). Incentive motivation in the mental retardate. In N. R. Ellis (Ed.), *International review of research in mental retardation* (Vol. 3, pp. 1-30). New York: Academic Press.
Siegel, P. S. (1979). Incentive motivation and the mentally retarded person. In N. R. Ellis (Ed.), *Handbook of mental deficiency, psychological theory and research* (2nd ed., pp. 1-61). Hillsdale, New Jersey: Erlbaum.
Sigelman, C. K., Schoenrock, C. J., Spanhel, C. L., Hroman, S. G., Winer, J. L., Budd, E. C., & Martic, P. W. (1980). Surveying mentally retarded persons: Responsiveness and response validity in three samples. *American Journal of Mental Deficiency*, **84**, 479-486.
Silon, E. L., & Harter, S. (1985). Assessment of perceived competence, motivational orientation, and anxiety in segregated and mainstreamed educable mentally retarded children. *Journal of Educational Psychology*, **77**, 217-230.
Simpson, N. (1962). *Short-term retention of paired associates by mentally retarded and normal children as a function of success or failure in original learning.* Master's thesis. University of Wisconsin, Office of Special Education.
Snyder, R., Jefferson, W., & Strauss, R. (1965). Personality variables as determiners of academic achievement of the mildly retarded. *Mental Retardation*, **3**, 15-18.
Spitz, H. H. (1986). *The raising of intelligence.* Hillsdale, New Jersey: Erlbaum.
Stark, J. A., Menolascino, F. J., Albarelli, M. H., & Gray, V. C. (Eds.) (1987). *Mental retardation and mental health: Classification, diagnosis, treatment, services.* New York: Springer-Verlag.
Stephen, W., Peck, J. R., & Veldman, D. (1968). Personality and success profiles characteristic of young adult male retardates. *American Journal of Mental Deficiency*, **73**, 405-413.
Sternlicht, M. (1964). A theoretical model for the psychological treatment of mental retardation. *American Journal of Mental Deficiency*, **68**, 618-622.
Sternlicht, M. (1967). *Adolescent retardates' values, as gleaned from sentence-completion responses.*

Paper presented at the meeting of the Eastern Psychological Association, Boston, April, 1967.

Sternlicht, M., & Deutsch, M. R. (1972). *Personality development and social behavior in the mentally retarded.* Lexington, Massachusetts: Lexington Books, Heath.

Switzky, H., & Haywood, H. C. (1985). *Self-reinforcement schedules in the mildly mentally retarded: Effects of motivational orientation and instructional demands.* Presented at Eighteenth Annual Gatlinburg Conference of Research and Theory in Mental Retardation and Developmental Disabilities, Gatlinburg, Tennessee, March.

Tramontana, I. (1972). Social versus edible rewards as a function of intellectual level and socioeconomic class. *American Journal of Mental Deficiency*, **77**, 33–38.

Vietze, P. M. (1985). Emotional development in retarded children. In M. Sigman (Ed.), *Children with emotional disorders and developmental disabilities* (pp. 23–43). New York: Grune & Stratton.

Viney, L. L., Clarke, A. M., & Lord, J. (1973). Resistance to extinction and frustration in retarded and nonretarded children. *American Journal of Mental Deficiency*, **78**, 308–315.

Webster, T. G. (1963). Problems of emotional development in young retarded children. *American Journal of Psychiatry*, **120**, 37–43.

Weiner, B. (1980). Human motivation. New York: Holt.

Weiner, B., Frieze, I., Kukla, A., Reed, S., Rest, S., & Rosenbaum, R. N. (1972). Perceiving the causes of success and failure. In E. E. Jones, D. E. Kanouse, H. H. Kelley, R. E. Nisbett, S. Valins, & B. Weiner (Eds.), *Perceiving the causes of behavior.* Morristown, New Jersey: General Learning Press.

Weisz, J. R. (1979). Perceived control and learned helplessness among mentally retarded and nonretarded children: A developmental analysis. *Developmental Psychology*, **15**, 311–319.

Weisz, J. R. (1982). Learned helplessness and the retarded child. In E. Zigler & D. Balla (Eds.), *Mental retardation: The developmental-difference controversy* (pp. 27–40). Hillsdale, New Jersey: Erlbaum.

White, R. W. (1959). Motivation reconsidered: The concept of competence. *Psychological Review*, **66**, 297–333.

Whitman, T. L., & Schibak, J. W. (1979). Behavior modification research with the severely and profoundly retarded. In N. R. Ellis (Ed.), *Handbook of mental deficiency, psychology theory and research* (2nd ed., pp. 289–340). Hillsdale, New Jersey: Erlbaum.

Windle, C. (1962). Prognosis of mental subnormals. *American Journal of Mental Deficiency, Monograph Supplements*, **66**, 1–180.

Wink, C. F. (1963). Mental retardation and learning under symbolic reinforcement in view of self-acceptance. *Dissertation Abstracts*, **23**, 2430–2431.

Yando, R. (1982). A behavioral approach to the treatment of the mentally retarded. In I. Jacob (Ed.), *Mental retardation* (pp. 142–163). Basel: Karger.

Yando, R., & Zigler, E. (1971). Outerdirectedness in the problem-solving of instutionalized and noninstitutionalized normal and retarded children. *Developmental Psychology*, **4**, 277–288.

Zakay, D. (1976). *Decision by meaning: A decision making model based upon the cognitive orientation theory.* Unpublished doctoral dissertation, Tel Aviv University (in English).

Zakay, D., Bar-El, Z., & Kreitler, S. (1984). Cognitive orientation and changing the impulsivity of children. *British Journal of Educational Psychology*, **54**, 40–50.

Zemet, R. (1976). *Cognitive orientation theory and patterns of behavior in conflictual situations in schizophrenic and normal subjects.* Master's thesis, Department of Psychology, Tel Aviv University (summarized in Kreitler & Kreitler, 1982).

Zigler, E. (1973). Why retarded children do not perform up to the level of their ability. In R. M. Allen, A. D. Cortazzo, & R. Toister (Eds.), *Theories of cognitive development: Implications for the mentally retarded.* Coral Gables, Florida: University of Miami Press.

Zigler, E. (1984). A developmental theory on mental retardation. In B. Blatt & R. J. Morris (Eds.), *Perspectives in special education: Personal orientations* (pp. 173–209). Glenview, Illinois: Scott,

Foresman.

Zigler, E., Abelson, W. D., & Seitz, V. (1973). Motivational factors in the performance of economically disadvantaged children on the Peabody Picture Vocabulary Test. *Child Development*, **44**, 294–303.

Zigler, E., & Balla, D. (1972). Developmental course of responsiveness to social reinforcement in normal children and institutionalized retarded children. *Developmental Psychology*, **6**, 66–73.

Zigler, E., & Balla, D. (1982). Rigidity—a resilient concept. In E. Zigler & D. Balla (Eds.), *Mental retardation: The developmental-difference controversy* (pp. 61–82). Hillsdale, New Jersey: Erlbaum.

Zigler, E., Balla, D., & Butterfield, E. C. (1968). A longitudinal investigation of the relationship between preinstitutional social deprivation and social motivation in institutionalized retardates. *Journal of Personality and Social Psychology*, **10**, 437–445.

Zigler, E., Balla, D., & Watson, N. (1972). Developmental and experimental determinants of self-image disparity in institutionalized and noninstitutionalized retarded and normal children. *Journal of Personality & Social Psychology*, **23**, 81–87.

Zigler, E., & Cascione, R. (1980). Overview of cognitive, behavioral and communicative disorders. In H. J. Grossman, E. M. Steindler, & C. Tarjan (Eds.), *The physician and the mental health of the child: The psychological concomitants of illness* (Vol. 2, pp. 3–10). Chicago: American Medical Association.

Zigler, E., & Cascione, R. (1984). Mental retardation: An overview. In E. S. Gollin (Ed.), *Malformations of development: Biological and psychological sources and consequences* (pp. 69–94). New York: Academic Press.

Zigler, E., & deLabry, J. (1962). Concept-switching in middle-class, lower-class, and retarded children. *Journal of Abnormal & Social Psychology*, **65**, 267–273.

Zigler, E., Hodgden, L., & Stevenson, H. (1958). The effect of support on the performance of normal and feebleminded children. *Journal of Personality*, **26**, 106–122.

Zigler, E., & Unell, E. (1962). Concept-switching in normal and feeble-minded children as a function of reinforcement. *American Journal of Mental Deficiency*, **66**, 651–657.

Ziv-Av, J. (1978). *Slowness in different types of action as a function of cognitive structures and contents*. Master's thesis, Department of Psychology, Tel Aviv University (summarized in Kreitler & Kreitler, 1982).

Mental Retardation, Analogical Reasoning, and the Componential Method

J. McCONAGHY

C.S.I.R.O. DIVISION OF HUMAN NUTRITION
ADELAIDE, AUSTRALIA

I. INTRODUCTION

The assumption that there are both quantitative and qualitative differences between groups with different verbal and spatial abilities but the same overall intelligence level has received considerable support (Cooper, 1982; Cooper & Regan, 1982; Hunt, 1978; Hunt, Frost, & Lunneborg, 1973; Hunt, Lunneborg, & Lewis, 1975; MacLeod, Hunt, & Matthews, 1978; Matthews, Hunt, & MacLeod, 1980; Pellegrino & Goldman, 1983; Pellegrino & Kail, 1982). Recently, R. J. Sternberg has developed a methodology, which he calls the componential method, to examine, both quantitatively and qualitatively, the processes used to perform tasks requiring analogical reasoning. Sternberg has concentrated specifically on the investigation of reasoning tasks because, like many others (Oppenheimer, 1956; Reitman, 1965; Spearman, 1927; Thurstone, 1938), he believes that an understanding of the processes used in these particular tasks can increase our understanding of general intelligence (*g*) (Sternberg, 1975, 1977, 1980, 1982, 1984). To this end, Sternberg has used the componential method to investigate the analogical reasoning skills of adults with different levels of reasoning ability and of children of varying ages (Sternberg, 1977; Sternberg & Rifkin, 1979; Sternberg & Nigro, 1980).

Of recent interest has been the proposal that quantitative and qualitative differences between groups of different overall intelligence levels might also be identified. Indeed, research into the cognitive processes of the mentally retarded has increased substantially in recent years (see Campione, Brown, & Ferrara, 1982; Detterman, 1979, for reviews), and much research points to the existence of quantitative differences between mentally retarded and nonretarded persons, with mentally retarded persons performing cognitive tasks slower (Jensen, 1982a; Jensen & Munro, 1979; Nettelbeck & Kirby, 1983).

Conversely, the examination of qualitative differences between mentally retarded and nonretarded persons has received less attention. Bray (1979) reviewed a number of studies using a directed forgetting task to examine the recall performance of mentally retarded and nonretarded persons. These studies indicated that while mentally retarded adolescents used a strategy to perform the directed forgetting task, this strategy was different from and less complex than the strategy adopted by nonretarded adolescents (Bray, Dann, & Gwartney, 1978; Bray, Goodman, & Justice, 1982). Belmont, Ferretti, and Mitchell (1982) used a self-paced memory task to examine qualitative differences in the spontaneous strategy usage of mentally retarded and nonretarded adolescents. To enhance spontaneous strategy usage by the mentally retarded adolescents, Belmont *et al.* presented these persons with a simpler version of the task compared to that presented to the nonretarded adolescents. Fewer of the mentally retarded adolescents spontaneously adopted a strategy for solution, even using the simpler task. Also, for those retarded persons who did spontaneously adopt a strategy, there were several trials between "strategic insight" and strategy usage, whereas these two events were virtually simultaneous for the nonretarded. Belmont *et al.* suggested that these differences indicated that mentally retarded persons "engaged in protracted tactical refinements following their initial strategic insights" (Belmont *et al.*, 1982, p. 208), which is suggestive of a qualitative differences between these and nonretarded persons in strategy development.

Finally, most research examining the cognitive processes of mentally retarded persons has been concerned with the examination of the performance of these persons on memory tasks, with very little research concerned with problem solving or analogical reasoning (Spitz, this volume). However, Spitz and colleagues (Borys, Spitz, & Dorans, 1982; Minsky, Spitz, & Bessellieu, 1985; Spitz, 1979; Spitz & Borys, 1984; Spitz, Minsky, & Bessellieu, 1985; Spitz, Webster, & Bory, 1985) have examined the performance of mentally retarded and nonretarded persons on a number of problem-solving tasks, and their work is suggestive of qualitative differences between these two groups. For example, in a review of this and earlier work on problem solving, Spitz (1979) found development lags of 1.5 to 4 years for mentally retarded persons compared to mental age (MA)-matched controls. The lag increased as the complexity of the task increased.

This article reviews research on quantitative and qualitative differences between intelligence groups on analogical reasoning tasks. Because of Sternberg's use of the componential method to study analogical reasoning, this method is briefly described [more detailed information can be obtained from McConaghy (1985) and Sternberg (1977)]. This is followed by a discussion of the results obtained from the application of this method to adults and children of normal intelligence. Then, data from the application of this method to groups with below-average intelligence and to mentally retarded groups are discussed, followed by an account of the effects of training on the performance of these groups on analogical reasoning tasks. Finally, an evaluation of the method is made, with regard to the study of mental retardation.

A. Sternberg's Componential Method of Analogical Reasoning

An analogy consists of four terms: A (the first term), B (the second term), C (the third term), and D (the fourth term). These terms combine in such a way that A is to B as C is to D. A higher order relationship must be extracted from the two lower order relationships between the A and B terms and the C and D terms.

Sternberg (1977) suggested that five processes or components are involved in analogical reasoning, including encoding, inference, mapping, application and preparation–response. The encoding component involves translating the analogy terms into internal representations for further processing. Inference involves the extraction of the relationship between the A and B terms. Mapping involves the extraction of the higher order relationship between the A and B terms and the C and D terms. Sternberg suggested that this occurs by extracting the relationship between the A and C terms. Application involves the extraction of the relationship between the C and D terms as well as the verification of the D term as true, or its rejection as false, by comparing it to an internal image of the correct D term. Finally, preparation–response includes such processes as preparing to solve the analogy, actually responding, and monitoring the response process. Sternberg suggested that these five components combine in an additive way to contribute to overall solution time. However, he also suggested that each of these components could be carried out in either an exhaustive or self-terminating manner. Exhaustive processing means that each analogy term is processed in full regardless of whether this is necessary to achieve a correct solution. Self-terminating processing means that only as many elements of each analogy term are processed as are necessary to arrive at a correct solution.

To examine whether processing is exhaustive or self-terminating, Sternberg used people-piece analogies made up of four two-dimensional elements; height (tall–short), weight (fat–thin), sex (male–female), and color (red–blue). Examples of these analogies are presented in Fig. 1. If all processes are exhaustive, then all four elements (height, weight, sex, and color) are encoded for all analogy terms; the relationship between all four elements is inferred

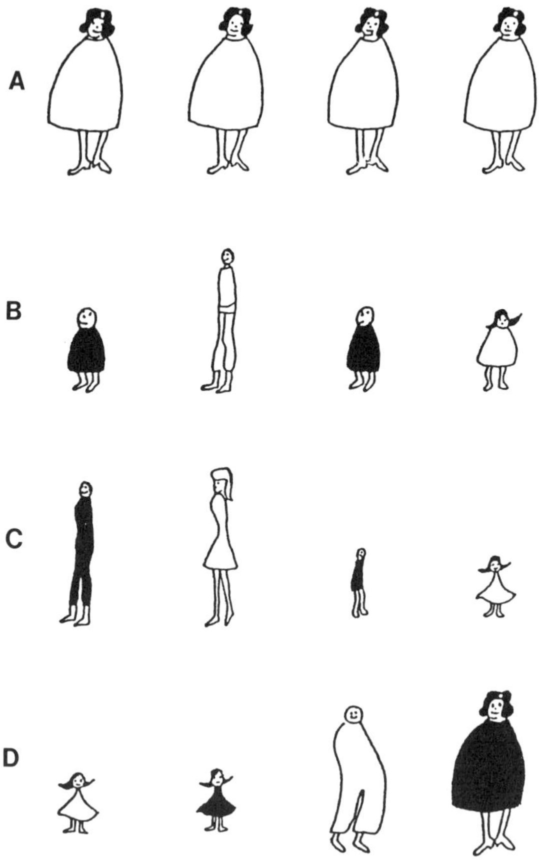

FIG. 1. Examples of the people piece analogy figures used by Sternberg (reproduced with permission from Sternberg, 1977, Fig. 7.2, p. 180). a, Denenerate analogy; b, semidegenerate analogy (A:B::A:B); c, nondegenerate analogy; d, nondegenerate analogy.

from the A to B terms; the relationship between all four elements is mapped from the A to C terms; and all four elements are applied from the presented D term to the internal image of the correct D term. Sternberg labeled this fully exhaustive model as Model I. Because it was unlikely that anyone processes analogies in this fully exhaustive way, Sternberg proposed three additional models, each containing the five component processes but varying the number of exhaustive processes (examples of all models are presented in Table I). Thus, in Model II, encoding, inference, and mapping are all exhaustive, but application is self-terminating with only as many elements in the presented D term being applied to the internal image of the correct D term as are needed to solve the analogy. In Model III, encoding and

TABLE I
EXHAUSTIVE AND SELF-TERMINATING COMPONENTS IN THE FOUR MODELS OF ANALOGICAL REASONING[a]

Components	Exhaustive components	Self-terminating
Model I	Encoding, inference, mapping, application	None
Model II	Encoding, inference, mapping	Application
Model III	Encoding, inference	Mapping, application
Model IV	Encoding	Inference, mapping, application

[a]Preparation–response was assumed to be a constant in all four models.

inference are exhaustive, but mapping as well as application is self-terminating with only as many elements as are required to solve the analogy mapped from the A to C terms and applied from the presented D term to the internal image. Finally, in Model IV, encoding remains exhaustive, but all of the remaining processes (inference, mapping, and application) are self-terminating with only as many elements as are required to solve the analogy being inferred from the A to B terms mapped from the A to C terms and applied from the presented D term to the internal image of the correct D term.

To obtain separate estimates of each of the component processes, Sternberg used a method called precuing. Each analogy or trial was presented in two parts, each part being separately timed. In the first part, either none of the analogy *or* 1, 2, or 3 analogy terms were presented. These were referred to, respectively, as the 0-, 1-, 2-, and 3-cue conditions. In the second part, the full analogy was presented in all cue conditions. The assumption was that processing in the first half of the trial should result in less processing in the second half. Thus, in the 0-cue condition or composite task with no terms presented in the first half of the trial, all processing presumably took place in the second half of the trial. In the 1-cue condition the first analogy term was presented in the first half of the trial so that encoding of that term could take place. Then, in the second half of the trial, the remaining 3 analogy terms could be encoded and the inference, mapping, and application component processes could occur. In the 2-cue condition the first 2 analogy terms were presented in the first half of the trial so that encoding of these 2 terms and the inference process could take place. Finally, in the 3-cue condition the first 3 analogy terms were presented in the first half of the trial, allowing encoding of these 3 terms plus the inference and mapping processes to take place.

Sternberg (1977) analyzed analogical reasoning with the people-piece analogies task using 16 young adults of above-average IQ. Half had higher reasoning ability scores and half had lower reasoning ability scores on subtests from Thurston's (1938) Primary Mental Abilities Test. Three types of analogies were used (See Fig. 1). Degenerate analogies were items where the first three analogy terms were identical. If the last term matched the first three terms, the analogy was true (Fig. 1a); if not, it was false. Semidegenerate analogies took two forms. In the first form the A and B terms were identical and different from the third term. If the last term matched the third term, the analogy was true; if not, it was false. In the second form the first and third terms were identical but differed from the second. If the last term matched the second term, the analogy was true; if not, it was false (Fig. 1b). Finally, in nondegenerate analogies all four terms differed and the relationship between terms had to be extracted and compared. A true and false example of this type of analogy is present in Fig. 1c and 1d, respectively. While these last analogies are essentially "real" analogies, the degenerate and semidegenerate analogies are not because they may be solved by matching the final term with one of the previous ones and, therefore, do not require the extraction of a higher order relationship.

From mathematical modeling of the solution time data, Sternberg found that all models accounted for large amounts of the variance, which suggested that the five component processes contained in them provided an adequate explanation of the processes used by above-average persons to solve analogies (see Table II). Further, since the partially exhaustive, partially self-terminating model (Model III) accounted for the largest amount of the variance (91.8%),

TABLE II

PERCENTAGE OF THE VARIANCE ACCOUNTED FOR BY MODELS I TO IV USING ABOVE-AVERAGE SUBJECTS[a]

	Model I	Model II	Model III	Model IV
People piece analogies				
Full analysis	75.5	84.7	91.8	90.8
Mean for individuals	66.0	74.0	80.0	79.0
Verbal Analogies				
Full analysis	83.2	84.7	85.6	84.8
Mean for individuals	46.2	47.4	47.8	47.6
Geometric analogies				
Full analysis	73.8	79.7	80.4	80.0

[a]Sternberg, 1977.

Sternberg concluded that this was the preferred model of analogical reasoning for these persons, although Model IV, accounting for 90.8% of the variance, could not be readily discounted.

Sternberg conducted further analyses to examine the reliability of the model-fitting procedure. These included model fits for the data from the 0-cue condition or composite task alone, the nondegenerate "real" analogies only, the first and last sessions separately, and the data from each individual separately. If the procedure was reliable, Models III and IV should remain the best-fitting models in these analyses. Indeed, Sternberg found that these additional analyses supported the use of either Model III or IV but did not allow a ready distinction to be made between them.

Sternberg (1977) then used the componential method to examine the performance of above-average young adults on verbal and geometric analogies. Results were consistent with those obtained using the people-piece analogies, although less robust (see Table II). Additional analyses, similar to those performed using the people-piece analogies, were also performed. The additional analyses emphasized the difficulty of distinguishing between the models (especially between Models III and IV) and confirmed the reduction in the reliability of the model fitting procedure using verbal and geometric analogies. For example, Sternberg noted that there was little to distinguish among the four models when analyzing the data from each individual separately, and for this analysis the amount of variance accounted for by the four models, for both verbal and geometric analogies, was poor (see Table II).

Examination of the parameter estimates for each component in each model indicated that persons with higher reasoning ability produced longer encoding times than those with lower reasoning ability and that this was especially apparent using the verbal analogies. In addition, the increased time spent on encoding by those with higher reasoning ability was coupled with less time spent on subsequent components and overall solution time. This finding led Sternberg to suggest that more time spent on encoding resulted in a positive advantage to overall performance. (A similar, although nonsignificant trend was apparent in the people-piece experiment.) Also, unlike the previous experiment, Sternberg found that data from the young adults with higher reasoning ability were, in general, better fitted by all of the models than the data from those of lower reasoning ability, which led him to suggest that more able persons were more systematic in their processing of the analogies. Both results are suggestive of qualitative differences between persons of different reasoning ability levels but the same overall level of intelligence.

B. Developmental Applications of the Componential Method

Two experiments by Sternberg and Rifkin (1979) and Sternberg and Nigro (1980) examined quantitative and qualitativve differences between children and adults using the componential method. Sternberg and Rifkin (1979) presented the people-piece analogies in booklet form instead of using the method of precuing described previously, which allowed group administration rather than individual testing. Sternberg and Rifkin used four groups; children in grades 2, 4, and 6, and college students. They found that both solution times and error rates decreased as age increased, with college students solving the analogies almost twice as quickly, on average, as the grade 2 children (4.82 and 8.42 seconds, respectively, for analogies solved correctly) and making far fewer errors.

Similar to the experiments by Sternberg (1977), all four models accounted for very similar amounts of the variance and the best-fitting model was not always apparent. Sternberg and Rifkin suggested that children in grades 2 and 4 used more self-terminating strategies, whereas children in grade 6 and adults used more exhaustive processing strategies. However, the results were difficult to interpret because, in some analyses, the self-terminating models provided excellent fits for grade 6 and adult subjects.

Despite these difficulties, the possible use of a more self-terminating strategy by both the grade 4 and grade 2 groups led Sternberg and Rifkin to suggest that this result was due to the load placed on short-term memory by the use of more exhaustive processes. In exhaustive processing all elements of each analogy term must be processed and presumably held in short-term memory while further processing takes place. In self-terminating processing, the number of elements held in memory depends on the stage of processing. This conclusion would suggest qualitative as well as quantitative differences between adults and children when solving analogies and that effective analogy solution depends, at least partially, on the effective use of short-term memory. However, the difficulty in distinguishing between the models weakens any conclusion concerning qualitative differences between adults and children. This may have been more of a problem in Sternberg and Rifkin's experiment than previously because of the presentation of analogies in booklet form.

Sternberg and Nigro (1980) used a modified form of the componential method to examine developmental changes in verbal analogical reasoning. The models they used included the same component processes described previously, but differed in how these components were derived (see Sternberg and Nigro for details). The models were referred to by Sternberg and Nigro as Models A, B, C, and D, with all processes being carried out exhaustively in Model A but in a fully self-terminating way in Models B and C. Model D was formulated subsequent to the data collection and was a mixed model, in that some processes were carried out exhaustively and some were assumed to be self-terminating. For example, in this model, it was assumed that exhaustive processing was used until the load on short-term memory became too great, whereupon self-terminating processing was used. Sternberg and Nigro also used a different method of data analysis, obtaining the best two predictor components for each model in each grade and calculating multiple correlations using these two predictors. As a consequence, they were unable to use this method to obtain separate time estimates for each of the components.

Sternberg and Nigro found that the data from the grade 9 and college student groups were best fitted by the fully exhaustive Model A, which accounted for 79 and 85% of the variance in the data from these groups, respectively. Conversely, the data from children in grades 6 and 3 were best fitted by the partially exhaustive, partially self-terminating model, Model D, which accounted for 77 and 72% of the variance in the data from these groups, respectively. These results suggest qualitative differences between the performance of adults and children, although as in previous experiments, all models tended to provide similar fits to the data. In addition, the use of the fully exhaustive model, Model A, by the two older groups is not entirely consistent with previous finds using the original componential method (Sternberg, 1977). The use of partially exhaustive, partially self-terminating model, Model D, by the grade 3 children is also not entirely consistent with the results obtained by Sternberg and Rifkin (1979) using people-piece analogies, where a fully self-terminating strategy seemed to be used by the children in grades 2 and 4. Direct comparisons among experiments are not possible because quite different methods of data collection and data analysis wwere used.

These experiments did, however, suggest that there was a developmental change in the time spent on processing, with older reasoners solving the analogies more quickly than younger reasoners. Both Sternberg (1977) and Sternberg and Rifkin (1979) found that initial encoding time was important, with those persons spending longer on this component producing better overall performances. This result may be related to the efficient use of short-term memory, the more mature or better reasoners being able to spend more time on encoding and storing the extracted information in short-term memory compared to younger and poorer reasoners, and may suggest, therefore, a qualitative difference between these groups.

II. USE OF THE COMPONENTIAL METHOD WITH PERSONS OF LOWER INTELLIGENCE

A. Initial Findings

Experiments by McConaghy and Kirby (1987a,b) and Smith (1981) are the only studies to date that have used the componential method to examine the analogical reasoning processes of below-average and mentally retarded young adults. Smith (1981) used the booklet form of presenting the analogies used by Sternberg and Rifkin (1979) and found that mildly retarded young adults produced longer solution times and higher error rates compared to a nonretarded group of similar chronological age, suggesting quantitative differences between the groups. However, of the four models of analogical reasoning described by Sternberg (1977), Smith tested only Model IV for the mentally retarded group and only Model III for the nonretarded group. In addition, the amount of variance accounted for by the models using the solution time data from both groups was not calculated, nor were parameter estimates for each component process obtained. Finally, not all analogies at each difficulty level were used, therefore introducing possible floor and ceiling effects for the groups. Thus, qualitative differences between the groups could not be examined.

McConaghy and Kirby (1987a), following Sternberg (1977), used the people-piece analogies and the method of precuing in experiments with young adults to examine processing differences between groups of different intelligence levels. The first experiment included an above-average group (IQ > 100) and a below-average group (IQ 70–100). In the second experiment, an above-average group and a mildly mentally retarded group were used.

McConaghy and Kirby (1987a) found that there were quantitative differences between the above- and below-average groups in the first experiment, with the below-average group producing longer mean solution times and higher error rates than the above-average group. The mildly retarded group in the second experiment performed similarly to the below-average group in the first experiment, although solution times were slower and error rates were slightly higher. Mathematical modeling of the solution times for all groups in both experiments indicated that, similar to the results obtained by Sternberg and colleagues, all models accounted for very similar amounts of the variance, although slightly more of the variance was accounted for by Models III and IV for the above-average and below-average groups compared to Models I and II (see Table III). Of interest was the finding that below-average and mildly retarded groups spent less time on encoding and more time on subsequent components and overall solution time than the above-average groups.

TABLE III

PERCENTAGE OF THE VARIANCE ACCOUNTED FOR BY MODELS I TO IV USING ABOVE- AND BELOW-AVERAGE GROUPS AND A MENTALLY RETARDED GROUP, EXPERIMENTS 1 AND 2[a]

	Model I	Model II	Model III	Model IV
Experiment 1				
Above-average	56.1	60.7	65.5	65.3
Below-average	26.0	32.1	37.9	38.1
Experiment 2				
Above-average	54.3	58.1	63.1	62.9
Mentally retarded	31.6	36.0	36.0	35.2

[a]McConaghy & Kirby, 1987a.

McConaghy and Kirby suggested that this was due to the increased load that would be placed on short-term memory by spending more time on encoding as Sternberg and Rifkin had suggested was the case with children.

Two results of the experiments by McConaghy and Kirby were inconsistent with those obtained by both Sternberg (1977) and Sternberg and Rifkin (1979). Much less variance was accounted for by all four models, especially for the below-average and mildly retarded groups (see Table III). In addition, the overall regression *F* ratios were lower and the standard errors of estimate were higher for all groups, especially for the below-average and mentally retarded groups. While it was expected that the model-fitting procedure would be less reliable for the below-average and mildly retarded groups, this was not expected for the above-average groups. Although design differences between Sternberg's and McConaghy and Kirby's experiments may partially explain this result, McConaghy and Kirby (1987a) suggested that all groups in both experiments made less use of the precued terms than the subjects tested by Sternberg (1977).

Sternberg's published works and Ph.D. dissertation did not mention instructions concerning use of the precued terms presented in the first half of the trial when using the method of precuing; therefore, no specific instructions were used in the first experiment by McConaghy and Kirby (1987a). Correspondence with Sternberg (January, 1983) indicated that he had provided specific instructions to use the precued terms. In their second experiment, therefore, McConaghy and Kirby gave specific instructions to use the precued terms. However, as can be seen in Table III, even with additional instructions the pattern of results is very similar to that obtained in the first experiment.

Less use of the precued terms than was predicted was especially evident in the 2- and 3-cue conditions. For example, in the 2-cue condition, cue and solution times should be approximately equivalent as they should both reflect similar amounts of processing (i.e., encoding 2 analogy terms and the inference process for the former, and encoding 2 analogy terms and the mapping and application processes for the latter). As can be seen in Table IV, this was the case for Sternberg's (1977) data, but was not the case for the data for both groups in McConaghy and Kirby's experiments. Especially in the below-average and retarded groups, solution times were substantially longer than cue times. Similar patterns were found in the 3-cue conditions.

McConaghy and Kirby concluded that while the above-average groups may have attempted to process the precued terms in the first half of the trial, they had also reprocessed these terms, to some extent, in the second half of the trial when the full analogy was present. Further, McConaghy and Kirby suggested that the below-average and mildly retarded groups used the precued terms even less. Thus, it appeared to be easier for all groups, but especially for the below-average and mildly retarded groups, to process each analogy when it was presented in full in the second half of the trial rather than to hold the precued terms for that analogy in short-term memory while processing the nonprecued terms.

TABLE IV
CUE AND SOLUTION TIMES (MSEC) FOR ABOVE- AND BELOW-AVERAGE GROUPS AND A MENTALLY RETARDED GROUP[a]

	Cue condition			
	0	1	2	3
Experiment 1[b]				
Above-average group				
Cue times	649	711	1023	1551
Solution times	2506	2418	2081	1732
Below-average group				
Cue times	894	839	875	1040
Solution times	3720	3624	3498	3412
Experiment 2[b]				
Above-average group				
Cue times	611	676	1171	1748
Solution times	2366	2212	1807	1581
Mildly retarded group				
Cue times	894	852	893	968
Solution times	3812	3760	3841	3678
Above-average group[c]				
Cue times	530	755	952	1174
Solution times	1423	1328	947	681

[a]Cue time is time spent on the first half of the trial; solution time is time spent on the second half of the trial.
[b]Data for above- and below-average groups and the mentally retarded group in Experiments 1 and 2 are from McConaghy and Kirby (1987a).
[c]From Sternberg (1977).

B. The Effects of Alterations to the Componential Method

Sternberg (1977) proposed an alternative method of presenting the analogies for precuing, although he did not actually test it. He did, however, suggest that this alternative method would not alter the way in which the task was performed. This method involved the presentation of the precued terms in the first half of the trial as previously, but only the nonprecued terms in the second half of the trial. McConaghy and Kirby (1987a) proposed that removing the precued terms in the second half of the trial would ensure use of these terms since it would prevent individuals from referring back to them in the second half of the trial. McConaghy and Kirby examined whether this was indeed the case in a third experiment using both an above-average and a borderline retarded group (IQ range 55–85).

McConaghy and Kirby found that the borderline retarded group was unable to perform this task. However, for the above-average persons this method greatly increased the use of the precued terms, their cue times showing the expected increase and their solution times the expected decrease from the 0- to 3-cue conditions. In addition, mathematical modeling of the solution time data indicated that much more of the variance was accounted for by the models. (Table V presents these results.) Also, overall regression F ratios were higher and standard errors of estimate were lower using this method. Finally, as found by Sternberg, all four models provided similar fits to the data from these persons, with there being little to separate Models III and IV as the best-fitting model. Overall, these results were very similar to those obtained by Sternberg using persons of similar ability, suggesting that if use of the precued terms could be ensured, then the componential method could be used effectively to examine the processes used in analogical reasoning by above-average young adults.

To use this method with mentally retarded young adults, McConaghy and Kirby (1987b) reduced the complexity of the task by reducing the number of cue conditions from 4 to 2, retaining the 0- and 2-cue conditions. The same group of borderline retarded young adults mentioned previously participated in this experiment, together with a group of young adults of above-average intelligence.

Cue times increased and solution times decreased from the 0- to 2-cue condition for both the above-average and borderline retarded groups, indicating use of the precued terms by both groups. In addition, the overall time taken to respond was increased for the borderline retarded group compared to the below-average and retarded groups in previous experiments, while it remained unchanged for the above-average groups. Models III and IV again provided similar fits to the data from the above-average group, and in contrast to the previous studies, a significant improvement in the amount of variance accounted for by the models was obtained for the borderline retarded group, with Model III being the best-fitting model and accounting for 64.5% of the variance. (Results for the remaining models for both groups are presented in Table VI). The overall amount of variance accounted for using the data

TABLE V
PERCENTAGE OF THE VARIANCE ACCOUNTED FOR BY MODELS I TO IV ABOVE-AVERAGE GROUP, EXPERIMENT 3[a]

	Model I	Model II	Model III	Model IV
Full analysis	77.1	79.1	84.1	83.6
Mean for individuals	50.1	52.3	55.0	54.1
Range	31.0–62.6	33.8–63.9	35.5–68.8	36.4–69.0

[a]McConaghy and Kirby (1987a).

TABLE VI
PERCENTAGE OF THE VARIANCE ACCOUNTED FOR BY MODELS I TO IV, ABOVE-AVERAGE AND MENTALLY RETARDED GROUPS, EXPERIMENT 4[a]

	Model I	Model II	Model III	Model IV
Above-average				
Full analysis	73.5	76.5	80.3	79.6
Mean for individuals	46.5	49.0	52.2	52.1
Range	18.8–66.8	23.6–66.8	24.8–66.6	27.1–69.6
Mentally retarded				
Full analysis	60.7	62.9	64.5	61.1
Mean for individuals	36.0	39.4	40.2	45.2
Range	21.3–47.9	25.8–51.4	25.9–52.1	37.6–52.3

[a]McConaghy and Kirby (1987a).

from the retarded persons was, however, still much lower than the amount of variance accounted for by the models using the data from above-average persons.

Examination of the time spent on each component indicated that the borderline retarded group spent much more time on encoding than had the below-average and mildly retarded groups in previous experiments. In fact, they spent more time on encoding than the above-average persons in this and all previous experiments. This increase in encoding time was not coupled, however, with a decrease in the time spent on subsequent components or overall solution time, as has usually been the case using older and better reasoners. This suggested that the increased duration for encoding obtained here reflected time spent attempting to maintain the encoded information in short-term memory after the disappearance of the precued terms in the 2-cue condition. A breakdown of the number of errors made in each cue condition provides support for this suggestion with a mean error rate of 9.2% being obtained for the 2-cue condition, compared to 4.5% for the 0-cue condition.

C. The Contribution of Short-Term Memory

The finding that more time spent on encoding was not coupled with less time spent on subsequent components or overall solution time, together with the finding that the below-average and mildly retarded persons in the earlier experiments made little use of the precued terms when these terms remained present in the second half of the trial, suggested that part of the difficulty that lower intelligence young adults experience with this type of task is the manipulation and maintenance of processed information in short-term memory. This suggestion is consistent with a number of findings from studies which have directly examined short-term memory in mentally retarded persons and have found them to perform poorly when compared to nonretarded, chronological age-matched controls (see Campione & Brown, 1979; Detterman, 1979; Ellis, 1978, 1982, for reviews). It is also consistent with the work of Spitz and Borys and colleagues (1984; Minsky *et al.*, 1985; Spitz *et al.*, 1985) who have highlighted the difficulty that mentally retarded persons experience in efficiently scanning and searching through an internally represented problem space while performing the tower of Hanoi problem-solving task. Results from these studies and the results obtained by McConaghy and Kirby are suggestive of a qualitative difference between nonretarded and retarded persons in the manipulation and maintenance of information in working memory.

The results of the experiments by McConaghy and Kirby (1987a) indicate that there are clear quantitative differences between groups with large differences in intellectual ability. In addition, their experiments suggest that there may be qualitative differences between these groups but that methodological limitations associated with the models in the componential method make it difficult to confirm differences in the processes used to solve the analogies.

III. TRAINING THE MENTALLY RETARDED USING THE COMPONENTIAL METHOD

A. Overview of Training Studies

In recent years, numerous training studies have sought to improve the performance of mentally retarded individuals on cognitive tasks (see Borkowski & Cavanaugh, 1979; Campione & Brown, 1979; Campione *et al.*, 1982; Sternberg, 1981, for reviews). There are three main criteria used to assess the success of a training procedure: (1) that after training, overall performance on the task is improved, (2) that the improved performance level is maintained over time, suggesting continued use of the trained skills, and (3) that the skills acquired during training are generalized to other tasks where they can also be used to enhance performance. Most training procedures used to enhance the performance of mentally retarded persons on memory tasks have been successful on the first (Butterfield, Wambold, & Belmont, 1973) and second criteria (Brown, Campione, & Murphy, 1977), but few have been successful in terms of the third criterion of generalization (see Belmont, Butterfield, & Borkowski, 1978; Brown, Campione, & Barclay, 1979, for notable exceptions). A distinction can also be made between near and far generalization or transfer. Near generalization is the transfer of skills to a task very similar to the training task, while far generalization is the transfer of skills to a task very different from the original training task. Both Borkowski and Cavanaugh

(1979) and Campione *et al.* (1982) make the point that not only is the generalization of trained skills by mentally retarded persons difficult to obtain but that this is especially so in the case of far generalization.

Most studies conducted in the area of cognitive skills training have used memory tasks, while comparatively few studies have been concerned with tasks where memory may be indirectly but substantially involved, such as analogies and other problem-solving tasks. Minsky *et al.* (1985), however, have examined the effect of training on the ability of mentally retarded young adults to solve the tower of Hanoi task. They found that training improved performance and that the improved performance level was maintained for periods of up to 9 and 13 weeks. Minsky *et al.* also examined generalization of the trained strategy to similar tasks but found only limited near generalization. The following section examines the effect of training, using the componential method and people piece analogies, on the analogical reasoning performance of mentally retarded persons.

B. Training and the Method of Presenting Analogies

McConaghy and Kirby (1987b) sought to improve the performance of mentally retarded young adults on the people-piece analogy task using a training program which incorporated an elaborative technique adapted from the work of both Evans (1968) and Borkowski and colleagues (Kestner & Borkowski, 1979; Kendall, Borkowski & Cavanaugh, 1980). Individuals were instructed to elaborate the changes and nonchanges in elements across analogy terms as they attempted to solve the analogies. The task used was that used by McConaghy and Kirby (1987a) in their final experiment with only the 0- and 2-cue conditions as the results of that experiment suggested that overall performance on an analogical reasoning task was enhanced by reducing task complexity. Both Bray (1979) and Belmont *et al.* (1982) have also obtained evidence which suggests that the adoption of both trained and spontaneous strategies by mentally retarded persons is enhanced by increasing the level of instruction and reducing the level of task complexity.

McConaghy and Kirby (1987b) initially examined the performance of three groups of borderline retarded young adults matched for IQ using the Wechsler Adult Intelligence Scale. The original method of presenting analogies (i.e. where the precued terms remained present in the second half of the trial) was used to examine if the simplified task would enhance use of precued terms without the need to use the alternative method of presenting analogies (i.e., where the precued terms were removed in the second half of the trial). The experimental group received the elaborative training procedure in two initial sessions. These sessions were followed immediately by two testing sessions, with two additional testing sessions being conducted approximately 4 months later. These latter 2 sessions were followed by a final session in which a test for "far" transfer (Campione *et al.*, 1982) was conducted, using the standard form of the Raven Progressive Matrices (see McConaghy, 1985, for details of this aspect of the experiment). Control group 1 received two initial sessions of practice, with no training on the people-piece analogies, followed by two testing sessions. It was not possible to examine this group's performance at maintenance as not all persons in this group were available at that time. Control group 2 participated in only one session, during which the standard form of the Raven Progressive Matrices was presented, at the same time as the experimental group participated in its seventh session.

In both initial and maintenance testing sessions using the people-piece analogies, the experimental group produced faster solution times and lower error rates than control group 1. While persons in the experimental group also made more use of the precued terms than those in control group 1, they made less use of these terms than had similar persons when the alternative method of presenting the analogies was used but no training was provided (McConaghy and Kirby, 1987a). Thus, even with a simplified task and a training procedure, mentally retarded young adults had difficulty using the precued terms. For model fitting, much more of the variance was accounted for by the models for the experimental group in the initial sessions compared to control group 1, and the relatively high amount of variance accounted for was maintained in the two testing sessions conducted 4 months later. Also, regression F ratios were higher and the standard errors of estimate were marginally lower for this group. These results, together with the lower solution times and error rates, suggested that training was successful in not only improving overall performance and in the maintenance of that performance over time, but also in producing more reliable data for model fitting from mentally retarded persons.

Interestingly, there appeared to be a slight trend toward more exhaustive processing in the initial testing sessions, where Model II accounted for marginally more of the variance than Models III and I. McConaghy and Kirby suggested that this was due to the training procedure, which encouraged, at least initially, more exhaustive processing of the analogy terms. Related to this may be the finding that the encoding times were longer in the initial testing sessions compared to the maintenance sessions, suggesting that additional time in these sessions was spent on maintaing encoded information in short-term memory. In addition, it is interesting to note that persons in the experimental groups spent more overall time on encoding than those in control group 1. Both of these results suggest that training may have had some effect on increasing the time spent on encoding by the experimental group, although not an enduring effect. Finally, McConaghy (1985) found no evidence to transfer to a far-generalization task, the Raven Progressive Matrices Test, when comparing the performance of persons in the experimental group to that of persons in control group 2.

McConaghy and Kirby (1987b) also examined whether the performance of a mentally retarded group on the people-piece analogy task could be enhanced by combining the training procedure with the alternative method of presenting analogies where the precued terms were removed in the second half of the trial. A mildly retarded group participated in two sessions of training, which were followed by two initial testing sessions and, finally, two maintenance sessions conducted 3 months later. As found by McConaghy and Kirby (1987a), precued terms were used effectively by the mentally retarded when this method of presenting analogies was introduced, with a clear increase in cue times and a clear decrease in solution times across cue conditions. However, the effective use of the precued terms also increased the difficulty of the task for this group as indicated by the increase in both overall interval scores (cue and solution times combined) and error rates. As found in the final experiment by McConaghy and Kirby (1987a), it appeared that this increase in task difficulty was due to the load placed on short-term memory by the disappearance of the precued terms in the second half of the trial. Finally, there was no increase in the amount of variance accounted for by the models when training and the altered method of presenting analogies were used in combination. Thus, similar amounts of the variance were accounted for by the models (see Table VII) compared to the experiments by McConaghy and Kirby (1987a,b).

Additional analyses were also conducted using the data from the mentally retarded group in both the initial and maintenance sessions, and again all

TABLE VII

PERCENTAGE OF THE VARIANCE ACCOUNTED FOR BY MODELS I TO IV, MILDLY RETARDED SUBJECTS, INITIAL AND MAINTENANCE SESSIONS[a]

	Model I	Model II	Model III	Model IV
Initial sessions				
Full analysis	61.8	62.7	61.3	56.9
Mean for individuals	31.4	32.1	31.5	28.8
Range	8.2–55.1	8.8–55.2	9.1–54.3	8.6–47.3
Maintenance sessions				
Full analysis	66.1	67.4	66.2	61.6
Mean for individuals	34.8	35.7	34.9	32.9
Range	7.1–63.6	8.6–64.6	9.1–62.0	8.9–55.2
Nondegenerate analogies	75.2	76.1	77.3	77.0

[a]McConaghy and Kirby (1987b).

models provided similar fits to the data as was the case in the full analysis. Similar fits were also provided by all models using the data from each individual analyzed separately in both the initial and maintenance sessions, although there appeared to be a trend toward more exhaustive processing, a result suggested in the full analysis but not apparent in the final experiment by McConaghy and Kirby (1987a) when they used the alternative method of presenting the analogies (see Table VII). Model II accounted for the most variance using the data from six individuals in the initial sessions, Model III for the data from three individuals, Model II for the data from two individuals, and Model IV for the data from only one person. In the maintenance sessions, Model II accounted for the most variance using the data from five individuals, while Models III and IV each accounted for the most variance using the data from three individuals and Model I accounted for the data from one individual.

In contrast to the results of the individual analyses, analyzing the nondegenerate "real" analogies separately revealed a trend toward more self-terminating processing. The contrast in these two results again raises questions about the reliability of the model-fittng procedure. Further, the amount of variance accounted for using the data for the nondegenerate analogies was only slightly less than the amount of variance accounted for using the data from these analogies for the above-average persons in the experiment by McConaghy and Kirby (1987a), where a similar experimental design was used (see Table VI). This result suggests that training significantly improved the performance of mentally retarded persons on the nondegenerate analogies.

Encoding time was found to be significantly increased compared to the experimental group in the previous experiment and was similar to the amount of time spent on this component by mentally retarded persons in McConaghy and Kirby's (1987a) final experiment, which used the alternative method of presenting analogies. Encoding time also increased in the maintenance sessions, increased rather than decreased as it had for the experimental group in the previous experiment. Further, the increase in encoding time here was accompanied by a reduction in the time spent on subsequent component processes and, to a lesser extent, overall solution time. That overall solution time was not greatly reduced, while subsequent component processing was, suggests that the additional time spent on encoding was disproportionately increased compared to the time spent on encoding by above-average groups in previous experiments. For these latter groups, an increase in encoding time was accompanied by a decrease in both overall solution times and subsequent component processing. This provides further evidence for the suggestion that the mentally retarded subjects experience difficulties when forced to hold processed information in short-term memory.

Thus, although there was no clear increase in the amount of variance accounted for when both training and the altered method of presenting analogies were used in conjunction, maintenance of the increased time spent on encoding was obtained under these conditions and this appeared to result in faster subsequent component processing. This result, together with the large amount of variance accounted for using the solution times to the nondegenerate analogies analyzed separately, suggests that the combination of training and the alternative method of presenting analogies produces the most favorable results among the mentally retarded.

C. Implications for Training

It appeared that training could be used to improve the performance of mentally retarded persons even on a complex cognitive task, but as many previous studies have found, there was little evidence for generalization. For example, as mentioned previously, Minsky *et al.* (1985) used another complex cognitive task (the tower of Hanoi) and failed to obtain transfer to a near-generalization task. Conversely, Kendall *et al.* (1980), using a paired associate-recall task, and an elaborative technique, on which the elaborative technique used by McConaghy and Kirby was based, obtained near generalization to a similar recall task. Campione *et al.* (1982) suggested that only training which included self-control skills (such as monitoring, checking, and evaluating in addition to task-specific skills) would produce far generalization. Alternatively, Belmont *et al.* (1978) have found evidence for successful far generalization of trained skills when simultaneous training on a number of related memory tasks is received by mentally retarded persons together with instruction on the similarity and transferability of the trained skills across these tasks. Further research is required to assess whether the lack of generalization in McConaghy and Kirby's experiment was due to the increased complexity of the task used or due to the need for refinement in training procedures and/or the test of generalization.

McConaghy and Kirby (1987b) also found that while the time spent on the encoding component by mentally retarded persons could be increased by training, the increase only produced a positive overall advantage to later processing when coupled with the altered method of presenting analogies (where the precued terms were removed in the second half of the trial). Further, training, both on its own or in combination with the altered method of presenting analogies, did not increase the overall amount of variance accounted for by the models to a level similar to that accounted for using data from above-average persons. Of interest, however, was the slight increase in the amount of variance accounted for by the models in the maintenance sessions for the mentally retarded groups receiving training. To some extent this was an unusual finding because it is more usual to find, as Minsky *et al.* did, that performance declines at maintenance. This may depend, however, on how many maintenance sessions are used. For example, Minsky *et al.* used only one session of maintenance while McConaghy and Kirby (1987b) used two maintenance sessions and found that the percentage of variance accounted for by the models was similar in both sessions. Phillips and Nettelbeck (1985), using S. Sternberg's (1969, 1975) memory-scanning task and several sessions of maintenance, found that although performance declined in the first maintenance session after a 3-month interim period, mildly retarded young adults had, by the second session, reached the same level of performance as they had attained at the end of the initial experimental sessions. Thus, a finding similar to that obtained by McConaghy and Kirby or Phillips and Nettlebeck may have been obtained by Minsky *et al.* if additional maintenance sessions had been used.

The number of training sessions provided may also have influenced the results obtained in these studies. For example, the mentally retarded young adults in the experiments by both Phillips and Nettelbeck and McConaghy and Kirby participated in at least four consecutive sessions of training and initial testing prior to their participation in maintenance sessions. In contrast, those in the experiments of Minsky *et al.* received one training session followed by one testing session conducted 3 weeks later, and then a maintenance session conducted 9 weeks later.

The differing results for these studies may be related to the influence of knowledge-base factors (Chi, 1981). Chi has suggested that mentally retarded persons required longer to build up an adequate knowledge base for a particular task compared to nonretarded persons, and this may be especially evident in a more complex reasoning task. Thus, mentally retarded persons in the studies by both McConaghy and Kirby and Phillips and Nettelbeck had more time in which to build up a knowledge base for the task used. Also consistent with the suggestion that mentally retarded persons required a longer time to acquire a knowledge base is the finding obtained by Phillips and Nettelbeck (1985) that mildly mentally retarded young adults had still not reached asymptotic performance after seven sessions of practice, while the performance of nonretarded young adults on the task did not change after the second session.

IV. CONCLUSIONS AND DIRECTIONS FOR ADDITIONAL RESEARCH

The research reviewed in this article demonstrates that the componential method can be used to examine the processes used in analogical reasoning by a wide range of ability and developmental groups. In addition, the method appears to be sufficiently flexible to allow alterations in design which do not affect the results obtained from most groups. Further, it is sensitive to changes in the type of model used by the groups in order to solve analogies. Finally, there is also some evidence that there are both quantitative and qualitative differences between subjects of different age levels and different intelligence levels when reasoning by analogy. However, while it is certainly the case that the componential method has many positive attributes, research with nonretarded and, especially, mentally retarded persons has tended to reveal a number of limitations. This section gives consideration to these factors.

A. Methodological Considerations

A review of the research by Sternberg and colleagues into analogical reasoning (Sternberg, 1977; Sternberg & Rifkin, 1979; Sternberg & Nigro, 1980) suggested that the most valid application of the componential method was that of Sternberg (1977). Attempts to adapt the method to the collection of data from groups (Sternberg & Rifkin, 1979) or alterations to the estimation of components and models used (Sternberg & Nigro, 1980) were not entirely successful, especially using the data from children. For example, Sternberg and Rifkin reported finding that young children used a more self-terminating model compared to adults, but this was only partially supported by examination of the data because more exhaustive models also account well for the data from children. The model fitting by Sternberg and Nigro only allowed the comparison of models with two components, rather than the usual four, and a new model had to be developed subsequent to the data analysis to explain the performance of children.

In Sternberg's (1977) original experiments the most successful application of the componential method was made using the people-piece analogies as opposed to the more complex geometric and verbal analogies. While the performance of above-average persons on these latter analogies was still well accounted for by the method, the reliability of the results was not as high. This was the case for both the full analysis using the group data and also for additional analyses using various separate aspects of the data. These results, together with those discussed previously, suggest that the componential method is more successful (1) if the comparatively simpler and more clearly quantifiable people-piece analogies are used, (2) if data is collected from individuals rather than groups, and (3) if the method of precuing is used.

Research by McConaghy and Kirby (1987a) has suggested, however, that even this method has inherent difficulties. For example, they were unable to obtain adequate use of the precued terms by persons with both above-average and lower intelligence using the original method of presenting the analogies where the precued terms remained present in the second half of the trial. Also, this was the case even when specific instructions were provided.

This led McConaghy and Kirby to alter the method of presenting analogies so that only the nonprecued terms, rather than the full analogy, were presented in the second half of the trial. This alteration produced much greater use of the precued terms by persons with above-average intelligence, but made the task too difficult for the mentally retarded. However, when the complexity of the task was reduced, it was found that this method of presenting analogies could be used to collect data from these persons. In addition, the use of this method, like the results for the above-average group, produced large increases in the percentage of variance accounted for by the models using the data from the mentally retarded. Overall cue and solution times were increased, however, suggesting that the altered method of presenting the analogies was still more difficult for these persons than the original method of precuing, even after a reduction in task complexity.

An increase in the amount of variance accounted for by the models was also obtained when mentally retarded young adults received training or a combination of training and the altered method of presenting the analogies. However, for mentally retarded young adults, the overall amount of variance accounted for by the models was never as great as that for above-average persons. It was suggested that the generally lower amount of variance accounted for by the data from mentally retarded persons was due to both the high level of consistency of performance required when using mathematical modeling and the difficulty of obtaining consistent performance from such persons. Further increases in the amount of variance accounted for by the models might be achieved by increasing the consistency of performance of the mentally retarded persons. In turn, increased performance consistency might be obtained through increased practice or training, although it is possible that these increases will be limited even after substantial practice and training. For example, Phillips and Nettelbeck (1985) noted that the consistency of the performance of mildly retarded young adults on the memory-scanning task increased over seven sessions of practice until it reached a level similar to that of a control group of the same mental age. However, the level of consistency evidenced by the mildly retarded group never reached that produced by a control group of the same chronological age. This contrasted with the results for this latter control group which indicated highly consistent levels of performance over seven sessions of practice.

An alternative interpretation is that the low percentage of variance accounted for by the models using the data from mentally retarded young adults may have been due to these persons using processes different from those proposed by the four models of analogical reasoning. Thus, the increase in the amount of variance accounted for by the models in later experiments using the data from mentally retarded persons may have been due to these persons having been forced to solve the analogies in a way predicted by the four models of analogical reasoning, with this, in turn, being a consequence of the introduction of training and the altered method of presenting analogies. Examination of the amount of variance accounted for by models of analogical reasoning developed by other researchers using the data from mentally retarded persons may indicate whether it is a lack of consistent performance on the part of mentally retarded persons or the predictions of the models proposed by Sternberg that are at fault. If inconsistent performance is responsible, then it would be expected that these other models would also account for little of the variance using the data from mentally retarded persons. Some of these models will be discussed briefly subsequently. However, few researchers to date have tested these models with the mentally retarded. If, however, it is assumed that the four models of analogical reasoning can be used to explain the performance of mentally retarded persons, it is clear that experimental interventions (such as the altered method of presenting analogies and increased instructions as well as training) have altered significantly the way in which these persons approach the task, while leaving unaffected the performance of those with above-average intelligence.

There is also difficulty in drawing any conclusions concerning the particular model used from all the studies reviewed here, and therefore the existence of qualitative differences in the processes used by different groups, because of the similarity of the amounts of variance accounted for by all four models. For example, only 0.9% of the variance accounted for separated Model IV for the below-average group in the first experiment by McConaghy and Kirby (1987a) from the next best-fitting model, Model III. In the same experiment, only 0.8% of the variance separated Models III and IV for the above-average group. As noted, a similar finding was apparent in most experiments conducted by McConaghy and Kirby (1987a,b) and by Sternberg and colleagues. Additional analyses for each individual separately tended to emphasize the similarity of all models (Models II, III, and IV in particular). As mentioned, it can be suggested that this is due to the fact that all models contain the same five components and only differ as to whether these components take an exhaustive or self-terminating form in each model. Alternatively, it might be the case that subjects alter the type of processing they use, whether exhaustive or self-terminating, depending on the level of difficulty in the analogy. Some support for this suggestion has been obtained by Bethell-Fox, Lohman, and Snow (1984), who found that above-average young adults used primarily self-terminating processing on simpler geometric analogies but mainly exhaustive processing on the most difficult of these analogies.

B. Theoretical Considerations

Applications of the componential method have suggested that the models of analogical reasoning developed by Sternberg provide a reasonable explanation of the way in which above-average adults and children solved analogies (1977; Sternberg & Rifkin, 1979; Sternberg & Nigro, 1980), and, to a lesser extent, how those with lower intelligence perform (McConaghy & Kirby, 1987a,b). In addition, early research by Sternberg and colleagues provided evidence for both quantitive and qualitative differences between adults and children when reasoning by analogy. However, a review of this work and additional research presented here suggests that, while the componential method can be used to clearly identify quantitive differences between adults and both children and mentally retarded individuals, it is less effective for providing evidence of qualitative differences between these groups. For example, when using this method it is not clear whether a more exhaustive or more self-terminating model is used by mentally retarded persons and, therefore, if mentally retarded persons use a different set of processes to solve analogies compared to nonretarded persons. In all the experiments conducted by Sternberg and colleagues and by McConaghy and Kirby, Models III and IV tended to be the best-fitting models using the data from above-average young adults. However, Models II, III, and IV all provided reasonable accounts of the performance of below-average, borderline, and mildly retarded groups at one time or another in the series of experiments by McConaghy and Kirby (1987a,b).

Other models have been developed which have attempted to identify the processes used in analogical reasoning. Mulholland, Pellegrino, and Glaser (1980) have developed a model of geometric analogy solution based on the work of Evans (1968). Rather than proposing the use of five processes as Sternberg does, Mulholland *et al.* suggest that only three processes are required: encoding, transformation, and a response process. Encoding was defined as the decomposition and input of analogy term, while transformation consisted of the discovery of the relationship between the A and B and C and D terms (similar to Sternberg's inference and application components). The response process (K) represented processes similar to those included in Sternberg's preparation–response component, such as preparing to solve the analogy, solving it, and monitoring the response process. Using a simple linear model [solution time = T (number of transformations) + E (number of elements to be encoded)], Mulholland *et al.* were able to account for 95% of the variance in solution times. This outcome was marginally improved (97%) when a more complex model was used, which took into account the increased load placed on short-term memory by an increase in difficulty level (solution time = $T + E + TE +$ K, where K represented the response process as a constant), which as N. W. Bray (1987, personal correspondence) suggests, may prove to be much more important in research with mentally retarded persons.

The result obtained by Mulholland *et al.* also compares favorably to the 80.4% of the variance accounted for by Model III found by Sternberg (1977) using geometric analogies. Some of the difference in the amount of variance accounted for by the two models must be attributed to differences in the actual geometric analogies used. For example, Sternberg selected analogies from the analogies subtest in a number of editions of the American Council on Education Psychological Examination for College Freshmen (see Sternberg, 1977), while Mulholland *et al.* constructed their own analogies based on the model they wished to test. Mulholland *et al.* also correlated performance on these analogies with performance on the 25-item geometric analogy subtest of the Cognitive Abilities Test (Thorndike & Hagen, 1971), obtaining a significant positive correlation of .69. While the experiment of Mulholland *et al.* could be criticized for using analogies specifically developed to test their model, this model is certainly more parsimonious and accounts for more of the variance than Sternberg's models using similar above-average persons.

Also using geometric analogies, Bethell-Fox *et al.* (1984) used the componential method to test Sternberg's four models of analogical reasoning. They found that all four models accounted for over 90% of the variance. This result led them to suggest that, since Models I and IM (a variant of Model I but with mapping excluded) were simpler in terms of the extraction of components and accounted for a similar amount of the variance to be the models including self-terminating processes, these models should be adopted as the preferred models of analogical reasoning.

Pellegrino and colleagues (Pellegrino & Goldman, 1983; Goldman, Pellegrino, Parseghian, & Sallis, 1982; Pellegrino & Glaser, 1980) have also constructed models of verbal analogical reasoning. This has proven problematic, however, due to the difficulty of quantifying verbal analogy terms. Pellegrino and Glaser (1980) make the point that the verbal analogies used by Sternberg (1977) had a low level of difficulty and that application of the four models of analogical reasoning proposed by Sternberg to more difficult analogies may not prove as successful. As mentioned, none of these alternative models has been applied to the data from mentally retarded persons.

Evidence for a qualitative difference between nonretarded and mentally retarded young adults was obtained when the time spent on the components was examined. In those cases where experimental intervention was minimal, persons of lower intelligence were found to spend less time on encoding and longer periods on subsequent processes and overall solution time than those of above-average intelligence. This finding, together with the finding that the time spent on encoding could be dramatically increased using the alternative method of presenting analogies (but without a concomitant reduction in the time spent on subsequent components and overall solution time), provides further evidence for the suggestion that mentally retarded persons are less efficient at maintaining encoded information in short-term memory. These findings also support the results obtained by Sternberg and by Sternberg and Rifkin that younger and poorer reasoners spend less time on encoding than older and better reasoners and that this is due to the increased load placed on short-term memory by encoding exhaustively. These findings are also consistent with the research by Spitz and colleagues which has suggested that mentally retarded persons are characterized by poor performance when the manipulation of information in short-term memory is required (Spitz & Borys, 1984).

C. Conclusion

The research reviewed here suggests that there are methodological limitations evident in the componential method which are related to the precuing techniques and to the mathematical specification of the models. In addition, it appears that these limitations are particularly highlighted when the method is used to examine the performance of persons with lower intelligence. The use of the method indicates clear quantitative differences between adults and children and also between persons with above-average intelligence and those with lower intelligence. However, evidence for qualitative differences between groups with different overall ability and developmental levels were more difficult to obtain. It appeared that there were qualitative differences between these groups in the manipulation and maintenance of processed information in short-term memory, such that younger and poorer reasoners experienced difficulties when required to do so. However, evidence for the existence of qualitative differences between the groups in terms of the particular set of processes used to solve the analogies (i.e., whether children and mentally retarded persons used a more self-terminating model than adults and those of above-average intelligence) was not apparent due to the similarity of the fits provided by all four models.. A further limitation of the componential method is that, because of the strict specification of the processes involved, it is not possible to examine the use of other processes to reason analogically. A clearer resolution of the degree of quantitative and qualitative differences between mentally retarded and nonretarded individuals may depend on the use of methods and models similar to those used by Mulholland *et al.* but not yet used with mentally retarded groups.

ACKNOWLEDGMENT

The author wishes to thank Dr. Ted Nettelbeck for his support and his helpful suggestions during the preparation of this manuscript.

REFERENCES

Baumeister, A. A., & Kellas, C. (1968). Reaction time and mental retardation. In N. R. Ellis (Ed.), *International review of research in mental retardation* (Vol. 3). New York: Academic Press.

Belmont, J. M., Butterfield, E. C., & Borkowski, J. G. (1978). Training retarded to generalise memorization methods across memory tasks. In M. M. Gruneborg, P. E. Morris, & R. N. Sykes (Eds.), *Practical aspects of memory.* London: Academic Press.

Belmont, J. M., Ferretti, R., & Mitchell, D. (1982). Memorizing: A test of untrained mildly retarded children's problem-solving. *American Journal of Mental Deficiency,* **87**, 197–210.

Bethell-Fox, C. E., Lohman, D. F., & Snow, R. E. (1984). Adaptive reasoning: Componential and eye movement analysis of geometric analogy performance. *Intelligence,* **8**, 205–238.

Borkowski, J. G., & Cavanaugh, J. C. (1979). Maintenance and generalization of skills and strategies by the retarded. In N. R. Ellis (Ed.), *Handbook of mental deficiency: Psychological theory and research* (2nd ed.). Hillsdale, New Jersey: Erlbaum.

Borys, S. V., Spitz, H. H., & Dorans, B. A. (1982). Tower of Hanoi performance of retarded young adults and nonretarded children as a function of solution length and goal state. *Journal of Experimental Child Psychology,* **33**, 87–110.

Bray, N. W. (1979). Strategy production in the retarded. In N. R. Ellis (Ed.), *Handbook of mental deficiency: Psychological theory and research* (2nd ed.). Hillsdale, New Jersey: Erlbaum.

Bray, N. W., Dann, L., & Gwartney, O. (1978). *The locus of task complexity in the directed forgetting task with retarded adolescents.* Unpublished manuscript, University of Alabama.

Bray, N. W., Goodman, M. A., & Justice, E. M. (1982). Task instructions and strategy transfer in the directed forgetting performance of mentally retarded adolescents. *Intelligence,* **6**, 187–200.

Brewer, N., & Smith, G. A. (1982). Cognitive processes for monitoring and regulating speed and accuracy of responding in mental retardation: A methodology. *American Journal of Mental Deficiency,* **87**, 211–222.

Brown, A. L., Campione, J. C., & Barclay, C. R. (1979). Training self-checking routines for estimating test readiness: Generalization from list learning to prose recall. *Child Development,* **50**, 501–512.

Brown, A. L., Campione, J. C., & Murphy, M. D. (1977). Maintenance and generalization of trained metamnemonic awareness by educable retarded children. *Journal of Experimental Child Psychology,* **24**, 191–211.

Butterfield, E. C., Wambold, C., & Belmont, J. M. (1973). On the theory and practice of improving short-term memory. *American Journal of Mental Deficiency,* **77**, 654–669.

Campione, J. C., & Brown, A. L. (1979). Toward a theory of intelligence: Contributions from research with retarded children. In R. J. Sternberg & D. K.. Detterman (Eds.), *Human intelligence: Perspectives on its theory and measurement.* Norwood, New Jersey: Ablex.

Campione, J. C., Brown, A. L., & Ferrara, R. A. (1982). Mental retardation and intelligence. In R. J. Sternberg (Ed.), *Handbook of human intelligence.* New York: Cambridge University Press.

Chase, W. G. (1978). Elementary information processes. In W. K. Estes (Ed.), *Handbook of learning and cognitive processes* (Vol. 5). Hillsdale, New Jersey: Erlbaum.

Chi, M. T. H. (1981). Knowledge development and memory performance. In M. P. Friedman, J. P. Das, & N. O'Conner (Eds.), *Intelligence and learning.* New York: Plenum.

Cooper, L. A. (1982). Strategies for visual comparison and representation: Individual differences. In R. J. Sternberg (Ed.), *Advances in the psychology of human intelligence* (Vol. 1). Hillsdale, New Jersey: Erlbaum.

Cooper, L. A., & Regan, D. T. (1982). Attention, perception and intelligence. In R. J. Sternberg (Ed.), *Handbook of human intelligence.* New York: Cambridge University Press.

Detterman, D. K. (1979). Memory in the mentally retarded. In N. R. Ellis (Ed.). *Handbook of mental deficiency: Psychological theory and research.* Hillsdale New Jersey: Erlbaum.

Ellis, N. R. (1978). Do the mentally retarded have poor memory? *Intelligence,* **2**, 41–54.

Ellis, N. R. (1982). A behavioural research strategy in mental retardation: Defense and critique. In E. Zigler & D. Balla (Eds.), *Mental retardation: The developmental–difference controversy.* Hillsdale, New Jersey: Erlbaum.

Evans, T. G. (1968). A program for the solution of a class of geometric-analogy intelligence-test questions. In M. Minsky (Ed.), *Semantic information processing.* Cambridge, Massachusetts: MIT Press.

Goldman, S. R., Pellegrino, J. W., Parseghian, P. E., & Sallis, R. (1982). Developmental and individual differences in verbal analogical reasoning. *Child Development,* **53**, 550–559.

Hunt, E., (1978). Mechanics of verbal ability. *Psychological Review,* **85**, 109–130.

Hunt, E., Frost, N., & Lunneborg, C. (1973). Individual differences in cognition. In G. Bower (Ed.), *Advances in learning and memory* (Vol. 7). New York: Academic Press.

Hunt, E., Lunneborg, C., & Lewis, J. (1975). What does it mean to be high verbal? *Cognitive Psychology,* **7**, 194–227.

Jensen A. R. (1980) Chronometric analysis of intelligence. *Journal of Social and Biological Structures,* **3**, 103–122.

Jensen, A. R. (1982a). Reaction time and psychometrics. In H. J. Eysenck (Ed.), *A model for intelligence*. Berlin: Springer-Verlag.

Jensen, A. R. (1982b). The chronometry of intelligence. In R. J. Sterberg (Ed.), *Advances in the psychology of human intelligence*. Hillsdale, New Jersey: Erlbaum.

Jensen, A. R., & Munro, E. (1979). Reaction time, movement time and intelligence. *Intelligence,* **3**, 121–126.

Kendall, C. R., Borkowski, J. G., & Cavanaugh, J. C. (1980) Metamemory and the transfer of an interrogative stategy by EMR children. *Intelligence,* **4**, 255–270.

Kestner, J., & Borkowski, J. G. (1979). Children's maintenance and generalization of an interrogative learning strategy. *Child Development,* **50**, 485–494.

MacLeod, C. M., Hunt, E., & Mathews, N. (1978). Individual differences in the verification of sentence-picture relationships. *Journal of Verbal Learning and Verbal Behaviour,* **17**, 493–507.

Mathews, N., Hunt, E., & MacLeod, C. M. (1980). Strategy choice and strategy training in sentence-picture verification. *Journal of Verbal Learning and Verbal Behaviour,* **19**, 531–548.

McConaghy, J. H. (1985). *Intelligence and analogical reasoning*. Unpublished doctoral dissertation, University of Adelaide, South Australia.

McConaghy, J., & Kirby, N. H. (1987a). Analogical reasoning and ability level: An examination of R. J. Sternberg's componential method. *Intelligence,* **11**, 137–159.

McConaghy, J., & Kirby, N. H. (1987b). Training the mentally retarded to solve analogies using the componential method. *American Journal of Mental Deficiency,* **92**, 12–23.

Minsky, S. K., Spitz, H. H., & Bessellieu, C. C. (1985). Maintenance and transfer of training by mentally retarded young adults on the Tower of Hanoi problem. *American Journal of Mental Deficiency,* **90**, 190–197.

Mulholland, T., Pellegrino, J., & Glaser, R. (1980). Components of geometric analogy solution. *Cognitive Psychology,* **12**, 252–284.

Nettelbeck, T., & Brewer, N. (1981). Studies in mild mental retardation and timed performance. In N. R. Ellis (Ed.), *International review of research in mental retardation* (Vol. 10). New York: Academic Press.

Nettelbeck, T., & Kirby, N. H. (1983). Measures of timed performance and intelligence. *Intelligence,* **7**, 39–52.

Oppenheimer, R. (1956). Analogy in science. *American Psychologist,* **11**, 127–135.

Pachella, R. G. (1974). The interpretation of reaction time in information processing research. In B. H. Kentowitz (Ed.), *Human information processing: tutorials in performance and cognition*. Hillsdale. New Jersey: Erlbaum.

Pellegrino, J. W., & Glaser, R. (1980). Components of inductive reasoning. In R. E. Snow, P. A. Federico, & W. E. Montague (Eds.), *Aptitude, learning and instruction*. Vol 1, *Cognitive process analyses of aptitude*. Hillsdale, New Jersey: Erlbaum.

Pellegrino, J. W., & Goldman, S. R. (1983). Developmental and individual differences in verbal and spatial reasoning. In R. F. Dillon & R. R. Schmeck (Eds.), *Individual differences in cognition* (Vol. 1). New York: Academic Press.

Pellegrino, J. W., & Kail, R., Jr. (1982). Process analyses of spatial aptitude. In R. J. Sternberg (Ed.), *Advances in the psychology of human intelligence*. Hillsdale, New Jersey: Erlbaum.

Phillips, C. J., & Nettelbeck, T. (1985). Mild mental retardation and memory scanning. In N. R. Ellis (Ed.), *International review of research in mental retardation* (Vol. 13, pp. 143–179). New York: Academic Press.

Reitman, W. (1965). *Cognition and thought.* New York: Wiley.

Smith, G. J. (1981). *Analogical reasoning profiles of mentally retarded and normal adults judged against Sternberg's unified componential theory of human reasoning.* Unpublished doctoral dissertation, University of Northern Colorado.

Spearman, C. (1927). *The abilities of man.* New York: Macmillan.

Spitz, H. H. (1979). Beyond field theory in the study of mental deficiency. In N. R. Ellis (Ed.), *Handbook of mental deficiency: Psychological theory and research* (2nd ed.). Hillsdale, New Jersey: Erlbaum.

Spitz, H. H., & Borys, S. (1984). Depth of search: How far can the retarded search through an internally represented problem space? In P. H. Brooks, R. Sperber, & C. McCauley (Eds.), *Learning and cognition in the mentally retarded.* Hillsdale, New Jersey: Erlbaum.

Spitz, H. H., Minsky, S. K., & Besselieu, C. L. (1985). Influence of planning time and first-move strategy on Tower of Hanoi problem-solving performance of mentally retarded young adults and nonretarded children. *American Journal of Mental Deficiency,* **90**, 46–56.

Spitz, H. H., Webster, N. A., & Borys, S. V. (1982). Further studies of the Tower of Hanoi problem-solving performance of retarded young adults and nonretarded children. *Developmental Psychology,* **18**, 922–930.

Sternberg, R. J. (1975). *The componential analysis of human abilities.* Unpublished doctoral dissertation, Stanford University.

Sternberg R. J. (1977). *Intelligence, information processing and analogical reasoning: The componential analysis of human abilities.* Hillsdale, New Jersey: Erlbaum.

Sternberg, R. J. (1980). Sketch of a componential subtheory of human intelligence. *Behavioural and Brain Science,* **3**, 573–614.

Sternberg, R. J. (1981). Cognitive-behavioural approaches to the training of intelligence in the retarded. *Journal of Special Education,* **15**, 165–183.

Sternberg, R. J. (1982). A componential approach to intellectual development. In R. J. Sternberg (Ed.), *Advances in the psychology of human intelligence* (Vol. 1). Hillsdale, New Jersey: Erlbaum.

Sternberg, R. J. (1984). Towards a triarchic theory of human intelligence. *Behavioural and Brain Sciences,* **7**, 269–315.

Sternberg, R. J., & Nigro, G. (1980). Developmental patterns in the solution of verbal analogies. *Child Development,* **57**, 27–38.

Sternberg, R. J., & Rifkin, B. (1979). The development of analogical reasoning processes. *Journal of Experimental Child Psychology,* **27**, 195–232.

Sternberg, S. (1969). Memory scanning: Mental processes revealed by reaction time experiments. *American Scientist,* **57**, 421–457.

Sternberg, S. (1975). Memory scanning: New findings and current controversies. *Quarterly Journal of Experimental Psychology,* **27**, 1–32.

Thorndike, R., & Hagen, E. (1971). *Cognitive abilities test.* Boston: Houghton Mifflin.

Thurston, L. L. (1938). *Primary mental abilities.* Chicago: University of Chicago Press.

Application of Self-Control Strategies to Facilitate Independence in Vocational and Instructional Settings

JAMES E. MARTIN, DONALD L. BURGER, SUSAN ELIAS-BURGER, AND DENNIS E. MITHAUG

SCHOOL OF EDUCATION
UNIVERSITY OF COLORADO
COLORADO SPRINGS, COLORADO 80933

I. ADAPTABILITY INSTRUCTION AND SELF-CONTROL STRATEGIES

Many community-based approaches have been suggested for improving educational and vocational outcomes for individuals who are mentally retarded (Brown, Ford, Nisbet, York, & Loomis, 1983; Halpern, 1985; Stainback, Stainback, Nietupski, & Hamre-Nietupski, 1986; Wehman, Kregel, Barcus, & Schalock, 1986). These approaches detail needed environmental components but have less to say about intervention procedures (Mithaug, Martin, & Agran, 1987). This is unfortunate because the traditional interventions used in these programs are often incompatible with community-based training efforts. The training techniques used may decrease the impact of changes in service delivery because they are based upon an instructional approach that requires dependency relationships. Because of this, behaviors incompatible with independence and self-initiative are often reinforced (Gifford, Rusch, Martin, & White, 1984; Rosenbaum & Drabman, 1979; Rusch, Martin, & White, 1985).

In educational settings for mentally retarded individuals, teachers and other changes agents typically determine what students should learn, how they will learn, and where the instruction should take place (Guess & Siegel-Causey, 1985). Mentally retarded students are not viewed as "self-directing and purposeful human beings" but as "objects of external manipulation" (Guess & Siegel-Causey, 1985, p. 234). As a consequence, children, adolescents, and adults with mental retardation may not acquire the ability to manage their own schedules and to solve problems across settings.

Clearly, a need exists for individuals who are mentally retarded to learn to control their own behavior with as little external influence as possible (Bandura, 1969). Interventions that increase self-direction and problem-solving ability in community work sites and classrooms seem necessary. Mithaug, Martin, and Agran's (1987) adaptability model focuses upon these generic skills. This should not imply that specific skill training is unnecessary, but rather that skill training is *not sufficient* for independent functioning and adaptation to new settings" (Mithaug *et al.*, 1987, p. 6).

Adaptability Instruction

Adaptability instruction consists of four components: (1) decision making, (2) independent performance, (3) self-evaluation, and (4) adjustment. Mithaug *et al.* (1987) suggested that

> Adaptability instruction establishes the problem-solving skills needed to perform different tasks in a variety of settings. Students who problem-solve have dynamic relationships with their. . .environment. They identify problems that may affect their success, define alternative solutions to those problems, determine a course of action, take that action, evaluate the consequences of their own performance, and then determine the need for adjustments and different decisions. (p. 501)

The adaptability instructional model details the critical concepts needed for students to become independent. Rather than teachers or trainers solving problems for students, adaptability instruction trains these skills. Students complete sequences of tasks independently and make decisions to work faster, slower, or to perform other tasks by using information from their self-evaluations.

The efficacy of the decision making, independent performance, self-evaluation, and adjustment components have been demonstrated with nonretarded individuals (Kanfer, 1980; Kurtz & Neisworth, 1976; Mithaug *et al.*, 1987). The independent performance and self-evaluation components of the adaptability model have been demonstrated with individuals who are mentally retarded primarily through the use of antecedent and consequent self-control procedures (Shapiro, 1981). These techniques facilitate independent functioning in the home, classroom, job setting, and across other community settings (Agran & Martin, 1987). In this article we will define self-control procedures and then review self-monitoring, self-reinforcement, and self-managed antecedent cue techniques with individuals who are mentally retarded.

II. SELF-CONTROL

"The ideal aim of education is the creation of the power of self-control" (Dewey, 1939, p. 75). For Dewey, self-control included the development of goals, assessment of progress, and arrangement of one's environment to reach these goals. This perspective emphasizes the importance of self-control for independent functioning, a trait equated with successful adjustment (Guess, Benson, & Siegel-Causey, 1985; Workman, 1982).

A. Definitions of Self-Control

Self-control has been associated with an individual's willpower, that is, the inner force that mysteriously guides one's destiny (Goetz & Elzel, 1978; Mahoney & Thoresen, 1974). In contrast, others believe the individual can be responsible for changing and managing his or her own behavior (Baer, 1984; Bandura, 1976; Bandura & Kupers, 1964; Brigham, 1983; Cole & Gardner, 1984; Goldiamond, 1965; Goldfried & Merbaum, 1973; Jeffery, 1974; Kanfer, 1975; Kanfer, Bradley, & Marston, 1962; Kazdin, 1980). According to Skinner (1974), self-control is a process whereby an individual's response alters the probability of another response. In order to ensure consistency, self-control used in this review refers to the process of managing one's own behavior through self-regulation of antecedent or consequent stimuli (Kurtz & Neisworth, 1976).

B. Self-Control Strategies

Several self-control techniques have been described in the literature, including self-observation, imagery, biofeedback, self-help books, self-recording, self-contract, and self-directed stimulus control (Goetz & Elzel, 1978; Kazdin, 1980; O'Leary & O'Leary, 1976). Of the available self-control strategies, Martin (1983) postulated that self-monitoring, self-reinforcement, and self-management of antecedent stimuli are especially useful with individuals who are mentally retarded. From 1973 to early 1987, 77 studies were conducted using these strategies with individuals who were mentally retarded. The greatest number of these studies were published between 1978 and 1984. Most studies examined the use of a single self-control strategy (see Fig. 1). Self-monitoring, picture cues, and overt self-instructional strategies have been examined most (see Fig. 2). Discussion papers, early research that

FIG. 1. Number of studies from 1973 to 1987 that used single or combined self-control strategies. Usually, the self-control strategy was combined with trainer interventions. When the review was completed, not all studies for the last year were published; thus the "incomplete data" caption.

involved nonretarded subjects, and reviews will be used to highlight specific points. The 77 mental retardation studies will be reviewed separately under categories that *appear to best fit* each individual investigation.

III. SELF-MONITORING

Self-monitoring is usually the initial step in establishing self-control (Rosenbaum & Drabman, 1979; Shapiro, 1981). In a two-stage process, the individual becomes aware of his or her own behavior by discriminating the occurrence or nonoccurrence of a specific behavior and then records or reports the observation (Nelson, 1977). Self-evaluation, an extension of self-monitoring, occurs when a person compares their performance to a standard that is either given (Browder & Shapiro, 1985; Kanfer, 1980) or self-determined (O'Leary & Dubey, 1979). Although self-recording may require an external cuing system, the individual still regulates the reporting of behavior (Howell, Rueda, & Rutherford, 1983). Self-monitoring can also play a role as an observational tool to evaluate on-going self-control efforts when the person collects their own data.

Self-monitoring may in and of itself change behavior by altering the

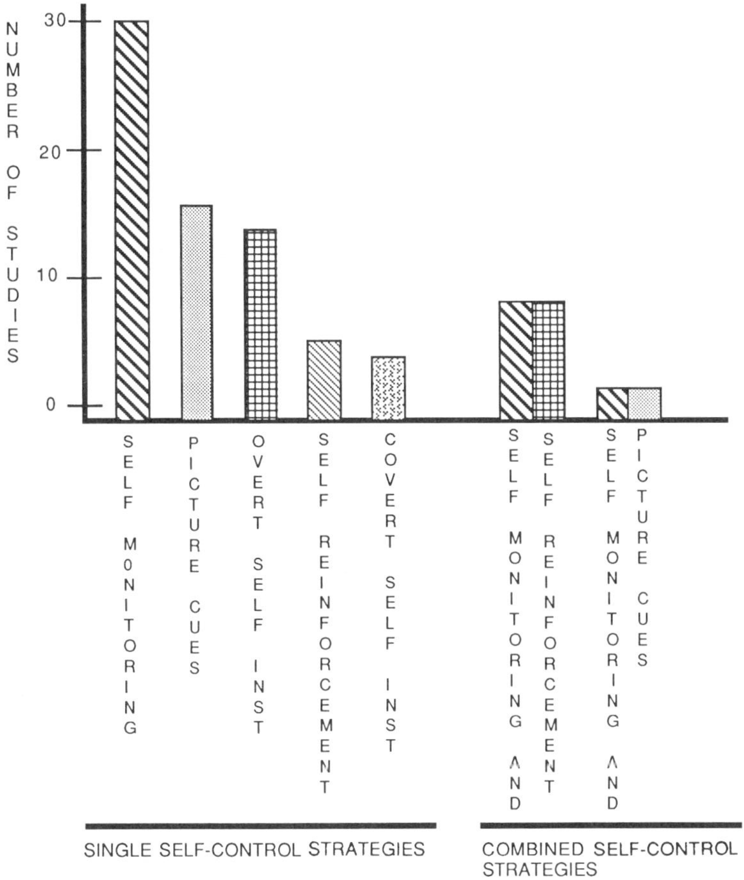

FIG. 2. Total number of strategies used from 1973 to 1987 by type of strategy.

characteristics of what is observed. Kazdin (1974) calls this reactivity and notes the self-monitoring process can change behavior simply because an individual becomes aware of the behavior under observation. Comparison to a standard, as done in self-evaluation, can take advantage of the reactive effect and may help increase performance to socially validated levels.

Six sections will examine and discuss self-monitoring. First, increases in target behaviors will be discussed followed by a section on decreases in target behaviors. Third, the effect of positive or negative values upon behavior change will be examined. Fourth, the ability of multiple behaviors to be self-monitored will be discussed, followed by a section on accuracy. Last, a summary section will tie all sections together.

A. Increases in Target Behaviors

The reactive effect of self-monitoring will be examined across increases in academic skills, work production rates, leisure skills, and physical fitness.

1. ACADEMIC SKILLS

To date, six studies have demonstrated an increase in academic skills. Knapczyk and Livingston (1973) investigated the effects of shifting the record keeping associated with a token program from teacher control to control by mildly mentally retarded students. Through a reversal design, token and self-recording phases yielded higher levels of correct recording of reading assignments than no-treatment baseline conditions. One experimental phase showed the addition of self-recording to the teacher-managed token program produced a noticeable increase in accurate responses. This increased accuracy is an example of moderate reactivity.

In a study involving four adolescents who were mildly mentally retarded, Long and Williams (1976) demonstrated more clearly than Knapczyk and Livingston (1973) the reactive effects of self-monitoring. A multiple-baseline design, with conditions presented successively in spelling and reading, showed improvement when students used a point sheet at their desks to record appropriate responses. This enabled three of four students to improve their classroom spelling behavior, while all four students gained in reading. Long and Williams suggested that recording of points immediately following the occurrence of a behavior provided performance feedback and that such knowledge of progress increased and maintained the desired behavior.

Horner and Brigham (1979) taught two mildly mentally retarded public school students how to self-monitor on-task behavior in two 40-minute sessions. As a result, each student doubled their on-task time. When feedback on accuracy of recording was removed, their performance decreased to near baseline levels. As soon as students gave themselves rewards, their performance increased dramatically. The authors concluded that the combined use of self-monitoring and self-reinforcement was more effective than the use of self-monitoring alone.

Chiron and Gerken (1983) examined the effects of self-monitoring on 91 educable mentally retarded students' locus of control orientation and academic performance. They received instructions to fill in a section of a chart after completing their assignment. In addition to significant increases in reading, the students indicated they were more in control of their environment.

Shapiro, McGonigle, and Ollendick (1980) studied the impact of self-monitoring and self-reinforcement upon classroom on-task behavior by examining the effect of self-assessment of five children who were mildly to moderately mentally retarded. Each received instructions to determine and record when they were on task. This process resulted in an increased level of on-task behavior. Most recently, Morrow, Burke, and Buell (1985) increased on-task behavior and the number of math problems completed by two emotionally disturbed moderately mentally retarded adolescents. An audio tape with random beeps was played. The two students were taught, when they heard a beep, to record a "+" or a "–" on a card taped to their desk to indicate if they were working or not.

2. WORK PRODUCTION RATES

The reactive effects of self-monitoring have been examined through eight studies undertaken in sheltered environments. Hanel and Martin (1980) used self-monitoring and self-reinforcement to increase the production rates of eight workshop clients who were mildly to severely mentally retarded. A marble-dispensing device was used as a token-reinforcement and self-monitoring system. The clients exchanged marbles for money at the end of each session. Productivity increased 43% over baseline. In addition, each client selected the condition they preferred to work under, either baseline or self-regulation. They selected the self-regulation package in 84% of the trials.

Through human intervention, Zohn and Bornstein (1980) used modeling and practice to teach self-monitoring to four sheltered workshop employees who were moderately mentally retarded. The dependent measures, including units completed, on-task behavior, and work quality, improved. Likewise, Ortega, Schultz, and Sanders (1976) combined self-monitoring with social reinforcement to enable a 27-year-old moderately mentally retarded sheltered workshop employee to almost double his production rate.

Unlike previous studies, Shapiro and Ackerman studied generalization and maintenance. Shapiro and Ackerman (1983) found that self-monitoring produced no significant production increases over a control condition in the training setting for 10 mild to moderately mentally retarded workers. Increases were noted, however, in a generalization setting. In a second study, Ackerman and Shapiro (1984) focused upon maintenance. First, the production rates of 5 mild to moderately mentally retarded workers were increased through prompts and praise. Second, self-monitoring was introduced. When the external prompts and praise were removed, the improved level of performance maintained.

More recently, self-monitoring, self-reinforcement, and performance feedback were used by McNally, Kompik, and Sherman (1984) to increase workshop production rates. A reversal combined with a changing criterion design yielded significant increases by 13 workers who were mild to moderately mentally retarded. Rudrud, Rice, Robertson, and Olson (1984) also investigated the effects of self-monitoring on workshop production rates; 16 work activity center clients, who were in the mild to severe range of mental retardation, learned to self-record on-task behavior when they heard a prerecorded tone. Production increased 11.2%.

In a study similar to the one undertaken by Horner and Brigham (1979), Mace, Shapiro, West, Campbell, and Allman (1986) investigated the role of self-monitoring and reinforcement with three moderately to severely mentally retarded sheltered workshop employees. Prior to the start of the study, each subject was taught how to self-monitor. Following baseline, two workers were given contingent praise and money for reaching individualized production rates. This intervention increased their rate. Next, the two subjects were introduced to self-monitoring and reinforcement. This increased their production rate further and decreased its variability. When reinforcement was withdrawn, performance rates returned to baseline levels. Reinstatement of reinforcement once agian increased their rates. The intervention order was different for the third worker. Following baseline, he was told to self-monitor and received no reinforcement. The addition of reinforcement once again increased productivity. As before, the removal of reinforcement decreased production and its reinstatement produced an increase. Interestingly, self-monitoring by itself produced little change. Reinforcement was needed to achieve increased production.

3. LEISURE SKILLS

Matson and Andrasik (1982) combined self-monitoring and self-reinforcement to increase leisure time conversational skills of mildly to moderately mentally retarded individuals. The conditions included social skill training, self-monitoring, and self-reinforcement. The authors concluded that self-monitoring was significantly more effective than either social skills training or self-reinforcement.

4. PHYSICAL FITNESS

Coleman and Whitman (1984) improved physical fitness through use of self-monitoring and self-reinforcement. Individuals (17) who were mildly to moderately mentally retarded increased the number of exercises completed during daily unsupervised exercise periods, improved their heart rate, respiration, and blood pressure, and acurately recorded their actual rate of exercising. During the first phase of treatment, the individuals were taught to self-monitor and to self-record their exercise activity. At the end of the exercise session, each person could place a sticker on the exercise chart. These were later converted into backup rewards based upon the accuracy of their self-recording. Improved results were maintained under the supervision of a new workshop supervisor.

B. Decreases in Target Behaviors

The results discussed in the preceding section suggest that self-monitoring does have a reactive effect in terms of increasing targeted behaviors. A number of other studies indicate that self-monitoring may also be effective in decelerating deviant behavior. The reactive effect of self-monitoring will be examined across decreases in self-stimulation, disruptive behaviors, tardiness, and tongue protrusion.

1. SELF-STIMULATION

Zegiob, Klukas, and Junginger (1978) examined the reactive effects of self-monitoring in an institutional setting. Two adolescents, one mildly and the other moderately retarded, were trained to record occurrences of their respective target behaviors. This procedure alone decreased one subject's severe nose and mouth picking and the other's consistent head shaking.

2. DISRUPTIVE BEHAVIORS

Self-monitoring alone or in combination with other treatment components decreased yelling, hitting, loud vocalizations, and out-of-seat behavior across five studies. Through the use of a multicomponent treatment package, Harvey, Karan, Bhargaya, and Morehouse (1978) reduced the yelling and hitting behavior of a 38-year-old mentally retarded woman in a sheltered workshop. The intervention components included self-monitoring, time out, covert self-instructions, and relaxation exercises. Self-monitoring was done two ways. First, she checked happy or sad faces after a brief period of time to indicate if she had an outburst or not. Second, at the end of each day she would chart her overall performance. Shortly after the intervention started, the frequency of outbursts decreased to zero. The results generalized from work to home and were maintained for up to 14 weeks. Likewise, Gardner, Cole, Berry, and Nowinski (1983b) reduced verbal disruptive and aggressive behavior of two moderately mentally retarded workshop employees. Self-monitoring was a component of a treatment package that included social reinforcement, corrective feedback, and a token economy. The training was effective in reducing and maintaining decreased levels of inappropriate verbalizations.

Unlike the previous studies, Robertson, Simon, Pachman, and Drabman (1979) used self-monitoring alone to reduce the frequencies of six classes of disruptive behaviors, which included out-of-seat, vocalization, noncompliance, and playing; 12 students, who ranged in age from 5 to 11 and had a mean IQ of 47, accurately evaluated and reduced their disruptive classroom behavior. Reese, Sherman, and Sheldon (1984) used peers to help prompt self-recording; 3 moderately mentally retarded residents of a group home were taught to self-record when they exhibited disruptive behavior, and peers helped remind the subjects to self-record. In each case, disruptive behavior was at its lowest frequency when self-recording was in effect.

Finally, out-of-seat behavior was the target of Sugai and Rowe's (1984) study of a 15-year-old student who was mildly mentally retarded. During baseline, this student was out of his seat 63% of the time. A kitchen timer was used to prompt recording. While the target behavior did not disappear completely, it was reduced.

3. TARDINESS

Shafer and Brooke (1984) examined the use of a self-recording procedure to increase the punctuality of a mildly mentally retarded employee who checked out early from work. In a reversal design, she was instructed to record her check-out time, which was validated against her time card. The intervention produced a rapid reduction of early check-outs.

4. TONGUE PROTRUSION

Rosine and Martin (1983) achieved reductions in the occurrence of inappropriate workshop behavior by using a multicomponent treatment package. Self-monitoring, self-instruction, and a token economy enabled three adults who were mildly to moderately mentally retarded to bring tongue chewing and tongue protrusion under control. Generalization to other settings, however, was limited.

Similarly, Rudrud, Ziarnik, and Colman (1984) used a self-recording procedure to decrease tongue protrusion in a woman who was moderately mentally retarded. First, they used discrimination training of visual cues to teach the subject when her tongue was in or out of her mouth. Then she was taught to self-record when an auditory cue was presented. Tongue thrust decreased to zero after 35 days of self-recording. The auditory cue was removed and the inappropriate behavior did not reappear.

C. Positive or Negative Value

In a few studies, researchers have manipulated the target behavior through the application of positive or negative values. For example, Nelson, Lipinski, and Black (1976) studied the relationship between the value of the behavior and degree of change. Moderately and mildly mentally retarded adults (15) were divided into three groups: face touching, object touching, and talking. Following baseline observation, each group was taught to record their target behavior. Those in the face-touching group were also told that this action may lead to infection. Members of the talking group learned that talking was desirable and they should do it more. Those in the object-touching group were told that such behavior was neither good or bad, and they should continue. Self-recording increased the frequency of the positive behavior (talking), decreased the neutral behavior (object touching), and decreased the negative behavior (face touching).

To further determine the effect of the value of behavior, Litrownik and Freitas (1980) examined the reaction of 40 moderately retarded adolescents who self-recorded positive, negative, or neutral behaviors. The subjects were divided into four groups who (1) recorded the completion of a bead-stringing task (positive behavior), (2) recorded not completing the task (negative behavior), (3) recorded the stringing of red beads (neutral behavior), and (4) did not not self-record. The group that self-monitored positive behaviors strung significantly more beads and made a greater degree of change than the other groups. The authors recommended that mentally retarded persons receive more opportunities to self-record their own behavior to facilitate independence.

D. Multiple Behaviors

Although the results on the reactive effects of self-monitoring is clear for a single behavior, little is known of this effect on several behaviors. In one of the few studies in this area, Hayes and Cavior (1977) determined that with nonretarded individuals self-recording one behavior produced greater reactivity than self-recording of two or three. To date, there are no studies of the reactivity of multiple tracking with mentally retarded individuals. Nonetheless, it appears that self-monitoring used alone or as a component in a package, can contribute to significant behavior change.

E. Accuracy of Self-Monitoring

A growing body of research has examined the accuracy of mentally retarded persons' self-monitoring. Fortunately, many of the studies reviewed included information on the accuracy of self-recorded behavior and a few specifically addressed accuracy. This section discusses the accuracy of self-monitoring in relation to academic tasks, training in how to self-record, value of behavior, limited accuracy outcomes, and with the severely disabled.

1. ACADEMIC TASKS

Knapczyk and Livingston (1973) were among the first to report that mildly mentally retarded individuals can accurately record information. In conjunction with a token program, their junior high school subjects were instructed to record the percentage of their correct responses to a daily reading assignment. At the same time, the classroom teacher maintained a record of student performance. Except for one instance, teacher records agreed with student recordings.

In more detail, Shapiro, Browder, and D'Hyvelters (1984) investigated the effects of a self-monitoring program on the completion of math and reading worksheets. A multiple-baseline design assessed training effectiveness. Following a baseline condition, the participants received stickers and other tangible rewards for accurate worksheets. Next, the children were prompted to self-monitor their performance, taking a penny from a container and placing it on a counting board after completing a worksheet. In the last condition, the children self-monitored without receiving any prompts. Maintenance and generalization effects were mixed. Only two of the four children accurately self-monitored, and only two generalized the skill to other tasks.

2. TRAINING IN HOW TO SELF-RECORD

Several studies focused on training their subjects to self-record. First, Nelson *et al.* (1976) found the accuracy of self-monitoring by mildly to moderately mentally retarded adults equal to that of college students. Following a brief training session that consisted of modeling, practice, and feedback, the subjects recorded a target behavior over several 10-minute trials. Next, they received a candy bar if they accurately self-recorded the target behavior. Contingent reinforcement significantly increased the accuracy of self-recording.

With laboratory tasks, Litrownik, Freitas, and Franzini (1978) studied the accuracy of self-monitoring in training and nontraining conditions. First, children demonstrated their ability to perform a self-monitoring task—placing a ring on a stick following the completion of a specific task. Second, the training group received an hour of instruction. Initially, the students could not self-monitor their behavior and verbal instructions did not improve performance. However, those who received a 1-hour demonstration program were able to acquire and maintain the self-monitoring response. The investigators concluded that most moderately retarded individuals can learn to monitor their own behavior accurately.

In one of the few *self-evaluation* studies, Litrownik, Cleary, Lecklitner, and Franzini (1978) taught moderately mentally retarded children to do a task and to evaluate its completion. When a task was completed, the children were to place a happy face on a felt board. A green square was placed on the board when a task was not completed. At the start of the study, all students could not self-evaluate. Following training in self-evaluation, their performance showed significant improvement.

Nelson, Lipinski, and Boykin (1978) examined the effects of training and obtrusiveness of recording devices on the accuracy of self-recording appropriate verbalizations. Nine mildly to moderately mentally retarded adolescents received limited self-monitoring training through videotaped feedback and in-class practice. During the self-recording phases, the subjects either held a counter in their hand (more obtrusive condition) or kept it in a pocketlike holder on their belt (less obtrusive condition). Self-recordings of appropriate verbalizations were significantly more accurate for trained than for untrained subjects. The obtrusive hand-held counters produced more accurate recordings than did the belt-worn counters.

Howell *et al.* (1983) studied the reliability of self-recording with five moderately mentally retarded students. The teacher tapped each student's shoulder at 4- to 10-minute intervals to prompt self-recording. Training was conducted in three phases. Rater agreement between the students and trainers across all phases averaged 92%. Reliability during the self-monitoring phase averaged 83%. The authors believed these figures to be educationally significant because they were above the 80% level generally used to define acceptable limits.

Shapiro *et al.* (1980) found that for students who were mildly to moderately mentally retarded, accurate self-assessments were minimal prior to training. After training, however, the accuracy of all subjects improved immediately. Interestingly, when general self-management instructions replaced self-assessment training, accurate self-assessment decreased slightly. When self-reinforcement was introduced, accurate self-assessment once again increased and was maintained when general self-management instructions replaced self-reinforcement. This suggests that maintenance of accurate self-assessment may require self-reinforcement. In a similar investigation, Shapiro and Klein (1980) found that during token reinforcement, four mildly to moderately retarded children could learn to self-assess on-task behavior accurately.

In contrast to studies that emphasized the importance of training, Bauman and Iwata (1977) found that two mildly disabled adults could record data on how they performed household tasks similar to that collected by trained observers.

3. VALUE OF BEHAVIOR

Litrownik and Freitas (1980) examined the effect of valence self-recorded positive, negative, or neutral behaviors. Their accuracy data revealed no differences between the three groups. Compared with data from trained observers, the groups' recordings were very accurate, ranging from 94 to 100%. However, this accuracy level was obtained only after the subjects received training in how to self-record.

4. LIMITED ACCURACY

Only one investigation determined that their subjects' self-recording accuracy was very low (Zegiob *et al.*, 1978). Other factors, however, may potentially confound this finding. For example, one subject received limited training on how to self-record, while the other received no training at all. Also, a combination of methodological problems were present, such as a lack of stimuli for self-recording, changes in the behavior definition, and different data collection systems.

5. SEVERELY DISABLED

Most accuracy studies have focused on individuals who are mildly to moderately mentally retarded. Relatively little is known about the self-monitoring skills of persons with moderate to severe mental retardation (Browder & Shapiro, 1985). Perhaps, the approach used by Matson and colleagues could encouage research in this area (Matson, 1980, 1981; Matson & Long, 1986; Matson & Marchetti, 1980; Matson, Marchetti, & Adkins, 1980). In a series of studies, the subjects were asked to verbally self-evaluate their performance. Responses were verified and the subjects received praise or correction for their self-evaluations. Unfortunatley, there were no data on the accuracy of self-monitoring. Even so, the studies demonstrate the use of self-reports when external recording is neither feasible nor desirable.

E. Summary

Most of the research reviewed in this section occurred in applied settings—schools, workshops, or community apartments. The studies employed a variety of procedures, including verbal self-reports, checking off items on a schedule, placing a tally mark on a card or piece of paper, using a belt-worn or hand-held counter, hand raising, and placing a marble into a glass tube or a ring onto a stick. They demonstrated that individuals who are mildly to moderately mentally retarded can monitor their own behaviors in different settings with a high degree of accuracy.

Several findings warrant special consideration. First, when mild to moderately mentally retaded persons self-monitor, reactivity will occur. This means that there is a corresponding change in the behavior being monitored. In several studies, self-monitoring was as effective and, at times, more effective than token programs. Second, mentally retarded individuals can be taught to monitor their own behavior accurately, often through the use of simple training procudures. Third, self-monitoring was reactive in the one study where the self-recordings were inaccurate, suggesting that self-monitoring may help change behavior even if the exact frequency is not correctly recorded. Fourth, self-monitoring tends to increase desirable and decrease undesirable behavior. Finally, future research needs to determine the effects of self-monitoring with persons who are severely mentally retarded.

IV. SELF-REINFORCEMENT

As a self-control strategy, self-reinforcement consists of the self-management of consequent stimuli through self-determined and/or self-administered reinforcers (Marston, 1964; Bandura, 1976; Wehman, 1975). Self-reinforcement is usually combined with self-monitoring procedures (Browder & Shapiro, 1985). Skinner (1953) noted an individual must be free to choose a reward at any time, regardless of whether or not he or she has performed the appropriate response. This means that "true self-reinforcement" occurs when the individual is free to "cheat." In the applied research literature, however, self-reinforcement seldom occurs in the absence of externally controlling influences—i.e., the subjects usually do not have control over available reinforcers, nor do they freely impose contingencies for their delivery (Jones, Nelson, & Kazdin, 1977). The presence of a high degree of external influence in most of the current research suggests that subjects may have not experienced "true" self-reinforcement (Morgan & Bass, 1973; Sohn & Lamal, 1982; Liberty

& Michael, 1985). This section will review the influence of motivation, examine studies where subjects determined their own rewards and administered their own reinforcers, discuss confounding variables, and summarize the major point.

A. Influence of Motivation

Bandura (1969) suggested that intrinsically motivated persons are less dependent on external reinforcement conditions than those who are extrinsically motivated. Switsky and Haywood (1974) found that under self-reinforcement conditions, intrinsically motivated children worked harder and changed and maintained behavior better than extrinsically motivated children. The extrinsically motivated children, however, did better under external reinforcement conditions.

As a followup to their earlier study, Haywood and Switsky (1985) examined the effect of external and self-reinforcement for intrinsically and extrinsically motivated mildly mentally retarded adults. Individuals (72) residing in a community care facility were tested to determine their motivation orientation. Each was assigned to control, self-reinforcement, and external reinforcement conditions. Subjects in the self-reinforcement condition set their own work goals, determined how many units they would produce, and then gave themselves as many tokens as they thought they deserved. Prizes were exchanged for the tokens at the end of each training session. In the external reinforcement condition, the researcher determined the goal and the number of tokens to be dispensed. Under the self-reinforcement condition, the intrinsically motivated subjects had higher production than those who were extrinsically motivated. The intrinsically motivated workers also did more in a no-reward condition. Interestingly, under external reinforcement conditions, both the intrinsic and extrinsic groups produced about the same amount. The authors concluded that since most persons who are mentally retarded tend to be extrinsically motivated, efforts to increase their independence may be frustrated until they learn to respond well to self-reinforcement.

Few self-reinforcement studies, however, have determined the motivational orientation of their mentally retarded subjects. As indicated in the Haywood and Switsky (1985) study, the orientation may make a difference with the intensity in which dependent measures change. The results from the following studies must be examined carefully in light of this information.

B. Self-Determined Rewards

In two studies, Wehman and associates examined the effects of external, self-administered, and self-determined reinforcement upon production rates of mentally retarded workers. In the first study, a worker who was severely mentally retarded experienced external, self-administered, and then self-determined reinforcement (Wehman, Schutz, Bates, Renzaglia, & Karan, 1978). During external reinforcement, he received verbal praise from a trainer for giving himself 3 pennies upon completion of a jump-rope assembly task. In the self-administered phase, there was no praise and the worker paid himself 3 cents for each completed unit. In the final phase, the worker determined the schedule and amount of reinforcement he would receive. While work production rates increased with the introduction of each condition, the self-determined reinforcement phase produced the highest level of production. Interestingly, the schedule and amount of reward during the self-determined phase was similar to the previous condition, that is, the worker gave himself 3 pennies whenever a unit was assembled correctly.

In the second Wehman *et al.* study, a mildly mentally retarded worker experienced three reinforcement conditions. During external reinforcement, he received a nickel for assembling two water softeners. In the self-administered phase, a box of nickels was placed on the work table and the subject was instructed to give himself a nickel for each two units completed. During the self-determined phase, he was given the box of nickels and told to pay himself. As in the previous experiment, each reinforcement phase produced higher production rates than baseline, with self-determined reinforcement being the most effective.

In summary, these two case studies suggest that mentally retarded workers can determine their own reinforcers. However, it is possible the two workers were responding to subtle influences that affected their choice of reward. Nevertheless, the self-determined condition produced the highest production rate, which suggests that self-determined reinforcement may be an effective strategy for use with workers who are mentally retarded.

C. Self-Administered Reinforcers

The effects of self-administered reinforcers will be examined across work production rates, inappropriate talking to self, and on-task behavior. All of these studies were undertaken in sheltered environments.

1. WORK PRODUCTION RATES

Three studies examined the effect of self-reinforcement upon production rates. The first two studies compared self-administered vs. externally delivered reinforcement. Helland, Paluck, and Klein (1976) divided 12 mildly to moderately retarded young adults into two groups. Members of the self-reinforcement group were trained to verbalize self-compliments and to select a reward upon completion of 10 sets of collated paper; subjects in the external reinforcement group were given a reward and praise following the completion of each 10 sets. Both conditions greatly improved performance, but there was no significant difference between the two methods. Members of the self-reinforcement group, however, accurately rewarded and praised themselves outside the training setting.

In the second study, McNally, Norusis, Gentz, and McConathy (1983) investigated the effects of a group contingency. Severely mentally retarded clients (10) attending a work activity center were trained to complete a packaging task using prompts and feedback. During the self-delivered reinforcement phase, the trainer instructed the clients to take a token for every 10 packages completed. During the group contingency phase, the clients formed two teams. The members of the team with the most tokens received extra leisure time regardless of their individual performance. The results indicated that while self-determined reinforcement increased production above the baseline level, the group contingent self-reinforcement intervention was more effective. It appears the group contingency enhanced the effectiveness of self-delivered reinforcement.

Third, self-reinforcement was the sole focus of a study completed by Bates, Renzaglia, and Clees (1980). Through the use of a changing criterion design, the use of self-reward by a woman who was severely mentally retarded was assessed. As a result of the intervention, each time the criterion was raised, the woman increased her production rate. This continued until her rate met a sheltered workshop's entrance requirements.

2. INAPPROPRIATE TALKING TO SELF

Gardner, Clees, and Cole (1983a) combined self-administered reinforcement with self-monitoring and self-evaluation procedures to reduce the inappropriate talking-to-self behavior of a 26-year-old moderately mentally retarded worker. During training, he was cued by a trainer to self-deliver a monetary reinforcer following an appropriate worker behavior, or to point to a picture of a frowning face after an inappropriate behavior. The trainer gradually faded the intervention as the client demonstrated independent self-management. Introduction of self-reinforcement procedures reduced inappropriate verbal behaviors from an average of 97.5% during baseline to near 0%. In addition, treatment effects were maintained over extended periods of time, with work productivity showing a gradual but steady increase as inappropriate behavior declined.

3. ON-TASK BEHAVIOR

Shapiro and Klein (1980) examined the effects of self-administered tokens by four mildly mentally retarded children. After baseline, a teacher provided tokens to students for being on task at the end of a brief period (30 to 90 seconds). Next, students were trained to assess and then reinforce their own behavior. In the subsequent phase, students accurately self-reinforced their behavior. On-task behavior remained at high levels during the self-managed phase and was maintained during a 2-month followup. One criticism offered by Sohn and Lamal (1982) suggested that external reinforcement was so gradually faded the subjects may have believed that external contingencies were still in operation. Nevertheless, the students demonstrated that they could manage important aspects of the token system.

In a subsequent study, Shapiro *et al.* (1980) examined the separate effects of five mildly or moderately mentally retarded children's self-assessment and self-reinforcement. Following the baseline period, a token economy was initiated. The teacher placed a star on a card taped to the desk of each student for being on task at the end of a brief period. If a child was not on task, the teacher provided feedback and removed a star. After a return to baseline, reinstatement of the token economy, and a self-management phase followed by self-reinforcement training, the children were trained to either place or remove a star on the chart depending upon their being on or off task. The results indicated that self-reinforcement was effective in maintaining behavioral improvements, even though only three of the five subjects reinforced themselves accurately. Overall, the study suggested that self-instruction in the management of a token economy was not sufficient to establish a high level of on-task behavior. However, when self-management followed self-assessment and self-reinforcement training, on-task behavior was maintained at a level comparable to the teacher-controlled phase. Although self-assessment training obviously increased self-management behavior, the role of self-reinforcement remains unclear.

D. Confounding Variables

The self-reinforcement studies show that self-determined or self-administered reinforcers result in behavioral change. Some of these changes may have been due to external contingencies not controlled in the investigations. These confounding variables may contribute substantially to the behavior change attributed to self-reinforcement. This issue and others identified by Jones *et al.* (1977) will be discussed in this section.

As mentioned earlier, self-monitoring is a powerful behavioral change strategy. In most of the self-reinforcement studies reviewed, subjects also monitored, to some degree, the target behavior (e.g., Gardner *et al.*, 1983b; Helland *et al.*, 1976; Shapiro & Klein, 1980; Wehman *et al.*, 1978). Even in the Shapiro *et al.* (1980) study, self-reinforcement was combined with self-monitoring. Hence, results attributed to self-reinforcement may, in part, be ascribed to self-monitoring.

An individual's reinforcement history, that is, reinforcing episodes prior to or earlier in the investigation, may enhance the effects of self-reinforcement. In most of the investigations there was a known history of reinforcement prior to the implementation of self-reinforcement. For instance, Shapiro and Klein

(1980) and Shapiro *et al.* (1980) introducted a token contingency before implementing the self-reinforcement procedures. Likewise, Wehman *et al.* (1978) interposed external or noncontingent reinforcement before self-reinforcement. These condition sequences make it difficult to determine the singular effect self-reinforcement. Note that an individual's freedom from external contingencies is a central dimension in current views of self-control. Even though freedom in determining and administering reinforcement is essential to the definition of self-reinforcement, the mentally retarded subjects in the studies reviewed were usually not free of externally delivered reinforcement. With the exception of the Wehman *et al.* (1978) study, not only were the subjects told how and when to self-reinforce, they were usually also observed while doing so. Under these conditions, it is doubtful the subjects felt free to decided for themselves when and how much to reinforce their own behavior. Clearly, researchers need to examine self-reinforcement systems that utilize reinforcers over which the subjects have greater control.

E. Summary

Self-reinforcement strategies have been successful with nonretarded persons across a wide variety of behaviors (Jones *et al.*, 1977), including classroom behavior, weight control, and depression. The literature reviewed here suggests that self-delivered reinforcement is an effective strategy for mentally retarded individuals as well. Additional research is necessary to examine the various aspects of managing one's own behavior and to determine the separate effects of the different self-management techniques. A question remains as to the status of "true" self-reinforcement (where the individual is free of subtle external influences). Nevertheless, the procedures have obvious and important implications worth further study.

V. SELF-MANAGED ANTECEDENT CUES

Antecedent discriminative stimuli control behavior by signaling the probable occurrence of reinforcing stimuli associated with certain behavioral responses (Reynolds, 1968). Self-management of antecedent cues is a self-control strategy that alters the conditons that preceded the target behavior (Kurtz & Neisworth, 1976). This strategy limits the range of discriminative stimuli that influence undesirable behavior by highlighting the discriminative stimuli that facilitate the occurrence of desired behavior (Burron & Bucher, 1978; Goetz & Etzel, 1978; Wehman, 1975). Both external and internal stimuli can be self-managed to produce or maintain desired behavior. The discussion of self-management of exernal or internal stimuli by mentally retarded individuals will focus first on self-management of antecedent cues through the use of visual cues. We will later discuss internal stimulus control strategies such as self-instruction, verbal mediation, and corresponding training.

A. Self-Management through the Use of Visual Cues

1. TASK COMPLETION

Several studies have been completed demonstrating the ability of visual cues to aid with task completion. The section will review these studies across meal preparation, vocational peer tutoring, grocery shopping, microcomputer, general task domains. Also, a sub-section study reviews a study which reported that visual cues provided no beneficial assistance.

a. Meal Preparation. Four studies have examined the use of picture recipe cards as cooking aids. In the earliest study, Robinson-Wilson (1977) taught three severely mentally retarded adults in a sheltered workshop to prepare simple food (hot chocolate, Jell-o, and hot dogs). The procedures consisted of hand-drawn picture recipe cards and color-coded stove dials and a timer. The recipes were introduced to each person in a different sequence. Subsequent recipes required fewer trials. Next, Johnson and Cuvo (1981) taught basic cooking skills in a workshop classroom to two mildy and two moderately mentally retarded adults. A multiple-baseline design across subjects was used to assess the dependent variables of broiling a hot dog and a muffin, boiling an egg and vegetables, and baking cornbread and a biscuit. Once again, picture recipes helped with meal preparation.

Third, Martin, Rusch, James, Decker, and Titol (1982) demonstrated the effectiveness of picture recipe cards as aids in the preparation of complex meals. During baseline, subject received instruction on how to complete each step of a meal and verbal praise or error correction for completed steps. Next, sequenced black-and-white photographs for each step of every meal were introduced. Each person was told to look at the card, do what was pictured, and then turn the page. These general instructions were followed by specific instructions on how to complete each step of the meal. Feedback was administered in the same manner as during the baseline phase. When the sequenced picture recipe cards were introduced, two of the three subjects immediately improved the percentage of steps completed independent of trainer assistance. The third individual's performance increased more gradually. When the picture recipe cards were removed for five meals, the percentage of steps completed independently decreased to near baseline levels, indicating the positive effects of the picture recipe cards. A partial-sequential withdrawal of all training components except the picture cues maintained performance levels for up to 8 months (Martin & Rusch, 1987).

b. Vocational Tasks. Four studies have demonstrated the efficacy of picture cues to aid in the completion of vocational tasks. First, Wacker and Berg

(1983) used a sequence of black-and-white photographs in conjunction with a three-step training package to teach five high school students, who were moderately to severely mentally retarded, to complete complex vocational tasks. The training program included contingent praise, verbal error correction, and separate picture books for two training tasks (a valve assembly and a circuit board assembly) and two generalization tasks (double valve assembly and a packaging task). First, students were taught to turn the pages of the picture books. Second, each student had to correctly select the item needed on each page. Third, they assembled the items shown in the photographs. The ability to use picture cues generalized to novel tasks. Although the sequenced pictures were not necessary to maintain performance on the training tasks, they were necessary for correct response to the generalization tasks.

In the second study, Wacker and Berg (1984a) demonstrated that high school students who were moderately to severely mentally retarded could use picture cues to set up work stations independently. The task involved the correct placement of 18 valve assembly pieces or 20 packaging pieces across 3 work tables of an assembly line operation. Following a baseline of modeling and instruction, the subjects received sequence photographs to guide them in the placement of the objects. The picture cues had an immediate positive effect upon the students' performance. Following the removal of cues, correct placement on the tables decreased. Unlike the previous Wacker and Berg (1983) study, performance decreased in the absence of picture cues. As before, once the students learned how to use the cues, this ability generalized to a novel task. In the third study, Wacker, Berg, Berrie, and Swatta (1985) examined the use of photographs to assist in the acquisition and generalization across settings of various vocational and domestic skills. This time, the initial training task generalized across settings. Additional training sessions, although substantially reduced in number, were necessary to obtain generalization across the other two tasks.

Finally, Fisher (1984) explored the use of isometric-projection exploded-view assembly drawing with moderately mentally retarded adolescents. These industrial-type drawings show a pictorial view of each part to the same scale and arrangement as the assembled item. During a pretest, the students were only given drawings of a roller skate board assembly; no teacher instruction in how to assemble the task was provided. No student in the control group ($n = 50$) or the experimental group ($n = 487$) was able to assemble the pretest task. Each student in the experimental group received daily 1-hour instruction in how to complete an easy-to-hard sequence of assembly drawings. Various teacher interventions to correct errors and prompt correct performance were used. Instruction continued until all 24 easy-to-complex tasks were completed or the student was classified as being unable to complete the task. Subjects who completed the sequence of instructional drawings ($n = 466$) and control group members were then asked to once again attempt to assemble the roller skate task. No control group member could assemble the task. Of the experimental group students, 85% could complete the post-test. Fisher concluded that students who are moderately mentally retarded could learn how to use technical drawings to prepare them for employment.

c. Peer Tutoring. Wacker and Berg (1984b) demonstrated that a peer trainer, in this case a 14-year-old student who was moderately retarded, could teach her classmates to use picture cues to perform janitorial tasks. The peer trainer used the same procedures as in Wacker's previous studies to assist the trainees to fill a soft drink machine and to do cleaning tasks correctly.

d. Grocery Shopping. Sarber, Halasz, Mesmer, Bickett, and Lutzker (1983) used picture cues to teach a 34-year-old mentally retarded mother to shop for groceries. A menu-planning matrix of four columns and three rows of various colors was used. Color-coded food cards with pictures of the food items assisted the subject in planning nutritious meals. When placed in a binder, the color-coded food cards helped the subject to make purchases at the grocery store. She was able to use the system with 100% accuracy after training. Followups at 8, 16, and 20 weeks indicated continued success in using the picture cue cards.

e. Microcomputer Skills. Frank, Wacker, Berg, and McMahon (1985) investigated the use of picture prompts to teach microcomputer skills. Five children, who were mildly mentally retarded, learned to perform various microcomputer tasks by following picture prompts. Frank *et al.* questioned the relative effectiveness of picture prompts in the acquisition phase, but supported their use to achieve maintenance and generalization.

f. General Task Acquisition. Martin, Mithaug, and Burger (1988) examined the effects of visual cues upon task acquisition. In a Latin square design that controlled for sequence effect, 20 students from the mild, moderate, severe, and profound mentally retardation levels were exposed to (1) easy, moderate, and difficult match–sort–assemble tool-use tasks and (2) modeling, exact-size photographs, exact-size line drawings, reduced-size line drawings, and reduced-size line drawings presented in vertical rather than horizontal position. The results demonstrated significant relationships between level of mental retardation, task complexity, and the type of visual cue. In general, the visual cues were more effective than modeling for the higher functioning students working more complex tasks, but not as effective with the lower functioning students across all tasks. For simple tasks, modeling the responses to be completed was as effective as using visual cues. However, as the task difficulty increased, modeling became less effective. This relationship was strongest with students who were mildly mentally retarded, somewhat robust for those who were moderately mentally retarded, and absent for students who were in the severe and profound levels. For those students in the severe group, training in how to use visual cues appears necessary.

g. No Effect. In contrast to the studies just cited, Gow and Ward (1984) concluded that pictures may be no more effective than traditional training techniques in completing vocational-like tasks. This study examined the effects of four training methods on the acquisition and generalization of skills required to pound nails in a set pattern. Training methods included viewing (1) the actual object, (2) photographic representation, (3) both the actual item and photographs, and (4) modeling how to do the task. The results indicated that acquisition of the skill was most rapid when the completed actual object or the actual object plus pictures could be viewed. Training with the actual object maintained and generalized performance better than the use of pictures alone. The use of photographs was superior only to modeling. The Gow and Ward study raises some interesting questions about the conditions under which picture cues are most effective. For example, the task in the study was very simplistic. Perhaps as demonstrated in the Martin *et al.* (1987) study, pictures cues are more appropriate for complex tasks that involve the sequence and placement of various parts and materials.

2. SEQUENCING OF TASKS

The most frequent target behavior assessed in vocational training studies has been the sequencing of tasks in response to performance or time dimensions. For example, Connis (1979) examined performance-based task sequencing by four mildly to moderately mentally retarded adults working in a nonsheltered vocational setting. Each person worked different task sequences, requiring from 9 to 14 steps to complete each workday. The training package consisted of photographs, instruction on how to use the picture cues, and self-recording. Task photographs taped on a wall in each subject's work area depicted the sequence. At the beginning of each workday, the subjects received instructions on how to use the picture cues. This included modeling, role playing, and a rationale. When starting a task, the subject placed an "X" on a blank piece of paper located below each picture. Independent movement from one task to the next was praised, and errors were verbally corrected. Following 3 to 4 weeks of picture cue training, the trainers discontinued instruction, praise, and corrective feedback, but continued to assess performance daily. Use of pictorial cues and self-recording procedures increased all four workers' ability to change tasks independently. Unfortunately, the use of a multiple-component training package precludes determining the effectiveness of any one component.

Sowers, Rusch, Connis, and Cummings (1980) trained three moderately mentally retarded cafeteria employees time-management skills. Each worker learned when to go to lunch, return from lunch, and return from break. Following baseline, a picture time card, verbal instructions, and feedback were introduced. The time card contained four clock faces and symbols representing lunch and break times. During instruction, subjects repeatedly matched times on the card to that on a real clock until each time was matched correctly twice. During the instructional feedback phase, subjects received praise for corrective feedback for time matches. Following training, each mentally retarded worker learned to go to and from lunch and break independently. Use of the time card enabled all workers to maintain their time-management skills for 23 days, at which point one worker began to make errors. Retraining corrected the errors and, subsequently the skill was maintained. Seemingly, the picture time cards regulated the antecedent cues that, in turn, controlled the maintenance of time-management responses.

Sowers, Verdi, Bourbeau, and Sheehan (1985) provided four workers, who were mildly mentally retarded, a photo sheet depicting the order of tasks to be completed. Each man was randomly assigned to 7 of 13 vocational tasks every day. The picture cue system enabled the workers to follow frequent changes in task sequences. The picture-following skill maintained and generalized to new tasks.

Martin, Elias-Burger, and Mithaug (1988) conducted a study similar to Sowers *et al.* (1985). The focus, however, was upon following a constantly changing sequence of tasks that varied by time and order. Five adolescents in a high school program for students who are moderately mentally retarded could not follow verbal instructions to complete the required sequence of tasks. Each student was first given a written list. Picture schedules were presented when the written schedules were not effective. Three of the students were able to do the job following the written schedule. Two students were aided by the picture schedule. Withdrawal and reinstatement of the successful schedule demonstrated their effect. All students maintained their performance in the absence of trainer instruction or feedback.

3. SCHEDULING

Another method of self-managing antecedent conditions is self-scheduling. Bauman and Iwata (1977) evaluated the effects of self-scheduling and self-recording on the maintenance of dining and housekeeping skills. Two men, one mildly mentally retarded and the other of normal intelligence (but with an institutional history), were capable of performing household tasks but failed to do so. Following baseline observations, they participated in a detailed counseling session focusing on the need to prepare well-balanced meals and keep their apartment clean. This intervention had no effect on 21 target behaviors. The experimenters then gave the subjects a written schedule for their dining and housekeeping chores and requested that they check off each item upon completion of the chore. The schedule plus self-recording increased the percentage of items completed. In the next two phases, the individuals also partially and then completely self-scheduled their tasks. The combination of self-recording and self-scheduling maintained the improved behavior.

4. SUMMARY

Most of the studies reviewed used multiple-component instructional packages, which obscured the independent effects of the visual cues. A few investigations, however, have established a definitive relationship between the use of visual cues and behavior improvement (Martin *et al.*, 1982, 1987, 1988; Sarber *et al.*, 1984). Combined interventions may be more commonplace because of their presumed power. What remains, of course, is further study of the independent effects of visual cues of performance relative to the contribution of other procedures.

B. Self-Management through the Use of Self-Instructions

Blackwood (1972) indicated that speech is a verbal chaining process that yields discriminative stimuli and conditioned reinforcers. Consequently, self-verbalizations should modify motor responses by mediating between stimulus situations and target behaviors (Bem, 1967; Birch, 1966; Burron & Bucher, 1978; Bornstein & Quevillon, 1976; Lovaas, 1964; Luria, 1961). Since the pioneering work of Meichenbaum and Goodman (1969a,b, 1971), a number of studies have established verbal mediated self-control (see Goetz & Etzel, 1978; Israel, 1978; O'Leary & Dubey, 1979; Rosenbaum & Drabman, 1979; Wong, 1986, for literature reviews).

According to Karlan (1980), the research on the use of self-instruction to modify behavior began by changing verbal behavior and then observing corresponding changes in the target behavior. Later efforts trained individuals to self-instruct as a means of modifying target behaviors. These approaches assumed a direct relationship between what a person said and what he or she did. Research has also examined the relationship between what a person says and does and the procedures that improve correspondence between the two (Risley & Hart, 1968; Karlan & Rusch, 1982).

Research has, for the most part, examined the use of self-management of verbal stimuli with children and adults of normal intelligence. Fortunately, a small but growing number of research investigations have studied individuals who are mentally retarded as well. These studies have used overt and covert verbalizations and instructions.

1. OVERT VERBALIZATIONS

Overt verbalization interventions have been used across several dependent variables. This section will review these studies across the following domains: motor movements, vocational tasks, on-task behavior, academic performance, leisure skills, daily living skills, and social skills.

a. Motor Movements. Bender (1977) investigated verbally mediated motor training, which is the use of speech to guide motor responses. In this study,

32 moderately mentally retarded children (4.5 to 17 years of age) were randomly divided (controlling for sex, setting, and prevalence of Down's syndrome) into three groups (1) verbal-mediated motor training, (2) motor training, and (3) in-class control. The verbal-mediated group was trained to say the name of the action while performing the movement. For example, as the child leaps, he or she would say "leap." The motor group performed without verbalizing. The in-class control received no training. The results indicated that verbal-mediated training did not facilitate motor behavior. Perhaps the statements were not explicit enough. As might be expected, verbal mediation training enhanced verbal performance.

b. Vocational Tasks. Five studies have examined the use of overt verbalization interventions; three of these were conducted in community training sites. Wacker, Carroll, and Moe (1980) trained four children who were moderately mentally retarded to assemble paper snowmen made from three different colored-paper circles. The students were taught, through a five-step training program, to verbalize the color of the circles before assembly. Praise, graduated guidance, and repeated demonstrations were also included within the training package. The intervention enabled the students to generalize their assembly skills across time and setting into the regular classroom. Since training involved several procedures, little is known about the independent effect of self-statements.

In a sheltered setting, Agran, Salzberg, and Stowitschek (1987) investigated the effects of overt self-instruction with three moderately to severely mentally retarded sheltered workshop employees. The study employed a self-instructional training package to increase the percentage of contacts the workers made with a supervisor in order to get materials and/or assistance. The self-instructional package consisted of verbal instructions, modeling, role playing, corrective feedback, and social reinforcement. The training increased the frequency of supervisor contacts for all workers. Further, the new skills generalized across settings and maintained at acceptable levels for up to 13 weeks.

In the first study of its kind conducted at a community job site, Crouch, Rusch, and Karlan (1984) reinforced verbal statements of mildly and moderately mentally retarded employees in order to increase their speed of task completion. Following baseline, each worker received co-worker coaching on how to use a wristwatch to complete the task on time. Next, the workers were individually prompted to say when they would start and complete their task by describing how their watch or clock would look. At the halfway point, each was also instructed to say when he or she would finish. Two of the three workers increased their performance rates to above the standard level.

In a community hospital vocational training program, Agran, Fodor-Davis, and Moore (1986) used self-instruction training to improve the job-task sequencing ability of four mild to moderately mentally retarded adults. Each worker had to complete a 10- to 16-step housecleaning or food-service task sequence. Unique to this study, self-verbalizations made prior to their performance of target responses were reported. Training package components included providing of a rationale, modeling, behavioral and verbal rehearsal, corrective feedback, and praise. In addition, the detailed instruction for one worker was changed to a short verbal label. During baseline, no worker self-instructed or completed the tasks in the correct sequence. Following training, correct performance increased and was strongly associated with the number of verbal self-instructions. The ability to complete the tasks in sequence and to emit self-instructions maintained for up to 3 months. Throughout the study, performance covaried with the number of self-instructions.

In a fast-food restaurant, Rusch, Martin, Lagomarcino, and White (1987) used a say-then-do procedure to assist a moderately mentally retarded woman to sequence tasks. Prior to starting her shift, the subject was told the tasks in the order they needed to be done. The worker was requested to repeat back the jobs in order. Errors were corrected, and she was given prompts if she did not state a task within 30 seconds. Once she learned the sequence, she was also told tasks not to do. Unlike earlier studies, she was required to verbalize before starting work rather than immediately prior to doing each activity. Interestingly, during the shift she would often be heard whispering the next step that had to be completed to herself. Her performance increased to near perfect levels. The verbal statements usually covaried with her performance.

c. On-Task Behavior. In a detailed and socially validated investigation, Burgio, Whitman, and Johnson (1980) used self-statements to increase the attending behaviors of two distractible, mildly mentally retarded children. Observations of two "no problem" students determined an acceptable standard for treatment success. During baseline, the experimenters observed the children during math, printing, and phonics tasks. During self-instruction training, the children were taught to verbally state needed rules. Next, attempts were made to distract the children from their tasks and verbal statements. Although the verbal self-instructions decreased off-task behavior, there were no effects on printing or phonics tasks. Math performance slightly increased.

Whitman, Scibak, Butler, Richter, and Johnson (1982) explored the use of correspondence training in three experiments. In Study one, overt self-instructions and contingent reward decreased the out-of-seat behavior of a mildly mentally retarded girl. The girl verbally stated at the start of each session that she was going to stay in her seat. If she did, this was acknowledged and she was rewarded. Out-of-seat behavior decreased and the results maintained at an 8-month follow-up check. In Study two, the same intervention increased the sitting posture of four boys who were mildly mentally retarded. The results generalized from math class to writing class, and the maintenance procedures transferred from the experimenters to the teacher. In Study three, the on-task behavior of three nonverbal mentally retarded children was improved. Since the children could not say all the steps involved in being on task, the procedure was modified so that each child could show what they were going to do. As before, if at the end of the observation period each child did what he or she said they were going to do, rewards were provided.

d. Academic Performance. Two studies have examined the use of overt instructions to improve academic skills. First, Albion and Salzberg (1982) assessed the effects of task-specific self-instructions on the rates of correct and incorrect math performance of five mildly to moderately mentally retarded children. The children were trained to verbalize task-specific self-instructions and score their own worksheets. Daily scores were displayed on charts. Math performance improved for all but one student. Again, the effects of self-instruction training or self-evaluation could not be isolated.

Second, Wacker and Greenebaum (1984) used "self-labeling" to improve performance on a shape-sorting task; 7 students who were moderately to severely mentally retarded and ranged in age from 19 to 22 years old participated in the investigation. The students received verbal and nonverbal training sequences. During nonverbal training, the correct sorting responses were demonstrated and contingent praise or error correction followed each response. During verbal training, each subject was taught to say the name of the shape of the initial card and then to sort all cards by shape. Both approaches enabled the students to acquire the skill; however, only the verbal labeling procedure enabled the students to generalize their performance to a novel shape and a new dimension.

e. Leisure Skills. Keogh, Faw, Whitman, and Reid (1984) taught complex game playing skills to two youths who were severely mentally retarded. The training package consisted of instructions, modeling, prompting, contingent praise, and verbalizations of game steps in a forward chaining procedure. Although the separate effects of the self-verbalizations were not evident, the boys did learn to self-instruct independently. The authors indicated that the self-statements were a crucial part of the training package. Although the two boys learned to play three games, they failed to generalize these skills to new games.

f. Daily Living Skills. Alberto, Sharpton, Briggs, and Stright (1986) used recorded verbal prompts to facilitate performance. Four high school students who were severely mentally retarded used a "Walkman" tape player to complete two of the following tasks: (1) operating a washing machine, (2) preparing a sandwich and a cup of soup, or (3) assembling a multipiece pipe unit. The tape provided verbal prompts needed to complete the tasks at appropriately timed intervals. At specific points in the tape, the verbal prompts directed the students to stop the activity, survey the materials, and determine the accuracy of completed steps. The recorded prompts enabled the four students to acquire the new skills and to perform without the use of the tape player.

g. Social Skills. Ralph and Birnbrauer (1986) used correspondence training to increase appropriate entry and exit behavior of three mild to moderately mentally retarded men. A social-skill training package consisting of role playing and verbal and video feedback served as the baseline condition. Next, correspondence training was used on one entry and one exit behavior. Each subject met with the researchers to state that he would perform the specific target behavior at the generalization location. The next night, each subject was asked to report their behavior and a trainer provided feedback on the accuracy of the report. Accurate reports were reinforced. In contrast to the results from social-skill training, correspondence training was more successful in improving the targeted skills, the behavior generalized from a treatment room to another room in the subjects' hostel, and it was maintained over time. The subjects also accurately reported their behavior.

2. COVERT INSTRUCTIONS

In comparison to overt instructional interventions, fewer studies have examined the use of covert self-instruction interventions by individuals who are mentally retarded. These studies will be reviewed across general task acquisition, academic skills, and vocational performance.

a. General Task Acquisition. In an early study, Guralnick (1976) compared the effectiveness of instructional feedback, modeling, self-instruction, and a control condition in learning a matching-to-sample task (nonsense line drawings). The self-instruction group used the general strategy developed by Meichenbaum and Goodman (1971), which involved fading a series of instructions and prompts (modeling and feedback) from speaking aloud (overt) to speaking internally (covert). Subjects in the modeling group observed the same verbalizations and behavior, but did not receive self-instruction training. The feedback group was asked to solve the matching-to-sample problems and were provided feedback on accuracy. The control group received no training. Although all groups performed at similar levels on the pretest, the self-instructional group far surpassed the other three conditions. On subsequent tests, including a generalization probe, self-instruction training was superior to the other groups as well. It appears that self-instruction focused attention skills, thereby facilitating the selection of relevant cues. Teaching the child to verbalize the problem-solving techniques as the problem is being solved apparently assists in developing correspondence.

b. Academic Skills. Johnston, Whitman, and Johnson (1980) examined the use of a self-instruction program for training addition and subtraction skills in 3-, 9-, and 10-year-old mildly mentally retarded children. Each worked a total of 30 single- and double-digit addition and subtraction problems presented randomly each day. During baseline, each child received feedback on their previous day's work. Next, they received 20- to 30-minute self-instructional training sessions based upon the procedures outlined by Meichenbaum and Goodman (1971). During overt verbalization each student was shaped to say each math step. A food reward along with verbal praise was given upon successful verbalization. The self-instruction strategy was successful. Although math performance was not directly assessed in the classroom, subjective teacher reports indicated that all children improved their math computation skills in their home classrooms. The authors noted that "having the child verbalize the self-instruction as he or she works a problem allows the teacher to quickly diagnose the child's difficulty and to focus remediation efforts at the specific point of difficulty" (Johnston *et al.*, 1980, p. 158).

c. Vocational Performance. Rusch, Morgan, Martin, Riva, and Agran (1985) examined the effects of self-instruction training on two mildly to moderately mentally retarded individuals. First, brief, massed-trial self-instruction periods were used rather than the typical spaced lessons. Second, the performance of nonhandicapped co-workers provided a standard to validate treatment goals and procedures. The percentage of 10-second intervals during which the two handicapped workers and their nonhandicapped co-workers were working was assessed. Each worker received only two 30-minute sessions before the lunch and dinner rushes. During baseline, the two handicapped workers were working below the rates of their nonhandicapped co-workers. After training, the handicapped workers either equaled or surpassed their co-workers' performance levels.

3. SUMMARY

The research conducted to date suggests that self-managed antecedent cues can enable individuals who are mentally retarded to improve their own behavior. Changes have been demonstrated across a variety of settings and a wide range of behaviors. Unlike the self-monitoring, self-reinforcement, and visual cue strategies, many have raised concerns about self-verbalization research (see Bornstein, 1985; Billings & Wasik, 1985; Martin & Mithaug, 1986, for addition discussion). Bender (1977) reported that verbal mediation did not produce greater gains than traditional approaches. Likewise, Burgio *et al.* (1980) noted little increase in performance across several measures. As suggested by Karlan and Rusch (1982), it is possible that the procedures will be more effective when the person is reinforced for first saying and then carrying out the target behavior.

VII. General Conclusions

The common theme of this review has been a focus on the use of self-control procedures to enable individuals who are mentally retarded to become more independent. Self-monitoring, self-administered and self-determined reinforcers, and self-managed antecendent cues have had a significant impact upon a variety of behaviors in the laboratory, classroom, and work setting. Maintenance and generalization checks were reported in 49% of the studies reviewed (see Fig. 3). In almost all cases the self-control strategy helped achieve maintenance and/or generalization. Interestingly, in the few studies that compared self-control strategies to traditional intervention, the self-control strategies were more successful than trainer-based traditional approaches.

Nevertheless, many questions remain to be answered regarding the separate effects of these procedure. First, what are the relative contributions of each procedure involved in various packages? Under what conditions is each of these procedures most effective? What are the precise factors involved in obtaining changes in behavior? Second, are combined procedures more effective than a single approach? Third, to what extent does learning these procedures generalize to other situations in which mentally retarded individuals must adapt? Fourth, can special education teachers, job coaches, residential staff, and other service providers develop and implement these procedures?

The work by a few researchers provides guidelines to help address these questions. The systematic line of work conducted by Wacker and associates, which has examined the use of picture cues, represents an excellent model for other self-control researchers to follow. Their studies demonstrated the efficacy of visual cues to facilitate maintenance and generalization across

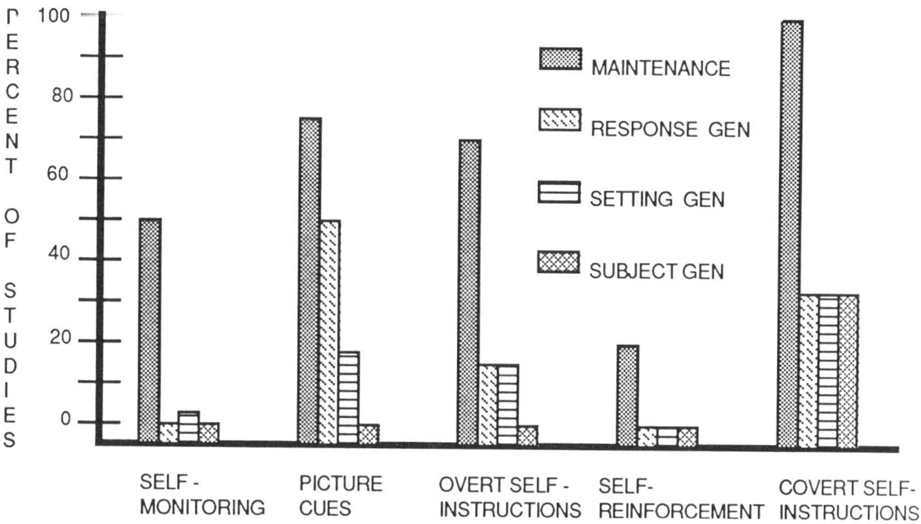

FIG. 3. Percentage of total studies by self-control strategy that included maintenance and/or generalization checks.

several dependent variables and to help individuals with mental retardation learn to learn. The self-control studies completed by Stevenson and Fantuzzo (1984, 1986) with underachieving school children represent the most complex and, we believe, the most interesting recent self-control research. They combined goal setting, self-evaluation, and self-reinforcement to increase the children's math performance, and the results generalized across 15 different generalization classes. Replication of their approach in combination with other components of Mithaug and co-workers' (1987) Adaptability Model is needed.

Rather than continue to use intervention approaches within community-based programs that often promote dependency, alternative strategies need to be considered. Adaptability instruction, which is based upon the use of self-control strategies, appears to be a means to help individuals with mental retardation become more independent. Infusion of self-control interventions within educational, vocational, and residential programs may help individuals who are mentally retarded become more a part of their community.

ACKNOWLEDGMENT

Preparation of this review was supported in part by a transition strategy research grant from the U.S. Office of Education, Office of Special Education and Rehabilitative Services (grant number G00A8430124).

REFERENCES

Ackerman, A. M., & Shapiro, E. S. (1984). Self-monitoring and work productivity with mentally retarded adults. *Journal of Applied Behavior Analysis,* **17**, 403–407.

Agran, M., Fodor-Davis, J., & Moore, S. (1986). The effects of self-instructional training on job-task sequencing: Suggesting a problem-solving strategy. *Education and Training of the Mentally Retarded,* **21**, 273–281.

Agran, M., & Martin, J. E. (1987). Self-control procedures with mentally retarded individuals. In M. Hersen, R. M. Eisler, & P. M. Miller (Eds.), *Progress in behavior modification* (Vol. 14, pp. 108–151). Newbury Park, California: Sage.

Agran, M., Salzberg, C. L., & Stowitschek, J. J. (1987). An analysis of the effects of a social skill training program using self-instructions on the acquisition and generalization of two social behaviors in a work setting. *Journal of the Association for Persons with Severe Handicaps,* **12**, 131–139.

Alberto, P. A., Sharpton, W. R., Briggs, A. H., & Stright, M. H. (1986). Facilitating task acquisition through the use of a self-operated auditory prompting system. *Journal of the Association for Persons with Severe Handicaps,* **11**, 85–91.

Albion, F. M., & Salzberg, C. L. (1982). The effect of self-instructions on the rate of correct addition problems with mentally retarded children. *Education and Treatment of Children,* **5**, 121–131.

Baer, P. M. (1984). Does research on self-control need more control? *Analysis and Intervention in Developmental Disabilities,* **4**, 211–218.

Bandura, A. (1969). *Principles of behavior modification.* New York: Holt.

Bandura, A. (1976). Self-reinforcement: Theoretical and methodological considerations. *Behaviorism,* **4**, 135–156.

Bandura, A., & Kupers, C. J. (1964). Transmission of self-reinforcement through modeling. *Journal*

of Abnormal and Social Psychology, **69**, 1–9.
Bates, P., Renzaglia, A., & Clees, T. (1980). Improving the work performance of severely/profoundly retarded young adults: The use of a changing criterion procedural design. *Education and Training of the Mentally Retarded,* **15**, 95–104.
Bauman, K. E., & Iwata, B. A. (1977). Maintenance of independent housekeeping skills using scheduling plus self-recording procedures. *Behavior Therapy,* **8**, 554–560.
Bem, S. L. (1967). Verbal self-control: The establishment of effective self-instruction. *Journal of Experimental Psychology,* **74**, 485–491.
Bender, N. N. (1977). Verbal mediation as an instructional technique with young trainable mentally retarded children. *Journal of Special Education,* **11**, 449–455.
Billings, D. C., & Wasik, B. H. (1985). Self-instructional training with preschoolers: An attempt to replicate. *Journal of Applied Behavior Analysis,* **18**, 61–67.
Birch, D. (1966). Verbal control of non-verbal behavior. *Journal of Experimental Child Psychology,* **4**, 266–275.
Blackwood, R. O. (1972). *Mediated self-control: An operant model of rational behavior.* Akron, Ohio: Exordium Press.
Bornstein, P. H. (1985). Self-instructional training: A commentary and state-of-the-art. *Journal of Applied Behavior Analysis,* **18**, 69–72.
Bornstein, P. H., & Quevillon, R. P. (1976). The effects of a self-instructional package on overactive preschool boys. *Journal of Applied Behavior Analysis,* **9**, 179–188.
Brigham, T. A. (1983). Self-management: A radical behavioral perspective. In P. Karoly & F. Kanfer (Eds.), *Self-management and behavior change* (pp. 32–59). New York: Pergamon.
Browder, D. M., & Shapiro, E. S. (1985). Applications of self-management to individuals with severe handicaps: A review. *The Journal of the Association for Persons with Severe Handicaps,* **10**, 200–208.
Brown, L., Ford, A., Nisbet, J., Sweet, M., Shiraga, B., York, J., & Loomis, R. (1983). The critical need for nonschool instruction in educational programs for severely handicapped students. *Journal of the Association for the Severely Handicapped,* **8**, 71–77.
Burgio, L. D., Whitman, T. L., & Johnson, M. R. (1980). A self-instructional package for increasing attending behavior in educable mentally retarded children. *Journal of Applied Behavior Analysis,* **13**, 443–459.
Burron, D., & Bucher, B. (1978). Self-instructions as discriminative cues for rule-breaking or rule-following. *Journal of Experimental Child Psychology,* **26**, 46–57.
Chiron, R., & Gerken, K. (1983). The effects of a self-monitoring technique on the locus of control orientation of educable mentally retarded children. *School Psychology Review,* **3**, 87–92.
Cole, C. L., & Gardner, W. I. (1984). Self-management training. *Psychiatric Aspects of Mental Retardation Reviews,* **3**, 17–20.
Coleman, R. S., & Whitman, T. L. (1984). Developing, generalizing, and maintaining physical fitness in mentally retarded adults toward a self-directed program. *Analysis and Intervention in Developmental Disabilities,* **4**, 109–127.
Connis, R. T. (1979). The effects of sequential pictorial cues, self-recording, and praise on the job task sequencing of retarded adults. *Journal of Applied Behavior Analysis,* **12**, 355–361.
Crouch, K. P., Rusch, F. R., & Karlan, G. R. (1984). Competitive employment: Utilizing the correspondence training paradigm to enhance productivity. *Education and Training of the Mentally Retarded,* **19**, 268–275.
Dewey, J. (1939). *Experience and education.* New York: Macmillan.
Fisher, M. K. (1984). Vocational assembly skills using isometric projection exploded view assembly drawings for mentally handicapped students. *Education and Training of the Mentally Retarded,* **19**, 285–290.
Frank, A. R., Wacker, D. P., Berg, W. K., & McMahon, C. M. (1985). Teaching selected microcomputer skills to retarded students via picture prompts. *Journal of Applied Behavior Analysis,* **18**, 179–185.

Gardner, W. I., Clees, T. J., & Cole, C. (1983a). Self-management of disruptive verbal ruminations by a mentally retarded adult. *Applied Research in Mental Retardation,* **4**, 41–58.

Gardner, W. I., Cole, C., Berry, D., & Nowinski, J. (1983b). Reduction of disruptive behaviors in mentally retarded adults. *Behavior Modification*, **7**, 76–96.

Gifford, J. L., Rusch, F. R., Martin, J. E., & White, D. M. (1984). Autonomy and adaptability in work behavior of mentally retarded clients. In N. R. Ellis & N. W. Bray (Eds.), *International review of research in mental retardation* (Vol. 12, pp. 285–318). Orlando, Florida: Academic Press.

Goetz, E. M., & Etzel, B. C. (1978). A brief review of self-control procedures: Problems and solutions. *Behavior Therapist,* **1**, 5–8.

Goldiamond, I. (1965). Self-control procedures in personal behavior problems. *Psychological Reports,* **17**, 851–868.

Goldfried, M. R., & Merbaum, M. (1973). A perspective on self-control. In M. R. Goldfried & M. Merbaum (Eds.), *Behavior change through self-control* (pp. 3–36). New York: Holt.

Gow, L., & Ward, J. (1984). The use of photographs as stimulus materials in programming for generalization with mentally retarded persons. *Australia and New Zealand Journal of Developmental Disabilities,* **10**, 69–79.

Guess, D., Benson, H. A., & Siegel-Causey, E. (1985). Concepts and issues related to choice-making and autonomy among persons with severe disabilities. *Journal of the Association for Persons with Severe Handicaps,* **10**, 79–86.

Guess, D., & Siegel-Causey, E. (1985). Behavioral control and education of severely handicapped students: Who's doing what to whom? and why? In D. Bricker & J. Filler (Eds.), *Severe mental retardation: From theory to practice* (pp. 230–244). Reston, Virginia: Council for Exceptional Children.

Guralnick, M. J. (1976). Solving complex perceptual discrimination problems: Techniques for the development of problem-solving strategies. *American Journal of Mental Deficiency,* **81**, 18–25.

Halpern, A. S. (1985). Transition: A look at the foundations. *Exceptional Children,* **51**, 479–486.

Hanel, F., & Martin, G. (1980). Self-monitoring, self-administration of token reinforcement, and goal-setting to improve work rates with retarded clients. *International Journal of Rehabilitation Research,* **3**, 505–517.

Harvey, J. R., Karan, O. C., Bhargava, D., & Morehouse, N. (1978). Relaxation training and cognitive behavioral procedures to reduce violent temper outbursts in a moderately mentally retarded woman. *Journal of Behavior Therapy and Experimental Psychiatry,* **9**, 347–351.

Hayes, S. C., & Cavior, N. (1977). Multiple tracking and the reactivity of self-monitoring. *Behavior Therapy,* **8**, 819–831.

Haywood, H. C., & Switzky, H. N. (1985). Work response of mildly mentally retarded adults to self- versus external regulation as a function of motivational orientation. *American Journal of Mental Deficiency,* **90**, 151–159.

Helland, C. D., Paluck, R. J., & Klein, M. (1976). A comparison of self- and external reinforcement with the trainable mentally retarded. *Mental Retardation,* **14**, 22–23.

Horner, R., & Brigham, T. A. (1979). The effects of self-management procedures on the study behavior of two retarded children. *Education and Training of the Mentally Retarded,* **14**, 18–24.

Howell, K. W., Rueda, R., & Rutherford, R. B., Jr. (1983). A procedure for teaching self-recording to moderately retarded students. *Psychology in the Schools,* **20**, 202–209.

Israel, A. C. (1978). Some thoughts on correspondence between saying and doing. *Journal of Applied Behavior Analysis,* **11**, 271–276.

Jeffery, D. B. (1974). Self-control: Methodological issues and research trends. In M. J. Mahoney & C. E. Thoresen (Eds.), *Self-control: Power to the person* (pp. 166–199). Monterey, California: Brooks/Cole.

Johnson, B. F., & Cuvo, A. J. (1981). Teaching mentally retarded adults to cook. *Behavior Modification,* **5**, 187–202.

Johnston, M. B., Whitman, T. L., & Johnson, M. (1980). Teaching addition and subtraction to mentally retarded children: A self-instruction program. *Applied Research in Mental Retardation,* **1**, 141–159.

Jones, R. T., Nelson, R. E., & Kazdin, A. E. (1977). The role of external variables in self-reinforcement. *Behavior Modification,* **1**, 147–178.

Kanfer, F. H. (1975). Self-management methods. In F. H. Kanfer & A. P. Goldstein (Eds.), *Helping people change* (1st ed., pp. 309–355). New York: Pergamon.

Kanfer, F. H. (1980). Self-management methods. In F. H. Kanfer & A. P. Goldstein (Eds.), *Helping people change* (2nd ed., pp. 334–389). New York: Pergamon.

Kanfer, F. H., Bradley, M. M., & Marston, A. R. (1962). Self-reinforcement as a function of degree of learning. *Psychological Reports,* **10**, 885–886.

Karlan, G. R. (1980). Issues in communication research related to integration of developmentally disabled individuals. In L. W. Heal & A. R. Novak (Eds.), *Integration of developmentally disabled individuals into the community* (pp. 121–137). Baltimore: Brookes.

Karlan, G. R., & Rusch, F. R. (1982). Correspondence between saying and doing: Some thoughts on defining correspondence and future directions for application. *Journal of Applied Behavior Analysis,* **15**, 151–162.

Kazdin, A. E. (1974). Self-monitoring and behavior change. In M. J. Mahoney & C. E. Thoresen (Eds.), *Self-control: Power to the person* (pp. 218–246). Monterey, California: Brooks/Cole.

Kazdin, A. E. (1980). *Behavior modification in applied settings* (2nd ed.). Homewood, Illinois: Dorsey.

Keogh, D. A., Faw, G. D., Whitman, T. L., & Reid, D. H. (1984). Enhancing leisure skills in severely retarded adolescents through a self-instructional treatment package. *Analysis and Intervention in Developmental Disabilities,* **4**, 333–351.

Knapczyk, D. R., & Livingston, G. (1973). Self-recording and student teacher supervision: Variables within a token economy structure. *Journal of Applied Behavior Analysis,* **6**, 481–486.

Kurtz, P. D., & Neisworth, J. T. (1976). Self-control possibilities for exceptional children. *Exceptional Children,* **42**, 212–217.

Liberty, K. A., & Michael, L. J. (1985). Teaching retarded students to reinforce their own behavior. A review of process and operation in the current literature. In N. Haring (Ed.), *Investigating the problem of skill generalization* (3rd ed., pp. 88–106). Seattle: University of Washington, College of Education.

Litrownik, A. J., Cleary, C. P., Lecklitner, G. L., & Franzini, L. R. (1978). Self-regulation in retarded persons: Acquisition of standards for performance. *American Journal of Mental Deficiency,* **83**, 86–89.

Litrownik, A. J., & Freitas, J. L. (1980). Self-monitoring in moderately retarded adolescents: Reactivity and accuracy as a function of valence. *Behavior Therapy,* **11**, 245–255.

Litrownik, A. J., Freitas, J. L., & Franzini, L. T. (1978). Self-regulation in mentally retarded children: Assessment and training of self-monitoring skills. *American Journal of Mental Deficiency,* **82**, 499–506.

Long, J. D., & Williams, R. L. (1979). The utility of self-management procedures in modifying the classroom behaviors of mentally retarded adolescents. *Adolescence,* **11**, 29–38.

Lovaas, O. I. (1964). Cue properties of words: The control of operant responding by rate and content of verbal operants. *Child Development,* **35**, 245–256.

Luria, A. R. (1961). *The role of speech in regulation of normal and abnormal behavior.* New York: Liveright.

Mace, F. C., Shapiro, E. S., West, B. J., Campbell, C., & Altman, J. (1986). The role of reinforcement in reactive self-monitoring. *Applied Research in Mental Retardation,* **7**, 315–327.

Mahoney, M. J., & Thoresen, C. E. (1974). *Self-control: Power to the person.* Monterey, California: Brooks/Cole.

Marston, A. R. (1964). Variables affecting incidence of self-reinforcement. *Psychological Reports,* **14**, 879–884.

Martin, J. E. (1983). *Time-setting generalization assessment of mentally retarded adults' acquired self-control in the preparation of complex meals after withdrawal of training components and trainers.* Unpublished doctoral dissertation, University of Illinois, Champaign.

Martin, J. E., Elias-Burger, S., & Mithaug, D. E. (1987). Acquisition and maintenance of time-based task change sequence. *Education and Training of the Mentally Retarded,* **22**, 250–255.

Martin, J. E., & Mithaug, D. E. (1986). Advancing a technology of self-control. *British Columbia Journal of Special Education,* **10**, 93–100.

Martin, J. E., Mithaug, D. E., & Burger, D. L. (1988). *Effects of picture cue types across levels of mental retardation and by difficulty of task.* Manuscript submitted for publication. Colorado Springs: University of Colorado.

Martin, J. E., & Rusch, F. R. (1987). Use of a partial-sequential withdrawal design to assess maintenance of acquired meal preparation skills. *Applied Research in Developmental Disabilities,* **8**, 389–399.

Martin, J. E., Rusch, F. R., James, Y. L., Decker, P. J., & Trtol, K. A. (1982). The use of picture cues to establish self-control in the preparation of complex meals by mentally retarded adults. *Applied Research in Mental Retardation,* **3**, 105–119.

Matson, J. L. (1980). Preventing home accidents: A training program for the retarded. *Behavior Modification,* **4**, 379–410.

Matson, J. L. (1981). Use of independence training to teach shopping skills to mildly mentally retarded adults. *American Journal of Mental Deficiency,* **86**, 178–183.

Matson, J. L., & Andrasik, F. (1982). Training leisure-time social interactions skills to mentally retarded adults. *American Journal of Mental Deficiency,* **86**, 533–542.

Matson, J. L., & Long, S. (1986). Teaching computation/shopping skills to mentally retarded adults. *American Journal of Mental Deficiency,* **91**, 98–101.

Matson, J. L., & Marchetti, A. (1980). A comparison of leisure skills training procedures for the mentally retarded. *Applied Research in Mental Retardation,* **1**, 113–122.

Matson, J. L., Marchetti, A., & Adkins, J. A. (1980). Comparison of operant and independence training procedures for mentally retarded adults. *American Journal of Mental Deficiency,* **84**, 487–494.

McNally, R. J., Kompik, J. J., & Sherman, G. (1984). Increasing the productivity of mentally retarded workers through self-management. *Analysis and Intervention in Developmental Disabilities,* **4**, 129–135.

McNally, R. J., Norusis, P. L., Gentz, S. A., & McConathy, L. C. (1983). Use of self-delivered reinforcement and group contingency management to increase productivity of severely retarded workers. *Psychological Reports,* **52**, 499–503.

Meichenbaum, D., & Goodman, J. (1969a). The developmental control of operant motor responding by verbal operants. *Journal of Experimental Child Psychology,* **7**, 553–565.

Meichenbaum, D., & Goodman, J. (1969b). Reflection-impulsivity and verbal control of motor behavior. *Child Development,* **40**, 785–797.

Meichenbaum, D., & Goodman, J. (1971). Training impulsive children to talk to themselves: A means of developing self-control. *Journal of Abnormal Psychology,* **77**, 116–126.

Mithaug, D. E., & Martin, J. E. (1988). *Why special education graduates fail. How to teach them to succeed.* Colorado Springs, Colorado: Ascent Publications.

Mithaug, D. E., Martin, J. E., & Agran, M. (1988). Adaptability instruction: The goal of transitional programming. *Exceptional Children,* in press.

Morgan, W. G., & Bass, B. A. (1973). Self-control through self-mediated rewards. In R. D. Rubin, J. P. Brady, & J. D. Henderson (Eds.), *Advances in behavior therapy* (Vol. 4, pp. 117–126). New York: Academic Press.

Morrow, L. W., Burke, J. G., & Buell, B. J. (1985). Effects of a self-recording procedure on the attending to task behavior and academic productivity of adolescents with multiple handicaps. *Mental Retardation,* **23**, 137–141.

Nelson, R. O. (1977). Assessment and therapeutic functions of self-monitoring. In M. Hersen, R. M. Miller, & P. M. Miller (Eds.), *Progress in behavior modification* (Vol. 5, pp. 263–307). New York: Academic Press.

Nelson, R. O., Lipinski, D. P., & Black, J. L. (1976). The reactivity of adult retardates, self-monitoring: A comparison among behaviors of difference valences, and a comparison with token reinforcement. *The Psychological Record,* **26**, 189–201.

Nelson, R. O., Lipinski, D. P., & Boykin, R. A. (1978). The effects of self-recording training and the obtrusiveness of the self-recording device on the accuracy and reactivity of self-monitoring. *Behavior Therapy,* **9**, 200–208.

O'Leary, S. G., & Dubey, D. R. (1979). Applications of self-control procedures by children: A review. *Journal of Applied Behavior Analysis,* **12**, 449–465.

O'Leary, S. G., & O'Leary, K. D. (1976). Behavior modification in the school. In H. Leitenberg (Ed.), *Handbook of behavior modification and behavior therapy* (pp. 475–515). New York: Prentice-Hall.

Ortega, D. F., Schultz, J. K., & Sanders, R. M. (1976). The use of social reinforcement to increase productivity and develop self-monitoring skills in a mentally retarded assembly-line worker. *Vocational Evaluation and Work Adjustment Bulletin,* **9**, 8–13.

Ralph, A., & Birnbrauer, J. S. (1986). The potential of correspondence training for facilitating generalisation of social skills. *Applied Research in Mental Retardation,* **7**, 415–429.

Reese, R. M., Sherman, J. A., & Sheldon, J. (1984). Reducing agitated-disruptive behavior of mentally retarded residents of community group homes: The role of self-recording and peer-prompted self-recording. *Analysis and Intervention in Developmental Disabilities,* **4**, 91–107.

Reynolds, G. S. (1968). *A primer of operant conditioning.* Glenview, Illinois. Scott, Foresman.

Risley, T. R., & Hart, B. (1968). Developing correspondence between the non-verbal and verbal behavior of pre-school children. *Journal of Applied Behavior Analysis,* **1**, 267–281.

Robertson, S. J., Simon, S. J., Pachman, J. S., & Drabman, R. S. (1979). Self-control and generalization procedures in a classroom of disruptive retarded children. *Child Behavior Therapy,* **1**, 347–362.

Robinson-Wilson, A. (1977). Picture recipe cards as an approach to teaching severely and profoundly retarded adults to cook. *Education and Training of the Mentally Retarded,* **12**, 69–73.

Rosenbaum, M. S., & Drabman, R. S. (1979). Self-control training in the classroom: A review and critique. *Journal of Applied Behavior Analysis,* **12**, 467–485.

Rosine, L. P., & Martin, G. L. (1983). Self-management training to decrease undesirable behavior of mentally handicapped adults. *Rehabilitation Psychology,* **28**, 195–205.

Rudrud, E. H., Rice, J. M., Robertson, J. M., & Olson, N. M. (1984). The use of self-monitoring to increase and maintain production rates. *Vocational Evaluation and Work Adjustment Bulletin,* **17**, 14–17.

Rudrud, E. H., Ziarnik, J. P., & Colman, G. (1984). Reduction of tongue protrusion of a 24-year-old woman with Downs Syndrome through self-monitoring. *American Journal of Mental Deficiency,* **88**, 647–652.

Rusch, F. R., Martin, J. E., Lagomarcino, T. R., & White, D. M. (1987). Teaching task sequencing via verbal mediation in a competitive employment setting. *Education and Training of the Mentally Retarded*, **22**, 229–235.

Rusch, F. R., Martin, J. E., & White, D. M. (1985). Competitive employment: Teaching mentally retarded employees to maintain their work behavior. *Education and Training of the Mentally Retarded,* **20**, 182–189.

Rusch, F. R., & Mithaug, D. E. (1980). *Vocational training for mentally retarded adults.* Champaign, Illinois: Research Press.

Rusch, F. R., Morgan, T. K., Martin, J. E., Riva, M., & Agran, M. (1985). Competitive employment: Teaching mentally retarded adults self-instruction strategies. *Applied Research in Mental Retardation,* **6**, 389–407.

Sarber, R. E., Halasz, M. M., Messmer, M. C., Bickett, A. D., and Lutzker, J. R. (1983). Teaching menu planning and grocery shopping skills to a mentally retarded mother. *Mental Retardation,* **21**, 101–106.

Shafer, M. S., & Brooke, V. (1984). The development of punctuality in a mentally retarded worker through self-recording. In P. Wehman & J. W. Hill (Eds.), *Competitive employment for persons with mental retardation* (pp. 265–297). Richmond, Virginia: Rehabilitation Research and Training Center.

Shapiro, E. S. (1981). Self-control procedures with the mentally retarded. In M. Hersen, R. M. Eisler, & P. M. Miller (Eds.), *Progress in behavior modification* (Vol. 12, pp. 265–297). New York: Academic Press.

Shapiro, E. S., & Ackerman, A. (1983). Increasing productivity rates in adult mentally retarded clients: The failure of self-monitoring. *Applied Research in Mental Retardation,* **4**, 163–181.

Shapiro, E. S., Browder, D. M., & D'Hyvetters, K. L. (1984). Increasing academic productivity of severely multi-handicapped children with self-management: Idiosyncratic effects. *Analysis and Intervention in Developmental Disabilities,* **4**, 171–188.

Shapiro, E. S., & Klein, R. D. (1980). Self-management of classroom behavior with retarded/disturbed children. *Behavior Modification,* **4**, 83–97.

Shapiro, E. S., McGonigle, J. J., & Ollendick, T. H. (1980). An analysis of self-assessment and self-reinforcement in a self-managed token economy with mentally retarded children. *Applied Research in Mental Retardation,* **1**, 227–240.

Skinner, B. F. (1953). *Science and human behavior.* New York: Macmillan.

Skinner, B. F. (1974). *About behaviorism.* New York: Knopf.

Sohn, D., & Lamal, P. A. (1982). Self-reinforcement its reinforcing capability and its clinical utility. *The Psychological Record,* **32**, 179–203.

Sowers, J. A., Rusch, F. R., Connis, R. T., & Cummings, L. E. (1980). Teaching mentally retarded adults to time-manage in a vocational setting. *Journal of Applied Behavior Analysis,* **13**, 119–128.

Sowers, J. A., Verdi, M., Bourbeau, P., & Sheehan, M. (1985). Teaching job independence and flexibility to mentally retarded students through the use of a self-control package. *Journal of Applied Behavior Analysis,* **18**, 81–85.

Stainback, W., Stainback, S., Nietupski, J., & Hamre-Nietupski, S. (1986). Establishing effective community-based training stations. In F. R. Rusch (Ed.), *Competitive employment issues and strategies* (pp. 103–113). Baltimore: Brookes.

Stevenson, H. C., & Fantuzzo, J. W. (1984). Application of the "generalization map" to a self-control intervention with school-aged retarded students through the use of a self-control package. *Journal of Applied Behavior Analysis,* **18**, 81–85.

Stainback, W., Stainback, S., Nietupski, J., & Hamre-Nietupski, S. (1986). Establishing effective community-based training stations. In F. R. Rusch (Ed.), *Competitive employment issues and strategies* (pp. 103–113). Baltimore: Brookes.

Stevenson, H. C., & Fantuzzo, J. W. (1984). Application of the "generalization map" to a self-control intervention with school-aged children. *Journal of Applied Behavior Analysis,* **17**, 203–212.

Stevenson, H. C., & Fantuzzo, J. W. (1986). The generality and social validity of a competency-based self-control training intervention for underachieving students. *Journal of Applied Behavior Analysis,* **19**, 269–276.

Sugai, G., & Rowe, P. (1984). The effect of self-recording on out-of-seat behavior of an EMR student. *Education and Training of the Mentally Retarded,* **19**, 23–28.

Switzky, H. N., & Haywood, H. C. (1974). Motivational orientation and the relative efficacy of self-monitored and externally imposed reinforcement systems in children. *Journal of Personality & Social Psychology,* **30**, 360–366.

Thoresen, C. E., & Mahoney, M. J. (1974). *Behavioral self-control.* New York: Holt.

Wacker, D., & Berg, W. (1983). Effects of picture prompts on the acquisition of complex vocational tasks by mentally retarded adolescents. *Journal of Applied Behavior Analysis,* **16**, 417–443.

Wacker, D., & Berg, W. N. (1984a). Training adolescents with severe handicaps to set up job tasks independently using picture prompts. *Analysis and Intervention in Developmental Disabilities,* **4**, 353–365.

Wacker, D., & Berg, W. N. (1984b). *The effectiveness of peer instruction for training use of picture prompts on complex vocational tasks.* Paper presented at the National Association for Persons with Severe Handicaps Conference, Chicago.

Wacker, D. P., Berg, W. K., Berrie, P., & Swalta, P. (1985). Generalization and maintenance of complex skills by severely handicapped adolescents following picture prompt training. *Journal of Applied Behavior Analysis,* **18**, 329–336.

Wacker, D. P., Carroll, J. L., & Moe, G. L. (1980). Acquisition, generalization, and maintenance of an assembly task by mentally retarded children. *American Journal of Mental Deficiency,* **85**, 286–290.

Wacker, D. P., & Greenebaum, F. T. (1984). Efficacy of a verbal training sequence on the sorting performance of moderately and severely mentally retarded adolescents. *American Journal of Mental Deficiency,* **88**, 653–660.

Wehman, P. (1975). Behavioral self-control with the mentally retarded. *Journal of Applied Rehabilitation Counseling,* **6**, 27–34.

Wehman, P. H., Kregel, J., Barcus, J. M., & Schalock, R. L. (1986). Vocational transition for students with developmental disabilities. In W. E. Kiernan & J. A. Stark (Eds.), *Pathways to employment for adults with developmental disabilities.* (pp. 113–127). Baltimore: Brookes.

Wehman, P., Schulz, R., Bates, P., Renzaglia, A., & Karan, O. (1978). Self-management programs with mentally retarded workers: Implications for developing independent vocational behavior. *British Journal of Social and Clinical Psychology,* **17**, 57–64.

Whitman, T. L., Scibak, J. W., Butler, K. M., Richter, R., & Johnson, M. R. (1982). Improving classroom behavior in mentally retarded children through correspondence training. *Journal of Applied Behavior Analysis,* **15**, 545–564.

Wong, B. Y. L. (1986). Metacognition and special education: A review and a view. *The Journal of Special Education,* **20**, 9–29.

Workman, E. D. (1982). *Teaching behavioral self-control to students.* Austin, Texas: Pro-Ed.

Zegiob, L., Klukas, N., & Junginger, J. (1978). Reactivity of self-monitoring procedures with retarded adolescents. *American Journal of Mental Deficiency,* **83**, 156–163.

Zohn, C. J., & Bornstein, P. H. (1980). Self-monitoring of work performance with mentally retarded adults: Effects upon work productivity, work quality, and on-task behavior. *Mental Retardation,* **18**, 19–25.

Family Stress Associated with a Developmentally Handicapped Child

PATRICIA M. MINNES

DEPARTMENT OF PSYCHOLOGY
QUEEN'S UNIVERSITY
KINGSTON, ONTARIO, CANADA

I. INTRODUCTION

In recent years, the study of stress from a life-span perspective has described a series of phases in which individuals and families undertake various developmental tasks. During this process, stress may arise with the occurrence of certain normative and unexpected events (Hetherington, 1984). The birth of a child and the transition to parenthood have been described as stressful life events (Gutman, 1975; Leifer, 1980; Osofsky & Osofsky, 1984). Several studies (Belsky, Spanier, & Rovine, 1983; Miller & Sollie, 1980; Waldron & Routh, 1981) however, have suggested that such stress is normative and that parents generally manage to cope with these events and make the necessary adjustments to maintain family stability. If, however, a child is born with a handicap, the unexpected, permanent, and involuntary nature of such an event greatly increases a family's vulnerability to stress and crisis (Adams, 1980; Price-Bonham & Addison, 1979; Willer, Intagliata, & Atkinson, 1981). Moreover, stress associated with the continuing burden of responsibility for a handicapped child living at home and the disruption of the normal family life cycle is reflected in the growing need for home- and community-based services such as parent relief and family support programs (Farber, 1975; Joyce, Singer, & Israelowitz, 1983; Upshur, 1982).

The impact of a handicapped child upon the family has been the focus of many articles over the past three decades. Research designed to document

INTERNATIONAL REVIEW OF RESEARCH IN
MENTAL RETARDATION, Vol. 15

the stress associated with a handicapped child, however, frequently has adopted a unidimensional perspective which focuses upon maternal behaviors and reactions (Beckman, 1983; Breslau, Staruch, & Mortimer, 1982). Although research has expanded to include fathers (Cummings, 1976; Goldberg, Marcovitch, MacGregor, & Lojkasek, 1986; Lamb, 1983; Price-Bonham & Addison, 1978) and siblings of handicapped children (Breslau, Weitzman, & Messenger, 1981; Brody & Stoneman, 1983; Simeonsson & McHale, 1981), the need for a multidimensional approach that incorporates the complexity of families and their dynamic qualities persists (Berger & Foster, 1976; Crnic, Friedrich, & Greenberg, 1983; Jacobsen & Humphrey, 1979). Research in this area also has been limited by conceptual and methodological problems. Many studies have had a strong clinical orientation characterized by the use of case reports and a tendency to focus upon maladaptive responses and pathology rather than coping and adaptation. Moreover, a strong theoretical base and operational concepts amenable to hypothesis testing have been used infrequently.

In the 1980s, the need for theoretically based research, the need for improved methodological rigor, and the need to focus upon the multiple factors that may mediate stress and facilitate coping with a handicapped child have been recognized increasingly (Byrne & Cunningham, 1985; Cole, 1986; Crnic *et al.*, 1983; Hetherington, 1984; McCubbin, Joy, Cauble, Comeau, Patterson, & Needle, 1980). In light of these concerns, the purpose of this contribution is to critically review research regarding family responses to a handicapped child using family stress theory as a framework. Moreover, in an attempt to adopt a positive and multidemensional perspective, this review will focus upon family coping as well as family stress and the factors which facilitate family adjustment to a handicapped child.

II. FAMILY STRESS THEORY

Despite a relatively well-developed body of theory in the field of family stress and crisis dating back to the 1940s (Burr, 1973; Hill, 1949, 1958; McCubbin *et al.*, 1980), the relevance of such theory to research on stress and coping in families of handicapped children has been noted only recently (Byrne & Cunningham, 1985; Cole, 1986; Turnbull, Brotherson, & Summers, 1984). The foundation for much family stress research since 1970 has been Hill's (1949) ABCX model of family stress and crisis. Based on studies of war-induced separations and reunions, this model describes family crisis as the degree of disruption or disorganization in a family system. Whereas Hill viewed stress as an imbalance between the demands made upon a family and their ability to cope, he saw crisis as involving a family's failure to restore equilibrium because of constant pressure to adjust the family system (McCubbin & Figley, 1983). According to Hill's ABCX model, a family's ability to cope with a potential crisis situation is dependent upon the interaction of three factors: (1) the stressor event, (2) the family's crisis-meeting resources, and (3) the family's interpretation or perception of the stressor event. When a stressor event disrupts family equilibrium and creates a potential crisis situation, a family's response to such events depends upon (1) the source of the event, i.e., within or outside the family; (2) the effects of the event upon the family's configuration, e.g., accession or dismemberment; and (3) the type of event, i.e., normative or expected, nonnormative or unexpected.

In a synthesis of family research, Burr (1973) emphasized not only a family's vulnerability to stress but also its regenerative power. The family is depicted as "a reactor to stress and as a manager of resources within the family unit with which to combat and control change within the family system" (McCubbin, 1979, p. 237). In the 1960s, the relationship between adaptation to stress and a family's internal resources was first clarified in four propositions: (1) adaptive behavior is more likely in families that are intact and well integrated than in families that are not; (2) adaptive behavior is more likely in families in which channels of communication are open; (3) adaptive behavior is more likely in families in which authority and status structures are flexible; and (4) adaptive behavior is more likely in families having successfully met past disasters (Hill & Hansen, 1964). However, McCubbin (1979) recognized the need to expand this conceptualization to include the coping strategies used by the family as well as their interactions with resources outside the immediate family unit in their attempts to reduce stress (see Fig. 1).

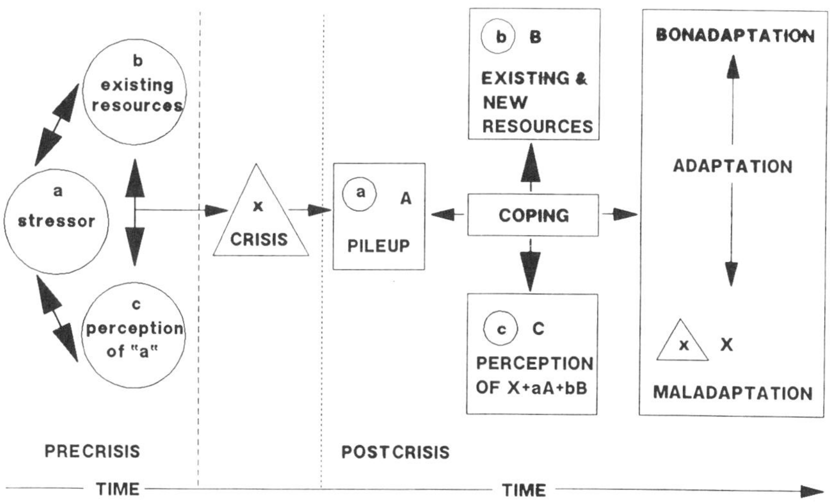

FIG. 1. The Double ABCX Model (McCubbin & Thompson, 1987).

Moreover, he noted the importance of the accumulation or "pileup" of various life stresses over time which might hinder family adaptation. McCubbin and associates, therefore, expanded Hill's original ABCX model to include a number of postcrisis variables, including (1) "additional life stressors and changes which may influence a family's ability to achieve adaptation; (2) the critical psychological and social factors families use in managing crisis situations; (3) the processes families undergo to achieve satisfactory resolution; and (4) the outcome of these efforts: (McCubbin & Figley, 1983, p. 11).

For purposes of this article, the Double ABCX Model will be used as a theoretical framework in view of the recent recognition of its usefulness in research concerning families of handicapped children (McCubbin, Nevin, Cauble, Larsen, Comeau, & Patterson, 1982; Minnes, 1984, 1986; Cole, 1986). Past research findings will be integrated under various components of the Double ABCX model, including the stressor event, the family's internal and external family resources, the perceptions of parents concerning the meaning associated with the handicapped child, parents' coping strategies, and the effects of stress pileup over time. Furthermore, this framework will be used as a guide to future research.

III. FACTORS ASSOCIATED WITH FAMILY RESPONSE TO A HANDICAPPED CHILD

A. The Stressor Event (the A factor)

The first component of the Double ABCX model, the A factor or stressor event, has been defined by McCubbin and Patterson as "a life event. . . impacting upon the family unit which produces, or has the potential of producing, change in the family social system. . . . Also part of this factor are family hardships defined as those demands on the family unit specifically associated with the stressor event" (McCubbin & Patterson, 1983, p. 7).

As in many areas of stress research, the study of stress in families of handicapped children has been plagued by definitional problems. Stress has been viewed both as a function of the event itself and in terms of the family's response to the event. Moreover, the hardships associated with the event, e.g., financial problems, frequently are included (McCubbin *et al.*, 1980). Various forms of the Questionnaire on Resources and Stress (QRS) (Holroyd, 1974, 1982; Friedrich, Greenberg, & Crnic, 1983) which have been widely used to measure stress in families of handicapped children (Beckman, 1983; Bristol, 1979; Friedrich, 1979; Friedrich & Friedrich, 1981; Friedrich, Wilturner, & Cohen, 1985; Holroyd & Guthrie, 1979; Holroyd & McArthur, 1976; Minnes, 1984, 1986) illustrate such definitional confusion in that they include stress associated with characteristics of the child (e.g., dependency and management, cognitive impairment) as well as the family's response to the child (e.g., pessimism, family disharmony) and hardships associated with the child, (e.g., financial stress).

Despite these problems, there is considerable evidence to suggest that families of handicapped children do experience stress (Beckman, 1983; Breslau *et al.*, 1982; Gallagher, Beckman, & Cross, 1983). In an attempt to clarify some of the issues in this area, the different characteristics of the child as the stressor event or A factor will be reviewed.

1. THE TYPE OF HANDICAP

Variations in parental stress according to the child's diagnosis or type of handicap have been reported in a number of studies which used the QRS (Holroyd, 1974, 1982) as the measure of stress. For example, in an early study designed to provide additional validation for the QRS, Holroyd and McArthur (1976) assessed levels of stress in mothers of autistic, Down's syndrome, and outpatient psychiatric clinic children. Significant differences were found in levels of family stress according to the child's diagnostic category. While families of autistic children reported the most stress overall, different patterns of parental response also were found. For example, mothers of autistic children reported more problems associated with their disappointment about the child, the child's dependency, family integration, physical disability, lack of available activities for the child, behavior problems of the child, and future vocational handicaps.

In a study of mothers of handicapped infants, Beckman (1983) also found a significant association between high family stress as measured by the QRS and specific characteristics of the infant, including difficult temperament, less social responsiveness, more stereotypic behavior patterns, and the presence of unusual care-giving demands. Moreover, care-giving demands alone were found to account for 66% of the variance in reported stress.

Similarly, the relationship between a child's diagnosis or type of handicap and parental stress was demonstrated in research by Minnes (1984, 1986). Scores on the QRS–Short Form (Holroyd, 1982) indicated that parents of mentally retarded children consistently reported higher stress than parents of normally intelligent children with a congenital limb deficiency. Significant differences in stress were reported in association with dependency and management issues, limits on family opportunities, life-span care, terminal illness stress, and personal burden.

From a clinical perspective, the information gathered from studies using comparison groups (e.g., Holroyd & McArthur, 1976; Minnes, 1984, 1986) provides valuable information concerning the stress experienced by parents of children with different types of handicaps. From a methodological perspective, however, the use of control groups of parents of children without handicapping conditions is also important. In one such study using the QRS

(Holroyd, 1974), Friedrich and Friedrich (1981) found that parents of handicapped children reported significantly more stress on all subscales of the QRS except pessimism, lack of social support, and financial problems. The authors suggested that the failure to demonstrate differences concerning financial problems may reflect the fact that the families in the study were not extremely poor and were not generally suffering from other stresses associated with lower socioeconimic status. Other findings concerning pessimism and lack of social support, however, were contrary to expectation. Although Friedrich and Friedrich (1981) suggested that these results reflect problems in the QRS, it could be that the results were affected by socially desirable responding by participants, although social desirability did not emerge as a significant factor in a later study by Friedrich *et al.* (1985).

Whereas Friedrich and Friedrich (1981) compared stress in parents of children ranging in age from 2 to 16 years, Wilton and Renaut (1986) compared the responses of mothers of handicapped and nonhandicapped preschool children on the QRS (Holroyd, 1974). Significant differences in reported stress were found on all but two subscales (i.e., excess time demands and limits on family opportunities). On each scale, mothers of handicapped children also reported more stress related to parent, family, and child problems than parents of nonhandicapped children. In view of the content of the QRS, which focuses primarily upon the experiences of parents of children with major disabilities, differences such as those reported by Friedrich and Friedrich (1981) and Wilton and Renaut (1986) are not surprising. The nonsignificant differences in reported stress may reflect the greater demands placed upon all parents of preschool children with or without handicaps. Unfortunately, however, the question of stress associated with normal parenting has been given relatively little attention in research with parents of handicapped children. Recent studies (Kazak & Marvin, 1984; Minnes, 1987) have used the Parenting Stress Index (PSI), which was developed by Abidin (1983), to measure parent–child systems under stress and at risk for the development of dysfunctional parenting or behavior problems in the child. Kazak and Marvin (1984) found significant differences in stress reported by mothers of physically handicapped and nonhandicapped children on both the parent and child domains of the PSI. For example, mothers of handicapped children saw their children as less adaptable to change, as more demanding, and as fulfilling fewer of the mother's expectations. Moreover, mothers of handicapped children were found to experience more depression related to parenting issues, felt less competent as mothers, and reported having significantly less time to spend by themselves or with their spouse than mothers of nonhandicapped children.

Unfortunately, Kazak and Marvin do not indicate whether the scores of their subjects on the PSI are within normal limits despite the significant group differences. However, in the Minnes (1987) study, the PSI profiles of 55 parents of mentally retarded children indicated child domain scores above the 80th percentile, whereas parent domain scores were within the normal range.

2. THE DEGREE OF HANDICAP

Although the type of handicap has been given considerable attention in the literature, few studies refer specifically to the degree of handicap. In the Minnes (1984, 1986) studies, degree of handicap was found to be significantly related to stress reported by parents on the QRS–Short Form (Holroyd, 1982). Parents of mildly retarded children reported significantly fewer limits on family opportunities than parents of moderately or severely retarded children and significantly less concern regarding life-span care and terminal illness stress than parents of severely retarded children. The parents of both mildly and moderately retarded children reported significantly less stress associated with physical limiations than parents of severely retarded children.

In contrast, rather than grouping children according to degree of handicap, Friedrich *et al.* (1985) focused upon child behavior problems associated with limited adaptive behavior. The results of regression analyses indicated that such behavior problems were a significant predictor of parental stress as measured by the Friedrich Short Form of the QRS (Friedrich *et al.*, 1983). Given Beckman's (1983) findings concerning the significant contribution of child dependency and management needs to parental stress and given the relationships between such needs and the severity of handicap, the Friedrich *et al.* (1985) findings are perhaps not surprising. However, research by Weller, Costeff, Cohen, and Rahmar (1974) and Bristol (1984) suggested that an inverse relationship between the degree of handicap and parental stress can occur. It has been argued that parents of more severely handicapped children are less able to deny their child's problems due to their appearance and behavior (Weller *et al.*, 1974) and, therefore, experience less stress associated with the acceptance of the handicap than parents of mildly retarded children who may hold unrealistic expectations due to diagnostic uncertainty and a more normal appearance.

In addition to more research that controls for the degree of handicap in a systematic fashion [i.e., stating the criteria to be used, such as IQ, mental age (MA), and adaptive behavior], there is a need for research that takes into account the parents' perceptions of their child's abilities. The important contribution of parental perceptions will be discussed further later in relation to the C factor in the Double ABCX model.

3. GENDER OF THE HANDICAPPED CHILD

The results of research on the relationship between parental stress and the gender of a handicapped child are unclear to date. As in Farber's (1959, 1960) early work which indicated that couples with male handicapped children experienced more marital disharmony than those with female handicapped children, Bristol (1979) found lower integration in families with male rather than female autistic children. Roesel and Lawlis (1983) found that young parents with a firstborn male child with a genetic handicap and mental retardation were at higher risk for divorce than parents of female children with similar handicaps.

In contrast, Friedrich (1979) found that mothers of female children reported more stress regardless of the nature of their child's handicap, whereas Beckman (1983) failed to find a relationship between the gender of the child and the amount of stress reported by mothers. However, as Beckman notes, this discrepancy may be a function of the ages of the children in her sample. Whereas the children in the Farber and Bristol studies represented a broad age range from 4 to 21 years, Beckman's sample included mothers of children 6.6 to 36.6 months of age. In light of these findings, Beckman suggests that the gender of the child may be less important to parents in the early stages of development than other characteristics such as the nature and degree of handicap.

Although Bristol controlled for the level of child dependency in her study, greater stress in parents of male children also may reflect greater management problems faced by parents of male children as they grow older and become stronger. However, the relationship between maternal stress and female children in the Friedrich (1979) study is difficult to explain.

As will be discussed later, parental perceptions of the child are likely to contribute to such differences. For example, Farber found differences in marital harmony only in lower class families with handicapped sons, whereas marital integration apparently was not related to the handicapped child's gender in middle class families. Farber (1959) suggests that such differences may be a function of parental expectations, e.g., a son would carry on family tradition and achieve success in the world. Moreover, marital disharmony may arise as a result of disagreements concerning child-rearing practices.

To date, little attention has been given to parental perceptions and expectations due, in part, to the problems of operationalizing such concepts. In addition, parents frequently are reluctant to discuss their hopes for and disappointments associated with a handicapped child. Clearly, this will be a challenging area for future research which should also take into account cultural differences and differential parental perceptions of the child.

4. AGE OF THE HANDICAPPED CHILD

While age has been included as a variable in many studies of stress in families of handicapped children, the results of research concerning this factor are limited due to methodological problems. Frequently, studies have been conducted using either a particular age group (Beckman, 1983; Waisbren, 1980; Wilton & Renaut, 1986) or a broad range of ages (Friedrich & Friedrich, 1981; Friedrich *et al.*, 1985; Holroyd & McArthur, 1986; Minnes, 1984, 1986, 1987).

Moreover, the relationship between parental stress and age would appear to be confounded by factors such as the nature and degree of handicap. For example, Minnes (1984, 1986) found that parents of normally intelligent, preschool-aged children with congenital limb deficiencies reported relatively low stress as measured by the QRS—Short Form (Holroyd, 1982) compared to the stress reported by parents of developmentally handicapped children of the same age. In contrast, while parents of primary-school-aged amputees were found to report stress levels on the QRS which were uniformly low, the scores of parents of mentally retarded children within this age range were significantly higher and associated primarily with physical limitation and life-span care. These findings are consistent with studies showing a strong relationship between the dependency and management needs of children and parental stress (Beckman, 1983). They also support prior studies demonstrating the tendency for severely handicapped children (especially males) to become increasingly disruptive to family life due to management problems (Farber, 1975).

In addition to focusing on the chronological age and functioning level of the child, future research should consider the life-cycle stage reached by the child's family. Older, well-established parents with grown children and a young handicapped child still living at home may respond quite differently from parents who have young normal children and an older child who is handicapped. Clearly, data obtained from longitudinal studies would be most valuable in this regard, especially if it is able to demonstrate changes in stress levels at various stages in the life cycle (Byrne & Cunningham, 1985).

B. Existing Resources (the B factor)

1. INTERNAL OR SYSTEMIC RESOURCES

Family resources have been described by McCubbin and Patterson (1983) as an important part of a family's ability to meet the demands and needs which arise in relation to a stressor event. Such resources include (1) the personal resources of individual family members, (2) the internal or systemic characteristics of the family which contribute to its role structure and organization, and (3) the social support received from extended family, friends, professionals, and agencies outside the immediate family.

In an analysis of family resources and health behaviors in the management of stress, Pratt (1976) described the "energized family" whose fluid internal organization, flexible role relationships and shared power facilitate personal growth and autonomy and reduce vulnerability to stress and crisis. Other aspects of family functioning which have been cited as resources include family affectional relations, marital adjustment, parent–child relations, power structures, decision-making patterns, previous experiences with crisis, communication patterns, self esteem, and the degree of independence in the family (Burr, 1973). Of these, particular attention has been given to family adaptability, cohesion, and communication by Olson and McCubbin (1982), who argue that families will adjust more readily and successfully to stress if they are both flexible and well integrated. In this context, adaptability is defined (Rodick, Henggeler, & Hanson, 1986) as the "capacity of the family system to change its power structure, role relations and relationship rules in response to situational and developmental stress" (p. 18). Cohesion is defined as "the emotional bonding family members have toward one another" (p. 18). Communication is described as being "important for facilitating a family's movement along the cohesion and adaptability dimensions" (Rodick, Henggeler, & Hanson, 1986, p. 18). These concepts were developed by Olson and associates as components of the Circumplex Model of family systems, which includes the two major dimensions of cohesion and adaptability. Using the four quadrants of the Circumplex Model, Olson, Sprenkle, and Russell (1979; Olson & McCubbin, 1982) emphasize that families which have achieved a balance between these two dimensions, e.g., moderately flexible (adaptable) and moderately cohesive (integrated), will adjust more readily and successfully to stress.

Given the hypothesized curvilinear relationship between cohesion, adaptability, and family functioning, Olson *et al.* (1979) and Olson & McCubbin (1982) suggest that families characterized by the extremes of these dimensions are likely to experience problems coping with change and restoring family equilibrium. Such balanced functioning may be particularly difficult to achieve and maintain in families disrupted by a handicapped child. Family members may become so involved in the care of and responsibility for a handicapped child (extreme cohesion–enmeshment) that individuation of family members is difficult. In contrast, families which have little cohesion, attachment, or commitment may be characterized by high levels of autonomy (disengagement) (Olson & McCubbin, 1982).

The importance of a family's resources for meeting a crisis has been demonstrated in a number of recent studies of families of mentally retarded children (Friedrich *et al.*, 1985; Mink, Nihira, & Meyers, 1983; Minnes, 1984; Nihira, Meyers, & Mink, 1980), autistic children (Bristol, 1984), and physically disabled children (McCubbin *et al.*, 1982; Minnes, 1984, 1986). One of the most frequently used measures of family functioning in this area of research has been the Family Environment Scale (Moos & Moos, 1981), a 90-item, true-false questionnaire developed to measure the social climate of the family, e.g., interpersonal relations (cohesion, conflict), communication patterns (expressiveness), family values (achievement orientation, intellectual–recreational orientation, moral–religious emphasis), and family structure (organization, control).

The results of these studies generally emphasize the importance of internal or systemic family resources in the management of stress associated with a handicapped child. In a number of studies of the relationships between home environments and parent–child adjustment in families of mentally retarded children (Nihira *et al.*, 1980; Mink *et al.*, 1983), the Moos scale was used to describe family environments. In the Mink *et al.* (1983) study, five clusters of family characteristics were described, including (1) cohesive and harmonious, (2) control oriented and somewhat unharmonious, (3) low disclosure and unharmonious, (4) child oriented and expressive, and (5) disadvantaged with low morale. Each cluster was found to be related to various child and family characteristics. For example, families who were cohesive and harmonious reported low levels of conflict and had high scores on moral religious emphasis. Low adaptive behavior and high maladaptive behavior were found in children of families which were control oriented and somewhat unharmonious. Families which were unwilling to disclose information were found to be unharmonious, whereas pride, warmth, and affection were expressed by more open and communicative child-oriented families.

In a further study of home environments of families of mentally retarded children, Blacher, Nihira, and Meyers (1987) compared profiles from the Family Environment Scale (Moos & Moos, 1981) for three groups of families having mildly, moderately, and severely retarded children. When compared to the Moos normative sample, the families of mentally retarded children in each group scored below the normative group on half of the subscales. Families with severely retarded children scored lowest on every subscale. Blacher *et al.* (1987) suggest that the lower cohesion scores may reflect the families' perceptions that they are more committed to the handicapped child than to one another, i.e., that they may be more child-focused than family focused. Similarly the lower scores on Independence may reflect the commitment to the child.

While these studies have provided valuable information concerning the family environments of mentally retarded children and their relationship to family and child adjustment, other studies (Friedrich *et al.*, 1985; Minnes, 1984, 1986) have explored the relationship between family environments (as measured by the Family Environment Scale) and stress associated with a handicapped child. Friedrich *et al.* (1985) for example, used the Family Relations Index from the Family Environment Scale (Moos & Moos, 1981) as a predictor of coping resources. The Family Relations Index is derived from the sum of scores on the cohesion, expressiveness, and conflict subscales of the Family Environment Scale. Using scores on Factor 1 of the Friedrich Short Form of the QRS (Friedrich *et al.*, 1983) as the dependent measure, the results of multiple regression analyses indicated that the composite score on the Family Relations Index was a significant predictor of coping (i.e., stress scores on Factor 1 of the Friedrich Short Form of the QRS were negatively correlated with scores on the Family Relations Index).

In a similar study by Minnes (1984, 1986) using the Family Environment Scale and QRS–Short Form (Holroyd, 1982), families with higher levels of cohesion as measured by the Family Environment Scale were found to report lower stress associated with dependency and management, life-span care, lack of personal reward, and personal burden. Similarly, families with high scores on the expressiveness subscale of the Family Environment Scale reported significantly less stress on the QRS than families with lower scores, indicating less direct and open patterns of communication. More specifically, the higher expressiveness groups reported less stress associated with family disharmony, life-span care, and limits on family opportunities. These findings may be explained by the greater tendency of the high expressiveness group to talk about their problems and to ask for help and support when needed. In such instances, caretaking responsibilities are more likely to be shared, which leads to fewer limits on family opportunities, less conflict over role distribution, and greater mutual support. Thus, stress may be reduced and the balance between family cohesion and adaptability maintained (Olson & McCubbin, 1982).

Minnes also found that families of retarded children with higher scores on independence reported lower stress associated with dependency and management, limits on family opportunities, and preference for instituational care. These results support the hypothesis that family independence (which on the Family Environment Scale refers to assertiveness, self sufficiency, and individual decision making) is an effective mediator of stress associated with a handicapped child.

Without a balance between family cohesion and independence, as well as open communication, conflict is likely to emerge as stress levels rise. Indeed, a recent study of the differential characteristics of low- and high-conflict families of children with cerebral palsy (McCubbin *et al.*, 1982), demonstrated a strong relationship between low conflict and greater internal family resources, including (1) family self esteem, (2) open communication, (3) mutual assistance, (4) optimism, (5) problem solving, and (6) autonomy and independence. Low-conflict families also were found to share (1) a sense of mastery over events and outcomes, (2) flexibility to adjust to demands, and (3) family mutuality with a sense of interpersonal support, togetherness, and cooperation. Similarly, studies of marital adjustment in families of handicapped children (Friedrich, 1979; Friedrich *et al.*, 1985) have demonstrated that a stable and satisfying marriage can mediate stress. Indeed, Friedrich (1979) found marital satisfaction to be the strongest predictor of successful coping in mothers of handicapped children.

Despite strong evidence to support the relationship between marital satisfaction and coping, the view that parents of handicapped children are more likely to experience marital problems continues to be the subject of debate. Whereas Friedrich and Friedrich (1981) found that parents of mentally handicapped children reported less marital satsifaction than parents of nonhandicapped children on the Locke–Wallace Marital Adjustment Inventory (Lock & Wallace, 1959), Waisbren (1980), using the same scale, found no differences between the scores of parents of handicapped and nonhandicapped children. In studies of stress in parents of children with and without handicaps, Kazak and Marvin (1984) and Williams and McKenry (1981) also found no differences overall between groups in marital satisfaction as measured by the Dyadic Adjustment Scale (Spanier, 1976). Indeed, the parents of handicapped children in the Kazak and Marvin study were found to report higher levels of marital satisfaction on some scales.

The lack of consensus in these studies may be a function of the instruments used to measure marital satisfaction. The validity of self-report measures frequently is limited by social desirability (Robinson & Anderson, 1983), especially when the focus of the instrument is personal (Quinton, Rutter, & Rowlands, 1976). Moreover, a brief questionnaire may not be able to tap the complexities of marital relationships adequately. Indeed, as Byrne and Cummingham (1985) have noted, marital satisfaction may decrease disproportionately over time in families of handicapped children. This factor may explain the differences in the Waisbren (1980) and Friedrich and Friedrich (1981) findings in that the mean age of the children in the former study was 13.5 months but 9.8 years in the latter. Given the accumulation of stress with the increasing burden of care and responsibility over time, it may be that parents of older handicapped children report less marital satisfaction than parents of both nonhandicapped children and younger handicapped children. Furthermore, parental age and birth order may be contributing factors. For example, Roesel and Lawlis (1983) found that mothers who gave birth to a firstborn genetically handicapped/mentally retarded child while in their thirties were at greater risk for divorce than mothers of similar age with later born children with such handicaps. While Waisbren did account for birth order, neither Friedrich and Friedrich nor Waisbren note parental age in their studies. To date, many studies have failed to account for the combined contributions of a variety of factors, including birth order, gender of child, type and degree of handicap, socioeconomic status, parental age, and gender (Roesel & Lawlis, 1983). Moreover, despite the problems of retrospective data, the degree of marital satisfaction prior to the birth of a handicapped child rarely has been assessed. Without careful control of such variables, contradictory results are likely to continue to emerge in studies of marital stress, conflict and adjustment.

While an increasing number of studies have recognized the importance of internal or systemic family resources in the management of stress associated with a handicapped child (Blacher *et al.*, 1987; Crnic *et al.*, 1983; Friedrich *et al.*, 1983; Mink *et al.*, 1983; Minnes, 1984, 1986; Nihira *et al.*, 1980), many have used questionnaires such as the Family Environment Scale (Moos &

Moos, 1981) to measure family process. However, given the limitations of such instruments, there is a need for studies that include behavioral observations of family interactions. In an early study by O'Connor and Stachowiak (1971) for example, videotaped family discussions were analyzed and the interactive patterns of families with an epileptic or mentally retarded child were compared with those of families without a disabled child. While interaction patterns in families of a retarded child were found to be different from those in a control group, they were not found to be dysfunctional. This technique, while time consuming, has considerable potential and would be an important adjunct to self report measures in family stress research.

2. EXTERNAL FAMILY RESOURCES

In addition to strengths and resources within the immediate family system, the Double ABCX Model (McCubbin & Patterson, 1983) includes social support systems outside the immediate family as an important component of family crisis-meeting resources. The contributions of kin, friends, neighbors, social service agencies and self help groups all have been found to have an important impact upon stress management in a variety of family situations (McCubbin *et al.*, 1980). While kin-embedded or large nuclear families frequently use extended family support (Lee, 1979; Lin, Ensel, Simeone, & Kuo, 1979), the small, individualistic nuclear family may be considerably more vulnerable to stress without such resources. Since the 1970s, however, self-help groups have become a popular form of social support for such families (McCubbin *et al.*, 1980).

Social support, defined by Cobb (1976) as the sum of emotional support, esteem support, and network support, has been shown to have beneficial effects on a host of health variables, various life transitions, and crises. According to French, Rodgers, and Cobb (1974), social support facilitiates stress reduction by improvement of the "person–environment fit." Not only does the social system provide cues for role performance in stressful situations (Kozloff, 1979), it also provides opportunities outside the family to gain encouragement and self-esteem while reducing feelings of isolation.

The importance of social support in the mediation of stress associated with a handicapped child has been noted (Bristol, 1979; German & Maisto, 1982; Kazak & Marvin, 1984; Minnes, 1984, 1986; Schilling, Gilchrist, & Schinke, 1984). In addition, a strong relationship between out-of-home placement of a handicapped child and limited availability of respite care, babysitting, and support from extended family and friends has been discussed (Cole, 1986; German & Maisto, 1982; Sherman and Cocozza, 1984).

Despite the potential benefits of social support, a number of studies have indicated that families of handicapped children suffer from social isolation (Kazak & Marvin, 1984). Indeed, Friedrich and Friedrich (1981) found significant differences in scores of families of handicapped and nonhandicapped children on the Social Support Index (Nuckolls, Cassell, & Kaplan, 1972). Lack of social support may be partly due to the unwillingness and inability of extended family and friends to help. However, as noted by Schilling *et al.* (1984), parents may lack competencies in developing social networks or simply may be unable to find the time and energy to maintain social contacts, seek such assistance, and act as educators (i.e., helping friends and relatives to feel more competent when dealing with a handicapped child).

Contradictory findings concerning social support and stress in such families (Friedrich, 1979; Friedrich and Friedrich, 1981; Minnes, 1984, 1986) may reflect the complexities of the relationship. While social support may help to mediate stress in some areas, such as limits on family opportunities and lack of personal reward (Minnes, 1984, 1986), stress may develop in response to efforts to find social support or in response to those providing the support. For example, while Kazak and Marvin (1984) found that the social support networks of parents were significantly smaller than those of the comparison group, they had networks that were significantly more dense, meaning that members of these networks tended to know and interact with one another. Such density may foster family cohesion, however, it may also be a source of additional stress. Whereas the importance of grandparents as a source of emotional support was indicated in a study by German and Maisto (1982), support from the father's parents would appear to be particularly important in terms of parents' positive feelings about their child (Waisbren, 1980). As Waisbren points out, however, such support also may be associated with marital stress. These findings are similar to those of early work by Farber (1960), which indicated that while frequent visits with the wife's mother could be potentially beneficial, especially in terms of her emotional support rather than her assistance with child care, frequent interaction with the husband's mother could add stress to the marital relationship. This finding is consistent with the results of studies of families without a handicapped child.

While there is growing interest among clinicians in programs to help families of handicapped children develop and benefit from social support networks (Schilling *et al.*, 1984), research is needed to evaluate the relative contributions of such resources to the coping process. Although various studies have included social support measures, few have been incorporated into a theoretical model. Moreover, there has been little consistency in the types of social measures used. Whereas Friedrich and associates used an adaptation of the Social Support Index (Nuckolls *et al.*, 1972), Minnes (1984, 1986) used the Social Support subscale of the Family Crisis-Oriented Personal Evaluation Scale (F-COPES) developed by McCubbin, Olson, and Larsen (1981). Waisbren (1980) used the Social Network Form adapted from Bott (1957). Contradictory findings in these and other studies may reflect differences in the measures used. In light of findings concerning the complexities of social support, future research should carefully consider the content of such measures. If the instrument yields only a total score, differences in the support received from grandparents, friends, and extended family may not be detected. Moreover, differences in the views of mothers and fathers as well as a measure of the stress involved in seeking or receiving social support would help to clarify the relationship.

In the absence of strong social support from extended family and friends, parents may turn to professionals and service providers for assistance. While interactions with professionals and community agencies are generally meant to be supportive of parents by providing counseling, encouragement, and information, reports to the contrary have begun to appear in the literature in recent years (Gallagher *et al.*, 1983; Minnes, 1984, 1986; Waisbren, 1980). Unfortunately, much of the available information has been provided in case histories and personal accounts. Some of the most convincing reports (Turnbull & Turnbull, 1978) have been made by professionals who, like parents of handicapped children, suggest that parent–professional interactions may provoke rather than reduce stress. For example, Roos (1978) has described how parental and professional values regarding what is best for a handicapped child may be incompatible and, therefore, may lead to conflicts regarding program objectives and long-range goals. Parents and professionals also may disagree about the amount of progress being made by a handicapped child as a result of differing views on the relative importance of specific programs. Finally, Roos cites lack of professional attunement to parents' anxieties, limited listening skills, reluctance to share all relevant information, and failure to communicate clearly due to unnecessary use of professional jargon as factors contributing to difficulties between parents and professionals.

Such parental views have been supported by a study by Huang and Heifetz (1984), one of the very few published attempts to investigate specific elements of professional support. Mothers of retarded children were asked to describe the characteristics of professionals who had been the most and least helpful to them. Both interview and checklist data emphasized the primary importance of the personal affective relationship between parents and professionals and the importance of a sense of collaborative partnership between parent and professional. Furthermore, mothers emphasized the value of professionals with skills and expertise in approaches pertinent to the particular needs of mentally retarded children. In each of these areas, mothers generally rated educational professionals as more helpful than medical professionals.

Although evaluations of early intervention and parent-training programs are appearing in the literature with greater frequency (Baker, Heifetz, & Murphy, 1980; Heifetz, 1977; Koegel, Schreibman, Britten, Burke, & O'Neil, 1982; Short, 1984), the focus of these studies tends to be on changes in either parental skill level or functioning of the child. With increasing numbers of parents bearing the responsibility of care for a handicapped child at home, there is a growing need for carefully designed studies that evaluate not only the quantity of service but also the quality of support available to parents as an important component of the family resource model. Without such information, the planning of future service delivery may well be inadequate.

C. Perceptions of the Handicapped Child

According to the McCubbin and Patterson (1983) formulation of family stress and coping, the meaning that a family attaches to a stressful event plays an important role in stress management. Whether or not an event leads to crisis, breakdown, or dysfunction in a family will depend upon the explanations used by the family to understand why it occurred and what can be done to alleviate the stressful situation.

Unfortunately, articles which have addressed this important factor frequently have been based upon the subjective and retrospective reports of parents and clinicians. For example, Ryckman and Henderson (1965) suggested that parents' interpretations of their child's handicap will be a function of their expectations of parenthood and the meaning which they attribute to the child in relation to themselves. Ryckman and Henderson described a number of expectations of children commonly held by parents, including (1) the child as a physical and psychological extension of the parent, (2) the child as a means of vicarious satisfaction, (3) the child as a means of attaining some measure of immortality, (4) the child as a personalized love object, (5) the child as a means of fostering parental self-worth, and (6) the child as an object of care and responsibility.

Parental reactions including shock, disbelief, grief, tension, loss, helplessness, confusion, disappointment, anger, sorrow, frustration, anxiety, and exhaustion all have been described as being experienced in response to a handicapped child. But the most commonly reported reaction would appear to be guilt (Eden-Piercy, Blacher, & Eyman, 1986). There is considerable confusion, however, concerning the features of these reactions. What one researcher may label "guilt" another may call "denial." Moreover, few have attempted to measure these emotions objectively (Eden-Piercy *et al.*, 1986). In addition to the absence of adequate instruments, the issue of social desirability has been addressed infrequently. Parents who wish to appear to be coping with their handicapped child may be reluctant to admit to such feelings even if only in retrospect. One approach, as suggested by Carr (1974), would be to ask parents whether they have ever experienced a given emotion but have said they did not. More indirect methods using a measure of socially desirable responding would be an alternative approach.

1. DIFFERENTIAL PERCEPTIONS OF MOTHERS AND FATHERS

Although both parents have been reported to pass through a similar sequence of reactions (Ryckman & Henderson, 1965), the manner in which a parent responds to a handicapped child has been found to differ between mothers and fathers. To date observational studies have not been conducted though there appears to be general agreement [based on research involving interviews and clinical impressions (Lamb, 1983)] that mothers and fathers initially respond differently to the birth of a handicapped child. Early studies (Gumz & Gubrium, 1972), for example, reported that fathers tended to respond less emotionally and were more concerned about the long-term economic and social dependency of their child. Mothers, on the other hand, were found to respond more emotionally and to express concerns about the time involved in caring for the child and the emotional strain of maintaining family harmony and integration.

Other early studies suggested that fathers, being more concerned about a child's roles outside the family, seem to be more affected than mothers by the physical attributes of their child and his or her behavior in public since the family's social and community image might be stigmatized (Price-Bonham & Addison, 1978; Tallman, 1965). In contrast, however, fathers have been reported to be more accepting of daughters than sons (Grossman, 1972), perhaps because daughters, despite their handicap, may be able to fulfill their expected roles more readily than a son.

Cummings (1976) has suggested that fathers who begin to question their biological capacities as a father following the birth of a handicapped child may suffer from considerably lower self-esteem than mothers. This may be because fathers frequently do not have as much direct involvement with the child as their wives and, thus, may have fewer indications of their value and ability as a parent. In a recent study by Goldberg *et al.* (1986), fathers were found to report fewer symptoms of distress, higher self-esteem, and greater locus of control than mothers despite the fact that they reported less support than their wives. Goldberg *et al.* suggest that these findings may reflect traditional divisions of roles whereby mothers' roles may be associated with less control and more distress than those of fathers. In instances where the mother bears the greatest responsibility for child care, her sense of well-being and control are more likely to be affected by the demands of the handicapped child despite greater support than fathers.

Despite changing family roles due to rising divorce rates, increasing numbers of women in the work force, and the increasing involvement of fathers in child care (Turnbull & Winton, 1984), the primary focus of research so far has been the mother–child dyad. Given available evidence to date regarding the differential experiences of mothers and fathers of handicapped children, it will be important for future research to include both parents not only to provide information concerning the impact of the child upon his or her father but also to study the effect of fathers' involvement upon a handicapped child as well as upon the perceptions and stress of mothers.

2. SPIRITUAL RESOURCES

Early studies of parental reactions to a handicapped child emphasized the relationship between spiritual or religious resources and acceptance of the child (Farber *et al.*, 1960; Zuk, 1959, 1962; Zuk, Miller, Bartram, & Kling, 1961). While religious association, particularly with the Catholic church, was shown to be correlated with successful coping with a handicapped child, the intensity of the association rather than frequency of church attendance was found to be particularly important. This distinction and other reported differences in acceptance and/or distress in Catholic, as opposed to Protestant and Jewish, families of handicapped children (Korn, Chess, & Fernandez, 1978) would seem to reflect the meaning which Catholic doctrine attributes to such a child. As Zuk *et al.* (1961) note, "Catholic doctrine is explicit that parents should not feel guilt for bearing a retarded child; indeed, they are asked to accept the child as a special gift of God. Protestant and Jewish doctrine is neither so explicit nor absolving. Emphasis in the Jewish group, particularly on intelligence as a special value, constitutes an additional handicap in acceptance." (p. 537) Unfortunately, such findings are limited by a number of methodological and design problems. The concept of acceptance, for example, is not clearly defined. Moreover, as Zuk *et al.* (1961) note, in view of cultural mores regarding parental feelings and behavior toward children, parents may well be reluctant to admit feelings of hostility toward a child, particularly if he or she is handicapped.

The results of more recent studies (Friedrich, 1979; Friedrich & Friedrich, 1982; German & Maisto, 1982; Minnes, 1984, 1986; Nihira *et al.*, 1980), however, have been contradictory. In some instances (Friedrich & Friedrich, 1982; Minnes, 1984, 1986; Nihira *et al.*, 1980) spiritual resources would appear to contribute to coping and stress management, whereas in others (Friedrich, 1979; German & Maisto, 1982) a significant relationship was not found. Such varying results may reflect the different measures used in these studies. Although the Religiosity Index developed by Zuk *et al.* (1961) was used by Zuk (1959), Friedrich (1979), and Friedrich and Friedrich (1982), German and Maisto (1982) used a standard interview which included questions concerning church attendance and emotional support gained from church. Minnes (1984, 1986) used the Spiritual Support subscale of the F-COPES (McCubbin *et al.*, 1981), and Nihira *et al.* (1980) used the Moral–Religious Emphasis subscale of the Family Environment Scale (Moos & Moos, 1981). While each of these scales has a similar focus, the varying emphasis upon faith in God, religious conviction, and religious affiliation, as well as involvement in church activities and support gained from these various aspects, may account for the contradictory findings to date. Furthermore, the criterion variables in these studies varied as well. Whereas Friedrich and associates (1979, 1982) used scores on the Questionnaire on Resources and Stress (Holroyd, 1974) as a criterion measure in multiple-regression analyses and Minnes (1984, 1986) used the QRS Short Form (Holroyd, 1982), German and Maisto (1982) focused upon group differences in various resources without actually measuring stress and Nihira *et al.* (1980) investigated the relationship between moral–religious emphasis as one characteristic of the home environment along with child development and family adjustment. Comparisons between these studies, therefore, are problematic. Further research on this variable is needed using clearly described samples of families representing various religious denominations and measures which assess both faith and church attendance. Moreover, social class and cultural differences must be taken into account.

3. SOCIOECONOMIC AND CULTURAL FACTORS

The impact of a handicapped child upon the family cannot be properly understood without giving due consideration to the social context. For example, as described earlier, Farber (1960) found that the gender of a handicapped child is perceived differently by various socioeconomic status (SES) groups, and these perceptions can have differential effects upon marital integration. Unfortunately, research findings concerning the responses of parents in different socioeconomic categories are contradictory. Whereas families seeking out-of-home placements are more likely to be from lower social classes (Cole, 1986; German & Maisto, 1982), Minnes (1984, 1986) found that despite lower financial stress, higher SES families expressed greater preference for residential care than parents in lower SES groups.

Such differences may reflect the different meanings atttributed to a handicapped child by these groups. For example, while early studies (Downey, 1965; Mercer, 1966; Farber, 1968) suggested that lower class families were more accepting of a handicapped child, they also were reported to seek out-of-home placement due to "role organization crises" (Farber, 1968) resulting from the excessive burden of care placed upon such families. In contrast, higher SES parents, despite greater access to resources (cognitive, financial, social) which could help them to cope with a handicapped child at home (Pearlin & Schooler, 1978), might prefer residential care for different reasons (Minnes, 1984, 1986). They may be concerned that a handicapped child could stigmatize the family's social or public image (Price-Bonham & Addison, 1978), or they may seek placement due to a "tragic crisis" (Farber, 1968) related to the frustration of the family's aims and aspirations for their child. Such responses were reflected in the Minnes (1984, 1986) finding that higher SES parents reported greater stress associated with the lack of personal reward. These differences may also have been accentuated by the tendency for higher SES parents to be more realistic about their handicapped child's abilities (Weller *et al.*, 1974; Wolfensberger & Kurtz, 1971).

Contradictory findings in such research may be explained further by a number of confounding variables. Cultural differences, for example, have been included in relatively few studies (Waisbren, 1980; Weller *et al.*, 1974), and the results once again have been conflicting. While earlier studies (Zuk, 1962) reported racial differences in levels of acceptance of handicapped children, cross-cultural studies have failed to find differences (Waisbren, 1980; Weller *et al.*, 1974). However, other factors, such as socioeconomic status and religious affiliation, as well as the characteristics of the handicapped child must be taken into account. For example, while Weller *et al.* (1974) did not find differences in the perceptions of Jews of European or Eastern descent, they did find an interaction between the social class of parents and the degree of handicap.

With the blurring of cultural boundaries, especially in North American society, the measurement of differential parental and family perceptions is becoming increasingly difficult. However, without careful consideration of the interactive effects of culture, religion, and socioeconomic status, research designed to study the perceptions of families will continue to yield inconclusive results.

IV. THE PROCESS OF ADJUSTMENT AND ADAPTATION

In expanding Hill's ABCX model, McCubbin and Patterson (1983) recognized the need to consider a family's response to stressor events over time. The Double ABCX Model, therefore, is divided into phases. The first involves initial adjustment to a stressor event, whereas the second involves adaptation following a crisis. The excessive demands of a crisis and the depletion of resources require a restructuring of family roles, rules, and goals as well as the adoption of new adaptive coping strategies.

Traditionally, the adjustment process following the birth of a handicapped child was viewed as a "well-circumscribed, definable and time-bound process" that can be divided into distinct stages (Menolascino, 1977). Moreover, the widely documented reactions, particularly of mothers, have been likened to those of the bereaved, and the process of individual adjustment has been compared to that observed during the resolution of grief (Solnit & Stark, 1961). As a result, many professionals have stressed the importance of acceptance in their work with parents and have tended to view parental failure to accept a handicapped child and the continuing use of defense mechanisms, such as denial, as neurotic or pathological manifestations (Darling & Darling, 1982; Wolfensberger, 1967).

In recent years, however, the importance of acceptance and the concept of time-bound adjustment have been challenged (Allen & Affleck, 1985;

Blacher, 1984; Searl, 1978; Wikler, 1981, 1986). Olshansky (1966), for example, has suggested that parents of a handicapped child, rather than progressing through the usual mourning process within a given time frame, often experience a state of "chronic sorrow," which is defined as the long-term internalization of a depressive mood. In contrast to the view that incomplete resolution of grief is evidence of neurosis or pathology, Olshansky has argued that chronic sorrow is a natural and understandable response to a tragic fact.

In a more recent attempt to investigate the adaptation process in greater depth, Wikler, Wasow, and Hatfield (1981) asked parents to graphically depict their feelings over time and at 10 specific points associated with developmental milestones when the child's deviance from normal would be particularly apparent. The concept of chronic sorrow was also described to parents who were then asked directly if they had experienced such a reaction. In contrast to Olshansky's view of a continuous response process, the results indicated that the majority of parents depicted a pattern of periodic adaptation with emotional distress and upheaval recurring at significant stages in the handicapped child's development. Although social workers who were asked by Wikler *et al.* (1981) to draw similar graphs indicated recognition of the chronic nature of stress experienced by parents, they were found to overestimate the stress experienced by parents in the early period and to underestimate the impact of later experiences.

In a later study, Wikler (1986) studied the relationship between stress and the later developmental transitions of entering adolescence (11–15 years) and entering adulthood (20–21 years). Parental stress as measured by the QRS (Holroyd, 1974) was assessed at the beginning and the end of a 2-year period in 60 families of mentally handicapped children divided into transition and nontransition groups. The results indicated a bimodal distribution with significantly higher stress reported by transition than by nontransition families.

Although such research is only in its early stages, the results to date suggest the importance of services which recognize the ongoing needs of parents and families, particularly at transition periods in the development of a handicapped child. Future research, in addition to assessing stress over time, will need to control for a number of important factors, including the nature and degree of the child's handicap as well as the family's internal and external resources. The use of families with nonhandicapped children as control groups also will be important in view of the lack of normative information on parental responses at these periods of transition.

1. PILE-UP (THE aA FACTOR)

In addition to recognizing the need to consider the experience of stress over time, McCubbin and Patterson (1983) included a "Pile-Up factor" which represents the accumulation of various demands and chronic stresses over time. These include "(a) the initial stressor and its hardships; (b) normative transitions; (c) prior strains; (d) the consequences of family efforts to cope and (e) ambiguity, both intrafamily and social" (McCubbin & Patterson, 1983, p. 14).

In addition to the initial stress associated with the birth and diagnosis of a handicapped child, parents must cope with stress associated with the increasing caretaking demands of the child, the need to find and coordinate services for the child, and increasing financial strain. In an attempt to cope with the additional demands of a handicapped child, parents may decide that they must move to a city closer to facilities and services for handicapped children, or the father may have to work overtime or the mother may have to return to work due to extra financial commitments associated with the child. In addition, prior strains in the marriage or problems at work may be exacerbated by a handicapped child and other family life-cycle changes (e.g., the birth of subsequent children, illness and death of grandparents, career changes) all contribute to pile up. Finally, there is a certain amount of ambiguity associated with every stressor (McCubbin & Patterson, 1983). In the case of families of a handicapped child, there frequently is uncertainty about the child's prognosis, future needs, and the availability of services. All of these factors contribute to the pile up of stress and increase a family's vulnerability to crisis.

Although the characteristics of the handicapped child have been studied frequently in relation to parental stress, clear descriptions of sample characteristics (e.g., diagnostic criteria) regarding the nature and degree of handicap and longitudinal studies which document the changes in stress (pile up) associated with a handicapped child over time are still required. The application of the Double ABCX Model has helped to draw attention to the importance of such a multidimensional approach.

2. CHANGING FAMILY RESOURCES OVER THE LIFE CYCLE (THE bB FACTOR)

According to the Double ABCX Model, when families under stress are no longer able to maintain stability using habitual coping strategies, a crisis may prompt restructuring of the family and modification of interaction patterns. Moreover, the family may call upon the support of external resources such as extended family, friends, and social service agencies. This process of adaptation in families of handicapped children has been described by Farber (1975) as following the "principle of minimal adaptation" whereby there is a gradual deceleration and, finally, the arrest of the family life cycle due to the limited or delayed development of a handicapped child. Relative to his or her normal siblings, the retarded child increasingly falls behind and eventually takes on the status of youngest child regardless of his or her original position. As a result, the family is never able to reach maturity; parents are never able to "retire" from child rearing, and, thus, they are prevented from pursuing their own life goals. In order to adjust to the disruption of family routines, family equilibrium, and the family life cycle, Farber (1975) argues that families will alter their patterns of living as little as possible. Following the "principle of minimal adaptation," families will proceed through a series of stages which represent various changes in family roles and relationships. Transitions from one stage to another, according to Farber, are likely to take place in periods of high stress when parents, in particular, are confronted by discrepancies between their own role expectations and role performance or those of their handicapped child.

While longitudinal research which follows changes in family roles, structures, and resources over the life cycle is still a developing area of research, a number of articles (Suelzle & Keenan, 1981; Turnbull *et al.*, 1984) have begun to address important issues pertaining to the changing needs and experiences of families over time. In the past, families who reached Farber's final elimination phase would attempt to restore family stability through institutionalization of the handicapped child. Indeed, the results of surveys cited by Seltzer and Krauss (1984) indicate that families continue to seek out-of-home placements for their children despite the deinstitutionalization movement. However, the limited availability of such placements is a source of continuing stress for parents, especially those who are elderly and concerned about the long-term welfare of their handicapped child. For those families who chose to institutionalize their child in the past, the move toward deinstitutionalization has created an additional potential crisis in the family life cycle (Willer *et al.*, 1981), and the majority of such families (72–86%) has been reported to oppose deinstitutionalization of their relatives (Conroy, 1985).

While considerable professional and research attention has been paid to the needs of parents of young handicapped children while they still are coping with the initial shock of the birth and diagnosis, Wikler (1986) has suggested that the needs of families at later stages in the life cycle have been underestimated. Moreover, Suelzle and Keenan (1981) found that parents' use of personal and professional support networks changes as their handicapped child grows older. In general, parents of younger children were found to use more services and support networks while parents of older children were less supported, more isolated, and in greater need of expanding services. However, it was not clear whether the latter findings were due to changing needs of older parents, the unavailability of appropriate services, or parental burnout.

With continuing trends toward deinstitutionalization and increasing numbers of families who are coping with a handicapped child at home, there clearly is a need for research which documents changes in family roles, relationships, and needs over time. To date, the majority of available research has been limited to cross sectional and retrospective studies without control groups. Without such research, the provision of an adequate continuum of services over the life span of handicapped people and their families will be difficult at best.

3. CHANGING PERCEPTIONS OVER TIME (THE cC FACTOR)

In order to insulate themselves against chronic stresses associated with a handicapped child, families frequently adopt coping strategies to alter their perceptions of the situation, which gives it a more acceptable meaning and thereby reduces the affective intensity and stress. If, over time, parents are unable to use defensive strategies such as denial, projection of blame, reaction formation (Boone & Harman, 1972), and/or sublimation to reduce guilt, they may come to rationalize their situation. They may justify and tolerate, if not accept, their child's disability.

Two such strategies are reframing and passive appraisal (McCubbin *et al.*, 1981). In the former, families may redefine their situation in more positive terms, e.g., as a "challenge" or an "opportunity for growth," whereas in the latter the family avoids taking action to resolve their problem believing that the situation will improve over time without their intervention. Voysey (1975) has suggested that parents of handicapped children frequently adopt strategies that contain elements of both reframing and passive appraisal. For instance, parents may use a strategy for coping that emphasizes the acceptance of the inevitable as expressed in the saying "it could happen to anyone." Parents might also use a strategy that incorporates a redefinition of "good" and "evil" by comparing their situation to others and noting that "there's always someone worse off." For such parents, death may come to be defined as a "blessing," and they may come to view themselves as being fortunate and say that they are "grateful for small mercies such as treatment facilities."

Research on the prevalence and usefulness of such strategies is underdeveloped. There is a need for empirical studies of the coping strategies used by parents and siblings of handicapped children and their relationship to family adjustment over time. In addition to providing valuable information on the experiences of families, the results of such research could have important implications for those counseling such families under stress.

V. DIRECTIONS FOR FUTURE RESEARCH

In view of the growing numbers of developmentally handicapped people living in the community in recent years, increasing demands are being made upon community services as families attempt to cope with stress and the potential crises associated with a handicapped child (Willer *et al.*, 1980). Theoretical models of family stress (Burr, 1973; Hill & Hansen, 1964; McCubbin *et al.*, 1980) have demonstrated the importance of a multidimensional approach. Moreover, they have emphasized the need to include coping strategies as well as stress-mediating factors in such models (McCubbin, 1979). While the stress experienced by mothers, fathers, and siblings of developmentally handicapped children has been widely documented in case studies and retrospective personal accounts over the past 25 years, more recent research has focused increasingly upon the relationships between family resources, coping strategies, and stress associated with a handicapped child.

To date, the majority of studies has obtained information on stress and/or coping from self-report measures. The use of questionnaires (which is common practice), however, poses a number of problems for researchers. Particularly in the area of stress, it is not always clear what is being measured. In addition, given the limitations of instruments designed to measure family variables, there is a need for studies which include behavioral observations of family interactions and more detailed analyses of family use of a variety of supports. Research on the assessment of family perceptions is still relatively new. Indeed, instruments which adequately measure the subjective C Factor in the Double ABCX Model have yet to be developed.

More rigorous research methodology and the further development of theory would accelerate the growth of research in this area. Methodological rigor could be increased by including larger, more representative samples matched for demographic and child characteristics as well as by using psychometrically sound measurement instruments, ideally in conjunction with behavioral observations. The use and refinement of the Double ABCX Model (McCubbin and Patterson, 1983) would facilitate analysis of the complex relationships between multiple factors contributing to family stress and coping. Furthermore, the use of such a model would encourage the implementation of longitudinal as well as cross-sectional studies that are needed to document not only the changes in stress over time but also changes in family resources, coping strategies, and perceptions.

With the growing need for community based support systems for families of developmentally handicapped children across the life-span, the data gathered from research that takes a multidimensional perspective should be of great value to professionals, caregivers, and parents as we continue to unravel the complex relationships between family stress, coping, and adaptation.

REFERENCES

Abidin, R. (1983). *Parenting stress index—Manual.* Charlottesville, Virginia: Pediatric Psychology Press.

Adams, B. N. (1980). *The family: A sociological interpretation.* Chicago: Rand McNally.

Allen, D. A., & Affleck, G. (1985). Are we stereotyping parents? A postscript to Blacher. *Mental Retardation,* **23**, 200–202.

Baker, B., Heifetz, L., & Murphy, D. (1980). Behavioral training for parents of mentally retarded children: One year follow-up. *American Journal of Mental Deficiency,* **85**, 31–38.

Beckman, P. J. (1983). Influence of selected child characteristics on stress in families of handicapped infants. *American Journal of Mental Deficiency,* **88**, 150–156.

Belsky, J., Spanier, G. B., & Rovine, M. (1983). Stability and change in marriage across the transition to parenthood. *Journal of Marriage and the Family,* **45**, 567–577.

Berger, M., & Foster, M. (1976). Family-level interventions for retarded children: A multivariate approach to issues and strategies. *Multivariate Experimental Clinical Research,* **2**, 1–21.

Blacher, J. (1984). Sequential stages of parental adjustment to the birth of a child with handicaps: Fact or artifact? *Mental Retardation,* **22**, 55–68.

Blacher, J., Nihira, K., & Meyers, C. E. (1987). Characteristics of home environment of families with mentally retarded children: Comparison across levels of retardation. *American Journal of Mental Retardation,* **91**, 313–320.

Boone, D. R., & Harman, H. (1972). The benevolent over-reaction. *Clinical Pediatrics,* **11**, 268–271.

Bott, E. (1957). *Family and social networks.* London: Tavistock.

Breslau, N., Staruch, K. S., & Mortimer, E. A. (1982). Psychological distress in mothers of a disabled child. *American Journal of Disorders of Childhood,* **136**, 682–686.

Breslau, N., Weitzman, M., & Messenger, K. (1981). Psychogenic functioning of siblings of disabled children. *Pediatrics,* **67**, 344–353.

Bristol, M. (1979). *Material coping with autistic children. Adequacy of interpersonal support and effects of child characteristics.* Unpublished doctoral dissertation, University of North Carolina, Chapel Hill.

Bristol, M. M. (1984). Family resources and successful adaptation to autistic children. In E. Schopler & G. Mesibov (Eds.), *The effects of autism on the family.* New York: Plenum.

Brody, G. H., & Stoneman, Z. (1983). Children with atypical siblings: Socialization outcomes and clinical participation. In B. B. Lahey & A. Kazdin (Eds.), *Advances in clinical child psychology* (Vol. 6). New York: Plenum.

Burr, W. R. (1973). *Theory construction and the sociology of the family.* New York: Wiley.

Byrne, E. A., & Cunningham, C. C. (1985). The effects of mentally handicapped children on families—a conceptual review. *Journal of Child Psychology and Psychiatry,* **26**, 847–864.

Carr, J. (1974). The effect of the severely subnormal on their families. In A. M. Clarke & A. D. B. Clarke (Eds.), *Mental deficiency: The changing outlook.* New York: Free Press.

Cobb, S. (1976). Social Support as a moderator of life stress. *Psychosomatic Medicine,* **38**, 245–258.

Cole, D. A. (1986). Out-of-home child placement and family adaptation: A theoretical framework. *American Journal of Mental Deficiency,* **91**, 226–236.

Conroy, J. W. (1985). Reactions to deinstitutionalization among parents of mentally retarded persons. In R. H. Bruininks & K. C. Lakin (Eds.), *Lifting and learning in the least restrictive environment.* Baltimore: Brookes.

Crnic, K. A., Friedrich, W. N., & Greenberg, M. T. (1983). Adaptation of families with mentally retarded children: A model of stress, coping and family ecology. *American Journal of Mental Deficiency,* **88**, 125–138.

Cummings, S. T. (1976). The impact of the child's deficiency on the father: A study of fathers of mentally retarded and chronically ill children. *American Journal of Orthopsychiatry,* **46**, 246–255.

Darling, R. B., & Darling, J. (1982). *Children who are different. Meeting the challenges of birth defects in society.* Toronto: Mosby.

Downey, K. J. (1965). Parent's reasons for institutionalizing severely mentally retarded children. *Journal of Health and Social Behavior,* **6**, 147–155.

Eden-Piercy, G. V. S., Blacher, J. B., & Eyman, R. K. (1986). Exploring parents reactions to their young child with severe handicaps. *Mental Retardation,* **24**, 285–291.

Farber, B. (1959). The effects of a severely retarded child on family integration. *Monographs of the Society for Research in Child Development,* **24** (2).

Farber, B. (1960). Family organization in crisis: Maintenance of integration in families with a severely retarded child. *Monographs of the Society for Research in Child Development,* **25** (1).

Farber, B. (1968). *Mental retardation: Its social context and social consequences.* Boston: Houghton-Mifflin.

Farber, B. (1975). Family adaptions to severely mentally retarded children. In M. Begab & S. Richardson (Eds.), *The mentally retarded in society: A social science perspective.* Baltimore: University Park Press.

French, J. R. P., Rodgers, W., & Cobb, S. (1974). Adjustment as person–environment fit. In G. V. Coelho, D. A. Hamburg, & J. E. Adams (Eds.), *Coping and adaptation.* New York: Basic Books.

Friedrich, W. N. (1979). Predictors of coping behavior of mothers of handicapped children. *Journal of Consulting and Clinical Psychology,* **47**, 1140–1141.

Friedrich, W. N., & Friedrich, W. L. (1981). Psychosocial assets of parents of handicapped and nonhandicapped children. *American Journal of Mental Deficiency,* **85**, 551–553.

Friedrich, W. N., Greenberg, M., & Crnic, K. A. (1983). A short form of the Questionnaire on Resources and Stress. *American Journal of Mental Deficiency,* **88**, 41–48.

Friedrich, W. N., Wilturner, L. T., & Cohen, D. S. (1985). Coping resources and parenting mentally retarded children. *American Journal of Mental Deficiency,* **90**, 130–139.

Gallagher, J. J., Beckman, P., & Cross, A. H. (1983). Families of handicapped children: Sources of stress and its amelioration. *Exceptional Children,* **50**, 10–19.

German, M. L., & Maisto, A. A. (1982). The relationship of perceived family support system to the institutional placement of mentally retarded children. *Education and Training of the Mentally Retarded,* **17**, 17–23.

Goldberg, S., Marcovitch, S., MacGregor, D., & Lojkasek, M. (1986). Family responses to developmentally delayed preschoolers: Etiology and the father's role. *American Journal of Mental Deficiency,* **90**, 610–617.

Grossman, F. K. (1972). *Brothers and sisters of retarded children: An exploratory study.* Syracuse, New York: Syracuse University Press.

Gumz, E. J., & Gubrium, J. F. (1972). Comparative parental perceptions of a mentally retarded child. *American Journal of Mental Deficiency,* **77**, 175–180.

Gutman, D. L. (1975). Parenthood: A key to the comparative study of the life cycle? In N. Datan & L. Ginsberg (Eds.), *Life span developmental psychology. Normative life crises.* New York: Academic Press.

Heifetz, L. (1977). Behavioral parent training for parents of retarded children: Alternative formats based on instructional manuals. *American Journal of Mental Deficiency,* **82**, 194–203.

Hetherington, E. M. (1984). Stress and coping in children and families. In A. Doyle, D. Gold, & D. S. Moskowitz (Eds.), *Children in families under stress. New directions for child development.* San Francisco: Jossey-Bass.

Hill, R. (1949). *Families under stress: Adjustment to the crises of war separation and reunion.* New York: Harper.

Hill, R. (1958). Generic features of families under stress. *Social Casework,* **39**, 139–150.

Hill, R., & Hansen, D. A. (1964). Families under stress. In H. T. Christensen (Ed.), *Handbook of marriage and the family.* Chicago: Rand McNally.

Holroyd, J. (1974). The questionnaire on resources and stress: An instrument to measure family response to a handicapped family member. *Journal of Community Psychology,* **2**, 92–94.

Holroyd, J. (1982). *Manual for the Questionnaire on Resources and Stress.* Los Angeles: UCLA Neuropsychiatric Institute.

Holroyd, J., & Guthrie, D. (1979). Stress in families with neuromuscular disease. *Journal of Clinical Psychology,* **325**, 743–749.

Holroyd, J., & McArthur, D. (1976). Mental retardation and stress on parents. *American Journal of Mental Deficiency,* **80**, 431–436.

Huang, L. N., & Heifetz, L. J. (1984). Elements of professional helpfulness. Profiles of the most helpful and least helpful professionals encountered by mothers of young retarded children.

In J. M. Berg (Ed.), *Perspectives and progress in mental retardation* (Vol. 1) *Social, psychological and educational aspects*. International Association for the Scientific Study of Mental Deficiency. Baltimore: University Park Press.

Jacobsen, R. B., & Humphrey, R. A. (1979). Families in crisis: Research and theory in child mental retardation. *Social Casework*, **60**, 597–601.

Joyce, K., Singer, M., & Israelowitz, R. (1983). Impact of respite care on parents' perceptions of quality of life. *Mental Retardation*, **21**, 153–156.

Kazak, A. E., & Marvin, R. S. (1984). Differences, difficulties and adaptation: Stress and social networks in families with a handicapped child. *Family Relations*, **33**, 67–77.

Koegel, R. L., Schreibman, L., Britten, K. R., Burke, J. C., & O'Neil, R. E. (1982). A comparison of parent training to direct child treatment. In R. L. Koegel, A. Rincover, & A. L. Egel (Eds.), *Education and understanding autistic children*. San Diego: College-Hill Press.

Korn, S. L., Chess, S., & Fernandez, P. (1978). The impact of children's physical handicaps on marital quality and family interaction. In R. M. Lerner & G. B. Spanier (Eds.), *Child influences in marital and family interaction: A life-span perspective*. New York: Academic Press.

Kozloff, M. A. (1979). *A program for families of children with learning and behavior problems*. New York: Wiley.

Lamb, M. (1983). Fathers of exceptional children. In M. Seligman (Ed.), *The family with a handicapped child. Understanding and treatment*. New York: Grune & Stratton.

Lee, G. (1979). Effects of social networks on the family. In W. R. Burr, R. Hill, F. I. Nye, & I. L. Reiss (Eds.), *Contemporary theories about the family:* Vol. 1: *Research based theories*. New York: Free Press.

Leifer, M. (1980). *Psychological effects of motherhood: A study of first pregnancy*. New York: Praeger.

Lin, N., Ensel, W., Simeone, R., & Kuo, W. (1979). Social support, stressful life events and illness: A model and an empirical test. *Journal of Health & Social Behavior*, **20**, 108–119.

Locke, H. J., & Wallace, K. M. (1959). Short marital adjustment and predictive tests: Their reliability and validity. *Marriage and Family Living*, **Aug.**, 251–255.

McCubbin, H. I. (1979). Integrating coping behavior in family stress theory. *Journal of Marriage and the Family*, **41**, 237–244.

McCubbin, H. I., & Figley, C. R. (1983). *Stress and the family:* Vol. 1: *Coping with normative transitions*. New York: Bruner/Mazel.

McCubbin, H. I., Joy, C. B., Cauble, A. E., Comeau, J. K., Patterson, J. M., & Needle, R. H. (1980). Family stress and coping: A decade review. *Journal of Marriage and the Family*, **42**, 855–871.

McCubbin, H. I., Nevin, R. S., Cauble, A. E., Larsen, A., Comeau, J. K., & Patterson, J. M. (1982). Family coping with chronic illness: The case of cerebral palsy. In H. I. McCubbin, A. E. Cauble, & J. M. Patterson (Eds.), *Family stress, coping and social support*. Springfield, Illinois: Thomas.

McCubbin, H. I., Olson, D. H., & Larsen, A. S. (1981). *Family crisis oriented personal evaluation scales (F-COPES)*. St. Paul: University of Minnesota, Family Stress Project.

McCubbin, H. I., & Patterson, J. M. (1983). Family transitions: Adaptation to stress. In H. I. McCubbin, & C. R. Figley (Eds.), *Stress and the family:* Vol. 1: *Coping with normative transitions*. New York: Bruner/Mazel.

McCubbin, H. I., & Thompson, A. I. (1987). *Family Assessment Inventories for Research and Practice*. Madison, Wisconsin: University of Wisconsin.

Menolascino, F. (1977). *Challenges in mental retardation: Progressive ideology and services*. New York: Human Sciences.

Mercer, J. R. (1966). Patterns of family crisis related to re-acceptance of the retardate. *American Journal of Mental Deficiency*, **71**, 19–32.

Miller, B. C., & Sollie, D. L. (1980). Normal stresses during the transition to parenthood. *Family*

Relations, **29**, 459–465.
Mink, I. T., Nihira, K., & Meyers, C. E. (1983). Taxonomy of family life styles—I. Homes with TMR children. *American Journal of Mental Deficiency,* **87**, 484–497.
Minnes, P. M. (1984). *Coping strategies and family adjustment to stress associated with a handicapped child.* Unpublished doctoral dissertation, York University, Toronto.
Minnes, P. M. (1986). *Family resources and stress associated with a handicapped child.* Paper presented at the A.A.M.D. Conference, Denver.
Minnes, P. M. (1987). *Stress and coping in rural families with a handicapped child.* Paper presented at the Ontario Chapter A.A.M.D. Conference, London, Ontario.
Moos, R., & Moos, B. H. (1981). *Family environment scale: Manual.* Palo Alto, California: Consulting Psychologists.
Nihira, K., Meyers, C. E., & Mink, E. T. (1980). Home environment, family adjustment, and the development of mentally retarded children. *Applied Research in Mental Retardation,* **1**, 5–24.
Nuckolls, K. B., Cassel, J., & Kaplan, B. H. (1972). Psychosocial assets, life crisis and the prognosis of pregnancy. *American Journal of Epidemiology,* **95**, 431–441.
O'Connor, W. A., & Stachowiak, J. (1971). Patterns of interaction in families with low adjusted, high adjusted and mentally retarded members. *Family Process,* **10**, 229–241.
Olshansky, S. (1966). Parent responses to a mentally defective child. *Mental Retardation,* **4**, 21–23.
Olson, D. H., & McCubbin, H. I. (1982). Circumplex model of marital and family systems. VI: Application to family stress and crisis intervention. In H. I. McCubbin, R. A. Cauble, & J. M. Patterson (Eds.), *Family stress, coping and social support.* Springfield, Illinois: Thomas.
Olson, D. H., Sprenkle, D., & Russell, C. (1979). Circumplex model of marital and family systems. I: Cohesion and adaptability dimensions, family types and clinical applications. *Family Process,* **18**, 3–28.
Osofsky, J. D., & Osofsky, H. J. (1984). Psychological and developmental perspectives on expectant and new parenthood. In R. Parke (Ed.). *Review of child development:* Vol. 7: *The family.* Chicago: University of Chicago Press.
Pearlin, L. I., & Schooler, C. (1978). The structure of coping. *Journal of Health & Social Behavior,* **19**, 2–21.
Pratt, L. (1976). *Family structure and effective health behavior. The energized family.* Boston: Houghton Mifflin.
Price-Bonham, S., & Addison, S. (1978). Families and mentally retarded children: Emphasis on the father. *Family Coordinator,* **27**, 221–230.
Quinton, D., Rutter, M., & Rowlands, D. (1976). An evaluation of an interview assessment of marriage. *Psychological Medicine,* **6**, 577–586.
Robinson, E. A., & Anderson, L. L. (1983). Family adjustment, parental attitudes and social desirability. *Journal of Abnormal Child Psychology,* **11**, 247–256.
Rodick, J. D., Henggeler, S. W., & Hanson, C. L. (1986). An evaluation of the Family Adaptability and Cohesion Evaluation Scales and the Circumplex Model. *Journal of Abnormal Child Psychology,* **14**, 77–87.
Roesel, R., & Lawlis, G. F. (1983). Divorce in families of genetically handicapped/mentally retarded individuals. *American Journal of Family Therapy,* **11**, 45–50.
Roos, P. (1978). Parents of mentally retarded children: Misunderstood and mistreated. In A. P. Turnbull & H. R. Turnbull (Eds.), *Parents speak out. Views from the other side of the two way mirror.* Columbus, Ohio: Merrill.
Ryckman, D. B., & Henderson, R. A. (1965). The meaning of a retarded child for his parents: A focus for counsellors. *Mental Retardation,* **3**, 4–7.
Schilling, R. F., Gilchrist, L. D., & Schinke, S. P. (1984). Coping and social support in families of developmentally disabled children. *Family Relations,* **33**, 47–54.
Searl, S. J. (1978). Stages of parent reaction. *The Exceptional Parent,* **8**, 127–129.
Seltzer, M. M., & Krauss, M. W. (1984). Family, community residence and institutional placements

of a sample of mentally retarded children. *American Journal of Mental Deficiency,* **89**, 257–266.

Sherman, B. R., & Cocozza, J. J. (1984). Stress in families of the developmentally disabled: A literature review of factors affecting the decision to seek out-of-home placements. *Family Relations,* **33**, 95–103.

Short, A. (1984). Short-term treatment outcome using parents as co-therapists for their own autistic children. *Journal of Child Psychology and Psychiatry and Allied Disciplines,* **25**, 443–458.

Simeonsson, R. J., & McHale, S. (1981). Review: Research on handicapped children: Sibling relationships. *Child: Care, Health and Development,* **7**, 153–171.

Solnit, A. J., & Stark, M. H. (1961). Mourning and the birth of a defective child. *Psychoanalytic Study of the Child,* **16**, 523–537.

Spanier, G. (1976). Measuring dyadic adjustment: New scales for assessing the quality of marriage and other dyads. *Journal of Marriage and the Family,* **38**, 15–28.

Suelzle, M., & Keenan, V. (1981). Changes in family support networks over the life cycle of mentally retarded persons. *American Journal of Mental Deficiency,* **86**, 267–274.

Tallman, I. (1965). Spousal role differentiation and the socialization of severely retarded children. *Journal of Marriage and the Family,* **27**, 37–42.

Turnbull, A. P., Brotherson, M. J., & Summers, J. A. (1984). The impact of deinstitutionalization on families: A family systems approach. In R. H. Bruininks & K. C. Lakin (Eds.), *Living and learning in the least restrictive environment.* Baltimore: Brooks.

Turnbull, A., & Turnbull, R. (Eds.) (1978). *Parents speak out. Views from the other side of the two-way mirror.* Columbus, Ohio: Bell & Howell.

Turnbull, A. P., & Winton, P. J. (1984). Parent involvement in policy and practice: Current research and implications for families of young severely handicapped children. In J. Blacher (Ed.), *Severely handicapped young children and the families: Research in Review.* New York: Academic Press.

Upshur, C. C. (1982). Respite care for mentally retarded and other disabled populations: Program models and family needs. *Mental Retardation,* **20**, 2–6.

Voysey, M. (1972). Impression management by parents of disabled children. *Journal of Health and Social Behavior,* **13**, 80–89.

Voysey, M. (1975). *A constant burden.* London: Routledge.

Waisbren, S. E. (1980). Parents reactions after the birth of a developmentally disabled child. *American Journal of Mental Deficiency,* **84**, 345–351.

Waldron, H., & Routh, D. K. (1981). The effect of the first child on the marital relationship. *Journal of Marriage and the Family,* **43**, 785–788.

Weller, L., Costeff, C., Cohen, B., & Rahman, D. (1974). Social variables in the perception and acceptance of retardation. *American Journal of Mental Deficiency,* **79**, 274–278.

Wikler, L. (1981). Chronic stresses in families of mentally retarded children. *Family Relations,* **30**, 281–288.

Wikler, L. (1986). Periodic stresses of families of older mentally retarded children: An exploratory study. *American Journal of Mental Deficiency,* **90**, 703–706.

Wikler, L., Wasow, M., & Hatfield, E. (1981). Chronic sorrow revisited: Parents vs. professional depiction of the adjustment of parents of mentally retarded children. *American Journal of Orthopsychiatry,* **51**, 63–70.

Willer, B., Intagliata, J., & Atkinson, A. (1981). Deinstitutionalization as a crisis event for families of mentally retarded persons. *Mental Retardation,* **19**, 28–29.

Williams, R. C., & McKenry, P. C. (1981). Marital adjustment among parents of mentally retarded children. *Family Perspective,* **15**, 175–178.

Wilton, K., & Renaut, J. (1986). Stress levels in families with intellectually handicapped preschool children and families with nonhandicapped preschool children. *Journal of Mental Deficiency Research,* **30**, 163–169.

Wolfensberger, W. (1967). Counseling parents of the retarded. In A. A. Baumeister (Ed.), *Mental retardation: Appraisal, education and rehabilitation.* Chicago: Aldine.

Wolfensberger, W., & Kurtz, R. (1971). A measurement of parents' perception of their child's development. *Genetic Psychology Monographs,* **83**, 3–92.

Zuk, G. H. (1959). The religious factor and the role of guilt in parental acceptance of the retarded child. *American Journal of Mental Deficiency,* **64**, 139–147.

Zuk, G. H. (1962). The cultural dilemma and spiritual crisis of the family with a handicapped child. *Exceptional Children,* **23**, 405–408.

Zuk, G. H., Miller, R. L., Bartram, J. B., & Kling, F. (1961). Maternal acceptance of retarded children: A questionnaire study of attitudes and religious background. *Child Development,* **32**, 525–40.

Physical Fitness of Mentally Retarded Individuals

E. KATHRYN McCONAUGHY AND CHARLES L. SALZBERG

DEVELOPMENTAL CENTER FOR HANDICAPPED PERSONS
UTAH STATE UNIVERSITY
LOGAN, UTAH 84322

I. INTRODUCTION

Physical fitness has received increasing attention over the past 20 years. The research indicates that numerous personal benefits result from regular physical activity: lower heart rates, lower percentage of body fat, lower blood pressure, increased oxygen supply to the organs of the body, and an increased immunity to heart-related illnesses (Fox, 1984; McArdle, Katch, & Katch, 1981; Thomas, 1979). Additionally, researchers have tried to relate fitness to IQ (Corder, 1966; Oliver, 1958; Solomon & Pangle, 1967; Tomporowski & Ellis, 1984, 1985), self-concept (Simpson & Meany, 1979), social status (Corder, 1966; Crain, McLaughlin, & Eisenhart, 1983; Gross & Johnson, 1984), adaptive behavior (Tomporowski & Ellis, 1984, 1985), and work absenteeism and production (Beasley, 1982; Morehouse, 1975). Although the nature of the relationships between regular exercise and these variables is equivocal (Moon & Renzaglia, 1982; Campbell, 1973; Thomas, 1979; Karper, 1981), the notion that fitness is important to the general quality of life remains strong (Thomas, 1979; Karper, 1981).

If fitness is important for the general population, it is no less so for mentally retarded individuals (Brown, 1977; Rarick, Widdop, & Broadhead, 1970; Nosek & Nofi, 1984). As early as 1963, Stein called for a greater emphasis on physical conditioning for mentally retarded youth. A review by Moon and Renzaglia (1982) indicated that studies completed since Stein's (1963) article

INTERNATIONAL REVIEW OF RESEARCH IN
MENTAL RETARDATION, Vol. 15

have repeatedly demonstrated that mentally retarded youth and adolescents have lower levels of fitness than nonretarded individuals. Few studies have examined the status of fitness in mentally retarded adults. However, the available information suggests that fitness levels continue to be low through adulthood (Beasley, 1982; Reid & Montgomery, 1983).

Mentally retarded people have more health-related difficulties than do their nonretarded counterparts. Nosek and Nofi (1984) indicated that disabled individuals often live in sheltered environments where their level of activity places few physical demands on them. As a result of lower activity levels, disabled individuals may be more susceptible to diseases. For example, the incidence of obesity among mentally retarded adults and children is greater than the incidence among nonhandicapped populations (Fox, Hartney, Rotatori, & Kurpiers, 1985). Further, lower activity levels in mentally retarded youth may adversely affect participation in normal school activities and employment.

Although the importance of physical fitness is generally accepted, a universal definition of fitness remains illusive. However, there is some agreement about the variables that make up physical fitness. This review will begin by defining the variables or components of fitness and briefly discuss their measurement. Studies that have examined the performance of mentally retarded and nonretarded adolescents and adults on fitness tests will then be reviewed. Finally, conclusions that can be confidently drawn from these studies will be discussed and recommendations will be made about further research.

A. Definition of Physical Fitness

There are many definitions of physical fitness. Guralnik (1976) defined fitness in Webster's New World Dictionary as "in good physical condition; healthy." Nosek and Nofi (1984) reported that the definition of fitness according to a Joint Committee of the American Medical Association and the American Association for Health, Physical Education, and Recreation (AAHPER) is "freedom from disease; enough strength, agility, endurance, and skill to meet the demands of daily living; sufficient reserves to withstand ordinary stresses without causing harmful strain; and mental development and emotional adjustment appropriate to the maturity of the individual" (p. 2). Interpretation of these definitions and others is difficult because words like "enough," "sufficient," "good," and "appropriate" must be understood in relation to standards that are not specified; that is, good enough for what? Further, fitness standards are linked to life-style. A sedentary person may display "good" fitness compared to other sedentary individuals but "poor" fitness compared to athletes. For this reason, researchers have defined fitness in terms of the components measured by physical fitness tests (Moon & Renzaglia, 1982; Speakman, 1977), and these components vary considerably from one study to the next.

B. Fitness Components

Fitness is generally thought to be composed of flexibility, strength, speed, and endurance (Moon & Renzaglia, 1982). These components are assessed in differing ways by fitness tests. In general, fitness measurements are linked to age and age-appropriate physical activities. Measures of youth and adolescent fitness tend to emphasize speed, strength, and flexibility, all of which are particularly salient for team sports and other youth-oriented recreational activities. Measures of fitness for adults, on the other hand, are weighted toward cardiovascular endurance. This emphasis is probably due to the inverse relationship between cardiovascular endurance and heart disease, a prime killer of middle-aged men and a growing number of women. Further, cardiovascular endurance is a prime component of many individual physical activities typical of adults (e.g., jogging, bicycling, etc.). The components of fitness and their measurement will now be discussed.

Flexibility refers to the range of motion of different body joints (Kusinitz & Fine, 1983). Although muscles, tendons, and ligaments all determine the range of motion that a joint is capable of, overly tight muscles and tendons are usually responsible for limited flexibility (Wilmore, 1982). An individual's flexibility may not be uniform throughout the body. One may demonstrate good flexibility of the upper arms but poor flexibility of knee and hip joints. Additionally, due to the number of joints, there is no singular measure of flexibility. One measure is the range of movements for different joints. For example, a normal range of motion for the arm is 90° of lateral movement when the arm is extended from the shoulder with the palm facing down (Kusinitz & Fine, 1983). Flexibility of the hip and knee can be measured by the angle that an individual achieves when asked to touch his or her toes in a straight-legged seated position (Wilmore, 1982). Tests of fitness often do not measure flexibility, presumably because there is no single indicator of flexibility and a comprehensive assessment of flexibility would be prohibitively time consuming.

Speed is the velocity of the body or any one of its parts (Wilmore, 1982). Since speed, like flexibility, can refer to specific body parts, there are a variety of ways to measure it. For example, the velocity of arm motion can be assessed by having an individual throw an object. In standardized tests, the focus is usually on whole body speed measured by the time it takes to run a specified distance, usually 50 yards. Speed combined with other fitness components, such as strength and flexibility, is often called agility and refers to the maneuverability of the individual (Wilmore, 1982). Again, agility can be specific to a particular body part. Most often, however, fitness tests evaluate agility of the whole body with an obstacle course or a shuttle run that requires an individual to run as quickly as possible between objects, bending down to touch each one.

The ability to apply or to resist force in a singular exertion is the usual definition of strength. For example, the maximal amount of weight that a person can lift with his or her arms is a measure of upper-arm strength. Strength required to lift an object is generally referred to as dynamic strength. Static strength is the ability to apply force against a fixed object and is measured with a dynamometer or a tensiometer in which the amount of force exerted is displayed on a meter.

Strength is often assessed in standardized tests of fitness; however, the measures are controversial. For example, sit-ups are used as a measure of abdominal strength. However, if the subject's feet are held while doing sit-ups, weakness of the abdominal muscles may be masked since the hip flexors may be performing some of the work (Safrit, 1973). The controversy over how to assess strength is not limited to sit-ups. Another example is pull-ups (Simri, 1974). In this exercise, individuals hanging from a bar by the hands attempt to lift their bodies so that their chins are above the bar. Essentially, persons are lifting their own body weight. Since weight varies, heavier people can do fewer pull-ups (Safrit, 1973). Moreover, if a person is not able to complete one pull-up, his or her maximal strength remains unknown. The fact that the range of scores in tests of pull-ups is limited and that many students get a zero score (Meyers, 1974; Safrit, 1973) verifies the problem. Similar problems exist for the flexed-arm hang (Meyers, 1974) frequently used with females and mentally retarded populations as an alternative to the pull-up.

When an exercise is performed more than once, muscular endurance is involved. Muscular endurance is the ability of muscles to sustain repeated movements or a fixed position for a prolonged period (Kusinitz & Fine, 1983; Wilmore, 1982). Muscular endurance, like strength and flexibility, is specific to different parts of the body. One may have good endurance of the leg muscles but poor endurance of the abdominal muscles. The maximal number of sit-ups and push-ups are examples of measures of muscular endurance. Endurance measures interact with strength since, invariably, a person must lift some proportion of his or her body weight in endurance tests. Some authors maintain that while muscular endurance is dependent on a person's strength, strength is not dependent on muscular endurance (Wilmore, 1982).

One very important type of endurance is cardiovascular endurance. Cardiovascular endurance is considered to be the best single indicator of overall health according to some fitness experts (Beasley, 1982; Cooper, 1968; Kusinitz & Fine, 1983; Newton, 1963). Measures of cardiovascular endurance reflect the maximal rate at which oxygen can be used to meet the demands of strenuous physical activity (Newton, 1963). During prolonged exercise, oxygen intake increases in a linear fashion until it reaches a peak; then it plateaus or falls slightly. Heart rate during exercise follows a similar pattern (Fox, 1984). The value at which oxygen intake peaks is known as the maximal oxygen intake, or $VO_{2\ max}$.

Oxygen intake sometimes is measured directly through air samples taken from exercising individuals. It can also be measured indirectly, or estimated, by requiring a person to exercise for a specified amount of time or to cover a certain distance. The 600-yard walk-run included in many fitness tests is an example of an indirect measure of cardiovascular endurance. Tests that directly measure oxygen consumption, such as a treadmill or bicycle test, express their results in milliliters of oxygen per kilogram of body weight per minute (or ml/kg/minute). The inclusion of body weight allows for more equitable comparisons between individuals of different sizes (Wilmore, 1982).

The components of fitness have been combined in various ways to produce fitness tests. These tests and their reliability and validity will be briefly discussed in the next section. Fitness tests that have been adapted for the mentally retarded will also be reviewed.

II. TESTS OF PHYSICAL FITNESS

Since fitness is a multiple-factor construct, fitness tests should independently assess a variety of components such as strength, muscular endurance, cardiovascular endurance, and flexibility. Many such tests have been developed by individual states or local school districts for their own use (Meyers, 1974). These will not be reviewed here; rather, only tests designed for nationwide use will be considered. These tests are summarized in Table I.

Tests of physical fitness differ in the number of components measured. There are general tests of fitness that measure several components, and others that measure only cardiovascular endurance. There is variation between the number of components assessed in a test and in the exercises used to assess each component. This lack of comparableness makes it difficult to validate fitness tests and has led some to suggest that the only type of validity pertinent to fitness tests is construct validity (Alderman & Howell, 1974). However, it is possible to assess concurrent validity since there are several instruments that all purport to measure physical fitness and several studies have compared the results of one or more tests against another. The reliability of multiple-component fitness tests has been well researched. Tests that measure fitness across multiple components along with their reliability and validity will be discussed first followed by a discussion of cardiovascular tests.

A. Multiple-Component Tests

The most widely used nationwide instrument is the AAHPER Youth Fitness Test (1976). While this test, normed on students from ages 9 to 17, does not measure flexibility (Speakman, 1977), it does measure arm and shoulder strength, abdominal strength and endurance, speed, power, agility, and cardiovascular endurance through the exercises summarized in Table II.

Test–retest reliabilities on the AAHPER range from .57 to .99 (Safrit, 1973) over 2-day intervals; the lowest score was in the sit-up subtest for tenth grade males, while the highest score was reported in the 600-yard run–walk subtest

TABLE I
SUMMARY OF COMPONENTS THAT ARE ASSESSED BY FITNESS TESTS

Tests	Components that are assessed					Population norms[a]			
						Youths		Adults	
	Strength	Muscular endurance	Flexibility	Speed	Cardiovascular endurance	nMR	MR	nMR	MR
American Alliance for Health, Physical Education, & Recreation (AAHPER) Youth Fitness Test	X	X		X	X	X			
AAHPER Special Fitness Test for the Mentally Retarded	X	X		X	X		X		
AAHPER Fitness Test for the Moderately Mentally Retarded	X	X		X	X		X		
Basic fitness tests	X	X	X	X		X			
Step tests (potpourri)					X	X		X	
Cooper's Aerobic Tests					X	X		X	
Treadmill tests (potpourri)					X	X		X	
Bicycle tests (potpourri)					X	X		X	
Canadian Public Health Association Standardized Test of Fitness	X		X		X			X	
Kraus–Weber Test	X		X			X		X	
International Committee for the Standardization of Physical Finess Tests	X	X	X	X	X	X		X	
Project Unique[b]	X	X	X	X	X	X			

[a]nMR, not mentally retarded; MR, mentally retarded.
[b]Normed on youths with auditory impairments, visual impairments, cerebral palsy, and spinal neuromuscular conditions.

TABLE II

SUMMARY OF EXERCISES IN TESTS OF PHYSICAL FITNESS

Exercises	Fitness tests								
	AAHPER Youth Fitness (nMR)	AAHPER EMR	AAHPER TMR	Basic fitness	Project Unique	Kraus–Weber Test	Canadian tests of fitness: PH	Canadian tests of fitness: RCAF[a]	Standardized Test of Fitness (ICSPHT)
Sit-ups	X	X		X	X	X	X	X	X
Flexed Arm Hang	X	X	X		X				X
Shuttle Run	X	X		X					X
50 Yard Dash	X	X	X		X				X[b]
Push-ups							X	X	
Softball Throw	X	X	X	X	X				
Pull-ups	X			X					X
Hand Grip				X	X		X		X
Broad Jump	X	X	X		X				X
Toe Touch				X	X	X	X	X	X
Distance Runs	X	X	X	X	X				X
Run In Place								X	
Leg Lift				X		X			
Step Test							X		
Head and Shoulder Lifts								X	

[a]RCAF, Royal Canadian Air Force; PH, Public Health.
[b]Test was 50 m.

for junior high males and females. Reliabilities computed between trials of the same subtest indicate that, in general, the more trials that are allowed for the exercises, the higher the reliability (Safrit, 1973). However, Meyers (1974) indicated that research on the number of trials necessary to establish acceptable reliability has been equivocal and, therefore, there is no reason to deviate from the number of trials specified for each exercise in the test manual.

The AAHPER test has been modified for use with mentally retarded populations. One variation (Johnson & Londeree, 1976) was designed for the moderately mentally retarded (see AAHPER TMR in Table II). This test measures strength, speed, muscular endurance, and cardiovascular endurance through a series of 6 exercises. Normative data, based on a sample of mentally retarded students in Missouri state schools, are provided for both genders from 6 to 20 years of age. Additional items (7), including tumbling, skipping, hopping, bob and reach, weight, and height, can be used as needed for establishing local norms. While there is no established reliability for the final 13 items, 6-month test–retest reliabilities were computed between 12 original items and 12 modified items of the final test. Of the 6 main items, 5 had reliability coefficients of .80 or greater. The 7 additional items had reliabilities that ranged from .60 to .90. Since the 300-yard run–walk was not administered on both occasions, no reliability was computed.

The AAHPER Special Fitness Test for the Mentally Retarded (see AAHPER EMR in Table II) is a variation that was designed for use with mildly mentally retarded populations and contains exercises similar to the other AAHPER tests. Norms are included for boys and girls aged 8 to 18. This adaptation of the AAHPER is reported to have test–retest reliability ranges of .60 to .95 with only the flexed arm hang, the 50-yard dash, and the softball throw having reliability coefficients consistently above .80 (Aufsesser, 1979).

Other fitness tests for youth have been developed that contain exercises similar to the AAHPER Youth Fitness Test. Fleishman (1964) designed the Basic Fitness Tests for youths 12 to 18 years of age. This battery is among the most comprehensive fitness assessment for youths (Meyers, 1974; Safrit, 1973). Exercises in this test have test–retest reliabilities that range from .70 to .93. The International Committee for the Standardization of Physical Fitness Tests (ICSPHT) designed a physical fitness test for use with individuals between the ages of 6 and 32 years. No reliability or validity figures were found. The Kraus–Weber test, originally designed for use with adult back patients, has also been used to test minimal muscular fitness of school-aged children (Safrit, 1973). Its six items are scored on a pass/fail system; that is, a failure on any single item is considered to be a test failure.

Few nationally used, multiple-component fitness tests are available for use with adults. Perhaps the best known and most widely used is the Royal

Canadian Air Force (RCAF) battery of exercises that measures flexibility, strength, and cardiovascular endurance. The Canadian Public Health Association has developed the Standardized Test of Fitness for use with adults over the age of 20. Sit-ups, push-ups, grip strength, a step test, toe touches, running in place, and head and shoulder lifts are the exercises included in these tests (see Table II).

Peries (1976) and Speakman (1977) have described fitness tests that have been specifically designed for mentally retarded populations. Five of the seven tests reviewed by these authors contained items similar to the AAHPER. No studies were found that examined fitness with those tests. The remaining two tests reviewed were the AAHPER versions for the mildly and the moderately mentally retarded. Additionally, Winnick & Short (1985) have recently designed a fitness test for use with people who have orthopedic, auditory, or visual impairments. The information provided with Winnick and Short's (1985) Project Unique Test for Disabled Youth does not describe how reliability was established or provide any reliability coefficients.

It is important to note that multiple component tests are, for the most part, tests of strength. While some tests purport to measure endurance, the type of endurance measured is usually that of a specific group of muscles (such as the abdominal muscles), not cardiovascular endurance.

B. Cardiovascular Tests

Although a few have been normed on adolescents, cardiovascular tests are used generally with adults (Cumming & Cumming, 1963). These tests, summarized in Table III, can be divided according to whether the results are obtained from performance measures (e.g., time it takes to run a specific distance) or from physiologic measures (e.g., heart rate).

The various performance-based tests included the Cooper Aerobic Tests and the 1- and 2-mile run (Dorociak & Nelson, 1983; Custer & Chaloupka, 1977; Beasley, 1982; Burke, 1976). One of Cooper's aerobic tests, the 12-minute run, was originally designed for the U.S. Air Force (Cooper, 1968). The distance covered during the run is directly related to maximal oxygen consumption and determines placement into one of five fitness categories. A person who covers less than 1 mile is estimated to have a maximal oxygen consumption below 25 ml/kg/minute and is categorized as being in "very poor" fitness. A person who covers 1.75 or more miles is in "excellent" condition with an estimated maximal oxygen consumption of 56 ml/kg/minute. Cooper's Aerobic Tests, including the 1.5-mile run and the 12-minute run, have been normed for junior high students (Meyers, 1974).

Although Cooper (1968) did not report a quantitative test–retest reliability score for his subjects, he noted that repeated testing at 3- to 4-day intervals had little effect on the performance of subjects who wanted to do well. Further,

TABLE III

CARDIOVASCULAR TESTS OF PHYSICAL FITNESS

Test	Measure of VO_2 max	Procedures for Administering Test
12-min run (performance test)	Indirect through distance covered	Person covers the longest distance possible in 12 min period running on a surface that is flat and well marked. Subjects should not have eaten for 2 hours prior to test.
1 & 2 mile run (performance test)	Indirect through time run completed	Person runs 1 or 2 miles as fast as possible on a surface that is flat and well marked. Subjects should not have eaten for 2 hours prior to test.
Step Test (physiological test)	Indirect through heart rate. Direct though air samples.	Person steps up and down a bench maintaining a specified stepping rate and continuing until a predetermined heart rate is achieved or until s/he can no longer continue.
Bicyle Test (physiological test)	Indirect through heart rate. Direct through air samples.	Person pedals at a specified rate and resistance. At intervals, the rate, the resistance, or both are increased. Example Protocols are:

Protocol	Stage	Rate	Resistance	Duration
ICSPFT	Rest	0	0	10-20 min
	Accom.[a]	50/60 rpm	1 watt/kg/lb	3 min
	Recovery	0	0	2 min
	Test	50/60 rpm	1 wat/kg/lb	2 min
	Resistance increases every 2 min by 1/3 body weight kg until test ends.			

		Astrand/Rodahl (1970)	Test	60 rpm	60 watts	2 min
			Resistance increases by 50 watts until heart rate is 140 BPM (under 50 years) or 120 (over 50 years). Then, level selected that the person can complete with difficulty in 2 min.			
Treadmill Test (Physiological test)	Indirect through heart rate. Direct through air samples.	Person walks on treadmill at a specified speed and elevation. At specified intervals, the speed, the elevation, or both are increased. Example Protocols are:				
		Protocol	Stage	Speed	Elevation	Duration
		ICSPFT	Rest	0	0	10-20 min
			Accom.	3mph	2.5%	3 min
			Recovery	0	0	2 min
			Test	3mph	2.5%	2 min
			Elevation increases 2.5% every 2 min until test ends.			
		Balke	Rest	0	0	2-3 min
			Accom.	2mph	0	2 min
			Recovery	0	0	2 min
			Test	2mph	0	2 min
			Elevation increases 2.5% every 2 min until test ends.			
		Balke & Ware	Rest	0	0	2-3 min
			Accom.	3mph	0	1 min
			Recovery	0	0	2 min
			Test	3mph	2.5%	2 min
			Elevation increases 2.5% every 2 min until test ends			

[a]Accom., Accommodation to familiarize subject with equipment.

he reported a test–retest reliability of .976 for 149 junior high school males in California. Other authors have reported test–retest reliabilities that range from .78 for college-aged women to .94 for ninth grade males (Katch, McArdle, Czula, & Pechar, 1973a; Safrit, 1973).

Physiologically based tests, also summarized in Table III, include the motorized treadmill, the bicycle ergometer, and the step test (Burke, 1976; Brouha, 1943; Cumming, Fisher, & Stasynec, 1978; Dolgener, 1982; Kasch, Phillips, Ross, Carter, & Boyer, 1966; Katch *et al.*, 1973a; Katch, Pechar, McArdle, & Weldman, 1973b; Shoenfeld, Keren, Birnfeld, & Sohar, 1981; Tomporowski & Ellis, 1984, 1985). In physiologically based tests, oxygen consumption is measured either directly or indirectly. When oxygen consumption is measured directly, air samples are usually taken during the final minute of each stage. A maximal limit is reached when the values of oxygen consumption remain constant for two consecutive stages. The International Committee for the Standardization of Physical Fitness Tests has also indicated that testing should be stopped if any of the following three conditions exist: the subject reports an inability to continue exercising, the presence of physiological indications that either maximal effort has been achieved or that the subject's health is in danger, or the sequential physiological measurements that allow for an extrapolation of maximal aerobic power are achieved.

Because it may be medically risky to have certain individuals exercise at levels required to assess their maximal oxygen consumption, methods of estimating $VO_{2\,max}$ from submaximal stress levels have been developed. Submaximal tests are usually terminated when the heart rate reaches a specific value (usually 160–170 beats/minute). Linear extrapolations between heart rate and oxygen consumption values are then made to determine the maximal oxygen consumption.

Due to the difficulty of taking air samples from a person who is continually moving up and down, indirect measures of oxygen consumption are usually taken with step tests (see Table III). Physiologically based tests done on a bicycle or treadmill allow for direct measurements of oxygen consumption since body position remains fairly constant. Because treadmills and bicycles allow for direct measurements of oxygen consumption, they are often used as the standard for comparisons to performance-based tests. A variety of protocols have been developed for both the treadmill and the bicycle. Sample protocols are given in Table III.

Despite the availability of standard protocols, many researchers develop their own (Coleman, 1976; Dolgener, 1982; Ribisl & Kachadorian, 1969). Further, even when standard protocols are used, they are often changed slightly to meet the needs of the equipment or subjects used in the study. For example, bicycles are used with persons who are obese and/or have orthopedic problems. The Balke protocol is used with elderly or less physically fit people because elevation is increased slowly and leg muscles do not easily fatigue, whereas a Bruce (1984) protocol is used for younger and more physically fit people because the elevation and speed are increased rapidly leading to greater muscle fatigue.

Because protocols are not consistently implemented, their reliability has not generally been reported. In one of the few exceptions, Bruce (1984) reported that maximal heart rate varied by 2% a year using his protocol. Occasionally, studies that have created their own protocols have examined test–retest reliability (Katch *et al.*, 1973a; Ribisl & Kachadorian, 1969) and obtained acceptable reliability (r = .95, r = .91 respectively). Despite their good internal reliability, the results across studies cannot easily be compared because the authors used different protocols.

Research has also examined whether fitness as measured by multiple-component tests is the same type of fitness as that measured by cardiovascular tests. In a study of 141 males from 16 to 59 years of age, Drake, Jones, Brown, and Shephard (1968) had subjects perform exercises similar to those in the AAHPER and a step test, from which maximal oxygen consumption was estimated. While some measures (sit-ups, standing broad jump, 50-yard dash, and 600-yard run–walk) were correlated significantly with estimated maximal oxygen consumption, all seven items of the AAHPER accounted for just 17.2% of the variance in maximal oxygen consumption. Other authors who have obtained higher correlations between multiple-component and cardiovascular tests have usually done so by using subjects with a restricted age range (Cureton, 1978). If, as some authors maintain, tests of maximal aerobic power are the best general indicator of fitness, then the AAHPER youth fitness tests may not be valid. At the least, the lack of a strong correlation between the two types of tests makes it difficult to examine how fitness develops over time. A decrease in fitness at age 18 may be due to a general decline in fitness or to differing measures.

Cardiovascular tests also do not always correlate highly among themselves. The question of how well performance-based tests relate to physiologically based tests has been the topic of many research articles. In Cooper's (1968) study of Air Force personnel, he obtained a correlation of .90 between the 12-minute run and treadmill measurements of oxygen consumption. However, recent research has questioned the high correlation obtained by Cooper (Burke, 1976; Custer & Chaloupka, 1977; Katch *et al.*, 1973b; Shoenfeld *et al.*, 1981). Correlations obtained in these studies ranged from .49 to .81.

Factors that appeared to influence the size of the correlation include the age of the subjects [a broader age range produces a higher correlation (Shoenfeld *et al.*, 1981; Katch *et al.*, 1973b; Maksud & Coutts, 1971)]; the level of fitness of the subjects [the more fit a subject is the higher the correlation (Bar-Or, Zwiren, & Dotan, 1978; Shoenfeld *et al.*, 1981)]; the percentage of lean body mass [a large amount of variance between maximal oxygen consumption and field-test performance can be accounted for by the amount of body fat (Dorociak & Nelson, 1983)]; the speed at which a run is conducted [the faster one begins a run, the faster he or she will tire, which results in poor performance and a low correlation—at least 5 minutes of running is needed to ensure an acceptable measure of maximal oxygen consumption (Katch *et al.*, 1973b)]; and the motivation of the subjects [poor motivation results in poor performance and a low correlation (Burke, 1976)]. Similar variability between tests of aerobic fitness has also been found for other field tests such as the 1- and 2-mile runs (Burke, 1976; Dorociak & Nelson, 1983; Ribisl & Kachadorian, 1969).

In one of the most extensive validity studies of cardiovascular tests, Burke (1976) compared 15 tests of fitness to each other as well as to maximal oxygen consumption measured by a treadmill test. Although all the findings cannot be described here, some of the more important ones will be mentioned. For instance, Burke found that the Cooper 12-minute run and the Balke treadmill protocol correlated highly with the treadmill test, $r = .90$ and $r = .77$, respectively. Short distance runs (10 yards, 50 yards) correlated highly with each other ($r = .84$) but poorly to treadmill tests ($r = -.18$), bicycle tests ($r = -.27$), and other field tests ($r = -.24$). Finally, there was no consistent pattern in the correlations of step tests with other tests. It appears from Burke (1976) that performance on one fitness test is not necessarily related to performance on another fitness test. Moreover, other studies that used subjects of different ages and fitness levels than those used by Burke (1976) have reported different correlations. For example, Kasch *et al.* (1966) reported a correlation coefficient of .95 between a step test and a treadmill test. Their subjects ranged in age from 7 to 57 and included both males and females, while Burke's subjects were males between the ages of 17 and 30 years.

Although maximal oxygen consumption measured on the treadmill or bicycle ergometer is used as a standard against which to compare other fitness tests, it is apparent that results from these tests also do not always agree. Generally, performance on bicycle tests produces lower levels of oxygen consumption than performance on treadmill tests (Newton, 1963). Cumming *et al.* (1978) reported that, with nonhandicapped adults, maximal oxygen consumption values were 40–50% higher on the treadmill than on the bicycle. The extent that treadmill and bicycle oxygen consumption values differ depends, in part, on the physical condition of the person being tested. A well-conditioned person will perform approximately the same on field and bicycle tests as they do on treadmill tests (Newton, 1963). Bicycle values may sometimes be lower due to leg muscles fatiguing or improper seat height (Astrand & Rodahl, 1977). Similar problems are noted on the treadmill when protocols are used that increase the speed and elevation rapidly.

Even though not all of the tests described previously have been normed on mentally retarded populations, many have been used to determine the fitness levels of people who are mentally retarded. In general, fitness levels of mentally retarded people are below those of nonretarded people. In the following section, research that has examined the status of fitness in mentally retarded populations will be reviewed.

III. RESEARCH ON FITNESS

Several studies have assessed fitness of both mentally retarded and nonretarded populations. Studies that examined multiple components of fitness will be reviewed first followed by those reporting only cardiovascular fitness.

A. Multiple Components of Fitness

The AAHPER (unmodified version) has been used in studies with both mentally retarded and nonretarded populations (Sengstock, 1966; Rarick *et al.*, 1970; Solomon & Pangle, 1967). Sengstock (1966) used the AAHPER test to compare fitness levels of mentally retarded and nonretarded adolescent males. One group consisted of thirty 10- to 15-year-old educable mentally retarded (EMR) males who had mental ages that ranged from 6 to 12 years. The second group of thirty males was matched to the first group on chronological age (CA, 10–15 years) but had normal IQs. Because some authors have questioned whether the poorer fitness levels may be due to limited cognitive ability, a third group of thirty males was included who matched the first group's mental age (6 to 12 years) but whose chronological age ranged from 5 to 13 years. Nonhandicapped males of the same chronological age exceeded EMR males in all exercises, and these comparative differences remained when factors such as height and weight were statistically controlled. The EMR males had greater speed, power, and cardiovascular endurance than chronologically younger males, but in two exercises designed to measure strength, the two groups did not differ. These results may be explained, in part, by the EMR subjects' greater height and weight. That is, height and weight are positively related to endurance (Cureton, 1978). Likewise, the greater weight of the EMR males may have contributed to their inability to do as well on the strength exercises (pull-ups and sit-ups). This study suggests that mentally retarded males do less well on tests of fitnesss than nonretarded males of the same age. Moreover, the poorer performance cannot entirely be attributed to the lack of cognitive ability since, on some exercises, mentally retarded males performed better than younger males with the same mental age.

In most studies, results for mentally retarded youth have been compared to normative data provided in the test manual (Rarick *et al.*, 1970; Solomon & Pangle, 1967). Rarick *et al.* (1970) conducted a nationwide study of 4235 mentally retarded students from 8 to 18 years of age using 7 exercises from the AAHPER Youth Fitness Test. Of the AAHPER exercises that subjects had difficulty with, 3 were modified, including timed sit-ups, flexed arm hang for both sexes, and a 300-yard walk–run. The remaining 4 exercises were not modified. In the nonmodified exercises where a direct comparison was possible, mentally retarded subjects performed 2 to 4 years behind the national norm. However, the developmental progression for many of the exercises were similar for the mentally retarded and the normative population indicating that fitness for mentally retarded subjects was delayed.

In another study, Londeree and Johnson (1974) used an adaptation of the AAHPER Youth Fitness Test developed especially for mentally retarded adolescents (the AAHPER–Kennedy Foundation Special Youth Fitness Test) to assess fitness levels in 1100 trainable mentally retarded (TMR) students from 6 to 19 years old. The fitness levels of the TMR subjects were compared to norms for EMR and nonretarded children. The results, reported by quartiles, indicated that TMR youth were even less physically fit than EMR youth. Except in the flexed-arm hang, there was no overlap in the quartile ranges (mean quartiles ± 1 SD) between TMR youth and the two comparison groups. On the flexed-arm hang, the upper quartile range for the TMR subjects overlapped with the bottom quartile range of the EMR subjects.

Based on these studies, it appears that while a nonretarded 16-year-old male could do an average of 20 sit-ups in 30 seconds, an EMR male of the same age could only do an average of 12 sit-ups in 30 seconds, and an average TMR 16-year-old male could do 10 sit-ups, in the same time. The performance of the average TMR would be half of that for a nonretarded 16-year-old male and about the same as an average, nonretarded 6 to 7 year old. An average 7-year-old TMR male cannot even do 1 sit-up. Nonretarded 16-year-old females average 14 sit-ups in 30 seconds, EMR females average 9 sit-ups, and TMR females average 7. For the flexed arm hang, an average nonretarded 10-year-old boy can hang for 20 seconds; an EMR boy can hang for approximately 7 seconds. Although females are able to hang for less time at every age than their male counterparts, the trend across handicapping conditions is parallel. Clearly, mentally retarded youths do not display even minimal fitness when compared to nonretarded youths.

Brown (1967) administered the Kraus–Weber test to 38 TMR children aged 8 to 16 years. These subjects' performance was then compared to that of nonhandicapped subjects included in four previous research articles. It should be recalled that one failure on any of the six components of this test is considered a test failure. In the Brown (1967) study, 78.9% of the TMR subjects failed compared to a 66.1% failure rate of nonhandicapped children in Iowa, a 45.1% failure rate of nonhandicapped children in Indiana, a 38.1% failure rate of nonhandicapped children in Oregon, and a nationwide failure rate of 57.9% (Kraus, 1954). Further, 43.4% of the TMR subjects failed one-half or more of the test items. Mentally retarded females in the Brown (1967) study fared better than their male counterparts, since 36.4% of the females failed one-half or more of the test items compared to 47.4% of the males.

With the exception of Brown (1967), the AAHPER or one of its modifications has been used exclusively for research on fitness of mentally retarded youth.

The paucity of studies that examine multiple components of fitness of mentally retarded individuals is greatest among adults. To begin with, there are few multiple-component fitness tests for mentally retarded adults. No multiple-component test was found that was normed on mentally retarded individuals above the age of 20. In the only study found that examined the fitness of mentally retarded adults across several components, Reid and Montgomery (1983) used the Standardized Test of Fitness, developed by the Canadian Public Health Association, with mentally retarded adults between 20 and 39 years of age. Although the level of retardation was not specified, all subjects were enrolled in sheltered workshops. Mentally retarded 20- to 29-year-old men placed in the first percentile of a normative distribution in two measures of strength, in the seventeenth percentile on a test of flexibility, and in the second percentile on a measure of cardiovascular endurance. Performance scores of mentally retarded women of the same age range placed them in the second and fourth percentile for strength measures, in the thirty-seventh percentile for flexibility, and in the fourth percentile for cardiovascular endurance. Older mentally retarded men (30–39 years) achieved the first and second percentile for strength, the twenty-sixth for flexibility, and the fourth for cardiovascular endurance while 30- to 39-year-old women achieved the first and fifth percentile for strength, the twenty-third percentile for flexibility, and the thirteenth percentile for cardiovascular endurance.

B. Cardiovascular Fitness

No studies have used performance-based tests of cardiovascular fitness with mentally retarded youths, probably because few cardiovascular tests have been normed for youth. Some studies that used physiological assessments of fitness for mentally retarded youth have been conducted. Maksud and Hamilton (1974) used a bicycle to measure the oxygen consumption of 62 educably mentally retarded boys (CA 10–13 years) in Milwaukee, Wisconsin. These subjects achieved an average maximal heart rate of approximately 187 beats per minute (BPM) and an average maximal oxygen uptake of 39 ml/kg/minute. Although maximal values for a nonretarded populaton were not reported, Maksud and Hamilton (1974) indicated that maximal values obtained by their subjects were lower than a nonretarded population of similar chronological age. Further, the authors attributed the poorer performance of the mentally retarded subjects to local muscular fatigue resulting in premature termination of the test.

Yoshizawa, Ishizaki, and Honda (1975) also used a bicycle to assess maximal oxygen consumption of 12- to 15-year-old Japanese mentally retarded boys. Mentally retarded boys had mean maximal oxygen consumption values of

42.43 ml/kg/minute compared to 51.24 ml/kg/minute for nonretarded boys. Girls in their sample demonstrated a maximal oxygen consumption of 33.17 ml/kg/minute compared to 41.38 ml/kg/minute for nonretarded Japanese girls. Yoshizawa *et al.* (1975) interpret their results with caution since the mentally retarded youths in their study also achieved lower maximal heart rates than their nonretarded counterparts. Average maximal heart rates achieved by their mentally retarded boys and girls were 186 and 184 BPM, respectively; values for nonhandicapped boys and girls were 191 and 190 BPM, respectively. Lower maximal heart rates may indicate that the mentally retarded youths stopped exercising before attaining their physiologic limit; that is, they were not as highly stressed as their nonhandicapped counterparts (Yoshizawa *et al.*, 1975). No studies have measured oxygen consumption while retarded youths exercised on a treadmill.

Generally, studies using cardiovascular tests are done with adults. Performance-based tests, such as the field tests, have been used extensively with nonretarded adult populations. In a study by Katch *et al.* (1973a), 36 women of a mean age of 21 years ran 12-minute distances that placed them in the "poor" to "fair" category of fitness. Other studies of nonhandicapped populations between the ages of 18 and 30 years generally found them to be in "fair" and "good" categories (Burke, 1976; Custer & Chaloupka, 1977).

Performance-based cardiovascular tests have been used to a lesser extent with mentally retarded adults. Beasley (1982) used the 12-minute run as a pre- and posttest measure of intervention with 30 mentally retarded sheltered workshop employees aged 16–50; 24 of the subjects were between 16 and 35 years of age. In the pretest, all but one subject covered distances that placed them in the "very poor" category of fitness. However, after 8 weeks of aerobic conditioning, experimental subjects covered distances that moved them up to the "poor" category. This study indicates that, in the 12-minute run, mentally retarded adults demonstrate relative fitness deficiencies similar to mentally retarded adolescents.

Studies using physiologically based tests have, for the most part, been limited to nonretarded adult populations. For example, only one study was found that used the step test with mentally retarded subjects. Reid and Montgomery (1983) measured oxygen consumption in mentally retarded sheltered workshop employees in Canada. Mentally retarded 20- to 29-year-old males obtained a mean $VO_{2\,max}$ of 35.6 ml/kg/minute, while mentally retarded females of the same age range obtained a mean of 32.5 ml/kg/minute. Males between 30 and 39 years of age obtained a mean value of 34.3 ml/kg/minute, while females of that age range obtained a mean oxygen consumption of 26.5 ml/kg/minute. Reid and Montgomery (1983) indicated that their subjects were between the second and the thirteenth percentile of a nonhandicapped population. However, a direct comparison may not be possible since the authors indicated that it was difficult to obtain rhythmic stepping with their retarded subjects.

Most work with mentally retarded adults has assessed maximal oxygen consumption through the use of a motorized treadmill or a bicycle ergometer. Several authors have used the Balke treadmill protocol to assess oxygen consumption with both mentally retarded and nonretarded population. Burke (1976) used the Balke protocol with 44 college-aged men who demonstrated an "average" level of fitness by exercising an average of 18.84 minutes; however oxygen consumption in milliliters per kilogram per minute was not reported. Katch *et al.* (1973a) used the Balke and Ware protocol with 36 college women who demonstrated an "average" level of fitness with a mean maximal oxygen consumption of 38.9 ml/kg/minute. In a study with mentally retarded sheltered workshop employees between the ages of 17 and 39 years, Tomporowski and Ellis (1984) used the Balke and Ware protocol to examine the effects of a 7-month exercise program. Although the authors note that treadmill performance improved after the program, the average time on the treadmill or the overall fitness level of subjects was not reported.

Oxygen consumption of mentally retarded individuals has also been measured while they exercised on a bicycle ergometer. Coleman, Ayoub, and Friedrich (1976) assessed the oxygen consumption of 37 educable and trainable mentally retarded individuals aged 16 to 25 years. In the protocol used by Coleman *et al.* (1976), subjects pedaled at work loads of 150 kg/minute, 300 kg/minute, and 450 kg/minute. The work loads were increased at 4-minute intervals and subjects were required to maintain a rate of 50 RPM's. If subjects achieved the 450 kg/minute resistance, the pedaling frequency was increased to 150 revolutions per minute (RPM). Exercising continued until subjects' heart rates reached 150 BPM. A linear extrapolation of oxygen consumption of 31.68 ml/kg/minute was calculated for these subjects. This rate was 20–30% lower than the values for nonhandicapped subjects reported by other authors and fell in the "low" range of fitness.

Custer and Chaloupka (1977) used the Astrand and Rhyming (1954) protocol with 40 nonhandicapped women aged 18–21 years. Maximal oxygen consumption values ranged from 20 ml/kg/minute to 60 ml/kg/minute reflecting "fair" to "high" fitness (Wilmore, 1982). A year earlier, Burke (1976) found the mean oxygen consumption of 44 nonhandicapped men from 17 to 30 years of age to be 42.93 ml/kg/minute, suggesting average levels of fitness. When these results are compared to the data from Coleman *et al.* (1976) it can be seen that, in general, oxygen consumption is higher for nonretarded individuals.

Despite the rather bleak status of fitness among most mentally retarded persons, several investigators have indicated that regular exercise does improve the fitness of mentally retarded individuals. Since fitness of nonhandicapped individuals improves with regular exercise (Fox, 1984), it is not surprising that fitness of mentally retarded individuals is also susceptible to systematic programming. Studies that have examined how fitness improves in mentally retarded individuals are reviewed in the following section.

C. Programs to Improve Fitness

Several studies have shown that regular participation in an exercise program, including training in athletic skills, improves fitness (Allison & Ayllon, 1980; Bundschuh, Williams, Hollingworth, Gooch, & Shires, 1972; Campbell, 1974; Crain *et al.*, 1983; Solomon & Pangle, 1967). In fact, Solomon and Pangle (1967) demonstrated that fitness of mentally retarded individuals can be improved to a level that compares favorably with nonretarded individuals. Mildly retarded boys (24) between the ages of 13.5 to 17.3 years participated in 45 minutes of daily exercise for 8 weeks, while 18 other boys of the same IQ and age range served as a control group and did not participate in the exercise program. The exercise program consisted of 15 minutes of warm-up and calisthenics, 15 minutes of individual and dual relay activities, and 15 minutes of group activities. Pre- to posttest gains on three items of the AAHPER test were statistically significant for the experimental group: 23 subjects achieved pretest scores that placed them in the bottom two quartiles, 1 subject placed in the third quartile, no subject scored well enough to be placed in the fourth quartile. On the posttest, however, 18 subjects achieved scores in the third and fourth quartile, 1 subject's score placed him in the bottom quartile, and 5 had scores in the second quartile. These scores are comparable to a nonretarded group, and, equally important, they were maintained over a 6-week follow-up period. The control group did not gain from the pre- to the posttest. Solomon and Pangle (1967) suggest that initial pretest scores may have been somewhat deflated because subjects were not familiar with the task. Hence, the gains may not be as great as they appear. However, this potentially confounding variable, to the extent that it is actual, may affect all fitness tests with mentally retarded individuals.

Unfortunately, trainable mentally retarded populations do not appear to gain in fitness as easily as mildly retarded populations. In Funk (1971), 18 trainable mentally retarded youths between the ages of 8 and 18 engaged in 30 minutes of daily exercise. Other youths (18) of the same IQ and age range served as a control group. The exercises consisted of balancing activities, agility games, relays, calisthenics, running, jumping, crawling, catching, throwing, and other similar activities. After 58 days, the experimental group had statistically significant pre- to posttest gains on sit-ups and a shuttle run but not on a straight-arm hang, standing long jump, or a medicine ball throw. Funk (1971) speculated that the lack of measured improvement was in areas in which the daily exercises were mismatched to the fitness test. For example, there were relatively few exercises that would be expected to increase arm and shoulder strength important to the arm hang and ball throw. Further, it is not clear whether it was the choice of activities or the relatively limited time spent doing them each day that was responsible for the lack of gains. This study serves as a reminder of the specificity of fitness measures. That is, exercises primarily related to one fitness component (i.e., endurance) will not necessarily produce gains in another fitness component (i.e., strength).

For both retarded and nonretarded populations, applying contingencies to exercise programs results in a greater improvement than when no contingencies are present (Allen & Iwata, 1980; Campbell, 1974; Wysocki, Hall, Iwata, & Riordan, 1979). For example, Campbell (1974) used the Royal Canadian Air Force exercises to improve fitness in 40 mentally retarded males aged 10 to 14 years with IQs from 20 to 84. Subjects were taught 5 exercises, including toe touches, sit-ups, head and shoulder lifts, push-ups, and running in place for 2 minutes. Subjects (20) received points based on the number of repetitions they completed within specified times. Points could later be exchanged for back-up reinforcers. The remaining 20 subjects also did the exercises daily, but did not receive points based on their performance. Although both groups improved, the contingent reinforcement group improved more on all exercises except running in place. Whether these gains would have continued in the absence of external contingencies is not known since Campbell (1974) did not present follow-up data. Since the contingent reinforcement group had greater improvements, physical ability may not be the only factor involved in doing exercises.

Adults' fitness also improves after exercise training (Beasley, 1982; Coleman & Whitman, 1984; Hussey, Maurer, & Schofield, 1976; Tomporowski & Ellis, 1984, 1985; Tomporowski & Jameson, 1985). Beasley (1982) instituted a 5-day-a-week jogging program with 15 educable and trainable mentally retarded adults between the ages of 16 and 50. The program consisted of having the subjects walk/jog 1.61 km at a pulse rate of 150 BPM. When subjects could do that in 10 minutes or less, the distance was increased to 2.44 km. Following 8 weeks of conditioning, the participants performed significantly better than a matched control group of mentally retarded adults on Cooper's 12-minute walk-run test. Further, the time it took the experimental group to complete the distance decreased by a mean of 2 minutes, 36 seconds. Although this was significant, nonretarded adults in a similar program typically reduced their time by even more (4 minutes, 3 seconds). It appears that mentally retarded adults require a longer period of time to achieve fitness levels similar to nonretarded adults. It is not known whether this is due to less fitness related activity in their daily life or to a physiological deficiency that prohibits normative progress.

It is known that longer exposure to exercise on a daily basis results in significant improvements in cardiovascular endurance. In Tomporowski and Ellis (1984), 20 moderately to profoundly retarded adults between 17 and 39 years of age exercised for 3 hours daily. Subjects had individualized training programs that typically consisted of 30 minutes of light calisthenics, 1 hour of exercise with a treadmill, bicycle, rowing machine, or a weight machine, and 1 hour of walking and running outdoors. Occasionally, subjects were exposed to other recreational activities such as group games or swimming. After 139 days of training, subjects significantly improved cardiovascular endurance as measured by pre- to posttest performance on a treadmill. A year later, Tomporowski and Ellis (1985) reported similar gains with a slightly different exercise program. Since neither article reported maximal oxygen consumption values, it is difficult to compare the fitness gains with a nonretarded population.

While few studies addressed improving fitness in severely retarded populations, those that did focused on adults (Caouette & Reid, 1985; Stainback, Stainback, Wehman, & Spangiers, 1983). From these articles, it seems that most work to date with the severely retarded has been confined to teaching subjects to do fitness exercises and has not produced measured improvements in their fitness levels. For example, Stainback *et al.* (1983) taught three 23- to 41-year-old profoundly retarded adults leg stretches, toe touches (legs positioned in a V while sitting), and knee bends through a combination of verbal cues, modeling, and physical prompts. Caouette and Reid (1985) increased the work output (measured in watts) on a bicycle ergometer of six severely retarded adults between 22 and 30 years of age through auditory and visual stimulation. Although total work output increased, heart rates were not affected. The authors concluded that to get an increase in physical fitness, contingencies would have to be applied to achieve work loads high enough to get a training effect.

The studies presented often compared the fitness of mentally retarded people to people who are not mentally retarded. Fitness of mentally retarded individuals does not compare favorably to nonretarded individuals. It would be helpful to know how fitness changes with age for the two groups. Research on that topic is reviewed in the next section.

D. Developmental Patterns of Fitness

In general, studies indicate that fitness levels of nonretarded individuals increase from 6 to 18 years of age. The amount of increase varies slightly with the component of fitness under study. For example, women and men both become stronger in the flexed-arm hang between the ages of 6 and 18 years, whereas endurance in males, measured by the 600-yard run–walk, increases until age 16 and then levels off at ages 17 and 18 years. Women's performance on the same test increases until age 10 and then remains level between the ages of 10 and 17. Women between the ages of 6 and 18 years usually score less well in the 600-yard run–walk than men.

Aerobic capacity also increases linearly with age. Iliev (1968) assessed the aerobic capacity of 430 boys and 330 girls between 9 and 16 years old. For boys, maximal aerobic capacity increased linearly with age at an average rate of 240 ml/year. For girls, it increased between the ages of 9 and 13 years, leveled off between the ages of 13 and 15, and then declined during the sixteenth year. At all ages, the girls had a lower aerobic capacity than boys. For example, the 9-year-old girls had a mean aerobic capacity of 1570 ml/minute compared to 1870 ml/minute for boys. At age 16, the mean aerobic capacity for the girls was 2300 ml/minute and 3480 ml/minute for the boys.

After age 18, fitness declines with age. In a study by Coleman and Burford (1971) of 35 sedentary men aged 24 to 66 years (mean = 37.09 years), estimated maximal aerobic capacities ranged from 25.57 to 65.12 ml/kg/minute, declining with increasing age. Men from 25 to 30 years of age had aerobic capacities between 25 and 65 ml/kg/minute; men over 50 had aerobic capacities between 25 and 50 ml/kg/min.

In an extensive study of aerobic capacity in men, Coleman, Burford, and Kreuzer (1973) found that the mean maximal oxygen uptake value of 26 to 30 year olds was 41.5 ml/kg/minute, of 31 to 40 year olds was 38.4 ml/kg/minute, of 41 to 50 year olds was 37.7 ml/kg/minute, and of 51 to 61 year olds was 33.6 ml/kg/minute. Coleman *et al.* (1973) noted that men who participated in regular physical activity (6 or more hours per week) deteriorated more slowly than their less active counterparts.

Although fitness declines with age, remaining physically active slows the rate of the decline. In a study of 86 physically active and inactive men from 40 to 70 years old, Dehn and Bruce (1972) also found that aerobic capacity declined at a mean rate of 0.28 ml/kg/minute/year. Although aerobic capacity declined in both active and inactive men, active males maintained their fitness longer. For example, active males between the ages of 50 and 69 years were doing as well or better than inactive males 10 years younger. Further, $VO_{2\,max}$ declines much faster in inactive than in active men. The annual decline in $VO_{2\,max}$ for inactive males was 1.32 ml/kg/minute compared to an annual decline of 0.65 ml/kg/minute for active males.

Most studies on development of maximal aerobic capacity over time have been done with men. However, it appears that the fitness of women also decreases with age. Further, $VO_{2\,max}$ is lower in women than in men across the entire developmental continuum (Dehn & Bruce, 1972). Astrand and Rhyming (1954) reported that healthy 20- to 30-year-old women had a mean maximal oxygen of 48.4 ml/kg/minute with a range from 42.0 to 54.8 ml/kg/minute, while men of the same age range had an overall oxygen intake of 58.6 ml/kg/minute with a range from 50.4 to 66.8 ml/kg/minute.

Unfortunately, there has been little developmental research on fitness in mentally retarded populations. Rarick *et al.* (1970) found that mentally retarded youths between the ages of 6 and 18 showed developmental patterns similar to nonretarded youths. That is, on exercises included in the AAHPER fitness tests, mentally retarded youths obtained performance curves that mimicked the curves obtained by nonretarded youths. Maksud and Hamilton (1974) found that oxygen intake values in EMR subjects followed typical trends for non-retarded subjects in that they increased between the ages of 10 to 13 years. Although no studies have examined the developmental patterns of fitness in mentally retarded adults, data reported by Reid and Montgomery (1983) suggest that $VO_{2\,max}$ declines with age in mentally retarded men and women. Mentally retarded men between the ages of 20 and 29 years had a mean oxygen consumption of 35.6 ml/kg/minute compared to the mean value of 34.3 ml/kg/minute for men 30 to 39 years of age. These values are about equal to the values reported by Dehn and Bruce (1972) for inactive 40 to 49 year olds. Mean values for mentally retarded women were lower than for mentally retarded men but showed the same trend. Mentally retarded women 20 to 29 years of age had mean values of 32.5 ml/kg/minute compared to the mean value of 29.5 ml/kg/minute for women aged 30 to 39 years.

Little is known about the fitness of mentally retarded populations according to gender. One study (Rarick *et al.*, 1970) demonstrated that both mentally retarded men and women between the ages of 6 and 18 were less fit than their nonretarded counterparts. The Reid and Montgomery (1983) study is the only one that reported gender differences in mentally retarded populations beyond the age of 18.

Despite the limited number of studies, it appears from the literature that people who are mentally retarded are much less fit than people who are not mentally retarded. Further, it appears that the relative fitness deficits of mentally retarded individuals continue through life and may increase with age relative to nonhandicapped people. However, since the amount of data is limited and there are questions about the reliability and validity of the instruments, these conclusions need to be held with reservations. Several variables affecting the conclusions that can safely be made from research on the fitness of mentally retarded populations will be discussed in the following section.

E. Factors That Affect Performance

Differences in test performance of mentally retarded and nonretarded individuals may reflect actual differences in physical fitness. However, they may also result, in part, from differences in motivation, in knowledge of the task requirements, in greater variability between individuals in test samples of mentally retarded people, or in the amount of lean body mass. In studies of fitness, these factors result in a retarded individual doing more poorly than a nonretarded person.

One assumption that underlies all tests of physical fitness is that the persons being tested have exerted themselves to their maximal limit. That is, individuals have covered the longest distance possible in the 12-minute run, pedaled or run for the longest time possible on the bicycle or treadmill, did the greatest number of sit-ups possible, etc. It is clear that motivation is directly related to performance on fitness tests since subjects may quit when they feel "exhausted" or "unable to continue." The role of motivation in fitness tests of mentally retarded populations has been discussed by many authors (Beasley, 1982; Burke, 1976; Cooper, 1968; Johnson & Londeree, 1976; Rarick *et al.*, 1970; Yoshizawa *et al.*, 1975) with general agreement that low motivation leads to poor test performance. Many authors working with mentally retarded subjects have had to modify the tests (Johnson & Londeree, 1976; Rarick *et al.*, 1970) or interpret their results with caution (Yoshizawa *et al.*, 1975) because of the subjects' inability to perform to the standards of nonhandicapped subjects. Additionally, rewards for achievement of certain scores have been built into the AAHPER Special Fitness Test (Johnson & Londeree, 1976; Speakman, 1977) as a motivational aid. Until more is known about the impact of motivation on performance, it will be difficult to say whether the performance of mentally retarded individuals reflects actual fitness levels or some unknown combination of fitness and motivation. Further, the validity of fitness tests used with mentally retarded populations remains questionable until comparable levels of motivation among subjects is adequately dealt with (Atha, 1974).

A second assumption underlying tests of fitness is that individuals know how to do the exercises. Many researchers address this factor by providing practice sessions for their subjects to familiarize them with the tests. However, because mentally retarded individuals have less opportunity than nonretarded individuals to engage in physical activities of the types called for in fitness assessments (Campbell, 1973; Moon & Renzaglia, 1983; Stein, 1963), equivalent knowledge between the handicapped and nonhandicapped cannot be assumed even with limited practice sessions.

A third assumption researchers make when using fitness tests is that subjects' performance of an exercise does not vary significantly from trial to trial. However, both mentally retarded and nonretarded subjects achieve more stable performance and higher reliabilities only after several trials are given (Porretta, 1985; Safrit, 1973). Performance remains variable even in tests that have been modified for retarded populations (Aufsesser, 1979).

Finally, the percentage of lean body mass influences results of fitness tests. Since retarded populations are more obese that nonretarded populations (Fox *et al.*, 1985), their relative fitness deficits may be, in part, due to their obesity. For example, the data presented by Londeree and Johnson (1974) indicated that, on the average, TMR youths are shorter than nonretarded youths, but their weight is equivalent. Therefore, an average TMR 15-year-old girl will be about 56 inches tall compared to 60 inches for a nonretarded 15-year-old girl. They will both weigh about 115 pounds. The differential weight of the retarded girl is likely to reflect a lower percentage of lean body mass which is negatively related to performance on fitness tests (Cureton, 1978). Since body fat and/or lean body mass percentages are typically not reported, we can't be sure of the extent to which retarded people are penalized by this factor.

Further, since the goal of many fitness programs is to increase the percentage of lean body mass while decreasing body fat, research on the interaction between these variables and performance in fitness tests with mentally retarded populations is needed.

It is clear that variables other than fitness influence scores on fitness tests. This fact, coupled with the lack of a universally accepted definition of fitness, makes it difficult to develop reliable and valid tests. However, such tests are needed to determine the status of fitness in mentally retarded populations. Reliability needs to be established for multiple-component tests that have been altered for mentally retarded populations. Cardiovascular tests are largely unstandardized, precluding assessment of reliability in either mentally retarded or nonretarded populations. In the absence of standardization, individual researchers will need to reexamine the reliability of their own instruments within each study and will have difficulty comparing their results to other studies.

More information is also needed to validate fitness tests. However, some basic work needs to precede validation studies. Few standardized cardiovascular tests exist, despite the general guidlines for the standardization of fitness tests from the International Committee for Standardization of Physical Fitness Tests (Larson, 1974). A standardized multiple-component test (the AAHPER) is available. However, it does not measure aerobic capacity and, thus, cannot be taken as a reflection of overall physical fitness. Further, researchers frequently alter standardized tests. Hence, there are few inferences that can be confidently made about the relative fitness of various populations or about how fitness changes over the life-span. A standardized comprehensive fitness assessment procedure needs to be established and validated.

IV. SUMMARY AND CONCLUSIONS

It is apparent that mentally retarded people have serious fitness deficits compared to people who are not mentally retarded. Further, as the level of retardation increases, the fitness deficits become more severe and more difficult to remediate. Although the research is limited, fitness of mentally retarded children appears to develop similarly, but more slowly and, on the average, to a more limited degree, to nonretarded children. The developmental pattern of fitness in mentally retarded adult populations remains largely unknown.

There may be numerous explanations for the relatively lower level of fitness demonstrated by mentally retarded populations. The pattern of slower development indicates that the relatively poorer performance of mentally retarded individuals on fitness tests may be due, in part, to their handicapping condition. However, it seems likely that environmental factors also play a major role in the fitness levels of mentally retarded people. Fitness is related to life-style, particularly to regular exercise. In fact, fitness tests measure physical attributes that grow naturally with participation in various sports activities such as racketball, skiing, softball, etc. Currently, the information needed to compare the fitness-related recreational activities of mentally retarded individuals to nonretarded individuals is lacking. Research that examines how life-style relates to fitness in mentally retarded individuals is clearly needed.

One's ability to function normally in life is also related to fitness. A person who habitually spends the day sitting may be unable to participate in sports or even perform most job activities over an 8-hour work day. For example, Wehman, Hill, Goodall, Cleveland, Brooke, and Pentecost (1982) reported that one major problem encountered by clients in an employment project was lack of sufficient strength and stamina to work in competitive jobs. The lack of fitness impaired the mentally retarded clients' ability to perform entry-level job tasks (U.S. Department of Labor, 1972), thereby decreasing their marketability. Wehman *et al.* (1982) attributed the lack of fitness to sedentary life-styles; that is, clients either sat in school or in sheltered workshops performing repetitive manual tasks. In short, fitness may be related in important ways to quality of life. However, the extent to which quality of life is impacted by fitness, the points of intersection between fitness and quality of life, and the ways that fitness affects (or, in turn, is affected by) other life domains (e.g., employment) is almost entirely unexplored.

It has been demonstrated that fitness of mentally retarded individuals can be improved through regular exercise programming. However, little is known about the amount and rate of improvement possible with individuals at different levels of retardation and ages. Further, fitness programs that are appropriate to retarded people of different ages have not been developed.

Mentally retarded children often may not have the skills or coordination to join with their nonretarded peers; moreover, they may not have other skills necessary to "fit in." As nonretarded children grow older, they frequently get involved in organized sports or activity programs. However, retarded children often lack the ability to compete and, again, they may not be welcomed for social reasons.

The problem grows in adulthood. Nonretarded adults who maintain exercise programs do so on their own initiative. They schedule exercise time, arrange for facilities and equipment, and structure their environment to provide the support and motivation to maintain a consistent exercise program. It seems unlikely that most mentally retarded adults will have either the necessary range of skills or sufficient control over their environment to develop and maintain their own exercise program. First, they do not have the skills to arrange for facilities (e.g., call for a racketball court), obtain information about recreational activities (e.g., find out about racketball leagues), and get the necessary equipment (e.g., purchase a racket). Second, mentally retarded individuals do not often control their own schedules; rather, parents, guardians, or residential providers determine how most of their time is spent each day. Third, they are not as likely as nonretarded individuals to be motivated to participate in fitness activities since their history of exercise is likely to be more limited and since they are less likely to understand that fitness can reduce serious health problems.

It is not clear who should be responsible for programming fitness activities for mentally retarded individuals. Mentally retarded individuals who have someone helping them attend systematically to their fitness and physical well-being are probably unusual. Even service agency personnel or residential providers who are cognizant of the need do not necessarily have the skills and resources to provide effective fitness programs, and no agency is currently obliged to assist them. Research on delivery of services to develop and maintain fitness in mentally retarded individuals is needed.

Finally, fitness research, in general, is plagued by measurement problems. These problems begin with the lack of a clear definition of fitness and are compounded by the variation among procedures used to assess fitness. Lack of a standardized assessment instrument makes it difficult to compare the results across studies, both from mentally retarded to nonretarded populations and from children to adults. A standardized instrument needs to be developed that assesses cardiovascular endurance and critical aspects of strength and flexibility. The instrument needs to have demonstrated reliability and validity and needs to be normed by age, gender, type of handicapping condition, and severity of handicap.

The rapid development of medical technology is resulting in more people living who would otherwise die. Many of those individuals will be handicapped, some severely. In addition, the technology is increasing the life-span of the mentally retarded. As more retarded people live longer, it will be even more important to find ways to help them achieve their maximal potential. Fitness programs are one way to enhance integration of retarded persons, and increased fitness may ultimately result in increased productivity. The design of an effective system to provide those programs awaits research about the development of fitness in mentally retarded people.

REFERENCES

Alderman, R. B., & Howell, M. L. (1974). Validity of human performance assessments. In L. A. Larson (Ed.), *Fitness, health, and work capacity: International standards for assessment*. New York: Macmillan.

Allen, L. D., & Iwata, B. A. (1980). Reinforcing exercise maintenance using existing high-rate activities. *Behavior Modification*, **4**, 337–354.

Allison, M. G., & Allyon, T. (1980). Behavioral coaching in the development of skills in football, gymnastics, and tennis. *Journal of Applied Behavior Analysis*, **13**, 297–314.

American Association of Health, Physical Education, and Recreation (1976). *Youth fitness test manual*. Washington, D.C.: Author.

Astrand, P. O., & Rhyming, I. (1954). A nomogram for the calculation of aerobic capacity (physical fitness) from pulse rate during submaximal work. *Journal of Applied Physiology,* **19,** 218-221.

Astrand, P. O., & Rodahl, K. (1977). *Textbook of work physiology: Biological bases of exercise.* New York: McGraw-Hill.

Atha, J. (1974). Physical fitness measurements. In L. A. Larson (Ed.), *Fitness, health, and work capacity: International standards for assessment.* New York: Macmillan.

Aufsesser, P. M. (1979). Effects of repeated testing on the reliability of fitness scores of institutionalized mentally retarded individuals. *American Journal of Mental Deficiency,* **84,** 313-315.

Bar-Or, O., Zwiren, D., & Dotan, R. (1978). Correlations among aerobic fitness tests and $VO_{2\,max}$ men who vary in aerobic power. In R. J. Shephard & H. LaVallee (Eds.), *Physical fitness assessment: Principles, practice and application.* Springfield, Illinois: Thomas.

Beasley, C. R. (1982). Effects of a jogging program on cardiovascular fitness and work performance of mentally retarded adults. *American Journal of Mental Deficiency,* **86,** 609-613.

Brouha, L. (1943). The step test: A simple method of measuring physical fitness for muscular work in young men. *The Research Quarterly,* **14,** 31-36.

Brown, B. J. (1977). The effect of an isometric strength program on the intellectual and social development of trainable retarded males. *American Corrective Therapy Journal,* **31,** 44-48.

Brown, J. (1967). Comparative performance of trainable mentally retarded on the Kraus-Weber test. *The Research Quarterly,* **38,** 348-355.

Bruce, R. A. (1984). Normal values for VO_2 and the VO_2-HR relationship. *American Review of Respiratory Disorders,* **129** (Suppl.), S41-S43.

Bundschuh, E. L., Williams, W. C., Hollingworth, J. D., Gooch, S., & Shirer, C. (1972). Teaching the retarded to swim. *Mental Retardation,* **10,** 14-17.

Burke, E. J. (1976). Validity of selected laboratory and field tests of physical working capacity. *The Research Quarterly,* **47,** 95-104.

Campbell, J. (1973). Physical fitness and the MR: A review of the research. *Mental Retardation,* **11,** 26-29.

Campbell, J. (1974). Improving the physical fitness of retarded boys. *Mental Retardation,* **12,** 31-35.

Caouette, M., & Reid, G. (1985). Increasing the work output of severly retarded adults on a bicycle ergometer. *Education and Training of the Mentally Retarded,* **20,** 296-304.

Coleman, A. E. (1976). Validation of a submaximal test of maximal oxygen intake. *Journal of Sports Medicine,* **16,** 106-111.

Coleman, A. E., Ayoub, M. M., & Friedrich, D. W.(1976). Assessment of the physical work capacity of institutionalized mentally retarded males. *American Journal of Mental Deficiency,* **80,** 624-625.

Coleman, A. E., & Burford, C. L. (1971). Aerobic capacity in sedentary adults participating in an adult fitness program. *American Corrective Therapy Journal,* **25,** 48-51.

Coleman, A. E., Burford, C. L., & Kreuzer, P. (1973). Aerobic capacity of relatively sedentary males. *Journal of Occupational Medicine,* **15,** 628-632.

Coleman, R. S., & Whitman, T. L. (1984). Developing, generalizing, and maintaining physical fitness in mentally retarded adults: Toward a self-directed program. *Analysis and Intervention in Developmental Disabilities,* **4,** 109-127.

Cooper, K. H. (1968). A means of assessing maximal oxygen intake. *Journal American Medical Association,* **203,** 135-138.

Corder, W. O. (1966). Effects of physical education on the intellectual, physical, and social development of educable mentally retarded boys. *Exceptional Children,* **32,** 357-365.

Crain, C., McLaughlin, J., & Eisenhart, M. (1983). The social and physical effects of a 10-week dance program on educable mentally retarded adolescents. *Education and Training of the Mentally Retarded,* **18,** 308-312.

Cumming, G. R., & Cumming, P. M. (1963). Working capacity of normal children tested on a bicycle ergometer. *Canadian Medical Association Journal,* **88,** 351-355.

Cumming, G. R., Fisher, J., & Stasynec, C. (1978). Comparison of maximal bicycle and treadmill exercise ECG tests in middle-aged males. In F. Landry & W. Orban (Eds.), *Sports medicine* (Vol. 5). Miami, Florida: Symposia Specialists.

Cureton, T. K. (1978). The A.A.H.P.E.R National Youth Fitness Test: Researched, slightly revised, and republished, 1976. In R. J. Shephard & H. LaValle (Eds.), *Physical fitness assessment: Principles, practice and application*. Springfield, Illinois: Thomas.

Custer, S. J., & Chaloupka, E. C. (1977). Relationship between predicted maximal oxygen consumption and running performance of college females. *The Research Quarterly*, **48**, 47–50.

Dehn, M. M., & Bruce, R. A. (1972). Longitudinal variations in maximal oxygen intake with age and activity. *Journal of Applied Physiology*, **33**, 805–807.

Dolgener, F. (1982). Oxygen cost of walking and running in untrained, sprint trained, and endurance trained females. *Journal of Sports Medicine*, **22**, 60–65.

Dorociak, J. J., & Nelson, J. K. (1983). The 1 mile and 2 mile runs as measures of cardiovascular fitness in college women. *Journal of Sports Medicine*, **23**, 322–325.

Drake, V., Jones, G., Bown, J. R., & Shephard, R. J. (1968). Fitness performance tests and their relationship to the maximal oxygen uptake in adults. *Canadian Medical Association Journal*, **99**, 844–848.

Fleishman, E. (1964). *The structure and measurement of physical fitness*. New York: Prentice-Hall.

Fox, E. L. (1984). *Sports physiology* (2nd ed.). New York: CBS College Publishing.

Fox, R. A., Hartney, C. W., Rotatori, A. F., & Kurpiers, E. M.(1985). Incidence of obesity among retarded children. *Education and Training of the Mentally Retarded*, **20**, 175–181.

Funk, D. C. (1971). Effects of physical education on fitness and motor development of trainable mentally retarded children. *The Research Quarterly*, **42**, 30–34.

Gross, A. M., & Johnson, T. C. (1984). Athletic skills and social status in children. *Journal of Social and Clinical Psychology*, **2**, 89–96.

Guralnik, D. B. (Ed.) (1976). *Webster's new world dictionary of the American language: Second college edition*. New York: Collins & World.

Hussey, C., Maurer, J. F., & Schofield, L. J., Jr. (1976). Physical education training for adult retardates in a sheltered workshop setting. *Journal of Clinical Psychology*, **32**, 701–705.

Iliev, I. B. (1968). Maximal aerobic power in girls and boys aged 9 to 16 years who participate regularly in sport. In R. J. Shephard & H. LaVallee (Eds.), *Physical fitness assessment: Principles, practice and application*. Springfield, Illinois: Thomas.

Johnson, L., & Londeree, B. (1976). *Motor fitness testing manual for the moderately mentally retarded*. Washington, D.C.: American Alliance for Health, Physical Education and Recreation.

Karper, W. B. (1981). The use of exercise in alleviating emotional disturbance: A review of the literature. *Journal for Special Educators*, **18**, 61–72.

Kasch, F. W., Phillips, W. H., Ross, W. D., Carter, J. E. L., & Boyer, J. L. (1966). A comparison of maximal oxygen uptake by treadmill and step test procedures. *Journal of Applied Physiology*, **21**, 1387–1388.

Katch, F. I., McArdle, W. D., Czula, R. & Pechar, G. S. (1973a). Maximal oxygen intake, endurance running performance, and body composition in college women. *The Research Quarterly*, **44**, 301–312.

Katch, F. I., Pechar, G. S., McArdle, W. D., & Weldman, A. L. (1973b). Relationship between individual differences in a steady pace endurance running performance and maximal oxygen intake. *The Research Quarterly*, **44**, 206–215.

Kraus, H. (1954). Minimum muscular fitness tests in school children. *Research Quarterly*, **25**, 178–188.

Kusinitz, I., Fine, M., & the Editors of Consumer Reports Books (1983). *Physical fitness for practically everybody: The Consumers Union report on exercise*. Mount Vernon, New York: Consumers Union.

Larson, L. A. (Ed.) (1974). *Fitness, health, and work capacity: International standards for assessment*. New York: Macmillan.

Londeree, B. R., & Johnson, L. E. (1974). Motor fitness of TMR vs. EMR and normal children. *Medicine and Science in Sports,* **6**, 247-252.

Maksud, M. G., & Coutts, K. D. (1971). Application of the Cooper twelve-minute run-walk test to young males. *The Research Quarterly,* **18**, 54-59.

Maksud, M. G., & Hamilton, L. H. (1974). Physiological responses of EMR children to strenuous exercise. *American Journal of Mental Deficiency,* **79**, 32-38.

McArdle, W. G., Katch, F. I., & Katch, V. L. (1981). *Exercise physiology: Energy, nutrition, and human performance.* Philadelphia: Lea & Febiger.

Meyers, C. R. (1974). *Measurement in physical education* (2nd ed.). New York: Ronald Press.

Moon, M. S., & Renzaglia, A. (1982). Physical fitness and the mentally retarded: A critical review of the literature. *The Journal of Special Education,* **16**, 269-287.

Morehouse, L. E. (1975). *Total fitness in 30 minutes per week.* New York: Simon & Schuster.

Newton, J. L. (1963). The assessment of maximal oxygen intake. *Journal of Sports Medicine and Physical Fitness,* **3**, 164-169.

Nosek, M. A. & Nofi, R. (1984). *The importance of physical fitness for persons with disabilities.* Washington, D.C.: The National Rehabilitation Information Center and National Council on Rehabilitation Education.

Oliver, J. N. (1958). The effects of physical conditioning exercises and activities on mental characteristics of educationally subnormal boys. *British Journal of Educational Psychology,* **28**, 155-165.

Peries, V. P. (1976). Fitness testing and evaluative procedures for mentally retarded children. *Journal for Special Educators of Mentally Retarded,* **12**, 192-195.

Pollock, M. L., Cureton, T. K., & Greninger, L. (1969). Effects of frequency of training on working capacity, cardiovascular function, and body composition of adult men. *Medicine and Science in Sports,* **1**, 70-74.

Porretta, D. L. (1985). Performance variability of mildly mentally retarded boys on a novel kicking task. *Adapted Physical Activity Quarterly,* **2**, 76-82.

Rarick, G. L., Widdop, J. H., & Broadhead, G. O. (1970). The physical fitness and motor performance of educable mentally retarded children. *Exceptional Children,* **36**, 509-519.

Reid, G., & Montgomery, D. L. (1983). Physical fitness of mentally retarded adults. *Medicine and Science in Sports and Exercise,* **15**, 182.

Ribisl, P. M., & Kachadorian, W. A. (1969). Maximal oxygen intake prediction in young and middle-aged males. *Journal of Sports Medicine and Physical Fitness,* **9**, 17-22.

Safrit, M. J. (1973). The assessment of physical fitness. In *Evaluation in physical education: Assessing motor behavior.* New Jersey: Prentice-Hall.

Sengstock, W. L. (1966). Physical fitness of mentally retarded boys. *The Research Quarterly,* **37**, 113-120.

Shoenfeld, Y., Keren, G., Birnfeld, C., & Sohar, E.(1981). Age, weight, and heart rate at rest as predictors of aerobic fitness. *Journal of Sports Medicine,* **21**, 377-382.

Simpson, H. M., & Meaney, C. (1979). Effects of learning to ski on the self-concept of mentally retarded children. *American Journal of Mental Deficiency,* **84**, 25-29.

Simri, U. (1974). Assessment procedures for human performance. In L. A. Larson (Ed.), *Fitness, health, and work capacity: International standards for assessment.* New York: Macmillan.

Solomon, A., & Pangle, R. (1967). Demonstrating physical fitness improvements in the EMR. *Exceptional Children,* **34**, 177-181.

Speakman, H. G. B. (1977). Physical fitness of the mentally retarded: A brief survey of the literature. *Canadian Journal of Applied Sport Science,* **2**, 171-176.

Stainback, S., Stainback, W., Wehman, P., & Spangiers, L. (1983). Acquisition and generalization of physical fitness exercises in three profoundly retarded adults. *The Journal of the Association for the Severely Handicapped,* **2**, 47-55.

Stein, J. U. (1963). Motor function and physical fitness of the mentally retarded: A critical review. *Rehabilitation Literature,* **24**, 230-242.

Thomas, G. S. (1979). Physical activity and health: Epidemiologic and clinical evidence and policy implications. *Preventive Medicine,* **8**, 89–103.

Tomporowski, P. D., & Ellis, N. R. (1984). Effects of exercise on the physical fitness, intelligence, and adaptive behavior of institutionalized mentally retarded adults. *Applied Research in Mental Retardation,* **5**, 329–337.

Tomporowski, P. D., & Ellis, N. R. (1985). Effects of exercise on the physical fitness, intelligence, and adaptive behavior of institutionalized severely and profoundly mentally retarded adults: A systematic replication. *Applied Research in Mental Retardation,* **6**, 465–473.

Tomporowski, P. D., & Jameson, L. D. (1985). Effects of a physical fitness training program on the exercise behavior of institutionalized mentally retarded adults. *Adapted Physical Activity Quarterly,* **2**, 197–205.

United States Department of Labor. (1972). *Handbook for analyzing jobs.* Washington, DC: U.S. Government Printing Office.

Wehman P., Hill M., Goodall P., Cleveland P., Brooke V., & Pentecost, J. H., Jr. (1982). Job placement and follow-up of moderately and severely handicapped individuals after three years. *Journal of the Association for the Severely Handicapped,* **7**, 5–16.

Wilmore, J. H. (1982). *Training for sport and activity: The physiological basis of the conditioning process* (2nd ed.). Boston: Allyn & Bacon.

Winnick, J. P., & Short, F. X. (1985). *Physical fitness testing of the disabled: Project Unique.* Champaign, Illinois: Human Kinetics.

Wysocki, T., Hall, G., Iwata, B., & Riordan, M. (1979). Behavioral management of exercise: Contracting for aerobic points. *Journal of Applied Behavior Analysis,* **12**, 55–64.

Yoshizawa, S., Ishizaki, T., & Honda, H. (1975). Aerobic work capacity of mentally retarded boys and girls in junior high schools. *Journal of Human Ergology,* **4**, 15–26.

Index

C

D

G

H

I

Q

R

Contents of Previous Volumes

Volume 7

Volume 8

Volume 9

Volume 10

Volume 11

Volume 12

Volume 13

Volume 14